David King is the author of *Vienna, 1814: How the Conquerors of Napoleon Made Love, War, and Peace at the Congress of Vienna* and *Finding Atlantis: A True Story of Genius, Madness, and an Extraordinary Quest for Lost World*. He is a Fulbright scholar with a master's degree from Cambridge University and lives in Lexington, Kentucky, with his wife and children.

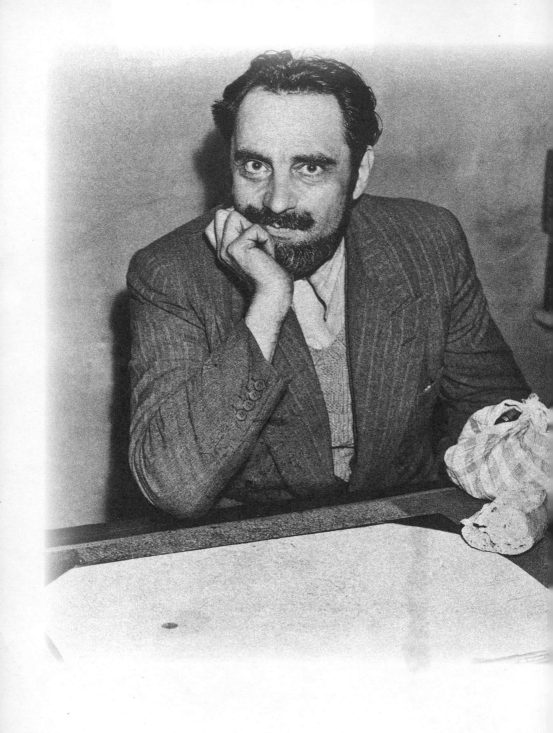

DEATH
IN THE
CITY OF
LIGHT

THE TRUE STORY OF THE
SERIAL KILLER WHO
TERRORISED WARTIME
PARIS

DAVID KING

sphere

SPHERE

First published in the United States in 2011 by the Crown Publishing Group,
a division of Random House, Inc., New York
First published in Great Britain in 2012 by Sphere

A CIP catalogue record for this book
is available from the British Library.

ISBN 978-1-84744-548-3

Printed and bound in Great Britain by
Clays Ltd, St Ives plc

Papers used by Sphere are from well-managed forests
and other responsible sources.

MIX
Paper from
responsible sources
FSC® C104740

Sphere
An imprint of
Little, Brown Book Group
100 Victoria Embankment
London EC4Y 0DY

An Hachette UK Company
www.hachette.co.uk

www.littlebrown.co.uk

To Julia and Max

With special thanks to the Préfecture de Police for granting me access to the entire Petiot dossier, which has been classified since the time of the events.

Contents

PREFACE

March 11, 1944

A THICK black smoke streamed into Jacques and Andrée Marçais's fifth-floor apartment at 22 rue Le Sueur in the heart of Paris's fashionable 16th arrondissement. The smoke had begun five days before, but now, in the unusually warm weather, it was getting worse, seeping through closed windows and soiling the furniture. In the air was a nauseating smell described variously as burnt caramel, burnt rubber, or a burnt roast of poor quality. The source of the disturbance, it seemed, was a building across the street. "Do something," Andrée Marçais told her husband when he returned home just before six o'clock that evening, and she sent him over to investigate.

Neither Jacques nor his wife knew who, if anyone, lived in the neighboring two-and-a-half-story town house at 21 rue Le Sueur. A man was sometimes seen riding there on a green bicycle, towing a cart whose contents were concealed under a heavy canvas. On rare occasions, he appeared to receive visitors, who arrived almost invariably at night curiously lugging a couple of heavy suitcases.

As Jacques approached the stately structure with its blackened gray stone façade, he could tell that the smoke was indeed pouring out of its narrow chimney. He could not, however, see inside the house. The shutters on the ground floor were closed, and the curtains on the second floor were drawn. Jacques rang the bell. After no response, he pressed the button a few more times. Then, noticing a small, weather-worn piece of paper attached to the large double door that had once served as a carriage entrance, he took it down and read: "Away for a month. Forward mail to 18, rue des Lombards, Auxerre."

Worried about a chimney fire blazing in an empty house, Jacques returned home and called the police.

Moments later, two bicycle patrolmen arrived on the scene. After trying in vain to enter the premises, the men, Joseph Teyssier and Emile Fillion, went looking for someone who could identify the owner of the property. The concierge at No. 23, Marie Pageot, informed them that the town house was unoccupied but belonged to a family physician named Marcel Petiot, who lived at 66 rue Caumartin near Gare Saint-Lazare, in a bustling commercial district just south of a seedy center of strip joints, brothels, and nightclubs.

With the physician's name and telephone number in hand, Teyssier entered the nearby grocer shop, Garanne, and dialed: Pigalle 77–11. A woman answered and then put Dr. Petiot on the line. Teyssier informed him of the fire at his property.

"Have you entered the building?" the physician asked.

"No."

"Don't touch anything. I will bring the keys immediately. Fifteen minutes at the most."

When Teyssier exited the shop, the unusual smoke had attracted a few residents onto the sidewalk. Other neighbors watched from upper-story windows, the officers and onlookers alike scurrying about as they awaited the arrival of the owner. Fifteen minutes passed, and Petiot was nowhere in sight. Another ten minutes passed, and still no Petiot. Biking from his apartment on rue Caumartin at that time of the evening should not have taken more than ten to twelve minutes.

After almost half an hour, the patrolmen decided that they could not wait any longer and called the fire department, which immediately dispatched a truck from the station at 8 rue Mesnil. The leader of the fire brigade, thirty-three-year-old Corporal Avilla Boudringhin, grabbed a ladder and climbed onto a second-floor balcony. Opening the wooden shutter, he smashed the glass, released the window lock, and stepped inside the darkened mansion. Two of his men followed. With the aid of a flashlight, the small team of firefighters traced the peculiar, nauseating smell to a small room in the basement. One of the two coal stoves there was roaring furiously. It was fireman Roger Bérody who opened the iron door.

Jutting out were the charred remains of a human hand. On the far staircase was a pile of debris, which turned out to be a skull, a rib cage, and several other recognizable bones. Arms and legs had been strewn about in parts. A split torso and two other skulls lay on the floor. The stench of scorched and decomposing flesh was overpowering. Horrified, the fire chief ordered his men out of the basement. As the firefighters exited the grisly site, one of the younger men leaned over an iron banister and vomited.

"Gentlemen, come and take a look," Boudringhin told the patrolmen once he emerged onto the street through the old carriage entrance. "I believe that your work will be cut out for you."

Teyssier was not the least prepared for the carnage that awaited him in the basement. He rushed back to Garanne and telephoned headquarters.

A large crowd soon gathered outside the town house, many of them curious about the smoke, the commotion, and now also the sight of a fire truck that was not yet extinguishing the fire. Among the arrivals was a slim, dark-haired man of medium height, pushing a bicycle through the throng of onlookers. He was pale and clean-shaven, and wore a dark gray overcoat and a fedora. He was sweating profusely.

When he reached the front of the crowd, he leaned his bike against the building, walked up to the fire chief, and identified himself as the brother of the owner. He demanded to be taken inside, speaking with such conviction that the fire chief waved him through to Patrolman Fillion. While the two men were talking, Patrolman Teyssier returned to the scene.

"Are you good Frenchmen?" the man asked.

"What kind of question is that?"

"Then listen carefully. What you see there are the bodies of Germans and traitors to our country." Discreetly, he asked if the authorities had been notified. Teyssier nodded.

"That's a serious mistake," the man said. "My life is at stake, as are the lives of several of my friends who serve our cause." He explained that he was in charge of a French Resistance organization and handed over a document to that effect, though the details were difficult to read in the darkness. In the meantime, he reached down and picked something off the ground, shoving it into his pocket.

The man then professed to have some three hundred secret files and identification cards of fellow Resistants at his house. "I must destroy them at once before they fall into the hands of the Germans."

Sympathetic to the work of the Resistance, Teyssier and Fillion had no desire to see so many patriotic Frenchmen handed over to the Nazis and carted off to prisons, concentration camps, or some other horrific fate. They agreed to allow the man to leave the scene of the crime, even though he clearly had information that could have helped the investigation. What's more, the officers agreed not to inform their superiors about his visit. The stranger biked away into the night.

Later, when Teyssier saw a photograph of the physician who owned the building, he was mortified to learn that the man on the bicycle had been Marcel Petiot.

ACROSS town, at 48–50 Boulevard Diderot, Commissaire Georges-Victor Massu, the chief of the Brigade Criminelle, had just finished dinner with his wife, Mathilde, and twenty-year-old son, Bernard. Massu had settled into his favorite chair to talk about the day's activities: a burglary, an assault case, and the usual routine of reports, interrogations, and seemingly endless paperwork. Bernard, a law student at the University of Paris, had retreated to his room to prepare for exams.

Minutes before ten p.m., after Massu had just climbed into bed, the telephone rang. "I still remember that call as if the crackle of the bell rang in my ears today," he said many years later. At that hour, he knew it could only mean one thing. This was not, as he put it, another "stabbing in the vicinity of Montmartre." Massu took the receiver with the steely composure of a gambler trying to bluff a rogue cardsharp.

On the line was Secretary Canitrot at the Brigade Criminelle. Without relaying the details of the discovery at rue Le Sueur, Canitrot urged the boss to come as quickly as possible and sent over a car right away. Fifteen minutes later, a long black Citroën 11 CV was waiting outside Massu's residence, the chauffeur with a hand at his cap.

Bernard wanted to tag along, as he sometimes did on the most serious or interesting cases. The commissaire agreed. Massu, a stocky man in his fifty-fifth year, with a shock of black hair and a dark mustache, put on his black overcoat and gray fedora. The two Massus, each wrapped up for the night chill, hopped into the car and drove across the city that, years before, would have been swirling with activity. That evening, however, Paris looked, as Massu put it, "somber and deserted."

The city was suffering the fourth year of the Nazi Occupation. Huge red and white banners emblazoned with a black swastika had flown atop the Eiffel Tower, the Arc de Triomphe, and many other landmarks and buildings near Petiot's town house. White placards with Gothic script directed traffic, mostly German and many of them, in that area, Mercedes-Benzes or Citroëns with small swastika flags on the fenders. The few people on the streets after the official ten p.m. curfew were Germans, "friends of the occupiers," and the "workers of the night." A brothel exclusively for Nazi officers was located just around the corner from Petiot's property.

As the car pulled up to 21 rue Le Sueur, a single streetlamp, hooded for the wartime blackout, cast a dim bluish light on the activities of the police, which, as Massu already realized, were inspiring an "uneasy curiosity" among the street's residents. Some officers controlled the crowd eager to watch from balcony windows; others followed the commissaire inside the town house. Policemen were now arriving every few minutes.

Massu entered the mansion, which had a grand salon, a petit salon, a large formal dining room, a billiards room, a library, six bedrooms, and two kitchens. The house had previously belonged to Princess Marie Colloredo-Mansfeld, a sixty-seven-year-old Frenchwoman whose husband's family had borne the title of imperial prince since 1763. The French actress Cécile Sorel, the comtesse de Ségur and doyenne of the

Comédie Française, had lived there in the 1930s, a neighboring concierge was telling people. This would be claimed for years, but it is not accurate. Sorel had only rented the house to store her extensive wardrobe and trunks of memorabilia from her long career on the stage.

The current owner of the property was far less known to the general public than either the princess or the actress. "The name Marcel Petiot meant absolutely nothing to me," Commissaire Massu admitted. It was the first time he had even heard it.

From what Massu could tell, the owner was an assiduous collector of fine art. Many of the rooms boasted a splendid array of crystal chandeliers, oriental rugs, antique furniture, marble statues, Sèvres vases, and oil paintings in gilded frames. At the same time, there was a startling state of neglect. The rooms were not only dusty and full of cobwebs, but also, in some cases, the furniture was turned over or stacked in corners as if at a flea market. In several rooms and corridors were torn wallpaper, loose baseboards, and dangling panels. Massu saw exquisite Louis XV furniture alongside filthy couches with visibly protruding springs.

When one officer warned that the case would most likely turn out to be appalling, Massu was unfazed. He had heard this before. In fact, almost every time a new crime was discovered, someone usually noted that it would be a *"terrible histoire."* He had no doubt that this might well be the case. As chief of the Brigade Criminelle, he was used to investigating disturbing affairs.

Still Massu was taken aback at the macabre spectacle in the basement of 21 rue Le Sueur: the half-burned skull in the furnace, the pile of tibias, femurs, and other bones on the floor. A foot, Massu saw, was "blackened like a log that had been slowly consumed." A dismembered hand, curled up tightly, "grasped the thin air in desperation." A woman's torso lay there, with the flesh "gnawed away to reveal the splinters of the ribcage." The stench—"the sinister odor of roasted human flesh," as he put it—gripped his throat.

A few steps away, Massu found a shovel, a dark-stained hatchet, and then, underneath the stone stairs, a gray bag containing the left half of a decomposed body, minus the head, foot, and internal organs. Massu did not know how to describe the ghastly site other than by using a reference to medieval literature. The basement of the elegant town house looked like a scene from Dante's *Inferno*.

EXITING into the courtyard, Massu, Bernard, and a couple of detectives, including Inspector Principal Marius Battut, entered one of the smaller buildings in the back. In the first room was a polished desk, along with two leather armchairs, a lounge sofa, and a small round table topped with magazines. A cupboard full of medical supplies stood against one wall; against another was a glass-lined bookcase in which medical treatises were shelved. What particularly struck the commissaire, however, was the room's appearance: It was cleaner, tidier, and in much better condition than the more stately main building. It also seemed to have been recently renovated.

Opening a second door, located near one of the bookshelves, Massu exited into a narrow corridor, about three feet in width, which led to another door, this one with a thick chain and padlock. The investigators entered. It was a small, triangular room, about eight feet on the longest side, six on the shortest. The walls were thick, two of them of rough cement and the third covered by beige wallpaper. There were no windows or furniture, only two unshaded lightbulbs and a plain metal cot. Attached near the corners of each wall, about one meter from the ceiling, were a number of iron hooks.

A gold-trimmed double wooden door on the far wall appeared to lead to some grand salon, but when one of the inspectors tried to open it, the doorknob simply turned around. With the help of a crowbar, the men ripped the door from the hinges to discover that it had been glued there. To the right of this false door was a bell, which did not work either. Actually it was not even connected, as its wires had been cut from the outside. As for the door through which the inspectors had entered, Massu noticed that it had no handle on the inside.

Examining the beige wallpaper, which looked freshly applied, Bernard peeled it back and discovered a viewing lens fitted in the wall at a height of almost six feet. The purpose of the room was not clear, but there was already a disturbing hunch that this small space with its iron hooks, many decoys, and virtually soundproof walls might well be where the victims had met their demise.

After retracing their steps to the courtyard, Massu and his team entered the old carriage house, which had been converted into a garage and crammed with tools, boards, slop pails, paintbrushes, gas masks, and old mattress springs. A sliding door in the back led to another building, probably the former stable. There, on the ground, beyond a pile of rusty scrap iron was a metal cover that hid the night's most horrific discovery.

It was the entrance to a pit. A newly greased pulley, with a hook and a thick rope tied to form a noose, hung over the hole. A horrible stench left little doubt as to what lay inside. Massu, nevertheless, climbed down the wooden ladder, watching each slippery step, and landed in the middle of a revolting mix of quicklime and decomposing bodies of varying stages—the dumping ground, in effect, of a veritable slaughterhouse.

But who could say how many bodies lay in the pit? With a depth estimated at ten to twelve feet, there were clearly many more here than in the basement. The bones crunched under Massu's foot on landing. When the commissaire exited, reeking from his descent, he ordered specialists to retrieve the bones for analysis at the police laboratory. His assistants, however, refused. They looked as frightened, Massu said, as if they expected a bomb to explode or had met the devil himself.

Commissaire Massu had made some 3,257 arrests in his thirty-three-year career investigating crime in the French capital, but he had never seen a case as heinous or as perplexing as this one. Who was responsible for this "nightmare house"? Who, for that matter, were the victims, how many were there, and how exactly had they died? Most perplexing of all, what was the motive? The murderer—whoever he was—was not just killing his victims, he was dismembering them. The attempt to solve what Massu soon dubbed "the crime of the century" had begun.

1.

GERMAN NIGHT

THE GERMAN NIGHT HAS SWALLOWED UP THE COUNTRY. . . .
FRANCE IS NOTHING BUT A SILENCE; SHE IS LOST
SOMEWHERE IN THE NIGHT WITH ALL LIGHTS OUT.

—Antoine de Saint-Exupéry, letter to the *New York Times
Magazine*, November 29, 1942

FOUR years before, many of Paris's richest and most privileged residents had begun fleeing the capital. The duke of Windsor; Prince George of Greece; Princess Winnie de Polignac and her niece, Daisy Fellowes, the heiress to the Singer sewing fortune, had all departed. The Aga Khan set out for Switzerland. Peggy Guggenheim stored her art collection in a friend's barn and drove away in her Talbot, in the direction of the Haute Savoie ski resort of Megève.

Not far behind were a number of writers, painters, and artists who had turned the City of Light into what *New York Times* art critic Harold Rosenberg called "the laboratory of the twentieth century." James Joyce left for a village outside Vichy before continuing into Zurich. Gertrude Stein and Alice B. Toklas departed for Culoz, near Annecy. Marc Chagall, Henri Matisse, René Magritte, and Wassily Kandinsky headed south. Vladimir Nabokov secured the last ocean liner to New York. Walter Benjamin hiked across a mountain passageway into Spain, but made it no farther than Portbou, where he committed suicide at age forty-eight.

The scale of departures from the French capital had accelerated in May 1940 with the Nazi invasion of Belgium, Luxembourg, and the Netherlands. On the afternoon of June 3, when the air raid sirens began to wail, the Luftwaffe pounded the Renault and Citroën factories, the bombs also falling onto the Air Ministry on Boulevard Victor. The one-hour raid left a trail of street craters, massive piles of rubble, and a block of apartment buildings looking, as journalist Alexander Werth put it, "like a badly-cut piece of cheddar." Two hundred and fifty-four people had been killed and another six hundred and fifty-two injured.

As the Nazi Wehrmacht advanced closer to the capital, nearly encircling it from the north, the east, and the west, the exodus soon reached epic proportions. Trains were booked far beyond capacity, forcing many Parisians to leave by motorcar, truck, horse-drawn cart, hearse, or any other contraption. More often, residents fled on foot, pushing selected personal belongings, from mattresses to birdcages, onto bicycles, motorcycles, prams, wheelbarrows, oxcarts, hay wains, coffee vendor carts—virtually anything with wheels.

Legions of refugees struggled, under the hot summer sun, against almost completely blocked roads, under the occasional strafing of the Luftwaffe and, after Mussolini declared war on June 10, the attacks of Italian planes. Automobiles were abandoned for lack of gasoline. Rumors thrived in the oppressive climate of heat and hunger, feeding on the painful memories of the First World War and the feelings of uncertainty that swirled around the present crisis. No one knew when, or if, they would be able to return home.

Of France's forty million people, an estimated six to ten million inhabitants clogged the roads. Paris saw its population fall from nearly three million to about eight hundred thousand. The mass exodus was replicated in cities all over northern and eastern France, as the population headed south or southwest. The pilot and future author of *The Little Prince*, Antoine de Saint-Exupéry, peering down from his observation mission on the 2/33 Reconnaissance Squadron, thought that the mass movements looked like "a boot had scattered an ant-hill," sending the unfortunate refugees dispersing "without panic. Without hope, without despair, on the march as if in duty bound."

Beginning on June 9, the French government itself fled the capital.

Heading south, first to Orléans and then to the châteaux of the Loire, the leaders retreated to Bordeaux. Five days after their flight, the first German motorcyclists reached Paris, rolling into the Place Voltaire from the northern suburbs of Saint-Denis. By the early afternoon, the Nazi Wehrmacht had staged the first of its daily marches goose-stepping to drum and fife down an otherwise silent Avenue des Champs-Élysées. "There never has been anything like the eerie atmosphere in Paris," Robert Murphy observed from his office at the United States Embassy on the Place de la Concorde.

At least sixteen people in Paris took their own lives that day. The neurosurgeon and head of the American Hospital, Comte Thierry de Martel, stuck his arm with a syringe filled with strychnine. Novelist Ernst Weiss, Franz Kafka's friend, swallowed a large amount of barbiturates, but when this overdose failed to have its intended effect, he slashed his wrists, dying twenty-four hours later. The sixty-four-year-old concierge at the Pasteur Institute, Joseph Meister, shot himself in the head rather than obey the German invaders—he had been the first person cured of rabies by Louis Pasteur.

Many Parisians were in shock. What the German army under the kaiser had failed to do in four years of vicious slaughter in the First World War had been accomplished under Adolf Hitler in six weeks. France had suffered the most humiliating defeat in its history. Worse, however, was to come.

THE Germans would occupy three-fifths of the country, seizing a vast swath of territory north of the Loire that included two-thirds of France's population, two-thirds of its most fertile agricultural lands, and three-fourths of its industry. The occupying power would control not only Paris but also the strategic Atlantic and Channel coastlines. France would have to pay the costs of the German Occupation, which were set at an exorbitant daily rate of 400 million francs and pegged to an inflated 20–1 franc-mark exchange rate. Over the next four years,

France would pay the Third Reich a total of 631,866,000,000 francs, or almost 60 percent of its national income.

The rest of France was to be carved up. Germany seized Alsace and Lorraine, as well as the northeastern territories of the Nord and Pas-de-Calais, the latter governed by Wehrmacht Command in Brussels, with entrance strictly forbidden to Frenchmen. A slice of territory from Menton to the southeastern border was handed over to Germany's ally, Italy. The remaining part, located south of the Loire, became the "free" or the unoccupied zone, a nominally independent state with its capital in Vichy, a spa and casino resort known for its mineral water. When the French government had resettled there in the summer of 1940, it had to acknowledge "the rights of the occupying power." Collaboration—once a benign word for "working together"—soon took on a sinister new meaning.

In Paris, the Blitzkrieg was rapidly followed by a Ritzkrieg. Nazi officials arrived en masse to take control of the capital and commandeer prime real estate in the elegant western districts. The High Command of the German Military Occupation, which would govern the occupied zone, moved into the Hôtel Majestic on avenue Kléber. The *Kommandant,* or governor-general, of Grand-Paris, chose the Hôtel Meurice on rue de Rivoli; the military intelligence and counterespionage organization, the Abwehr (Abwehrstelle Frankreichs), set up headquarters in the Hôtel Lutétia nearby on the Boulevard Raspail. The Luftwaffe took over the Palais Luxembourg, while the Kriegsmarine settled into various properties on and around the Place de la Concorde.

For Nazi officers and their favored French collaborators, Paris had become the Babylon of the Third Reich. There were lavish champagne-and-caviar parties hosted by Ambassador Otto Abetz on rue de Lille, and equally extravagant affairs organized by Luftwaffe General Friedrich-Carl Hanesse in the Rothschild mansion on Avenue de Marigny. Famous restaurants, like Maxim's, Lapérouse, and La Tour d'Argent, catered to every whim, as did cabarets, nightclubs, and brothels, many of which enjoyed exemptions from the official curfew. As *New*

York Times correspondent Kathleen Cannell put it, at the time of the discovered bodies on rue Le Sueur in March 1944 Nazi-occupied Paris seemed to be "dancing with false gaiety on a rumbling volcano."

For most Frenchmen, however, the last four years represented fear, cold, hunger, and humiliation. No group of people, of course, fared worse than the Jews. Almost immediately after the conquest, the 200,000 Jews of France began losing their basic civic rights. As of October 3, 1940, they could no longer serve in positions of authority in government, education, publishing, journalism, film, and the military. The following day, civil authorities were granted the power to intern foreign-born Jews in "special camps." Three days later, the repeal of the Crémieux Act stripped citizenship from another 1,500 Algerian Jews.

The flurry of discriminatory laws was relentless. By early 1941, Jews could no longer work in banking, insurance, real estate, or hotels. Quotas restricted the number of Jews allowed to practice the legal and medical professions to 2 percent, though this, too, was later expanded into an outright ban. Jewish shops were soon to be "Aryanized," that is, seized by the state and the ownership handed over or sold at a bargain rate to non-Jews. The aim was to "eliminate all Jewish influence in the national economy."

It was not long before the *rafles,* or roundups, began. On May 14, 1941, the first *rafle* resulted in the arrest and internment of 3,747 innocent Jewish men. Ten months later, on March 27, 1942, "special train 767" left France with the first convoy of 1,112 Jews packed into overcrowded third-class passenger cars, bound for the new extermination camp of Auschwitz-Birkenau. Eighty-four deportations would follow, most of them in sealed cattle cars. SS Lieutenant General Reinhard Heydrich and his deputy Adolf Eichmann would continually press French authorities to quicken the pace. In all, 75,721 Jewish men, women, and children would be deported from France to Nazi death and concentration camps in the east. Only 2,800 of them would return home.

Paris under the Nazi Occupation was, in the words of historian Alistair Horne, the four darkest years of the city's two-thousand-year history. For many Parisians indeed, it was a nightmare of tyranny and terror, resulting in a desperation to escape that would be ruthlessly exploited by one man in its midst.

W HAT Massu did after his initial search of the town house might seem peculiar at best. He did not go straight to rue Caumartin to look for Dr. Petiot, nor did he send any detectives there. Instead, he went home.

A French law, dating back to December 13, 1799 (22 Frimaire of the French Revolutionary Calendar), prohibited the police from barging in on citizens during the middle of the night unless there was a fire, flood, or an invitation from inside the residence. Article 76 of the Constitution of Year Eight, as it was known, had been written to stop the late-night arrests that occurred during the Reign of Terror. But in a case of this magnitude, Massu could have simply posted men outside Petiot's apartment to wait for the legal hour. Clearly, there was another explanation for his inaction.

The commissaire suspected that 21 rue Le Sueur had been used by the Gestapo, the German secret state police, that had seized control of French internal affairs. Established in April 1933 to eliminate "enemies of the state" as part of Adolf Hitler's consolidation of power, the Gestapo had swelled from some three hundred officials in a former art school on Prinz-Albrecht-Strasse in Berlin to a total of forty thousand agents and many more informers across Occupied Europe. In the name of law and order, they could spy, arrest, imprison, torture, and kill with almost complete impunity. The organization was above the law, and there was no appeal.

Massu had reasons for presuming a possible Gestapo connection. There was not only the butchery and brutality of the crime scene, but also the fact that the German security forces had preferred to set up its offices in the chic 16th arrondissement. Around the corner on the Avenue Foch, for instance, were Gestapo buildings at Nos. 31, 72, 84, and 85, along with offices of the related SS secret service the Sicherheitsdienst, or SD, at Nos. 19–21, 31 bis, 53, 58–60, 80, and 85. Many other German military, counterespionage, and Nazi Party offices were located on this street as well.

A swastika had flown over the building across from Petiot's property. The garage at No. 22 had been appropriated by Albert Speer's Organization Todt, a vast supply company that supervised German construction projects in Occupied Europe. In Paris, this group was doing everything from melting down bronze statues for armaments to sending laborers north to construct the Atlantic Wall against an Allied invasion.

The French police, of course, had no authority over the Gestapo or any of its activities. In a protocol signed with SS Brigadier General Karl Oberg on April 18, 1943, the secretary general of the French police, René Bousquet, had to agree to work with the occupying power to maintain "calm and order in an always efficient manner." Specifically, the French would have to help German police combat the "attacks of the communists, terrorists, agents of the enemy and saboteurs as well as those who support them: Jews, Bolsheviks, Anglo-Americans." To add further insult to humiliation, French policemen had to salute German officials whenever they encountered them in the street—this was the notorious *Grusspflicht*.

This subordination was to be endured, the argument went, because it was preferable to the alternative: namely, a police force staffed only by the occupying power and the many extremist militaristic organizations that collaborated with the Nazis. Such circumstances would not only lead to frightening police brutality, but also offer few chances to sabotage German authorities. Many members of Resistance organizations, on the other hand, scorned this position as a mere rationalization of a cowardly, self-interested collaboration between enemy and traitors.

Still, despite his initial hunch that the human remains on rue Le Sueur were somehow tied to the Gestapo, Massu had some nagging doubts. For one thing, he had not been warned off the site, as surely would have happened in advance or soon after the discovery of the bodies on its premises if there had been a Gestapo affiliation. Nor had he encountered any Gestapo agents on the property, which also would likely have occurred if the building had served as an extension of the secret state police. Hours after the initial phone call from his secretary, Massu had still not received any communication from German authorities.

C OMMISSAIRE Massu arrived at his office at 36 Quai des Orfèvres on the Île de la Cité about nine o'clock on the morning of March 12, 1944. His windows on the third floor of the sprawling Police Judiciaire overlooked the horse chestnut trees of the place Dauphine, the restaurant Le Vert-Galant, and the Pont Neuf, the oldest bridge in Paris and still standing despite the increased threat of Allied bombing raids.

Some inspectors were drawing up reports; others looked after detainees in the corridors, none of whom, unfortunately, would turn out to have anything to do with 21 rue Le Sueur. Picking up the Petiot file, which was begun the previous night, Massu prepared to return to the town house to meet a team of dignitaries and officials that included his immediate superior, the prefect of police Amédée Bussière, who was eager to inspect the site for himself as he would have to report to both French and German authorities.

At ten o'clock that morning, the German-controlled broadcasting organization Radio Paris first announced the gruesome discovery of the charnel house on rue Le Sueur. "Petiot has fled Paris," the presenter said, not wasting any time to speculate on the suspect's whereabouts. "He will likely return to the terrorist bands of *Haute-Savoie*," as officials dubbed the Resistance fighters in the Alpine region bordering Switzerland, "and resume his position as médecin-major." In this initial broadcast, as well as many others that followed that day, the radio station painted a portrait of the killer as an outlaw terrorist who opposed the Third Reich.

But Radio Paris had a poor reputation as a source of information. "Radio Paris lies, Radio Paris lies, Radio Paris is German" was a popular refrain sung to the tune of "La Cucaracha." Was Petiot really with the Resistance? Rumors inside the police force already circulated of the suspect's ties to clandestine patriotic organizations. Massu had also heard that a leader of a Resistance network had arrived at the crime scene, spoken with police officers, and then, after having been shown inside the building, left with their permission. Patrolmen Fillion and Teyssier still denied this allegation, but Massu planned to question the patrol officers himself.

As news of the discovered human remains spread, many people began to take detours to see the building on rue Le Sueur, a short walk from the Arc de Triomphe, the Avenue des Champs-Élysées, and the Bois de Boulogne. Many women with handbaskets stopped by on the way to and from the daily ritual of standing in long lines at the bakery, the dairy, the butcher, the greengrocer, the tobacconist, and elsewhere, where they hoped to obtain expensive, often poor-quality rationed goods, if they were still available. When one of Petiot's neighbors, Madame Legouvé, went for a walk with her daughter that morning, she heard two people speak of the discovery. One gasped at the stench outside the physician's town house, claiming that "it smells like death," and the other replied that "death has no odor."

Inside Legouvé's rue Le Sueur apartment building, discussion was more animated. One of her neighbors noted that the smell on the sidewalk was of no consequence compared to the courtyard: "There, it is truly, truly foul." Another neighbor, Monsieur Mentier, shrugged his shoulders, unwilling to speculate other than to state that the smell might well be explained by a crack in the main line of the sewer. The concierge hinted at something more sinister: "If I told you everything I know, it is likely that you would change your opinion."

2.

THE PEOPLE'S DOCTOR

ALL THINGS TRULY WICKED START FROM AN INNOCENCE.

—Ernest Hemingway, *A Moveable Feast*

DR. Marcel André Henri Félix Petiot had seemed a respectable family physician with a flourishing medical practice. He adored his wife, Georgette Lablais Petiot, an attractive thirty-nine-year-old brunette whom he had married almost seventeen years before. They played bridge, often went to the theater or the cinema, and doted on their only son, Gérard (Gerhardt Georges Claude Félix), one month from his sixteenth birthday. All of this made the discoveries at rue Le Sueur even more inconceivable.

The physician had grown up in Auxerre, an old medieval town just under one hundred miles southeast of Paris. At its center, amid the half-timbered buildings on the winding cobbled streets, stood the imposing Gothic Cathedral of St. Étienne and the large Benedictine Abbey of Saint-Germain, with its late-fifteenth-century clock tower. The Yonne River runs through this wine-growing district famous for its Chablis, branching out into the surrounding wooded region that produces its second-leading export, timber.

Petiot's father, Félix Iréné Mustiole, worked at the Auxerre postal and telegraph office. His mother, Marthe Marie Constance Joséphine Bourdon, or Clémence as she preferred to call herself, had also worked there, as a young postal clerk before his birth. Petiot, the older of two children, was born January 17, 1897, just over ten years before his brother Maurice was born in December 1906. Petiot had lived his earliest years in the family's rented apartment on the top floor of a house at 100 rue de Paris.

In 1912, his mother died from complications of a surgery. "At the death of my sister," Henriette Bourdon Gaston told the police in March 1944, "I raised my nephews." Many villagers, on the other hand, would claim that the brothers had lived with her much longer, Marcel for extended periods of time since the age of two. Was Gaston ashamed of the man he had become and therefore downplaying her involvement in his upbringing?

It was difficult, for Massu and historians alike, to navigate through the layers of rumor, gossip, and myth that surrounded Petiot's childhood. As with many other accused murderers, former neighbors dwelled upon tales of his sadism and antisocial behavior. Young Petiot, it was said, liked to capture insects and pull off their legs and heads. He snatched baby birds from nests, poked out their eyes, and laughed as they shrieked in pain and stumbled into the side of the cage. Then, withholding food, he watched them starve to death.

Even his favorite cat was not immune to his cruelty. In one of several variants of the story, when Henriette Gaston was preparing to wash clothes, she put a tub of water on the stove and went to fetch the linen. Marcel was playing on the kitchen floor with the cat. When Gaston returned, the young boy was holding the animal by the neck and attempting to dip its paws in the scalding water. She screamed. Marcel, changing abruptly, hugged the cat to his chest and yelled back that he hated her and wished she were dead. The next morning, after she tried to teach him a lesson in empathy by allowing him to sleep with the cat, she awoke to find the boy covered with scratches and bites. The cat had been smothered to death.

A plethora of anecdotes was easily obtained in the gossip that circulated about the physician, but they were often difficult to verify. By most accounts, Petiot was precocious and highly intelligent. He read at an advanced level all his early years, and later, it was said, he devoured a book a night. His reading was said to be wide-ranging, though this was not reflected in his library, which had a disproportionate number of police novels, studies in criminology, and books about murderers, such as Henri Landru, Jack the Ripper, and Dr. Crippen.

As a child, Petiot had been easily bored in the classroom and often got into trouble. The French police would later learn that he was disciplined for bringing pornographic materials into his elementary school. As several of his former classmates would inform inspectors, young Petiot liked to read about the sexual habits of famous people, dwelling upon what was often then regarded as aberrational behavior. He spoke with relish about the homosexuality of Julius Caesar and Alexander the Great, or the bisexuality of Giacomo Casanova. One of his personal favorites was the Chevalier d'Eon, the transvestite fencer and spy who dazzled eighteenth-century French aristocratic circles.

The Petiot patriarch wanted his boys to follow him into the postal service. But Marcel was not interested in, as he put it, wasting away in an office waiting for old age. He wanted something greater.

Petiot had been an ambitious boy who yearned for power, wealth, and fame, and yet, ultimately, he proved to be a loner. Few friends from childhood would be uncovered. One friend was known only for allowing Petiot to stab a knife between his outstretched fingers on a table or throw them at him, like a circus performer. A former lover was found, a cabaret dancer named Denise, whom he met in his teens in Dijon. She left him one day, prompting Petiot later to quip that that was the only disappearance the police or press did not blame on him.

One former classmate, Jean Delanove, remembered how Petiot sometimes took a gun to school, showing it off to other children on the playground and pointing it at stray cats. Petiot was eventually expelled for bringing the weapon into the classroom and then, in the middle of a lecture, firing it into the ceiling.

Athanise Berthelot, a teacher at Auxerre who knew Petiot between the ages of thirteen and sixteen, summed him up as "intelligent, but not enjoying all his mental faculties. In a word, he was a bizarre character." The assistant principal, Marcel Letrait, agreed. Petiot was smart, but when it came to his studies, he was "incapable of [making] a sustained application."

At age seventeen, Petiot was arrested. In a crime that must have particularly angered his father, still a postal employee, Petiot was caught stealing mail with a contraption he made from a fishing pole with an adhesive at the end. He was believed to be looking for cash, money orders, or just salacious gossip, which he could spread in anonymous letters, perhaps even accompanied by threats of blackmail. The psychiatrist appointed to examine the young delinquent, as required by French law, concluded that Petiot suffered from hereditary mental illness. Petiot's father protested that that was not possible.

Young Petiot seemed to crave attention. As he later said, he had felt abandoned by his parents. When his mother died, his father, grieving, shut himself off further from his two boys. Marcel Petiot would say that he believed that he had been conceived by mistake, and his birth had probably been illegitimate. In any case, he had felt lonely, rejected, and unloved. His first known close relationship was with his younger brother, Maurice. The Petiot brothers would, for the most part, remain close their entire lives.

AFTER a few more unsuccessful stints in school, with probably additional expulsions at Joigny and Dijon, Petiot received his secondary school diploma (Bachot d'Enseignement Secondaire) on July 10, 1915, by studying at home in Auxerre with his uncle, Vidal Gaston, a mathematics teacher. By this time, with the First World War raging, Petiot had volunteered for the army, receiving the early enlistment number at Auxerre of 1097. On January 11, 1916, he began his military training at Sens, a tranquil village with a cathedral designed by the architect William of Sens, better known for his supposed work on Canterbury Cathedral.

Ten months later, Petiot saw his first action, in the muddy, bloody, rat-infested trenches of the Western Front. This was the beginning of four grim months of aerial bombardments, artillery shellings, and vicious close-range fighting. All around young Petiot, in the Eighty-ninth Infantry Regiment, bodies were mangled, bones smashed, and entrails disgorged. The ghastly slaughter of the war of attrition was immense. The Parisian doctor Sumner Jackson, who drove an ambulance on the same battlefield as Petiot's regiment, estimated that the French there lost one hundred men a minute. On May 20, 1917, in a trench at Craonne, along the Chemin des Dames, a strategic passageway to the Aisne, Petiot was wounded. A hand grenade tore an almost three-inch gash in his left foot.

This was a curious wound. A hand grenade, lobbed into a trench, would likely explode upward, not downward into his foot, and indeed, at least one soldier in his unit claimed that Petiot had wounded himself. According to this allegation, Petiot had placed a grenade into a pipe and then put his foot in front of its opening. Petiot adamantly denied this accusation, dismissing it as a malicious fabrication of a man who envied his education.

It was at this time that Petiot started to show pronounced signs of imbalance. Like many shell-shocked soldiers, a term that derives from the First World War, Petiot could not sleep or eat, and he suffered agonizing headaches and vertigo. He lost weight. He would tremble, or startle at the slightest noise. He also burst into fits of unrestrained crying and suffered bronchial complications, probably from an earlier poison-gas attack. The head of the medical team at the hospital in Orlé-ans diagnosed Petiot as showing "mental disequilibrium, neurasthenia, depression, melancholia, obsessions, and phobias."

Over the last twenty-four months of the war, Petiot was shuffled between medical clinics, army barracks, mental asylums, and even a military jail for theft. He was accused of stealing blankets, morphine, and other army supplies, as well as wallets, photographs, and letters. One soldier remembered encountering Petiot for the first time when he returned to his hut and found the smiling stranger stretched out on a nearby cot, reading a book by candlelight. The soldier recognized the book as his own, as was the candle. Petiot, showing no embarrassment, said only, "Here, what is yours is mine." The soldier asked if that principle worked both ways and, receiving the answer that it did, went to rummage through Petiot's haversack. He found only a miniature chess set.

After Petiot's arrival, the unit began to enjoy an unaccustomed variety of dry sausages, cheeses, candy, wine, and other luxuries, no doubt obtained from daily and nightly foraging excursions. Petiot seemed to glow after each triumph. The soldier remembered one conversation about the morality of theft, Petiot arguing that it was completely natural. "How do you think that the great fortunes and colonies have been made? By theft, war, and conquest." Then morality does not exist? No, Petiot answered, "it is the law of the jungle, always. Morality has been created for those who possess so that you do not retake the things gained from their own rapines." Petiot would later claim that he learned a lot from war.

He would have one last stint (September 1918) in active duty, as a machine gunner with the Ninety-first Infantry Regiment at Charleville in the Ardennes. This was in the Second Battle of the Marne, and the Germans were coming as close to taking Paris as they had since the First Battle of the Marne four years before. But here, too, Petiot ran into trouble with authorities, and his panic attacks returned. The physician later claimed that he had faked mental illness to avoid combat and had used knowledge gained in the hospital's library, particularly its medical journals, to embellish his performances. The doctors who diagnosed him, on the other hand, were convinced it was no act.

Petiot would be institutionalized in not one, but several different mental hospitals over the next three years, including Fleury-les-Aubrais, Bagnères, Évreux, and Rennes. Five months after the armistice, Petiot was still institutionalized in the psychiatric division of Rennes Military Hospital. He was diagnosed as suffering from "mental imbalance, along with sleepwalking, melancholia, and depression marked by a tendency towards ideas of persecution and suicide." Petiot was discharged in July 1919 with a 40 percent disability pension, though in September 1920 he was given full disability. Examiners believed that Petiot was unable to work and required institutionalization with "continuous surveillance." After later medical tests, his disability was reduced in March 1922 to 50 percent. This rate was confirmed again in July 1923.

In evaluating his mental health, army investigators had interviewed many family members. His grandmother, Jeannquin Constance Bourdon, told them that Petiot had always been a "delicate and nervous" child. He wet the bed and soiled his clothes until the age of ten or twelve. At night, he would not sleep, but always wanted to "go for a walk." His uncle and teacher, Vidal Gaston, described him as "very intelligent and understands well," but added, "what bizarre behavior." No friends visited him, and Gaston had not seen him either since he helped him pass his exams. He said that he could "provide no information on his mental state."

But the army board was not the only institution evaluating the patient at this time. Petiot was also, remarkably, a medical student at the University of Paris. After his discharge from the military, he had joined an accelerated course intended to help French veterans readjust to civilian life. The first two years of the program were at Dijon, where he studied osteology, histology, anatomy, biological chemistry, physiology, and dissection. He completed his third and final year in Paris, graduating on December 15, 1921, with honors. His thesis, *A Contribution to the Study of Acute Progressive Paralysis,* discussed "Landry's disease," named after the physician who, in 1859, first diagnosed the symptoms of nerve degeneration.

Questions were later raised about his degree. Could he really have passed the exams after such a brief period of study? The eminent psychiatrist Paul Gouriou later expressed skepticism that Petiot had written his thesis, noting a lively market for buying and selling theses near the university. But he did not cite any evidence for this claim, nor has anyone else. In fact, as the dean of the Faculty of Medicine at the University of Paris confirmed to the French police, Petiot was a legitimate degree-holder. Whether he deserved the distinction of honors for the thesis, which was a mere twenty-six pages in length and described by a later physician as "very banal," is more debatable.

At any rate, Petiot now enjoyed a moment of triumph. His father organized a celebratory dinner for his graduation, borrowing silver from neighbors and bringing out china not used since his mother's death. Maurice, too, waited anxiously for the return of the older brother he adored. Petiot, who still felt that his father had never expected much of him, arrived punctually and behaved in a formal, if cold and distant, manner. He initiated no conversation and answered most inquiries with only a few words. Then, before the dessert was served, the older Petiot son announced that he had an appointment elsewhere and walked out of the room.

TWENTY-FIVE-YEAR-OLD Marcel Petiot first set up his medical practice in the old town of Villeneuve-sur-Yonne, some seventy-five miles southeast of Paris and just over twenty-five miles from Auxerre. He moved into a small house on the cobbled rue Carnot, which was flanked on one end by the Gothic Church of Notre Dame, begun by Pope Alexander for the king of France Louis VII in 1163, and on the other by the "House of Seven Heads," a mansion with marble busts looking out from under second-floor windows.

Petiot had chosen this small town mainly because it lay close to home and had fewer doctors in residence. Indeed, there were only two, and both were elderly. Petiot's advertisement, which he distributed upon arrival, summed up his talents at the expense of his rivals: "Dr. Petiot is young, and only a young doctor can remain up to date on the latest methods born of a progress which marches with giant strides." Petiot promised to treat, not exploit, his patients. He soon flourished, drawing a variety of patients who praised his work.

The young physician was kind, courteous, and charming. He listened well and, for many, seemed remarkably adept at diagnosing illnesses. "I know exactly what you mean," he often said, "I know just what your trouble is," before launching into a description of his patients' suffering, often with astonishing accuracy. One recurring rumor was that Petiot had hidden a small microphone under a table in the waiting room. Petiot comforted many patients with his uncanny diagnostic abilities and convinced many Villeneuve-sur-Yonne residents that he was the best doctor in town.

Madame Husson later told how he, with the help of a homemade ointment, managed to remove a growth on a child's forehead that had long defied medical treatment. Monsieur Fritsch recalled how Petiot offered to treat one of his neighbors who had been diagnosed with an unidentified terminal illness. Petiot said that he knew of a new, risky experimental drug that could either kill or cure, and asked if the patient wished to try it. He did. The patient would live another quarter of a century.

What's more, Petiot opened his office on Sunday, for workers who could not visit him during the week, and made house calls, riding his bicycle long distances to treat the sick, particularly children. He gave discounts to older and poorer patients, and sometimes waived the fees entirely. Veterans of the First World War also paid much less, if anything. Petiot became known as the "worker's doctor" or "people's doctor." He soon traded his bicycle for a yellow sports car, a Renault 40CV. Over the next few years, Petiot would own a series of them, including an Amilcar, Salmson, and a Butterosi.

Petiot was enjoying his newfound success. He dined regularly at the Hôtel du Dauphin on rue Carnot and delved into the history of his adopted town, reading books by its famous residents, such as the *philosophe* Joseph Joubert and the romantic poet François-René de Chateaubriand. Petiot sang, sculpted, painted, played chess, and one year he won the town's checkers tournament. He took pride in his cravats, the one item of fashion he permitted himself, and often indulged in late-night walks, usually wrapped up in a black coat with his hat pulled down over his eyes.

Yet there were already concerns about the brash young doctor. Advertising his services was frowned upon by colleagues as undignified, and the way he presented himself at the expense of his rivals was deemed even more so. Petiot's tendency to prescribe strong, unorthodox medications worried Villeneuve-sur-Yonne's pharmacists. "Horse cures!" Dr. Paul Mayaud called them. Unfazed, Petiot replied that pharmacists and drug companies had long diluted their medications to increase profits, and this forced him to strengthen the dosage to obtain its intended effect. Pharmacists, besides, had no right to criticize medical treatment ordered by a licensed physician.

A pharmacist later told how he once refused to fill one of Petiot's unorthodox prescriptions—a dose for a child, he said, "that could kill an adult." Petiot's alleged response was chilling, if he was serious, as his enemies claimed that he had been: Isn't it better to do away with this kid who does nothing but annoy his mother?

It was curious that Marcel Petiot, known to be frugal to excess, would offer so many discounts and waive so many fees in his practice. Actually, Petiot had found a way to beat the system, which was something that appealed to him immensely. So while he enjoyed the reputation of offering free or discounted medical service, Petiot was signing up his patients for public assistance without their knowledge, and being reimbursed by the state. Even a few people who paid him in goods, trinkets, or produce, including cheese, eggs, and poultry, were added to the social register. In those cases, the "people's doctor" was receiving double payment for his services.

But there was another implication to this fraud.

RENÉ-GUSTAVE Nézondet, a clerk at the town hall of Villeneuve-sur-Yonne, was Petiot's oldest known friend. They had met in 1924, when Petiot came to an auction looking to buy furniture for his newly purchased house, a three-story structure on rue Carnot. "It was a veritable bewitchment," Nézondet said, trying to describe the sense of camaraderie that the two bachelors shared. "I could never find the cause of this voiceless attraction that drew me towards him, almost despite myself and any rational consideration which would have called for me to stay out of his way."

Curiosity piqued, Nézondet came to see more of his new friend. Petiot was polite, eloquent, charming, an excellent conversationist, and above all, very intelligent. At the same time, Nézondet said his "exuberant vitality" could soon disappear, plunging him into severe "childlike rages and despair." The two men enjoyed weekend trips to surrounding villages for dinner, which Nézondet always paid for. They also spent long hours at cafés, Nézondet always drinking wine and Petiot a small black coffee. Again, Nézondet picked up the tab.

In 1926, over one of these meals, Petiot suddenly turned to his friend and said, "I think I will get involved in politics." It was such an abrupt and unexpected announcement that Nézondet doubted that he was serious. But sure enough Petiot registered as a candidate for that spring's council election and hit the campaign trail with ferocity. He would run as a member of the Socialist Party, which in Villeneuve-sur-Yonne, as in many parts of France in the mid-1920s, was thriving. Petiot believed that this was the party of the future. The increasing power of the "have-nots," with whom he identified, would, he thought, eventually overwhelm rivals with the strength of numbers.

Petiot had gotten to know many of these have-nots in his medical practice. He paid attention to his patients' concerns and put many of them in his debt for "free" medical care. Now, if elected, Petiot promised to make the rich and privileged citizens pay for more social services, ranging from a new sewer system to playgrounds for the children. Many people listened. Petiot developed a reputation for lively conversation, both far-ranging and free-spirited, punctuated only by a bizarre unrestrained laughter that came at unexpected or awkward moments. It was compared to the howl of a shipwrecked man who had lost everything.

So far from hurting his chances at election, Petiot's eccentricities sometimes proved beneficial on the campaign trail. He was a night owl who slept little and often had great difficulty winding down. He poured this restless energy into the campaign. His mind always seemed to be racing ahead to solve the next problem. In the meantime, he continued providing free and discounted medical service to patients, thereby building his practice and political base of loyal supporters, all the while keeping on, secretly, being reimbursed for his services by the state.

Petiot, no surprise, won the election; the only surprise was the margin of victory. It was a landslide. Marcel Petiot, only thirty years old, was about to be inaugurated as mayor. He would soon follow up this success by winning an election for Yonne's *conseil général,* the approximate equivalent of a US congressman. When one friend congratulated him, Petiot was blunt. "That's nothing. I am going to go very far."

3.

PRELIMINARY FINDINGS

ALL EVENING, I HAVE RECEIVED TELEPHONE CALLS AND
REPORTS. IT IS CLEAR THAT WE ARE IN THE PRESENCE OF
A STRANGE AFFAIR WHOSE SIGNIFICANCE IS GOING
TO INCREASE.

—Amédée Bussière, prefect of police

IT was the afternoon of March 12, 1944, that the first printed account of the sinister discovery on rue Le Sueur hit the streets. The brief mention in *Paris-Midi* managed to garble the few facts known at the time. According to this report, employees of the gas company, investigating a gaslike odor, entered the building and discovered "the charred remains of two people in the boiler." No other information was provided, other than the equally false statement that several tramps had been found on the premises, and one of them started the fire.

Outside 21 rue Le Sueur, the crowd had begun to grow. The smell—described as a sickening sweet smell that permeated everything—was now worse than it had been the previous night. One First World War veteran outside the property was reminded of his experience spending several days in a shell hole with five dead bodies. "After two days," he said to Jean-François Dominique, a young journalist with Toulouse's *La Républic du Sud-Ouest,* "it smelled just like this."

About two dozen police officers, faces pale with fear, tried in vain to usher along the crowd. Behind the barricades, while Massu showed police and legal dignitaries around the property, pointing out where they had found "a pile of skulls, tibias, humeri, broken thigh bones, and human debris of all kinds," a team of four men continued the excruciating work of sifting out the remains from the lime pit. Massu's assistants were horrified at the task, so the commissaire had hired gravediggers from Passy cemetery.

Petiot's neighbors talked to the police and to one another. Some residents claimed not to know that the house at No. 21 was inhabited, or at least not regularly by "respectable people." Others discussed the owner's strange behavior. A nearby concierge described how Petiot would enter or depart from his courtyard, invariably on a bicycle with a cart in tow. Each time, the physician nervously glanced over his shoulder and all around him to check that no one was watching him. The concierge at No. 22, Marie Lombre, agreed, noting that the man came almost daily and usually wore a Basque beret and workman's clothes. His cart was often filled with furniture, works of art, and items of value. But sometimes, she said, "it was impossible to tell."

Victor Avenelle, a fifty-three-year-old professor of Romance languages who lived on the sixth floor of 23 rue Le Sueur, claimed often to hear shouts and disturbing "cries for help." He had heard this screaming three or four times since Christmas, usually between eleven and midnight or perhaps one in the morning. The voice was always female. Another tenant in that building, Count de Saunis, said that he sometimes could not sleep for the yelling, or the odd hammerlike sounds that emanated from the house. Others claimed to hear laughter of women, strange popping noises that resembled the uncorking of champagne bottles, or even the sounds of an old horse-drawn carriage clip-clopping down rue Le Sueur about eleven thirty at night before stopping outside No. 21. The police, at this point, had no idea what to make of these statements.

Massu's detectives powdered for fingerprints and continued to search through the town house for any evidence of the crime or its victims. In one of the buildings in the back of the courtyard, police found a second, smaller pile of lime about fifteen to twenty inches high, six feet wide, and six to nine feet long. It, too, was filled with human bones. Nearby was a cart lacking a wheel. Was this the one neighbors had seen? At various other places of the mansion, agents found workman's clothes, soiled with lime. In the entrance was a darkly stained brown suitcase that contained a nail file, an eyelash brush, the sheath of an umbrella, and eleven pairs of women's shoes. The dark stains on the suitcase were almost certainly blood.

In Dr. Petiot's consulting room, police found a Czechoslovakian-made gas mask, which, they concluded, was used as protection against "the odors of the cadavers" as he transported them to the stove. A "needle for injections" was also found, as was a small bust of a woman made in wax.

Agents Petit and Renonciat discovered a black satin dress with deep décolletage and adorned with two golden swallows, designed by Silvy-Rosa at rue Estelle in Marseille. The garment was still scented with perfume. Another officer uncovered a small, round, old-fashioned woman's hat, in brown velvet with a peacock feather, made by Suzanne Talbot, at 14 rue Royale in Paris. A woman's nightgown with the initial "T" was also discovered in Dr. Petiot's consulting room, along with a man's gray dress shirt with red stripes and red embroidered initials "K.K.," which someone had tried to remove. Two other items bearing the same initials were also found: a white shirt with dark blue stripes and a pair of undershorts.

It was another find, however, that underlined the sheer extent of the human tragedy. Concealed in a cupboard in Petiot's basement were some twenty-two toothbrushes, twenty-two bottles of perfume, twenty-two combs and pocket combs, sixteen cases of lipstick, fifteen boxes of face powder, and thirty-six tubes of makeup, mascara, and other beauty products. There were also ten scalpels, nine fingernail files, eight hand mirrors, eight ice bags, seven pairs of eyeglasses, six powder puffs, five cigarette holders, five gas masks, four pairs of tweezers, two umbrellas, a walking cane, a penknife, a pillowcase, a lighter, and a woman's bathing suit. Clearly there were many women among the victims, and the killer appeared to be hoarding their personal belongings. Had he also been sadistically inflicting pain or sexually abusing them before chopping them into pieces and dumping the remains into a lime pit?

The question became more charged when police found something else at rue Le Sueur: two specimens of human genitals preserved in jars of Formol.

A T some point that morning—the time is disputed—a black Citroën pulled up to 21 rue Le Sueur with four German officers, obviously of high rank. They entered the building and then quickly returned to the car. By the early afternoon, the time also unclear, a telegram from the High Command of the German Military Occupation reached Massu's offices on the Quai des Orfèvres. It read in full: "Order from German Authorities. Arrest Petiot. Dangerous Madman."

As Commissaire Massu prepared his arrest warrant, an officer telephoned police headquarters with something he'd uncovered in Petiot's home region of Yonne. In 1926, just one year before he married Georgette, Petiot's lover, Louisette Delaveau, had disappeared under mysterious circumstances.

Louisette Delaveau, or Louise as he called her, had worked as a housekeeper with one of Petiot's patients. She and the doctor had met at a dinner in 1924, when Delaveau, then a twenty-four-year-old brunette with dark eyes, served the meal. Petiot was obviously attracted. His friend René Nézondet said that he had never seen him so carefree.

Petiot had used his contacts around town to find out more about this woman. He learned that she liked to shop on rue Carnot, attend mass at Notre Dame, and occasionally relax at Frascot's bistro. The proprietor of that establishment, Léon Fiscot, or "Old Man Frascot," also happened to be one of Petiot's patients. Surprised and apparently enjoying the opportunity to play matchmaker, Frascot agreed to serve as a go-between. Petiot wrote her a letter and asked his friend to deliver it. Louise, if she was interested, should telephone him at his medical practice or show up at his house on rue Carnot.

When she called the next day, they arranged a meeting for the evening at Frascot's bistro. The date went well, ending with a romantic walk back to Petiot's house. They would continue to sneak away for arranged and impromptu dalliances, until not long afterward, Louisette moved in with the doctor. For the sake of appearances, she became his cook and maid.

The difficulties of living with Petiot—obsessive, compulsive, and already demonstrating a passion for purchasing "bargains" at auctions—soon took their toll. Other sources of tension surfaced, not least of which was that Petiot had begun an affair with another patient. Delaveau may have been pregnant, too, as she had confided to one of her friends, adding that Petiot would take care of it. The young physician was already suspected of supplementing his income with illegal abortions.

But in May 1926, Louisette Delaveau disappeared. To friends, Petiot explained her departure as the result of a quarrel so uproarious that she had stormed out of town without saying where she was headed. René Nézondet remembered how distraught his friend appeared after her disappearance. At one meeting over lunch not long afterward, Petiot had been weeping. He stared into the distance aimlessly. His hands trembled even more than usual.

Apparently Louisette had not said good-bye to her friends or anyone else in town, either. She left no forwarding address and did not pack her personal belongings. "If she returns to the house when I am not here," Petiot told Suzanne, who replaced her as cook and maid, "her things are there and you should give her this envelope." The new employee did not know what was in the envelope. Louisette never returned.

Few at the time suspected anything sinister. One anonymous letter to the police did accuse Petiot of murdering his lover, but investigators did not find any evidence of foul play. The official search was abandoned after a few months.

Not long after Louisette's disappearance, it had been reported, Petiot was seen loading a large wicker basket into the trunk of his sports car. This testimony gained additional relevance a few days later, when the body of a young woman in her mid-twenties was retrieved from the same kind of basket outside Dijon. What's more, Commissaire Massu was in a position to appreciate the importance of something that had escaped investigators at the time. The corpse in the basket had been decapitated, the body had been dismembered, and the inner organs and intestines had been cut out.

M ASSU approached crime methodically and with as little emotion as possible, trying not to differentiate between major and minor crimes, or what he called interesting and uninteresting ones. In each case, it was only a matter of victims and criminals—the former had to be identified and the latter apprehended and brought to justice. No more, no less. "A murder is a murder," he said.

Massu was a native Parisian, born on December 9, 1889. His father had died in Massu's second year, and his mother had supported the family by working at a grocer's shop. At the age of thirteen, Massu had gone to work for a butcher on rue des Capucines. He would spend the next five or six years working for various butchers around the capital. In January 1908, just after his eighteenth birthday, Massu volunteered for the army, joining the 117th Infantry Regiment. He was discharged two years later with the rank of sergeant and eventually found work again in the credit office of the large department store Galeries Lafayette, just a few steps from Dr. Petiot's future home. Massu stayed there until his application to the police was accepted.

On December 16, 1911, at age twenty-two, Massu began work under Charles Vallet in the Brigade Mobile, which had been established to supervise the 1900 Paris Universal Exposition. His first days on the force coincided with the pursuit of the infamous band of anarchists known as the Bonnot Gang.

Viewing theft as liberation, Jules-Joseph Bonnot and his men had stolen automobiles and rapid-reloading rifles, which they then used to burglarize everything from shops to homes. On December 21, 1911, for instance, when they robbed a Montmartre branch of the Société Génerale Bank, they fled in an automobile; the police, at the time, pursued criminals on horseback and bicycle. The reign of the "Motor Car Bandits," as the press dubbed them, ended with its leaders killed or captured, all during Massu's first year on the force.

After years of chasing pickpockets, which he called "good training" for teaching him how to follow a suspect, watch that person closely, and ultimately catch him or her in the act of committing a crime, Massu had developed into a patient and observant detective with a mastery of police procedure. He was praised for his psychological insight into the criminal mind. As he gained more responsibilities, rising to secretary in August 1921 and eventually commissaire of police in January 1933, Massu would also earn a reputation for his ability to recognize the strengths and weaknesses of the men who served on his team. Some superb interrogators, Massu said, could not catch a pickpocket, and many detectives, veritable bloodhounds in the hunt for a criminal, would be lost in the interrogation room. His job was to delegate the tasks of an investigation accordingly.

Massu's own specialty was interrogation. He placed an enormous value on its importance to an investigation. Evidence at a crime scene was often complicated, subject to a variety of interpretations; witnesses may lie, mislead, or make mistakes, and science, even in the best of circumstances, was not infallible. But an interrogation could produce a detailed confession—and this, when corroborated by outside verification, represented the most certain way to determine if someone was guilty and, what's more, ensure that justice was in fact being served.

Success in the interrogation room meant tailoring his strategy to suit the suspect sitting in the green velvet chair in his office. Whether dealing with a thug or a sophisticated swindler, it was always essential to create a calm environment for questioning. A glass of beer or a dry white wine, the commissaire said, was more productive than screaming in the suspect's face, threatening reprisals, or resorting to blows. Massu prided himself not only on gaining the most confessions at the Quai des Orfèvres, but, more important, on the fact that he had achieved these results "without raising the voice or the hand."

In 1937, when the International Exposition had returned to Paris, Massu established the "Brigade Volante," a mobile police squad to fight crime, which had risen dramatically at the 185-day World's Fair that drew some 31.5 million registered visitors. Massu tried to make sure that this "ritual of Peace and Progress" would not be scarred by murder or tragedy. He averaged about three hundred arrests per month, but in one key respect, Massu and all his colleagues had not succeeded.

A German drifter named Eugen Weidmann had been luring tourists away to a small villa west of Paris, at St. Cloud, where he killed and robbed his six victims and then buried most of them in his basement. Weidmann was eventually caught, sentenced to death, and guillotined in June 1939. The massive, unruly crowd outside St. Pierre's prison at Versailles that day would prompt the French president LeBrun, nine days later, to abolish public executions.

Now, four and a half years after Weidmann, there was another serial killer in Paris, this one more prolific and far more disturbing.

WITH the order from the German authorities in hand, Commissaire Massu hurriedly drafted a warrant for the arrest of Marcel Petiot and his wife, Georgette. The latter was described as "about forty years old, small stature, light complexion, thin face." Dr. Petiot, age forty-seven, was presented as being "about 180 cm [just under 5'11"], rather corpulent, dark chestnut brown hair, thrown back, slight frontal baldness, clean-shaven, strong jaw, chin slightly prominent, and wearing a large overcoat." Petiot is, the notice warned, "considered dangerous."

"The steps of an investigation," Massu said, "are always the same: statements, interrogations of witnesses, picking up clues and fingerprints at the scene of the crime and everywhere it seems necessary." All of this would be "compared and examined scientifically," looking for "anything that can be useful to the demonstration of the truth." As for finding the suspect, Massu was confident. No matter how clever a murderer had been, how perfect his plan, or flawless its execution, a murderer was always, at some point, "an idiot." A mistake would eventually be made and he would pounce.

Investigator Marius Battut and a couple of homicide detectives headed to Petiot's apartment on rue Caumartin, which was not too far from the métro stations Caumartin and Saint-Lazare. The apartment was in the middle of the lively Opera District, full of hotels, restaurants, cafés, theaters, nightclubs, brothels, and many other commercial establishments on and around the Boulevard Haussmann.

The officers walked up to the five-story building at No. 66. Two businesses were on the ground floor: the hairdresser salon Gaston Coiffure and the bistro La Chope du Printemps. An air raid shelter was in the basement. To the right of the front door was a black marble plaque with engraved gold letters advertising the medical practice and office hours of Dr. Petiot, a graduate of the University of Paris Medical School.

The bistro, the hair salon, and Petiot's practice were all closed. The concierge, Raymonde Denis, happened to be away from her lodge when the police team arrived. Her twelve-year-old daughter, Alice, on the other hand, told the officers that she had seen Marcel Petiot and his wife, Georgette, about nine thirty the previous night, when they had returned home together on foot. She thought that they might still be in their apartment.

The officers walked up two flights of stairs and knocked. No one answered. The door, the officers discovered, was unlocked. Later the police would learn that Petiot never locked his doors, because a skilled burglar, he reasoned, would always find a way inside, and this way, he would not have to make repairs. The police, however, did not enter.

Although they held a warrant for the arrest of the couple, and authorization to search rue Le Sueur, they did not have permission to search Petiot's apartment. The Germans might flaunt French laws, but Battut was determined to follow procedure. On their way back to the headquarters to obtain the necessary paperwork, the officers met Petiot's concierge.

"Yesterday evening," thirty-nine-year-old Raymond Denis said, "I saw Dr. Petiot for the last time at seven o'clock." He was leaving the apartment on his bicycle. About eight o'clock, Georgette had stopped by the concierge lodge with some cakes for her daughter. Madame Denis did not know anything else about the evening, other than the fact that at about nine thirty p.m., after she had gone to bed, her daughter said that she had seen Marcel and Georgette come home.

When the police officers returned to rue Caumartin the following morning with the search warrant, there was no one there. In contrast to the chaos at rue Le Sueur, the rooms here were neat and tidy. Papers, personal belongings, and other objects of value were conspicuously absent. What they did find was a large supply of coffee, sugar, chocolate, and spirits, all difficult to obtain in wartime Paris—a veritable prewar café, Massu said. There was also a variety of prescription drugs and narcotics, including peyote, a hallucinogenic drug popular in Parisian nightclubs, and some 504 vials of morphine, worth a fortune on the black market.

This was a large amount, even for a physician who, as reports indicated, claimed to treat drug addicts in his practice. Was Petiot a drug user himself? Was he dealing in drugs on the side? Early rumors suggested that Petiot catered to a diverse clientele, and his office was located in a notorious drug district. Physicians, too, investigators knew, were the most readily available source of illegal drugs in Occupied Paris.

In addition, the inspectors found a collection of bizarre artwork and a number of masks described as "diabolical and grimacing." On a pedestal in the doctor's office, between the cupboard and the wall, was a wooden statue, about two feet in height, of a beast, a devilish or Pan-like creature with a grotesquely large phallus. Dr. Petiot, police soon learned, was the artist.

4.

TWO WITNESSES

THE REIGN OF BEASTS HAS BEGUN.

—Albert Camus, *Notebook*, September 7, 1939

MARCEL Petiot had indeed been selling drugs. By March 1944, no fewer than ninety-five registered drug addicts were attending his "detoxication program" at rue Caumartin, ostensibly to be cured of their addiction by a series of increasingly smaller doses. Petiot had gained a reputation for this treatment and also for being a sympathetic doctor who indulged his patients. His waiting room was regularly packed. Georgette, who did the bookkeeping for the practice, was busier than ever.

Massu now learned that Petiot had a sizable file with the Brigade Mondaine, a specialized force of the Police Judiciaire that dealt with, among other things, prostitution, procurement, pornography, and drugs. In early 1942, in another periodic clamp-down on the rampant illicit drug trade in Paris, the Brigade Mondaine had launched a campaign to arrest suspected addicts. Among the people taken into custody was one of Petiot's patients, and the subsequent inquiry had raised a number of questions about the physician, which, in light of the later investigation, would prove to be a key piece of evidence.

The patient was Jean-Marc Van Bever, a forty-one-year-old coal deliverer. This was his first steady job, gained only a few months before, with the rising demand for this scarce resource to heat offices, apartments, and other buildings. Previously Van Bever had invested his inheritance into a number of printing businesses that had gone bust. For most of the late 1930s, he had lived in poverty, eking out an existence thanks to social welfare and various charities. This was an unexpected result for a man of his background.

After graduating from the prestigious Louis-le-Grand Lycée, Van Bever had studied at university, including a year in law school. He spoke English and knew a smattering of Spanish and Italian. His father, Adolphe Van Bever, had coedited a noted anthology of French poets, and his great-uncle was the painter La Quintinie.

At the time of his arrest, Van Bever had protested that he was not an addict himself, claiming only to have mixed in the environment thanks to his relationship with a prostitute named Jeannette Gaul. At thirty-four years of age, Gaul had a severe addiction to morphine and one of its more potent derivatives, heroin, which had grown in popularity in Paris after expanding beyond its original use as a cough suppressant and cure for a variety of diseases of the "air passages," ranging from bronchitis to pneumonia. Both morphine and heroin flourished in the demimonde, not least among prostitutes trying to escape hazards of the trade.

After working as a chambermaid with a family in Fontainebleau and later moving on to a number of brothels in Nantes, Clamecy, and Auxerre, Gaul had arrived in Paris just after the Occupation. Her last pimp, Henri "The Jailbird" Baldenweek, had abandoned her and she became an unlicensed streetwalker, the most exposed and dangerous of the main types of prostitution that flourished in the Occupation. In November 1941, not far from La Madeleine, Gaul met Van Bever. After three weeks of regular visits, he asked her to move in with him in his small rented room at 56 rue Piat in the 20th arrondissement. She promised to quit her job. This was two days before Christmas 1941.

Gaul, however, remained an addict. To obtain narcotics, she had exploited the lack of control in the system by obtaining heroin prescriptions from five different doctors. One of them was Marcel Petiot. In the first month and a half of 1942, specifically the last twenty-two days, Petiot had written five prescriptions for her and two more in the name of Van Bever.

On February 19, 1942, Inspectors Dupont and Gautier of the Brigade Mondaine arrested Gaul in her room. Van Bever was also apprehended, and then after being held in custody for almost four weeks, he was released on bail. Discovering Petiot's name as the physician who prescribed the drugs, the Brigade Mondaine sent this information to Achille Olmi, the *juge d'instruction,* an investigating magistrate who would decide whether or not the state would prosecute. Olmi summoned Petiot for questioning.

The prescriptions were legal, Petiot argued. He was merely attempting to cure his patient by prescribing progressively smaller doses of the drug. This method was superior to having the addict "go out and steal, or even kill to get it" and, even more, remained "the only known cure." The state was wrong to suspect him of trafficking. If he had been doing that, Petiot said, he would not have charged a mere 50 francs for a visit and 200 for a substance that would fetch far more on the black market.

As for writing prescriptions to Van Bever, Petiot said that he had been told that he was an addict, and after a physical examination, he had believed it was true. He had, however, become suspicious on their third visit, when Van Bever, claiming to be deaf, answered the doctor's questions only after his girlfriend whispered in his ear. At this point, Petiot refused to sign any more prescriptions. Both Van Bever and Gaul later acknowledged that this was accurate. Van Bever defended his deception by saying that he had been surprised when his girlfriend claimed that he was a deaf addict and had not known what to do. On the spur of the moment, he had gone along with the scheme.

Van Bever and Gaul later changed their story in certain respects to create just enough confusion that the magistrate felt compelled to indict the patients as well as the physician. The crux of the matter was that Van Bever now claimed that Petiot knew all along that he was no drug addict and that the drugs in his name would go to his lover. If the patients were found guilty, they would go to prison; if Petiot were found guilty, he would, at minimum, lose his medical practice. The trial, which would take place at the Tribunal Correctionnel, was set for May 26, 1942.

Two months before the trial, however, Van Bever disappeared.

=

VAN Bever was last seen at a café on rue Piat on the morning of March 22. He was having a drink with his friend and fellow coal deliverer, a former Italian hatter named Ugo Papini. During their conversation, Van Bever was called away to meet a tall man in his mid-forties, dark-haired, clean-shaven, and wearing a beret. Not long afterward, Van Bever returned and said that he had to leave with the stranger. It was all very mysterious, Papini acknowledged. Van Bever said only that the man was a friend of Jeannette Gaul, or more exactly, the husband of one of her friends. "Perhaps Jeannette had some debts that they want me to pay," Van Bever said, promising not to be gone long.

When Van Bever failed to return that night, or show up for work the following day, Papini entered his room, which looked untidy as usual. Strangely, Van Bever, a smoker, had not taken his tobacco with him. Earlier, he had told Papini that he had to mail an urgent letter, but it was still in the room. Papini wrote immediately to Van Bever's lawyer, Maître Michel Menard, who suggested that he report the missing person to the *procureur de la République,* or public prosecutor.

On March 26, 1942, Papini filed a report, elaborating on his fears for his friend's safety. He never suspected Dr. Petiot, nor did the police. At the time, there was a more likely suspect.

Over the past few months, Van Bever had been visiting another prostitute, France Mignot. In November 1941, he had accompanied her to her family's house in Troyes. As he prepared to have sex with her, Mignot's brothers and mother attacked. Van Bever was stabbed, beaten, and robbed. After his release from the hospital, he pressed charges. The girl, her mother, and her brothers had all been arrested, with a trial scheduled to begin on Tuesday, March 24, 1942. So when Van Bever suddenly disappeared two days before that, Papini suspected that the culprit was someone in or close to that family.

But then, on March 26, while Petiot's case was still pending, an unknown man delivered two letters to the office of Jeannette Gaul's public defender, Maître Françoise Pavie on Boulevard Saint-Germain. Both letters were purportedly written by Van Bever. The first one, addressed to his attorney, Maître Menard, informed him that his services were no longer needed—an odd way to end a business relationship with an old family friend. The second letter, addressed to Jeannette Gaul, was even more peculiar.

"It is no longer necessary to tell any stories," the writer began. He then claimed to be a drug addict who required one to four shots a day and admonished her to tell the truth. There was little here about Van Bever's lover, but a great deal instead about his physician:

> *You know that Dr. Petiot examined me in the next room. The proof is that he saw the scabs of my hypos. If I made false statements, it was to get temporary freedom to make a new life for myself somewhere else. We will meet on your release to try to make a new life together, far from all filth. I kiss you warmly.*

The letter was signed "Jean Marc van Bever."

Why would Van Bever go to the trouble of writing to his lover only to spend two-thirds of his letter confessing to an addiction that either he did not have or that, if he did, would not be news, and then proceed to make points that corroborated Petiot's position? Why, too, in a letter to his lover, was he signing his full name? Van Bever's attorney, for one, doubted that these letters were written by his client.

The police continued to search for Van Bever in bars, prisons, hospitals, asylums, morgues, and other likely places around the capital and surrounding country, without success. His trial with Petiot, meanwhile, came up, as scheduled, at the Tenth Police Court. Van Bever was pronounced guilty in absentia and sentenced to a year's imprisonment with a fine of 10,000 francs. He was never found.

As for Jeannette Gaul, she received a fine of 2,400 francs and a sentence of six months in prison, though she would be released after serving only three months (in May 1942), counting from her arrest in February. She returned to the streets and her drug habit, even visiting Dr. Petiot again. She died three months later of tetanus, a complication from an unclean hypodermic needle.

Petiot argued that Van Bever's disappearance—"he did not dare to show up"—was proof of his own innocence. He was let off with a fine of 10,000 francs, which his lawyer, René Floriot, appealed and soon managed to reduce to 2,400 francs. Dr. Petiot had emerged from a potentially disastrous narcotics charge with his record untarnished.

A S the Van Bever–Gaul investigation was winding down, Petiot was implicated in a second narcotics case. The circumstances were similar. He was allegedly attempting to cure a patient, who had then tried to circumvent his treatment and gain more drugs by deception. But as the case emerged, there would be even more striking similarities.

The patient in the investigation was the twenty-eight-year-old Régine or Raymonde Baudet. In early 1942, when Petiot had prescribed Sonéryl, a mild sleeping pill, Baudet had attempted to replace the word "Sonéryl" with "14 vials of heroin." The pharmacist on rue des Écoles was not fooled by the unsophisticated tactic. He notified the police. Baudet was taken into custody on March 16, 1942, her fourth arrest on drug charges, two of which had previously led to convictions.

Once again hauled into court for a drug case, Petiot freely admitted trying to cure Baudet of her addiction. He had written four prescriptions for heroin for her already under the name that she had given him, Raymonde Khaït, the last name borrowed from her stepfather. Petiot had refused, he further stated, to write any more prescriptions, offering instead a sedative. It was hardly his fault that his patient, in conjunction with one of her lovers, a man named Daniel Desrouët, had tried to alter his prescription.

There is no evidence that Petiot was involved in the attempted forgery, but what he did next was surprising to say the least, and the case becomes more convoluted. According to the police report filed by Raymonde's half brother, Fernand Lavie, a thirty-six-year-old clerk at the Préfecture de Police, Petiot went over to the home of their mother, fifty-three-year-old Marthe Antoinette Khaït, at 27 rue de la Huchette, in the Latin Quarter. Passing the cabaret El Djezair in the same building, an Abwehr-controlled establishment, Petiot entered the apartment and berated Khaït for her daughter's preposterous mistakes. Then Petiot offered to help. They would first need to hire a good attorney, and he offered to pay the expenses.

The physician then advised that Raymonde could best escape a long prison sentence if Madame Khaït claimed that she was herself a drug addict. The authorities would believe it, he explained, because Raymonde had already told the police that she and her mother shared the prescriptions, which had been made to the name of Khaït. Then, to make this claim more credible should the police examine her, Petiot offered to make a dozen injections in her thigh. The injections, he promised, would be innocuous.

Khaït's son was shocked by the doctor's proposal. Under no circumstances, he told her, should she be a party to such fraud. Madame Khaït, however, was eventually won over by Petiot's apparent generosity and adamancy. After many years of helping her daughter, Khaït said that she would not stop now in this time of need. Petiot and Khaït went into another room. A few minutes later, the doctor left the apartment.

At some point that week, probably one or two days later, Khaït decided that she did not want to follow through with their plan and deliberately mislead authorities. Her son had rebuked her for her complicity, as had her husband David and her physician, Dr. Pierre Trocmé, who was appalled to learn about the behavior of his medical colleague. In fact, Trocmé refused to believe that a licensed doctor would give such advice. He urged Madame Khaït to report the matter to the police. If she refused, he would do so himself.

About seven o'clock in the evening of March 25, 1942, Madame Khaït left her apartment, telling her husband that she had to see Dr. Petiot and then stop by the office of her daughter's lawyer. It would be a quick errand, she said. She did not state the purpose of the visit. Nor did she take any identification papers, ration cards, or even her purse. A large pot of water was boiling on the stove.

On the following morning, when she had still not returned home, an envelope containing two letters had been slipped under the door of Madame Khaït's residence. One was for her husband David, a Jewish tailor, and the other for her son Fernand. Both were allegedly written by Marthe Khaït. Opening the envelope addressed to himself, David Khaït read with surprise:

> *Do not trouble yourself on my account. Do not say anything to anybody and above all, don't go to the police. What I'm doing is in the interest of Raymonde. Dr. Petiot was right. It is better for the police to believe that I am a drug addict. I am not able to withstand an interrogation. I am going to escape to the Free Zone. You will definitely be able to come and join me by adopting the same means. Later, Raymonde will rejoin us.*

Bizarrely, she then confessed to having taken drugs for years as a painkiller for a heart ailment. The letter to Fernand was similar. And both letters bore a striking resemblance to the letter in the Van Bever case, in everything from confession and explanation of the disappearance (which in both cases involved leaving abruptly without packing), to the method and timing of the letters' delivery (which in both cases had the person signing his or her full legal name). Some experts would extend the similarities further, concluding that the handwriting appeared to be from the same person, though this would be disputed.

The handwriting actually seemed to be his wife's, David Khaït acknowledged, and he eventually concluded that she had in fact written the letters. He also thought that she had delivered them herself. The family dog, which always barked at the approach of a stranger, had not stirred. Even the stubborn latch on the door in the courtyard had posed no problem. Someone familiar with the building must have delivered the letters. Khaït also recalled his wife's earlier frustrations about her daughter's predicament and some conversations when she claimed that she had considered fleeing to the unoccupied zone for the duration of the trial. But at the same time, he knew, she was no drug addict.

Also that morning, two other letters were delivered to the home of Raymonde's attorney, Maître Pierre Véron. Both of them—one to the attorney, the other to Raymonde—duplicated the information contained in the letters to her family. Three one-hundred-franc notes were enclosed for the attorney's fee.

The maid, who received the letters, first said they had been delivered by Marthe Khaït. She was certain, she said, because she recognized the woman from previous visits. Later she changed her statement, claiming that the letters were delivered by someone who resembled Madame Khaït. As with the first two letters, the tone of these two was more formal than usual and devoid of the usual nicknames for members of Madame Khaït's family. Handwriting experts again disagreed on the authenticity of the letters.

Why had Madame Khaït gone to Petiot anyway? Was it to report her decision not to participate in his fraudulent scheme? Was it to pick up the money to pay the attorney, as he had earlier promised, or was there yet some other, unknown reason?

Madame Khaït's husband, David, uncertain how to proceed, listened to the pleas in the letters and refrained from approaching the police, which was only done by Fernand on May 7, 1942. David Khaït, being Jewish, had good reasons for avoiding contact with authorities and had first gone to Petiot, who claimed not to have seen his wife on the day she disappeared. He had not seen her, he added, since the day he visited her house after Raymonde's arrest. "All that I know," Petiot told him in his office, "is that she wanted to leave for the Free Zone."

Petiot did say that he had earlier given her a contact in the unoccupied zone, should she want to flee. While David Khaït waited, Petiot grabbed a postcard, addressed it to "Monsieur Gaston," Plagne, near Loupiac, Cantal, in southwest France, and scribbled the single line: "Have you seen the party I sent to you?" Petiot placed a stamp on the card and gave it to Khaït.

The following month, when David Khaït visited Petiot a second time, the doctor said he had not heard from his contact. On a third encounter, in Olmi's office at the Palace of Justice in early May, Petiot said that he had just learned that his associate in the unoccupied zone had not seen Madame Khaït.

"You wretch! You criminal!" Khaït shouted. "It's you who killed my wife!" He could read it in the physician's eyes, he said. Petiot replied calmly that the man was crazy and needed to be locked up.

When questioned by the police, Petiot said he had no idea what happened to Marthe Khaït and denied that he had given her any injections. He also alleged that he had received a letter from Madame Khaït's daughter, threatening to blackmail him if he did not say that the original prescriptions were genuine. The story of his injections, Petiot said, was simply the lie of a drug addict desperate to save her own skin.

Baudet was found guilty on July 15, 1942. Petiot was also fined and sentenced for drug trafficking, though his attorney, René Floriot, succeeded in January 1943 in having the fines of the Van Bever and Khaït cases combined for a total of 2,400 francs. Despite the verdict, many who worked on the case remained suspicious. Maître Véron, for one, urged Magistrate Olmi to charge Petiot with kidnapping or murder. He would later come to play an important role in the suspect's life.

The police continued to look for Madame Khaït, under that name as well as several possible aliases suggested by her family, including her maiden name, Fortin, and variations of her earlier name by marriage, Lavie, such as Lavic, Laric, and Lepic. They never found her. So just three days after Van Bever vanished, another witness in a separate case against Dr. Petiot had disappeared.

The police eventually searched Petiot's apartment on rue Caumartin, finding nothing whatsoever to implicate him in the disappearance of either person. They did, however, find a surprising number of jewels, linen, and other objects of value in an office drawer, which Petiot explained as "gifts of clients" who could not afford his fees. Almost apologetically, as the search failed to turn up any evidence of the missing persons, the presiding officer, Achille Olmi, turned to Petiot and said, "Rest assured, no one is accusing you of burning them in your stove."

5.

"100,000 AUTOPSIES"

MY DEAR COMMISSAIRE, I DO NOT ENVY YOU INVESTIGATORS
WHEN IT COMES TO PUTTING NAMES ON THIS DEBRIS.

—Dr. Albert Paul

PARIS'S newspapers devoured the story of the monster in the elegant 16th arrondissement. Marcel Petiot was dubbed "The New Landru," after the infamous French murderer who had been convicted in 1921 for killing eleven people, ten of them lovers. *Le Petit Parisien* chose that sobriquet for its two-inch-high headlines on Monday, March 13. *L'Oeuvre* used it that morning as well, reporting that some twenty-five or perhaps thirty women had been killed or "burned alive" in the charnel house. *L'Oeuvre* and its many rivals in the capital competed in depicting the killer as a sadistic sex fiend who tortured women before he watched their "throes of agony" in his viewer and then mutilated their bodies.

Le Matin was also emphasizing the "demonic, erotic" nature of the crimes. All the bodies found at rue Le Sueur—that is, those that were not chopped up, burned, or caked with lime—were naked. When exactly had the killer removed the victim's clothes? Was it before or after he latched them to the hooks of his padded cell? To complete the nightmare image, *Le Matin* was also reporting that Dr. Petiot would wear a frightening mask as he tortured and finished off his victims.

As the controlled French press covered the Petiot case for the home market, the official state-run German news agency DNB, Deutsches Nachrichtenbüro, broadcast the news internationally of the "charred and dismembered skeletons of 25 women" found on the physician's property. Almost every night, its bulletins detailed how Petiot pedaled to the empty house near the Arc de Triomphe to conduct the grim business that filled his lime pit and produced the nauseating smoke that emanated from his chimney.

The DNB, like the Parisian press, sometimes reported that Georgette Petiot knew or participated in her husband's activities; other times, she was presented as oblivious to his double life. Usually, however, the German-controlled press emphasized that Petiot preyed on women. The physician was described as leaving his wife at home as he arranged nightly rendezvous on rue Le Sueur. Neighbors looked away, disinclined to interfere with the physician's presumably romantic liaisons.

The female visitors to his property—often assumed to be "shady ladies of the demi-monde"—sought packets of heroin, cocaine, or some other narcotic. What they received, however, was not "the white powders of forgetfulness, but death itself." Petiot, with his hypodermic needle, was quickly deduced to have injected a poison into the veins of his victims. Whether it was a yet-to-be-identified substance, an overdose of some generic drug, or perhaps a concoction of his own invention was not clear.

Thanks to his connections, a German journalist for the DNB, Karl Schmidt, received one of the first tours of the triangular room. The butcher, he speculated, drugged his victim and then dragged her into the dark room, where she was tied up and suspended from the hooks on the back wall. The murderer projected two spotlights onto her face, watching the "human agony until the last convulsion." The physician, using his medical skills, proceeded to inflict torture, presumably prolonging the pain as long as possible. He then dissected "the twisted corpse" and tossed it into the lime pit.

Massu, however, was far from ready to draw any conclusion. Known for his caution, the commissaire preferred to move slowly, building his case piece by piece and proceeding with as much certainty as possible, rather than rushing into a mistake. He was skeptical, particularly of evidence that seemed too clear or obvious. "You have often heard me say," Massu said to Brigade Secretary Canitrot, "it is necessary to be suspicious of the so-called evidence." When policemen make hasty conclusions based on "the evidence," Massu believed, they often fall into a river of error, with potentially "catastrophic" results. The fundamental problem for a detective was how to interpret the evidence.

On one hand, Massu was relieved to receive unambiguous instructions from the Gestapo, hoping of course that it would mean that German authorities would not interfere with or obstruct his investigation. At the same time, there was another concern. The Gestapo rarely expressed immediate interest in a French criminal case. When they did, particularly when ordering an arrest, it was usually to catch a culprit whose crime consisted of little more than opposing the Nazi regime. Did this mean that the owner of the house at No. 21 rue Le Sueur possibly served the French Resistance?

The case was certainly perplexing. Unlike the case of the infamous French serial killer Henri Landru or the recent murder spree of Eugen Weidmann, it was not clear how exactly Petiot or the murderer had either killed or disposed of his victims. There was no sign of stabbing or physical blows, and there was no blood found on the bodies of the victims or in the basement. As the journalist Jacques Perry put it, there were many bodies, but no signs of a murder.

O N the morning of March 13, a saleswoman at the department store Grand Magasins du Printemps on Boulevard Haussmann contacted the police to tell her story. "I should have been killed this afternoon at three o'clock," she said. Based on a referral from her pharmacist, she claimed to have consulted Petiot about a sore wrist on the afternoon of March 11. Petiot, she thought, looked more like a mason than a medical doctor, and his suit was supposedly stained with lime.

"A shiver ran down my spine," she claimed, describing her unease as the physician, staring intensely at her, touched her wrist to examine it. "His black eyes," she said, "bored into me with such impertinence that I thought he was mad." Petiot allegedly X-rayed her hand, diagnosed a sprain, and told her that her delicate bones needed more calcium. He prescribed treatment. But as he did not have the necessary equipment at his office, he asked her to consult a "special clinic." The address was 21 rue Le Sueur.

Although it was not easy to sift out the valuable pieces of information in the barrage of rumors and allegations already coming to his attention, Massu now had many leads. The chief priority, of course, was locating the physician. The obvious place to check was the forwarding address posted on the front door at rue Le Sueur: 18 rue des Lombards, Auxerre, just under one hundred miles to the southeast, in the central Burgundian region of Yonne. In addition, examining the note, Massu learned that there had originally been a different address—one that had been removed and then replaced, in a different handwriting. The original was 55 or 56 rue du Pont, Auxerre.

Massu asked one of his assistants to make the travel arrangements. Trains ran less regularly during the Occupation, only twice a week to Auxerre, and the next one did not leave for a few days. But Massu obviously did not want to wait. He called a friend in the garage of the préfecture de police and obtained car number 3313 and gasoline for his trip, which, in the strict rationing system, was not always an easy prospect even for the head of the Brigade Criminelle. The brigade secretary and two inspectors joined him. By six o'clock that morning, they were on the road.

Massu was still trying to figure out how the murderer selected his victims, lured them into the town house, and, as he imagined the terrifying scenario, pulled out a long syringe to deliver a deadly injection. The killer then chopped up the bodies, disposed of the internal organs, and dropped the remaining debris into the lime pit, which would further dehydrate the bodies and make them easier to burn. Massu's hypothesis sounded, as he put it, as "horrible and icy as any story of Edgar Allan Poe."

Massu needed to find out how and when the doctor obtained his lime, and who had helped him. Clearly the doctor—or whoever the murderer was—could not have killed so many people on his own.

How, too, could he have escaped detection by his neighbors? Massu was nowhere near understanding the case, let alone finding the killer and the evidence to convict him. For the first time in his career, the commissaire was having trouble sleeping.

"Boss," the secretary asked in the car, "is it true, as it's said, that some engravings of the devil were found in the office at rue Caumartin?"

"Yes," Massu said. "There was better than that, or worse, depending on your view." The commissaire did not elaborate more than mentioning some "bestial and smutty drawings" found in Petiot's office.

"Is the doctor a drug addict?" another inspector wondered, picking up on another rumor.

"It's almost certain," Massu answered, probably too hastily. Drugs were too easy an explanation for how a respectable physician by day could become a monster at night.

Before reaching Auxerre, the investigators stopped at Villeneuve-sur-Yonne, the town where Dr. Petiot had served as mayor. Chief Inspector Marius Battut and Inspector Rochereau went first to the murder suspect's former home at 56 rue Carnot. The current occupant, another physician, told them that he had lived there since July 1934. He had seen Dr. Petiot only once and had never had any dealings with him. The home owner, Battut summed up in his report, "did not want to provide any interesting information."

The gendarmes at the Villeneuve-sur-Yonne police department, however, were more helpful. They told the officers of the Brigade Criminelle that Petiot suffered from a "very bad reputation." During his term as mayor, he had been suspected of committing a number of thefts, including cans of oil and gasoline. One time, he was charged with stealing electricity by tampering with the meter attached to his property. What's more, the brigade inspectors learned that another one of his suspected lovers had died in mysterious circumstances.

ON March 11, 1930, fourteen years to the day before the discovery at rue Le Sueur, Armand Debauve, the owner of a dairy cooperative outside Villeneuve-sur-Yonne, was having a drink at Fras-cot's bistro. About eight o'clock that evening, a villager arrived with news that his dairy was on fire. Debauve rushed home to find his house in flames and his wife, firefighters informed him, sprawled out dead on the kitchen floor, her head covered in blood.

It did not take long for detectives to conclude that the fire had been intentionally set, and the victim, forty-five-year-old Henriette Debauve, had received a series of blows to her skull. The size of the wounds suggested that the weapon had been a hammer. Indeed, of the handful of objects missing from the property, one of them was a hammer.

Not long afterward, neighbors reported seeing Mayor Petiot drive by the ruined farmhouse with his wife. He had come, eyewitnesses first deduced, to express his condolences to the family of the victim. For an experienced doctor and veteran of the First World War, however, he seemed strangely uneasy, even nervous. Then, to further surprise, the mayor returned to his car and drove into the town of Sens to take his wife to the cinema.

Petiot certainly knew the victim. The two had been introduced several years before by "Old Man Frascot"—the same man who had introduced Petiot to his previous lover, Louisette Delaveau. Frascot, moreover, had joined the doctor and Henriette for dinner a few times, and they had appeared to hit it off. She became his patient, and, as police investigators later believed, almost certainly his lover.

There were many curiosities about this case. The fire occurred on a Tuesday evening, when Debauve's husband went out to the bistro. This was also the second Tuesday of the month, the day before the dairy paid the farmers for milk. The safe had been forced open, but no money had been found there, because Debauve had hidden it earlier that day under the kitchen cabinet.

Interestingly, too, the police had uncovered a clear set of finger-prints on an iron engraving tool that had been removed from the shed and probably had been used to pry open the safe in the bedroom. Fin-gerprints were taken of the dairy's twenty-one employees, but there was no match. When Petiot was asked for fingerprints, he refused. Robert

Seguin, his successor as mayor in Villeneuve-sur-Yonne, later described the uproar when Petiot finally complied. He lost his temper and ripped out a page from the town's official register (*registre officiel des délibera-tions*). "Furiously, he pressed his fingers into the ink himself and affixed his fingerprints onto the legally inviolable register. Then he threw it on the table saying, 'Do what you want. You'll see that it will not get you anywhere.' " He stormed out of the room, slamming the door.

When Commissaire Massu requested the file on the Debauve murder from the investigators of the Brigade Mobile of Dijon, it was not found, and detectives began to grow suspicious. Speculations rose about the missing documents, and many people believed that the mayor had used his power to destroy them. Years later, the dossier was actually located—filed not under D for Debauve, but M for murder. Curiously, too, it was slim, containing no record of any interviews or even a refer-ence to Petiot's arrival on the scene.

Of course, a crime of this nature had attracted a great deal of atten-tion from police, press, and townsmen. One freelance reporter for the local paper, *Le Petit Régional,* was particularly well informed. His reporting was soon filling in details that perplexed even the main inves-tigators. Among other scoops, he retrieved the hammer used in the mur-der, from a stream close to the farmhouse, dropped there likely so that the rust would remove any trace of fingerprints. The journalist never signed his name to any of the articles. His identity was only revealed in 1945. It was Marcel Petiot.

Frascot, in the meantime, had been claiming that he knew some-thing about the case that no one else did, insinuating that he had seen Petiot at the dairy before the fire and implying that the hunt for the mur-derer should begin in the mayor's office.

What exactly Frascot knew about that night may never be revealed because, a few weeks after Debauve's death, he agreed to meet with Petiot for a drink at the bar of the Hôtel du Dauphin. During the course of the conversation, Frascot told his doctor that he was suffering from a painful bout of rheumatism. Petiot informed him of a pioneering new drug from Paris that would likely relieve the symptoms, if not also cure him. As a favor to his old friend, Petiot offered to administer the injection for free. They walked to Petiot's office down the street. Three hours later, one of the most promising witnesses in the murder investigation was dead.

The official cause of Frascot's death was an aneurysm, or "by accident . . . from a heart shock, or some unknown side effect resulting from a hypodermic injection." This is of course possible, but the person who conducted the postmortem and signed the death certification was Villeneuve-sur-Yonne's medical coroner. And that position—Massu learned with disbelief—was held by Dr. Marcel Petiot.

AFTER finishing a funeral at Passy cemetery, the gravediggers returned to their sieves at the Petiot town house, retrieving the bones and rotten limbs from the pit, placing them in wooden boxes that resembled coffins, and then transporting them to the Institut médico-légal on the place de Mazas in the 12th arrondissement.

The Institut médico-légal (IML) boasted one of the most celebrated forensic laboratories in the world. After moving to this location in 1914, from its previous site just behind Notre Dame, the IML had expanded from its original role as a morgue to being an advanced institution that pioneered the use of science in criminal investigation. One of the groundbreaking investigators was Alphonse Bertillon, an early proponent of what he called "anthropometric" techniques: that is, learning how specific measurements uniquely identify individuals.

As nineteenth-century French law differentiated between first-time and repeat offenders, allowing for more lenient penalties for the former, criminals regularly adopted false aliases to pose as first-timers. Bertillon's method consisted of measuring every criminal upon arrest on eleven points: height, width of outstretched arms, length and breadth of head, as well as length of the foot, the middle finger, the little finger, the arm from elbow to middle finger, and so on—the left side being preferred in the measurements because it was the least likely to change if the suspect engaged in hard physical labor. Together, these precise measurements would uniquely identify a person. Two people, Bertillon reasoned, may share one, two, or perhaps three of the same measurements, but not all eleven. The odds, he calculated, were 268,435,456 to 1. And then, to address this possibility, he added three additional descriptive points of reference: the color of the suspect's eyes, hair, and skin.

In February 1883, after years of cataloguing and refining his classification system, Bertillon successfully identified a repeat offender, an achievement that has been heralded as the first use in history of scientific detection to identify a criminal. Over the next few years, Bertillon would repeatedly demonstrate the value of this method, identifying no fewer than 241 offenders in 1884, 425 in 1885, and by the end of the decade, some 3,500. By the mid-1890s, the French police had five million measurements on file.

Bertillon would pioneer a number of other changes as well, from standardizing the photograph of the criminal upon arrest into a front and side "mug shot," to bringing a camera to document the scene of the crime. He would eventually support the use of fingerprints, though he had first resisted this tool as a challenge to his own identification system. Bertillon's esteem had risen quickly. Sir Arthur Conan Doyle would make Sherlock Holmes show "enthusiastic admiration of the French savant," and then, in *The Hound of the Baskervilles,* Dr. Mortimer credits Holmes and Bertillon as being the two best detectives in Europe.

The current head of the IML was Paris's chief medical examiner, Dr. Albert Paul, a renowned sixty-five-year-old forensic scientist who came from a family of doctors and lawyers. After studying under Paul Brouardel, a leading expert on forensic pathology and forensic entomology, Paul had become professor of forensic medicine at the Sorbonne in 1918 and worked on many high-profile cases, most famously the Henri Landru case in 1920–1921. Landru had eluded authorities for years as he killed wealthy women, robbed them, and then burned their bodies.

Dr. Paul had cracked the case when, replicating Landru's technique of disposing of his victims, he burned human body parts in a kitchen stove. "A right foot," Paul learned, "disappears in fifty minutes, a half skull with brains taken out in thirty-six minutes, the whole skull in one hour ten minutes. A human head with the brain, hair, tongue, etc. disappears in about one hour forty minutes." The most difficult to dispose of were the trunk and thorax, possibly explaining why the murderer at rue Le Sueur chopped the bodies up before feeding them to the fire.

A legend in his field, Dr. Paul was also no small sensation in Parisian society, where he was known for a wealth of tales, often spiced up with his macabre sense of humor. Commissaire Massu had a great respect for Dr. Paul, whom he called "the doctor of a 100,000 autopsies." Massu and Paul had met thirty-two years before, in the spring of 1912, when both were starting their careers, Massu at the brigade and Paul at the old coroner's office on quai de l'Archevêché, before he moved to the Institut after the First World War. Massu had learned among other things that the coroner was a touchy eccentric who hated long questions and could not stand "chatterboxes." Massu always kept this in mind in his dealings with the temperamental expert.

On the rue Le Sueur case Paul would be assisted by a talented forensic team that included Professors Léon Dérobert and René Piédelièvre of the Museum of Natural History. Both Dérobert and Piédelièvre were specialists in the area of reconstructing fossil remains—an expertise that would prove invaluable in the Petiot investigation. Paul already suspected that work on this case would be more difficult than even Landru.

The coroner's office was being asked to identify human beings from a horrid mass of decomposed and mutilated remains retrieved from the lime pit, the stove, and the basement of rue Le Sueur. They would have to match arms, legs, torsos, and thighs—much as they might do for a dinosaur skeleton at the museum. They were asked to determine, among other things, the number of victims, identifying them by age and gender as well as cause and time of death. Their report would be crucial evidence to authorities struggling for fundamental facts.

Hard at work, Paul sorted through a heap of "thigh bones, craniums, shinbones, ribs, fingers, knee caps, and teeth" at his large marble table. There were two nearly complete skeletons and two half torsos. In most cases, however, they were dealing with bones, such as the ten collarbones, nine sterna, six shoulder blades, and one complete pelvis that had been found, or, more often, fragments too small or deformed to be identified. There were many of those pieces or, as Dr. Paul put it, "three garbage cans full." There were also several human scalps. The collection of hair alone weighed eleven pounds.

"It's not an autopsy," Paul said. "It's a puzzle." A puzzle, or rather, as investigators would soon learn, a set of different puzzles with many missing pieces.

6.

THE WOMAN WITH THE
YELLOW SUITCASE

I AM A SPECIALIST IN DESTINY AND ITS MYSTERIES,
BELIEVE ME. SEIZE YOUR CHANCE. IT'S HERE.

—Jean Cocteau, "Address to Young Writers,"
La Gerbe, December 5, 1940

A STONE'S throw from Marcel Petiot's apartment on rue Caumartin, Jean-Paul Sartre was teaching philosophy at the Lycée Condorcet. Outside of class, which was held three and a half days a week during term, Sartre enjoyed spending time in a number of cafés around town. One of his favorites, in the spring of 1944, was Saint-Germain-des-Prés's then little-known Café de Flore, where he liked to arrive early in the morning and head for his table in the back on the second floor. There, the short, balding, and bespectacled thirty-nine-year-old sat in a red chair, puffing on his pipe and scribbling away with his fountain pen, racing to capture his thoughts in small, tidy letters. Given the wartime shortage of tobacco, Sartre would stop from time to time to retrieve cigarette butts from the floor to stuff into his pipe.

At the other end of the room, at a mahogany marble-topped table, preferably near the stove, sat his friend and lover Simone de Beauvoir. The two deliberately staked out territory at opposite ends of the café to concentrate on their work. About lunchtime, they would break for a meal, most often in Beauvoir's corner flat on the third floor of the La Louisiane on the rue de Seine. Conversation, no surprise, flowed.

"I realized," Beauvoir once said, "that even though we went on talking till Judgment Day, I would still find the time all too short."

Sartre was entering into a very productive period that would ultimately send him to the heights of intellectual stardom. In the summer of 1943, he had published his monumental *Being and Nothingness,* a 722-page philosophical treatise about freedom and responsibility that would become a sensation in the immediate postwar period. At first, however, it was largely ignored. There had only been one review thus far, in René-Marill Albérès's *Etudes et Essais universitaires.* Sartre's friend Jean Paulhan joked that the bulky work would be useful for weighing fruits and vegetables.

That summer, Sartre had also just completed his first major play, *The Flies,* which was staged at the Sarah Bernhardt Theater, then renamed Theatre de la Cité by the Nazis, to remove the Jewish reference. In this play, which reinterprets the myth of the House of Atreus, young Orestes returns home to Argos amid a plague and the tyrannical rule of Aegisthus, his father's murderer and now his mother's lover. Orestes obtains his revenge, murdering the hated usurper and freeing the city from the curse—an appropriate subject for the Occupation that was also subtle enough in its ancient Greek setting to pass the censors.

On the opening night, which, because of electricity cuts, was actually held during the afternoon of June 2, 1943, Sartre was standing in the theater lobby, when a handsome, elegantly dressed young man with gray-green eyes walked up and introduced himself. It was Albert Camus, the twenty-nine-year-old novelist who had the previous year published his first novel, *The Stranger.* Camus had left his native Algeria in March 1940 to seek a cure for pulmonary tuberculosis at the mountain retreat at Le Panelier near Chambon in Vichy. In November 1942, he had become virtually stranded when the Allies invaded North Africa and the Germans seized the unoccupied zone.

Sartre had reviewed *The Stranger* in a mostly positive six-thousand-word essay; he was in fact one of the first people to do so, that is, except for the reviews by Camus's friends or by journals owned by his publisher, Gallimard. The two thinkers, Sartre and Camus, shared many interests, from literature and social justice, to explorations of freedom and absurdity. But the ice really broke, as Simone de Beauvoir put it, when they discussed the theater. Sartre was writing a new play, the future *No Exit,* and wanted Camus to act in and direct it. Sartre insisted.

As rehearsals began over Christmas 1943, Camus joined Sartre's circle at Café de Flore, and their friendship grew quickly enough to evoke Beauvoir's jealousy. Later, she acknowledged that she worried about how Sartre, "the strongest heterosexual I knew," could fall so completely for the charming stranger. "We were like two dogs circling a bone," she said of her rival. What Beauvoir did not mention, however, was that she had also been attracted to Camus and once tried to seduce him, only to be rebuffed. "Imagine what she might say on the pillow afterwards," Camus told his friend and fellow writer Arthur Koestler.

Another place Sartre, Camus, and Beauvoir could be seen that spring was at the restaurant the Catalan, on rue des Grands-Augustins, sometimes seated at the table of their new friend, Pablo Picasso. Despite many invitations to come abroad, the Spanish artist had remained in Paris during the Nazi Occupation, painting in his two-story studio on rue Saint-Augustin, on the Left Bank. The sixty-two-year-old Picasso, with long white hair falling onto his shoulders, was surrounded by his work and his women, including his latest lover, twenty-two-year-old painter Françoise Gilot.

In the eyes of Nazi authorities, Picasso was a highly suspect artist. He had supported Spanish republicans in the Civil War, raised money for their cause, and published caricatures of the military dictator in his *Dream and Lie of Franco.* He had commemorated the German firebombing raid of the Basque city of Guernica on the afternoon of April 26, 1937, on a three-hundred-square-foot canvas that had dramatically raised awareness of the tragedy. Hitler, of course, had placed the painter on a list of modern degenerates, and the Nazis banned all his exhibits in Paris.

The French police had actually collected a sizable file on the Spanish painter, a dossier that was only discovered in 2003, when 140 cardboard boxes were returned to Paris from Moscow. The Russians had seized the archive in 1945 from the Germans, who in turn had taken it after the Liberation. As historians then learned, Picasso had applied for French citizenship in April 1940, but the state had rejected the application on grounds that he was suspected of being an anarchist or communist, or harboring sympathies leaning in that direction. "He has no right to be naturalized," an official wrote on the form, and "should even be considered suspect from a national viewpoint."

Picasso had not told even his closest friends about this request. He had, however, let them know about his fears: namely, that his authorization to remain in the country was about to expire and he had sworn never to return to Spain as long as Franco was in power. Fortunately for Picasso, a sympathetic police official intervened. "Very illegally," Maurice Toesca wrote in his diary in September 1943, "I have prolonged his stay for three years."

The Germans who visited Picasso's studio during the Occupation were not the SS men who were rumored to be slashing his paintings, but instead a number of officials who admired his work. One frequent visitor was Lieutenant Gerhard Heller of the Referat Schriftum (Literature Section) of the Propaganda-Staffel. After his introduction in June 1942, Heller, a censor, would take a break from the stacks of manuscripts overflowing on the shelves, tables, chairs, and floors at his office at 52 Champs-Élysées to climb the spiral staircase, heart beating with excitement at another chance to observe the most infamous example of modern degenerate art at work.

As usual, Picasso was experimenting with color, texture, and form. In addition to woodcuts and pen-and-ink drawings, he worked on cardboard, matchboxes, cigarette boxes, even food, like a piece of bread—a reflection of his creative zeal as well as the shortage of canvases under the Occupation. Many of the objects of his paintings—sausages, legs of lamb, grand buffet tables, and the empty cooking pot—reflect the preoccupations and hardships of the period, as did the death's-heads and grotesque monsters reminiscent of his early cubist days. Even his choice of colors, more black, gray, and beige, seemed to parallel the drab palette of the Occupation.

Sartre, Camus, Beauvoir, and the literary world of the Left Bank were gearing up for a novel event: a new play scheduled to debut on March 19, 1944. The author was Pablo Picasso. The Nazis had refused to allow him to exhibit his paintings in Paris, but they had said nothing about plays.

AFTER leaving Villeneuve-sur-Yonne, Massu and his colleagues reached Auxerre on Monday, March 13, about one o'clock in the afternoon. Along the way, they had stopped by a roadside restaurant, where they encountered a scarcity of food options and jokingly complained about the difficulty, as policemen, of cashing their ration tickets on the black market.

After finishing their coffee, or "roasted barley," the officers visited the police station, informing the local authorities of the objectives of their mission and obtaining reinforcements to watch railway stations and quays for possible escape. Both Dr. Petiot and Madame Petiot were officially "in flight."

The rue des Lombards address listed on the note attached to the door at rue Le Sueur belonged to Marcel Petiot's younger brother, Maurice, who owned a number of properties. He lived, however, in an apartment above his electronics shop on 56 rue du Pont with his wife and two kids, thirteen-year-old Ghylaine and eight-year-old Daniel. A third minor was staying in there: Marcel and Georgette's son, Gérard, who was studying at the nearby sixteenth-century school, Lycée Jacques Amyot.

The home address was the one that police discovered had first been scribbled on the note and then erased. The detectives were eager to visit, but they first checked out the owner, Maurice Petiot, a thirty-seven-year-old electrician by trade who, in his photograph, looked like a taller, darker, and more handsome version of his older brother. Maurice had struggled financially for a number of years and had declared bankruptcy. More recently, his business had improved dramatically and he had begun investing in properties in the region.

When police arrived at his shop, its shelves stocked with a range of radio and electronic goods in high demand due to the popularity of the BBC and Radio Berlin, Maurice Petiot was not there. His wife, the thirty-one-year-old Marie Angèle Le Guyader Petiot, or Monique, received the officers cordially. She allowed them to look around the premises without a permit. She also agreed, when asked, to escort the detectives three blocks away, to the property at 18 rue des Lombards.

What Massu and his team found was a small château. Built atop a hill, with a gate and metal grilles over the windows, the estate had a labyrinthine cellar with two long corridors that connected into a series of Roman catacombs. How could Maurice Petiot afford this property? Clearly the profits from selling radio and electronics equipment would not have sufficed. Monique explained that the building had been purchased by her father-in-law, Felix Petiot, in the name of her son Daniel.

No one lived at the estate, Monique Petiot said. Indeed, despite its grand exterior, the inside was dusty and untidy, with broken panels and furniture sometimes piled in heaps in the corners, strangely reminiscent of rue Le Sueur. Upstairs, the state of disuse also resembled the Paris town house. There was, as Pierre Malo of *Le Matin* would later describe it, "the most extraordinary collection of works of art and garbage that it is possible to imagine." The property, however, did not seem as uninhabited as Monique Petiot claimed.

In a small room on the ground floor near the staircase was a bed with the covers pulled back and the sheets ruffled. Massu asked who had slept there. Was it Marcel or Georgette Petiot? Monique shook her head, saying only that the guest was a family friend, a forty-seven-year-old businessman named Albert Neuhausen, who lived in Courson-les-Carrières, a small town about ten miles south. She had forgotten to mention that.

The inspectors made the short drive to verify the claim. Neuhausen, also in the electronics business, admitted that he knew Maurice and Monique Petiot well. Yes, he had recently stayed with them, he said, as he often did when he took the train to Paris.

Neuhausen had something else to tell the detectives. Although he did not know Dr. Petiot well and certainly had no information on his whereabouts, Neuhausen admitted seeing the murder suspect on the morning of Saturday, March 11. Neuhausen had been in Paris on business, and as a favor for Monique, he had stopped by Petiot's apartment on rue Caumartin about eleven o'clock to fetch a pair of shoes for Gérard.

"We spoke of things without importance," Neuhausen said. "The doctor gave me the shoes for his son and a quarter of an hour later, I left." He took the 5:20 train at Gare de Lyon, arriving at Auxerre at 9:40, and while he had intended to bike home, it was raining and he decided to stay the night at rue des Lombards, just as Monique said. He told detectives that this was all he knew about the matter.

ON Tuesday, March 14, an investigator spotted an attractive woman in a black skirt and a black astrakhan coat, carrying an expensive yellow leather suitcase. She was standing on the platform waiting for a train at the Auxerre station. Slim and petite, she had deep brown eyes and black shoulder-length hair with a few locks falling onto her forehead. She was just four months shy of her fortieth birthday, though she looked much younger. When the policeman approached, the woman did not deny her identity. "I have done nothing wrong," Georgette Petiot protested, before collapsing on the platform. Two gendarmes carried her out of the station. One young man assisted the police, crying all the while. This was her son, Gérard.

Massu, informed of the arrest, returned at once to the Auxerre police station. Georgette was taken to his car. Already in the vehicle was her brother-in-law Maurice, who had been apprehended the previous night when he returned home from the nearby villages of Cheney and Joigny. Georgette rested her head on his shoulder. Her "short sobs" broke up the otherwise silent ride back to Paris.

7.

"BESIDE A MONSTER"

HELP US FIND YOUR HUSBAND. WE'LL HELP YOU
ESTABLISH THE TRUTH.

—Commissaire Massu to Georgette Petiot

NEWS of the arrests spread quickly, and when Massu's car approached his office on the Quai des Orfèvres, a crowd of reporters and photographers was already waiting. Commissaire Massu helped Georgette and Maurice Petiot out of the car, trying to shield them from the cameras popping and flashing in a disorienting barrage of blue magnesium light.

Massu was particular about how he wanted to question suspects. For one thing, he preferred to interrogate them alone, or in the company of a deputy who remained silent. A room full of police officers and observers posed far too many problems. Countless interrogations, Massu knew, had been derailed by an untimely interruption from an aggressive yet inexperienced officer.

Above all, Massu believed in dealing mainly in hard evidence and rational deductions grounded in fact. He would first attempt to gain an early admission, however insignificant, that would penetrate the defenses a suspect had almost invariably constructed. Then he would proceed as soon as possible to the moment that he called "the intrusion of an elephant into a porcelain shop"—that is, the awkward question, based on evidence and the suspect's previous admissions, that simply could not be parried without making a major contradiction or otherwise losing credibility.

The commissaire showed Georgette Petiot to her seat in his office and asked her if she would like a drink, which she refused. Then, as customary, Massu stalled a few minutes before launching into his questions. He tidied the papers on his desk, walked to the window, and gazed out onto the Pont Neuf. He saw cyclists crossing the bridge, some of the two million bicycles in Paris, the new ones then selling for almost as much as an automobile had only five years before. Massu wondered if Marcel Petiot had also biked across the bridge, towing who knows what in his cart.

Massu turned back to face the suspect's wife. "Well, Madame Petiot, what do you know? No need to rush, we have a lot of time. Begin where you would like."

"I must say that I was unaware of his business," Georgette Petiot said, referring to her husband. She sat with her elbows on his desk, staring aimlessly ahead. In her right hand was a small handkerchief. Speaking in a low, barely audible voice, Petiot explained that she knew that her husband had purchased a property at 21 rue Le Sueur two or three years before (it was three years). Massu, settling into a chair near her, noted the beads of sweat on her forehead. He asked if she was warm and wanted to take off her coat. She did, revealing a tight red-and-white checkered sweater.

She had only been to rue Le Sueur one time, about two years before, Georgette Petiot said, but she had not gone inside. She had never liked the house. It was too large and expensive, costing nearly half a million francs. Moreover, it would mean that her husband would be home even less. Still, despite her misgivings, she had not protested at the purchase of the property because, as she put it, her husband attracted a large clientele at his medical practice and made a lot of money.

As for the renovations to the property, Georgette knew that Dr. Petiot was skilled enough to perform much of the interior work himself, such as the painting, the installations, and the decorations. She then bragged about his talent at sculpture, particularly working in wood, but did not provide any specific information about possible renovations to rue Le Sueur.

Massu asked about her husband's bicycle and trailer. Georgette Petiot claimed not to remember exactly when he bought them, though she believed that they had been acquired together. She knew that he used them when he went to the auction houses, where he often indulged his hobby of purchasing "old books and antiquities." Above all, in response to Massu's probing, Georgette defended her husband as a "very gentle man" who took care of his family. His patients adored him. And if they were poor, or unable to pay his medical fees, she added, Petiot would not take a sou.

There was a problem about eight years ago, Georgette acknowledged. Her husband had ended up in a mental institution because, she told Massu, of "some troubles he experienced following the accidental death of one of his clients." Georgette was referring to the thirty-year-old woman Raymonde Hanss, who had lost consciousness after Dr. Petiot treated an abscess in one of her teeth. Hanss's mother blamed the physician for her death, but an investigation was never made with any thoroughness.

WHEN Massu asked about the events of March 11, 1944, Georgette said that her husband had spent the morning making house calls. They had eaten lunch together at the apartment and then, about three or three thirty, he left again "without telling me where he was going." Marcel refused to keep her updated on his activities, she said, and this was her one reproach with their marriage.

About six that evening, Petiot returned home and received a client who had been waiting for a consultation. One hour and a half later, about seven thirty p.m., as she and her husband dined together, they were interrupted by the telephone call from the police, informing them of the chimney fire. As Massu called for specifics about her and her husband's response immediately afterward, he observed that his questions disturbed Georgette. She sank into the chair and, raising her hand to her eyes, began to cry. Massu later said that he thought she would crack at any moment.

"Pull yourself together. We do not want anything from you. We only want to know the truth. What did your husband say?"

"I heard the word 'police.' Marcel immediately grabbed his hat and left."

"Did he not say where he was going?"

"No, he didn't give me an explanation."

"Did he often leave without saying where he was going?"

"Sometimes. I never questioned him."

Georgette would only admit to following him down the stairs to see which direction he went, later adding that she had accompanied him around the corner onto rue Saint-Lazare. She never said anything about their conversation along the way.

When Massu asked her what she did after her husband's departure, Georgette Petiot said that she had "waited all night in an armchair." Did she always do that whenever Dr. Petiot left without giving any information on his destination? No, that night was different. "It was the word 'police' that disturbed me."

"But this word should not have disturbed you since you know your husband is incapable, as you say, of doing an evil deed. Was there something else that bothered you?"

"You never know, these days, what is going to happen to a man who has business with the police."

Georgette Petiot was right. The Nazi Occupation had vastly complicated criminal investigations, tarnishing respect for law and the police who enforced it. Massu later said that he admired her for her candid remark, which was uttered at no small risk to herself. He pressed on, however, with questions about her actions immediately following the discovered remains at the town house.

"That morning, did you think of going to rue Le Sueur to find your husband?"

"No, I decided to return to Auxerre," she said, eager to be with her son, who then studied in that town and lived with her husband's brother Maurice. She went to Gare de Lyon, looking for the seven or eight o'clock train, but learned that there were none leaving until Monday evening. "I returned to the neighborhood of rue Caumartin, but without returning to my apartment."

"Why?"

"I do not know. . . . A feeling told me that there was danger there for us."

"Was it not rather the sight of two policemen at the door that made you turn back?"

"I do not know. Yes perhaps." She also said that she had hoped, despite everything, to find her husband somewhere on the street.

Georgette Petiot explained that she went to church, attending several masses, and then spent the rest of the afternoon at the busy train station Gare Saint-Lazare. She was not waiting for anyone, she told the commissaire, and she had not gone there to avoid being recognized. "I was afraid, and I felt more security in the middle of the crowd."

Asked what exactly she feared, Petiot said that the evening newspapers had appeared at the train station kiosk about six o'clock, and she had panicked when she saw her name on the front page of *Paris-Soir*. That night, she went to one of her husband's properties, at 52 rue de Reuilly, thinking that he might come there and give her an explanation. He did not. And as she did not know anyone there, she hid on a staircase near the attic, fleeing into the shadows when a door opened, or occasionally into the courtyard of the neighboring building, which her husband also owned. Fearing detection, she had not slept well.

Early Monday morning, she had gone back to the Gare de Lyon and found the train schedules. As the next departure was not until 5:20 p.m., she spent most of the day at a small hotel restaurant, the Hôtel Alicot at 207 rue de Bercy. She bought her ticket at the last minute and boarded the train for Auxerre. Arriving at 9:00 p.m., she went over to the apartment of her brother-in-law Maurice on rue du Pont. She hoped to find her husband, she repeated, but no one was home. She waited, terrified and uncertain of her next move.

"Perhaps rue des Lombards?" Massu asked.

The mention of this property shook her. She also seemed disturbed by the fact that the address had been posted on a sheet attached to the carriage door. As Massu described the scene, Petiot's hand opened, her handkerchief fell to the floor, and she fainted. This would not be the last time she would collapse—or pretend to collapse—in the middle of an interrogation.

W IVES of criminals, Massu later reflected, were indeed an interesting lot.

> *There are those who, real panthers in madness, defend their men with claws out; there are the cold and insensitive ones, who wrestling step by step, discuss each argument and answer your questions with other questions; there are the stubborn ones who can pass the entire night in total silence against the light of the interrogation; there are still others, who, shaken and in distress, discover as you do that they have lived for years beside a monster.*

In which category did Georgette Petiot belong? And what about Maurice? Massu was eager to find out.

The commissaire began the first interrogation of Maurice by exploring his background, establishing that he had, like his older brother, been raised by his aunt Henriette Gaston and educated by his uncle, Vidal Gaston, now deceased. The Petiot brothers had been close, but, in the early 1930s, Maurice told the commissaire, they had drifted apart. His relationship and then marriage to Monique had resulted in what he called "a little chill." After the wedding on September 22, 1934, the brothers did not speak for five years.

After the exodus in the summer of 1940, Maurice claimed that he had returned home to find that his warehouse had been sacked. He had begun to make regular trips to Paris to replenish his stock and, in the process, mend his relationship with his brother. "I have eaten lunch with him on each trip," Maurice said, adding that this was often followed by dinner with Marcel, his wife, and son. This occurred about every two weeks.

Massu asked what he knew about 21 rue Le Sueur. Maurice replied that he remembered his brother, or perhaps Georgette, speaking at some point, probably in 1942, about the purchase of a new property in Paris. Maurice emphatically denied having any further information on the topic. "I have never known which street this private mansion was on, and I have never been there."

When pressed, however, Maurice soon qualified this statement. Yes, he knew the address and he had in fact been there three or four times. In July or August 1943, Maurice had applied anti-mite treatment on the bug-infested furniture and rugs. A few months later, probably December 1943, he had gone to shut off the water in case of an accident with the sudden arrival of cold weather. The last time, January 1944, he had brought an architect to look for possible leaks that might be causing humidity problems in a neighboring building on rue Duret.

Asked if that was all he knew about the town house, Maurice Petiot said that it was. Massu, however, would soon have good reason to be skeptical.

8.

A DELIVERY

MY HUSBAND GAVE ME A ROSETTE NECKLACE, A RING
WITH A SOLITAIRE OF FIVE CARATS, I BELIEVE . . .
AND A CROSS MADE OF GOLD.

—Georgette Petiot

CURFEW, blackouts, air raid sirens, long lines outside shops, and the daily risk of unwarranted denunciations, which poured in to German authorities at a staggering rate, all compounded the hardships suffered from a lack of food and fuel. "Paris had been reduced to a sham," Jean-Paul Sartre said. He compared the occupied city to "empty bottles of wine displayed in the windows of shops which could no longer manage to stock the real thing."

As a result, many Parisians resorted to Système D, a colloquial expression for a "do it yourself" approach that involved stretching meager resources as far as possible and finding the least unacceptable substitutes. Coffee was brewed with chicory, chickpeas, or roasted acorns. Tea was made from apple skins, and milk was skimmed and watered. Cigarettes were rolled with Jerusalem artichoke or nettles. Potatoes were peeled after boiling to make them last longer. Thin leek soup was often served as dinner, accompanied by new dishes like turnips, previously viewed only as "cow food." Chestnuts spiced up bland desserts, which were otherwise expensive and difficult to obtain.

Carrots, beans, and a variety of vegetables were grown in window boxes, on rooftops, and in large public spaces like the Tuileries, Luxembourg Gardens, and the Esplanade des Invalides. Rabbits and hens were raised on balconies and in broom closets. Pigeons became an increasingly rare sight in parks. The prefect of Paris warned against the health hazards of eating "stewed cat." During the Nazi Occupation, French men and women were consuming an estimated half the total calories that they had in the Depression, circa 1935–1938. Wartime diets in France were probably the lowest in calories in Western Europe.

By March 1944, the cold winter was at last giving way to the arrival of spring, the "ballet of buds," as Massu put it, that danced on the quays, parks, and windowsills around Paris. Alas, the commissaire did not have time to enjoy it as much as he would have liked. There were seemingly endless meetings with the heads of brigades and principal inspectors—a council of ministers for the police, he joked. "I have never loved these chitchats where you lose precious time." he said. He often arrived late, left early, and in the meantime, kept his eyes glued to the clock. Above all, he was consumed by the Petiot case.

After Madame Petiot recovered from her faint, or feint, at Massu's office, the commissaire asked her to accompany him to her family's apartment on the second floor at 66 rue Caumartin. Massu exited his office first, landing in a crowd of reporters and photographers who fired questions rapidly. "Did she confess?" one journalist yelled. "Did she help dispose of the bodies?" another asked. "Did she help her husband flee?"

"Gentlemen," Massu said. "My secretary is going to speak to you." As the reporters rushed off to hear the announcement, thinking no doubt of impending deadlines, the commissaire escaped down the corridor with Madame Petiot and slipped into a car waiting outside on the quay.

A few miles away, at rue Caumartin, a crowd of about one hundred people jammed the sidewalks and spilled over onto the road, and onto the nearby rue Saint-Lazare. Photographers and reporters were there looking for a scoop. "Those lads are everywhere like mushrooms," the chauffeur said to Massu in the car. A motion picture camera was set up to shoot their arrival.

"Assassins!" Georgette Petiot screamed as she tried to make her way to her apartment. "You are the assassins! You are jeering at my distress." She had only gone to Yonne to see her son, she yelled.

After a locksmith hired by the police opened the door, which had been locked since the last visit, Commissaire Massu, Georgette Petiot, and a team of investigators entered the apartment. While detectives searched, Petiot sat in an armchair in her living room, adorned with Chinese vases, fine porcelain, and tapestries on the wall. The commissaire resumed his questioning: "How did you live here?"

"As the good middle-class citizens that we were," she said in an angry tone that Massu suspected had been inspired in part by her encounter with the hostile mob. "We often went to the theater and the cinema. It is not forbidden, as far as I know." Massu asked if her husband had a lot of free time. "Obviously," she answered, although he often had to leave in the middle of a performance.

"Did he say where he went?" Massu asked.

"To the sick, of course."

"Were you ever astonished by the jewels and the linen that your husband often brought in his cart?"

"Sometimes."

"Did he ever give any explanations?"

"Yes, completely valid ones." She told how he often made purchases at the House Drouot, France's oldest and most prominent auction house, established in 1852 by Napoleon III and located a few minutes' walk from the Petiot apartment. Both the auctioneers and the famous black-clad porters with the red collar could well vouch for him. Petiot spent a great deal of time there huddled in a corner like many other dealers, presumably discussing lots and bids.

"What about the many erotic prints that we found?" Massu asked.

"Simple mania of a collector."

By the end of the visit, the police had uncovered nothing whatsoever to implicate Georgette Petiot in the murders. All they found was a five-carat diamond ring that she could not explain other than say it was a gift from her husband. On this basis, the French police would later charge her with receipt of stolen property. In the meantime, Massu made no charge. He asked her to pack a bag to return to the station. After escorting her through the crowds and into the car, the commissaire was struck by the many curious people who peered in through the window. Georgette shielded her face behind a handkerchief. The driver blew the horn several times to clear a path through the crowds blocking the way.

Georgette Petiot was driven to the Hôtel-Dieu, the oldest hospital in Paris. Located in the shadow of Notre Dame Cathedral on the Île de la Cité, the hospital held the sick and wounded in wings that segregated French and German patients. It also held important witnesses in criminal trials. Here, it was reasoned, Madame Petiot would be able to answer questions, safe from the reporters, photographers, camera crews, crowds, or anyone, for that matter, who might try to avenge a missing person blamed, rightly or wrongly, on her husband. Massu also hoped that, with close surveillance, he might be able to protect this important source of information from a possible suicide attempt.

MARCEL and Georgette Petiot had been married in her hometown of Seignelay on June 4, 1927. Georgette's father, Nestor Lablais, a former porter of a wagon-lits company, owned a local tavern-inn there, and her mother, Anna Villard Lablais, had been his chambermaid before their marriage. By the time Georgette was fourteen, the family had moved to Paris, and her father purchased the restaurant Côte d'Or in the 7th arrondissement, next to the parliament, the Chambre des Députés. Nicknamed "Long Arm" for his influence with his restaurant patrons, many of whom were prominent politicians, businessmen, and other leading figures of society, Lablais had recognized the talents and potential of his son-in-law.

Other people had also envisioned a bright future for Villeneuve-sur-Yonne's young mayor. Petiot's supporters compared him to another French physician-turned-statesman, Georges Clemenceau. One politician at the Petiot wedding, Henri Chéron, told the groom that if he ever had the chance to lead the government, he would appoint him as one of his ministers. Chéron would later serve in several positions, including two stints by 1934 as both minister of justice and minister of finance. By then, however, Petiot's promising career of the "New Clemenceau" had ended in scandal.

During Petiot's term as mayor, small items had often disappeared from City Hall. Sometimes it was funds, other times simple trinkets, like a spoon, an ashtray, or a small keepsake that would fit into his pocket. Townspeople soon whispered about the mayor's peculiar habit. A Villeneuve-sur-Yonne blacksmith, Depond-Clément, remembered Petiot coming to his forge looking for parts to repair his sports car—the mayor drove fast and recklessly, and thus became a frequent visitor there. Petiot would show up, "humming, whistling, and joking," while also gossiping and showing interest in the workers. Almost every time, afterward, something small, like a tool or a key, would be missing. When a forge employee went to confront him, the mayor simply returned the item, laughing and making no excuses.

Petiot was accused of some other bizarre crimes during his term. One time, the mayor was suspected of stealing a drum. The band for his rival right-wing party had set up the night before a concert at the Salle des Fêtes in the town hall. The next morning, band members arrived to find their bass drum missing. Within days, another band in town, which often played at political functions in support of Petiot's socialist party, received a new, recently painted drum, the same size instrument as the one that had disappeared. It was a gift from the mayor.

Petiot polarized the town, leading some to praise his achievements, such as his reform of the elementary school system, his modernization of the sewer system, his improvement of garbage collection, and his building of other urban amenities, like a tennis court and a playground. Petiot also gained more railway stops for his town. At one point, he was said to have convinced railway executives of the stops' necessity by throwing himself from a moving train.

Other people criticized the mayor for his unscrupulous actions, mostly involving corruption and his almost dictatorial control of the city council. Controversy would surround the rest of his term. Funds

DEATH IN THE CITY OF LIGHT • 79

and property continued to disappear. At least one member of City Hall, Léon Pinau, quit, claiming that he did not want to be engulfed in any of the many scandals likely to ensue in the mayor's office.

Sure enough, after surviving several lengthy investigations into his accused thefts of oil and gasoline, a small scandal in the summer of 1931 resulted in Petiot's resignation. A routine audit of his office had found 2,890 francs in fees, from 138 alien-registration applications, that had not been forwarded to the necessary officials. Petiot blamed his secretary for this simple mistake, and the man accepted full blame, pointing to his age, his poor eyesight, and exhaustion as a result of being too long overworked. But in late August, Petiot was suspended. On the twenty-sixth, the day before the suspension took effect, he resigned from office.

Petiot, however, came back in full force, waging another intense, passionate, and controversial campaign for reelection. He told how his experience in war had made him "love the people" and aspire to a career as a physician to improve their well-being. He targeted First World War veterans and workers with appeals to the common man against Parisian decadence and corruption. His opponents returned the criticism: "Drain Petiot out of his graft-built sewers," as one poster put it.

Petiot's brazen confidence and unorthodox tactics provided some advantages. At a late-season candidate debate at town hall, he offered to allow his opponent, Henri Guttin, to speak last. Petiot then delivered an enthusiastic address, outlining his many achievements and work on behalf of the poor. When Guttin stepped up to the podium and took out his notes to read his prepared statement, the room suddenly lost power. The candidate fumbled through his speech in the dark, an awkward contrast to the dynamic Petiot. The source of the outage was later traced to the physician's residence.

In the end, Petiot was defeated. Prepared for the possibility, he had already entered a second campaign for office, this time as general councillor, the rough equivalent of a US congressman. Petiot won this contest, becoming the youngest of thirty-four representatives from Yonne. This position would not last long.

Petiot was again accused of theft, this time in the form of using a combination of cables, plugs, and pins to rewire electricity meters on his house and steal electricity. "It's a vile political hazing," Petiot said, blaming the charges on his enemies. The evidence against him, however, was overwhelming. On July 19, 1933, the tribunal at Joigny pronounced him guilty, sentencing him to fifteen days in prison and fining him 300 francs with another 200 in damages. Petiot appealed, and the court waived his prison sentence and reduced the fine to 100 francs, but upheld the verdict.

This conviction—the first to stick against the young politician—led to a temporary loss of his voting rights, which, in French law, required a mandatory removal from office. And so once again, before the inevitable occurred, Petiot resigned. The political career of the "New Clemenceau" was over. Another phase was about to begin.

B ACK at headquarters, after a beer in a brasserie on place Dauphine and a quick telephone call to his wife, Commissaire Massu sent a couple of inspectors to check out Georgette Petiot's claims. No one had seen her at 52 rue de Reuilly, but this did not necessarily discredit her statement, as she had been trying to hide and none of the twenty-one residents in the building knew her. Even the concierge barely recognized her.

Another detective, Inspector Hernis, checked out the Hôtel Alicot at 207 rue de Bercy, where she claimed to have eaten before leaving for Auxerre. The owner, Henri Alicot, confirmed that Madame Petiot had arrived at his restaurant, as she had claimed, on the morning of the thirteenth, looking bewildered and exhausted. He could also confirm that she had spent the day there, distraught about the news.

It was not possible, she had said, that her husband, "who is so good to me," could have done those things reported in the newspapers. In the seventeen years of marriage, Georgette Petiot added, she had not once seen him angry. Her immediate plans were to travel to Auxerre to be with her son. Madame Petiot had napped in one of the rooms, but declined food until Alicot had convinced her to eat a bowl of soup before leaving for the 5:20 train to Auxerre. Clearly she had feared being arrested.

Perhaps the restaurateur's most interesting revelation concerned not the suspect's wife, but his brother. According to Alicot, Maurice Petiot came to Paris almost every week for business, usually arriving on a Wednesday and staying at his hotel until Saturday. Alicot claimed not to have seen him since the previous month, but he could date the event because it had been so peculiar.

During his stay February 19–22, 1944, Alicot recalled, a truck driver and a workman had appeared in his hotel lobby to deliver a message to Maurice. Their truck, which contained a delivery for the younger Petiot, had broken down at the corner of Boulevard Saint-Michel and Boulevard Saint-Germain, and the two men had been forced to leave it there. What particularly struck Alicot, however, was not the message, though he did wonder why they would abandon a truck loaded with goods. It was how frightened the men looked when they relayed the news and then how quickly they departed afterward.

9.

EVASION

DR. PETIOT WAS A CLEVER MAN.

—René Piédelièvre

EXAMINING the black satin dress found in the basement of rue Le Sueur, Massu's men had identified a possible victim. Detectives had contacted the Marseille designer listed on the fashion tag, Silvy-Rosa, whose real name was Sylvie Givaudan, and she remembered the dress. Givaudan had made it about three and a half years before and sold it to a woman named Paulette from a nearby brothel, whom she described as young and beautiful.

The Marseille police department was able to provide more information about this woman. Her real name was Joséphine Aimée Grippay. She had been given the name Paulette by a pimp who thought "Joséphine" sounded old-fashioned. "It was good one hundred years ago," he had reportedly told her, "[but] men like easy names to remember." Grippay had gained a number of other sobriquets, including "La Chinoise" for her long black hair, high cheekbones, and other facial features deemed Asian, though she was actually from Corsica.

Born January 7, 1917, in the port of Bonifacio (Bunifaziu), to a Corsican mother and a Breton father, Grippay had begun working in a brothel in Ajaccio before reaching Marseille, where she settled into an upscale brothel on rue Venture. Grippay soon made connections with many figures in the underworld, including, most prominently, Joseph Piereschi, known variously as "Joseph le Marseillais," Dionisi, or Zé. By the time World War II broke out, Piereschi had been sentenced to prison a number of times, mostly for petty theft, though there was one murder charge and his participation in a train robbery that netted 983,000 francs. During the German Occupation, he started running a brothel for Nazi officers at Aire-sur-la-Lys. Eventually accused of defrauding German authorities, Piereschi fled, bringing Paulette Grippay with him. They worked their way north. Grippay had been in Paris just over one year when the police found her dress in Dr. Petiot's basement.

How had Petiot come to know her? Was he one of her clients, or was she one of his? Rue Caumartin, after all, was located in the middle of a lively district full of nightclubs, bars, and brothels.

Not far away, on rue Provence, tucked into a discreet building with closed white shutters, was the One Two Two. The seven-story brothel, once the home of Napoleon's marshal Joachim Murat, catered to an exclusive clientele that included royalty, statesmen, film stars, and eventually, many tourists. Each room upstairs projected a different theme. There was an Orient Express suite, a luxurious ocean liner cabin, and a Cloth of Gold Room inspired by the famous celebration by King Francis I and King Henry VIII in the summer of 1520. The Arctic igloo came with reindeer antlers and a polar bear rug, and the "sunny farmhouse" was surrounded by a white picket fence with a mock hayloft above the bed. Two rooms were covered completely with mirrors. The top floors contained the more risqué rooms, including the popular torture chamber, with its whips, chains, handcuffs, and leather thongs.

Since his arrival in Paris eleven years before, Petiot had drawn many clients from this environment. He had also attracted women from far less luxurious brothels, and many of them, like Jeannette Gaul, were outside the system of regulation altogether. Antonie Marguerite Bella, a thirty-six-year-old former chambermaid who became addicted to heroin and then worked as an unlicensed street walker, often visited his practice. She had no difficulty whatsoever in obtaining drugs from Dr. Petiot, she told Inspector Jean Prigent when he questioned her in prison. She had been referred to his practice by a friend in the same line of business, who consulted the doctor for "the same reasons" and, she added, found the "same satisfaction."

There was no shortage of witnesses ready to testify about Petiot's clientele, which seemed overwhelmingly female, with many of them addicted to morphine, heroin, or cocaine. As one patient later put it, Dr. Petiot was known to "nearly all the drug addicts of Montmartre." And if these women could not pay his rates, Petiot was not averse to cutting a deal or trading services. The physician credited these women with teaching him invaluable lessons, not least in how to impose his will on other people. "It is through them that you learn to dominate," Petiot said, calling prostitutes "the harems which make the great conquerors."

One unidentified prostitute and client later told a reporter of her experiences with Petiot. "We were all a little afraid of him. He always asked for tricks that we did not like or sometimes that we did not know. Then, he would explain it to us with a funny laugh." He was often rough and liked to bite or "pinch nipples with all his might." Some prostitutes, like Marguerite la Poupée or Annette "Chouchou," frequented his clinic for ointments. Petiot had a reputation for treating venereal diseases, particularly gonorrhea and syphilis, the latter being an especially difficult and lengthy procedure. There was, in short, no lack of opportunities for Petiot to gain insight and influence into the Parisian underworld.

Was this how the physician had met Paulette Grippay? The brothel where she worked was located just one street away, on rue Godot de Mauroy. Had Petiot sold her drugs, treated her for disease, or was there some other still-unknown link? The police would soon have their answer, and it would not be at all what Massu expected.

"ALL human preoccupations, all the difficulties, and all the worries of life—in order to end up there," René Piédelièvre, a forensic expert working on the Petiot case, later reflected after his forty-five years of experience at the autopsy table. By "there," he meant a lifeless body lying "among the debris which is going to crumble and disappear progressively into a microbial rot in the earth among the devouring insects and their larva, the workers of death."

Piédelièvre had never forgotten his first trip to rue Le Sueur. Walking across the courtyard, he had stumbled upon what he thought was a pebble. He reached down to examine it and found instead a "fragmented vertebra where one could still see through the ligament." He had "trampled in the dust of bones" and then, once the debris arrived at the Institut médico-légal, examined the "portions of scalps with the hair completely impregnated by a foul magma." But, as with Commissaire Massu, the most troubling discovery for Piédelièvre was the drainage pit in the back building, where he saw the many twisted bodies, "cooped together like herring and partially burned by the lime which whitens them like sparrows."

Some of the bodies were nearly intact, others were dismembered, and an early examination proved to him that the suspect was a skilled dissector. Like his colleagues on the case, Dr. Paul and Dr. Dérobert, Piédelièvre was not yet prepared to state that the murderer was an anatomist, or a forensic specialist, but he was clearly a doctor. "The dislocations were well done," Piédelièvre said, noting how the suspect had carefully removed the *pulpes digitales* to prevent fingerprint identification and then removed the face mask in a single cut. Piédelièvre marveled at the "extreme skill" of the murderer.

As forensic scientists, Piédelièvre's team would serve as an important "auxiliary to justice." The goal was to render a carefully weighed opinion that, given the hard evidence, they would not soon "be obliged to contradict." The task in the Petiot case was excruciatingly complicated, as they tried to reconstruct the bodies among the scalped craniums, the broken thighbones, and what Piédelièvre called a "foul muddle" of lime-caked flesh and debris. And when they could not reconstruct, they would resort to calculating the number of victims by weighing the bone fragments.

They were asked to determine the number and gender of the victims. This was difficult enough, but possible by concentrating on certain bones, such as the pelvis, the thighbone, and the femur, all of which were wider and more spread out in the female. Far more difficult, however, was trying to determine the time and cause of death. Most of the remains were not only savagely mutilated, but also in an advanced state of decomposition.

To complicate matters further, the forensic team had found no evidence of a bullet, knife, bludgeon, or other violent wound. A few of the victims had broken arms or legs, but the angle of fracture suggested that this had probably happened after death, and clearly after the skin and muscles had been removed from the bone. The implication was that the breaks had occurred when an arm or leg had been crammed into the small space of the basement stove.

Nor were there bloodstains, smears, drops, splashes, or even a trace of poison. In most cases, the internal organs had been cut out. Disemboweling the victim had certainly diminished the stench; it would also multiply the difficulties of finding the cause of death. In the few instances when they found internal organs, it was feared that the fire, the lime, and the advanced putrefaction would prevent the organs from yielding any significant conclusions.

The unanswered questions were certainly accumulating. Massu needed to learn everything he could about the suspect and who, if anyone, might be helping him. "The smallest testimony can have its importance," Massu said, sending detectives across the city looking for anyone who might have known the doctor.

M AURICE Petiot, meanwhile, was brought in for a second interrogation.

"Would you please indicate how you spent your time during the days of March 11 through March 13?"

On the eleventh, Maurice answered, he had stayed the entire day in Auxerre. He had made some repairs in the neighborhood, and then, in the evening, he received his friend Albert Neuhausen, who arrived on the 9:30 train from Paris. As he had "no means of returning home to Courson," Maurice had invited him to stay the night at one of his properties.

On Sunday the twelfth, Maurice worked on the central heating of his property on rue Sous-Murs. In the evening, he and his wife, Monique, went to an auction house and purchased a rug. On the thirteenth, he remained at home on rue du Pont until three in the afternoon, when he biked to Seignelay to visit a farm that Georgette Petiot had inherited from her father after his death in October 1943. "I did not find anyone there," Maurice said, adding that it was only that day that he heard the news of the police investigation.

"Contrary to what you claim," Massu said, "you have sent certain products or material to the property at rue Le Sueur. Would you like to explain?"

"If I have sent any materials, it is for you to prove it."

"You have sent some, including lime."

"It is for you to prove."

Massu was well on his way to doing just that. The truck driver who came by the Hôtel Alicot looking for Maurice about a delivery, Jean Eustache, had already contacted the police with a major revelation. Eustache, age twenty-two, informed detectives that he had made deliveries for Maurice Petiot on four or five occasions. Mostly it was electronics or furniture, but the last time, in mid-February 1944, Eustache and a fellow worker named Robert Massonière had picked up Maurice Petiot in truck number 290-ZU-4 and driven him to a quarry outside Aisy-sur-Armançon, where they had collected four hundred kilograms of quicklime.

"He told me it was for whitewashing the property," Eustache said. Upon arrival in Paris about ten o'clock on the morning of February 19, 1944, the three men had unloaded the sacks just inside the carriage entrance to a private mansion somewhere in the city. Eustache was not sure exactly where. Maurice did not pay him anything for the transport, he said, and he assumed that the price had been negotiated with his employer.

Massu did not specifically question Maurice yet about the lime, as he did not have the deposition in front of him. Instead, the commissaire pressed on, preparing the ground for the future confrontation.

"Have you seen any lime on the property at rue Le Sueur?"

"No," Maurice answered. "I have never seen any there."

Massu asked about his whereabouts on February 19. Once again,

Maurice claimed to have spent the day at home. Did he know a man named Jean Eustache? Yes, Maurice said, but not very well, and he could not say for sure the last time he had seen him.

How about on the nineteenth?

Maurice hesitated, removed his scarf, and then calmly said that he would now tell the truth. He had come to Paris about that time, probably the nineteenth, in a small truck driven by Eustache. Maurice then claimed that he had been dropped off at the Place de la Concorde, while Eustache and a coworker at the delivery firm proceeded to make deliveries. The three of them were to meet the following day about two o'clock at the intersection of rue Le Sueur and the Avenue Grande Armée. Maurice was then supposed to direct them to a warehouse, where they would haul away "the electrical material that I had bought."

But Eustache did not arrive at the designated time, Maurice said, and so he went to dine with his brother at rue Caumartin and then afterward to a vaudeville show at the A.B.C. on the Grands Boulevards. Later, at the Hôtel Alicot, Maurice said, he learned that Eustache had not shown up at the rendezvous because his truck had been involved in an accident.

Massu interrupted to ask if Maurice had been to 21 rue Le Sueur at any point during this trip to Paris.

"I did go to rue Le Sueur," Maurice now admitted, but he had not entered the house. He said that he had to return a set of keys to his brother—a statement that Massu thought had been uttered accidentally. It certainly did not help his claims about not knowing much about the building.

"I should tell you," Maurice added, "that in the truck were about thirty bags of coal which were supposed to be returned to Auxerre." After the accident, Maurice said that he had offered to allow Eustache to store this cargo at his brother's town house at rue Le Sueur while they waited on repairs or the arrival of a new vehicle. He had not mentioned this incident earlier, he said, because he could not have imagined that it could have had any significance for the investigation.

As for his brother's whereabouts, Maurice said that he did not know. He had not received any news and could only guess, envisioning three possibilities: he was hiding out with the Resistance, he had taken flight abroad, or he had committed suicide.

Massu asked an officer to lead Maurice into a holding cell. How long would he be held? he asked.

"As long as I am permitted by law." Massu needed to follow up on details, which "however unimportant for you, are essential for the investigation." Maurice Petiot, protesting his innocence, was led away.

At this time, almost midnight, Massu returned home. Bernard, he knew, would still be awake, studying in his room and waiting to hear the latest news about the case. Massu felt that they were approaching a major breakthrough. That night, he and Bernard discussed serial killers. Petiot had not killed over a long period of time like Henri Landru, the commissaire said. Instead Petiot had attempted too much too soon, and as a result, his killing spree had lasted only a short while. Massu, clearly, had a lot to learn about this case.

10.

"GOODBYE ARROGANCE"

AFTER HAVING HAD THE LEISURE TO STUDY THE DEPTH
OF HIS THOUGHT, I AM CONVINCED THAT HIS GREATEST
PLEASURE WAS TO PLAY WITH OTHER PEOPLE'S MINDS.

—René Nézondet on Marcel Petiot

PROFILING—the practice of drawing up a psychological portrait of a criminal based on behavioral clues and evidence—was not used in this murder investigation or in any other during the Occupation. Although already occasionally employed, most famously in Walter Langer's profile of Adolf Hitler for the Office of Strategic Services (OSS) in 1943, profiling's heyday would come much later. The FBI's elite Behavioral Science Unit, which opened in 1972 in Quantico, Virginia, would have many first-rate identifications—a success popularized in Thomas Harris's harrowing 1988 novel *The Silence of the Lambs* and the subsequent film starring Anthony Hopkins as Dr. Hannibal Lecter.

A veteran of this unit, Special Agent John Douglas, widely regarded as the basis for the fictional detective Jack Crawford in the Harris novel, described what he referred to as the "homicidal triad" of behaviors that suggest future violent crime—namely, cruelty to small animals, bedwetting at a late age, and arson. Two of these applied to Marcel Petiot. And the third was not far off. Police already knew of the fire at the dairy following the murder of its owner, Petiot's patient and possible mistress, Henriette Debauve. They would also soon learn that, not long after the disappearance of another lover, Louisette Delaveau, a mysterious fire had destroyed the home of her former employer.

The French police continued the difficult task of trying to understand this man. Detectives searched banks and insurance companies to find his account and look for any suspicious transactions. They solicited information from government agencies overseeing hospitalizations, accidents, prisons, and passports, the latter under his name as well as several others, such as his wife's maiden name, Lablais. Detectives continued to speak with neighbors, while also staking out the auction houses Petiot liked to frequent, the train stations he might use to flee Paris, and the various properties he owned around the city. The only visitor they noted was a forty-eight-year-old woman named Marie Julienne Le Roux. She had come to clean Petiot's office.

When questioned, Le Roux told inspectors that she worked at rue Caumartin weekday mornings from ten to twelve and then again in the afternoons from two thirty to five thirty, with an additional short shift on Saturday mornings. During this time, she would receive patients, which, she confirmed, included more women than men. She also cleaned the apartment and office—everything, that is, except for the linen, which Georgette Petiot preferred to wash herself. Le Roux had not seen Dr. Petiot since her shift Friday night.

On Saturday, March 11, 1944, when she worked the morning as usual, Petiot had not arrived. "I have never noticed anything suspicious either in his office or his X-ray rooms," Le Roux said. Her testimony, though, was of limited value because she had worked in Petiot's office for only three weeks.

There was another woman, however, who might have more valuable information for the investigation; this was Geneviève Cuny, who had worked in Dr. Petiot's office and household for a couple of years. She was no longer at rue Caumartin and, apparently, not in Paris either. Massu sent detectives to find this woman.

BY March 16, 1944, when Massu called in Maurice Petiot for another interrogation, Inspector Battut and several detectives from the Brigade Criminelle had searched his property on rue du Pont. They had gone through the ground floor with its electronics boutique, the dining room, and the kitchen, followed by the cellar and the three bedrooms on the top floor. As the police report of the search summed it up, they found "nothing suspicious."

The detectives had also searched Maurice's property on rue Sous-Murs. At first, they found mainly tools, firewood, and more antique furniture. Then, in one of the bedrooms, an inspector discovered a curious locked cupboard. After locating the key in a drawer, he opened it and found a number of papers belonging to Dr. Petiot: a diploma, an insurance policy, acts of sale for a couple properties, two address books, and the identity card of the late French actor Harry Bauer. A closet in the room also contained an astrakhan coat, two furs, and several other articles of women's clothing in a small size.

When asked about these discoveries, Maurice said that he had no idea that they were there. He imagined that they had been left a few months before, when Marcel and Georgette had come to Auxerre and stayed several nights in the room. As for Bauer's identity card, Maurice suggested that it must have been a gift to his brother. Maurice was also still denying any knowledge of lime at rue Le Sueur. This time, however, Massu read aloud the signed testimony of the truck driver Jean Eustache.

Looking him straight in the eye and calmly changing his story again, Maurice admitted that Eustache was correct. According to the account he now told, Maurice had delivered four hundred kilograms of lime to the town house. His brother Marcel had requested the material to "kill the bugs in the attic of rue Le Sueur and to whitewash the façade." "Goodbye arrogance," Massu said afterward. Maurice Petiot was another witness "caught in the trap of his own lies."

As Maurice explained to the commissaire, he had failed to answer honestly because he feared that the information would give a false impression. He was also trying to protect the truck driver, who had been sworn to secrecy about the lime. Maurice acknowledged that he had made a mistake in covering up his involvement in the delivery, but he was no murderer and knew nothing about bodies in his brother's town house.

"My brother did not keep me informed of his business," Maurice said. What he did know was that Dr. Petiot had wanted the building on rue Le Sueur to establish "a clinic for cancer and tumor research." Georgette Petiot, he added, had certainly visited the property, because his brother would not have bought it without showing it to her.

Asked about his own visits to rue Le Sueur, Maurice said that he had never seen anything unusual. Nor had he been surprised by the disorder and bric-a-brac that prevailed, as his brother was an avid collector who enjoyed purchasing items at auction houses. He had, he now admitted, entered the triangular room, which he described as "a sort of cabinet noir." While he claimed not to recall any hooks on the walls, he had seen the false door, which had intrigued him, and he had tried to open it with an iron bar. He had concluded that it was merely decorative.

It was during this interview that Maurice admitted that he had learned of the discovery of the crime scene not on Monday, March 13, as he had claimed, but actually on March 11. He had received a late-night anonymous telephone call. Adamantly and repeatedly, he swore that it was not his brother who made the call.

Massu asked if Maurice had questioned the caller, and his response was curious. "I wanted to know how the bodies had been discovered, but nothing was said on the subject." If Maurice did not know anything about the murders, it is striking that this was his first question. It is also striking that, as Massu soon learned, this so-called anonymous phone call had lasted almost eight minutes: 9:54:36 to 10:02:32.

Massu took Maurice down the corridor, past a line of photographers to the *juge d'instruction,* or examining magistrate, where he was booked for complicity.

"I am convinced," Massu soon told reporters, "that the refuge of the doctor is known by his brother and also his wife."

11.

SIGHTINGS

BLOOD, MORE BLOOD, STILL MORE BLOOD.

—Commissaire Massu

THE extensive coverage of the Petiot affair soon escalated into a full-blown media circus. Newspapers dubbed the doctor the Butcher of Paris, the Scalper of the Étoile, the Monster of rue Le Sueur, the Demonic Ogre, and Doctor Satan. One of the first and more popular sobriquets was the Modern Bluebeard, comparing Petiot to the rich aristocrat in a late-seventeenth-century folk tale who killed his wives and hung their bodies on hooks in a room underneath his castle. Later, other names would be proposed for the murder suspect, from the Underground Assassin to the Werewolf of Paris.

Speculation was rampant. Petiot was discussed in sidewalk cafés, smoky cabarets, and brothels that flourished day and night around the city. In the métro during an air raid alert on March 24, 1944, a journalist for *Paris-Soir* noted that people spoke only about Marcel Petiot. Many Parisians were reminded of a popular movie, two years before, Henri-Georges Clouzot's *L'Assassin habite au 21* (The Murderer Lives at No. 21). In the film, Scotland Yard struggled to catch an elusive London killer who teased authorities by leaving behind his calling card "Monsieur Durand." The motive for the murders in the film was profit. Petiot's motive, on the other hand, was not so easily determined.

Rumors circulated that the physician was an "insane sadist" who tortured his victims savagely before burying them alive in quicklime. He was, it was also asserted, a sexual predator who slaughtered for thrills or, as Jean Boissel put it in *Le Réveil du Peuple,* sought raw material for his black mass ceremonies. *Le Cri du Peuple* was focusing on his scalping of the victims. Other people suggested that the suspect was a mad inventor who conducted gruesome experiments to perfect his torture devices, including a distance-operated syringe that injected poison into his victim. The police, *Le Cri du Peuple* reported, were trying to track down the craftsman Petiot supposedly hired to build the machine.

Photos of the grinning monster with the hypnotic eyes appeared regularly on the front pages. *Le Petit Parisien* reported that Petiot took "sadistic pleasure in listening to the pitiful confidences" of his patients in drug treatment before finally writing them a prescription, which, *Paris-Soir* noted, was often adorned with obscene rhymes. Petiot was "Satan in person," a former schoolmate at Auxerre told a journalist for *A Matin*. Sales of French newspapers soared, soon reaching their highest levels since the Occupation.

The sensational tales, however, hardly helped the police sort through the layers of mystery that surrounded the case. Readers sent in tips, some of them bizarre. A psychic claimed that Petiot was hiding in the Neuilly district of Paris, either at No. 4 or No. 20 boulevard d'Inkermann, or No. 2 or 4 rue de Chartres. A radiesthesist, using his pendulum to detect energy vibrations from a map, declared that Petiot had fled to his home region of Auxerre. Another seer reported having visions of the dead physician, poisoned and abandoned on a country road in Yonne. Other people speculated that he had committed suicide, perhaps using one of his own injections.

A small book printed on rue d'Enghien in Brussels that March noted the widespread belief that Petiot would likely soon die at the hands of his drug suppliers or some other shady accomplice who would be unnerved by the prospect of Petiot revealing everything he knew. Many policemen had already expressed a similar fear, not least Massu. "If Petiot is still alive," the commissaire said, "we will not take long to catch him." In the meantime, the sightings continued. Fifty thousand concierges and countless shop workers across Paris would be on the lookout for the serial killer, predicted Maurice Toesca of the Préfecture de Police.

The lack of information on the doctor's whereabouts only fueled the rumors. Someone believed he had seen Petiot handing out candy to children in a Parisian square, and an anonymous caller to the police reported seeing him enter a building in the northwestern suburb of Asnières. A journalist at *L'Oeuvre* thought that he spotted Petiot on a métro quay, wearing dark glasses and a beard.

Petiot was spotted all over Paris, or headed north to Brussels, west to Andorra, or south to Morocco or Algeria. A man in Orléans was sure he had seen Petiot at his inn. The physician, he said, had arrived on a black bicycle, breathless and lost in his thoughts. Intrigued, the innkeeper had invited him for dinner. Petiot had said nothing coherent other than ask where he might obtain a boat. The innkeeper was certain that he had dined with the Vampire of rue Le Sueur.

It was not always easy to confirm or refute the many stories that circulated in the aftermath of the discovery. Two women, for instance, were also positive that they had spotted Petiot that March at a central train station, booking passage to Anvers. While one of them followed the suspect, keeping him in sight, her friend rushed to a nearby kiosk for reinforcements. The crowd accosted the fellow, only to find that the alleged mass murderer was a Spanish merchant on a business trip. "Pity," one of the women was overheard saying, "I would have liked so much to have seen him."

The reason no one had found Petiot, some Parisians speculated, was that he dressed up as a woman, adding new relevance to the collection of blouses, skirts, and lingerie uncovered in his closets at rue Le Sueur. Other people believed that he had evaded detection by moving in with a lover, one of his "freemason brothers," or, as the press initially reported, with a band of Resistance fighters in the countryside. Still others, hardened by years of press manipulation, believed that the real Petiot had already been arrested in Vichy, or that he never existed other than as a fabrication by the German authorities to distract Parisians from the hardships of war. "It is a myth inspired by the Landru Affair," the historian Léon Werth wrote, noting the rumor in his diary March 29, 1944. "There has never been the shadow of a cadaver at rue Le Sueur."

As the police stumbled on in the search, appearing no closer to finding Petiot, the bestselling mystery novelist and creator of Inspector Maigret, Georges Simenon, volunteered his detective skills to his old friend Commissaire Massu. The French police certainly looked like they could use the help. Petiot seemed to be taunting them. Was he really the person who sent authorities cryptic notes of his whereabouts or teasing reminders that "Petiot, he runs, he runs, he runs"? Massu certainly thought so.

The international press also seized on the story. In Switzerland, Belgium, and Scandinavia, the Petiot affair dominated headlines on a daily basis. In the issue of March 27, 1944, *Time* magazine traced the source of the killings to "fatal injections" with the victim "chained to the wall of a soundproof 'death chamber' " and the murderer watching "the last agonies through a peephole." The report continued:

In the underheated rooms and overcrowded subways, clerks and salesgirls read the gory details. Fleshy black-marketeers and their flashy molls exchanged sadistic tidbits over champagne and caviar.

The slaughterhouse on rue Le Sueur, *Time* correctly noted, "crowded war news from headlines."

Cabaret acts incorporated the grisly material into its shows. "Madame, your bones need some lime" was one example. "*La femme au foyer . . .*" was another. The story of the "real-life equivalent of Jekyll and Hyde" gave Parisians, in the words of Steward Robertson of the *St. Petersburg Times*, "a thrill, running second only to the feats of Allied bombers." No one yet knew the scale of the crimes, but Paris seemed obsessed with Petiot Mania. "Will Dr. Petiot be found?" *Paris-Soir* asked on March 18, 1944, only to answer that it was doubtful.

"WHO would have believed that this is possible," the concierge at 66 rue Caumartin, Raymonde Denis, told Massu when he and one of his officers returned to the suspect's apartment. Petiot, she said, "was so nice, so sweet"—he was one of her kindest tenants. She was still in disbelief. Massu muttered something polite about how it is possible to rub shoulders with someone for years without ever realizing that that person conceals dark secrets, but the concierge stuck to her opinion of the alleged killer.

Not far away, at 17 rue Darcet, the location of a bistro that had until recently been run by Petiot's patients and friends Louis Albert and Emilie-Justine Bézayrie, Inspector Battut questioned someone who might have seen the murder suspect on the night of the discovery. The new bistro manager, Maria Vic, said that a man had come into her establishment about nine fifteen or nine twenty p.m. and asked to use the telephone. When she agreed, he told her the call was to the region of Yonne. She was not sure who he was, whom he called, or what they discussed. She went to wash the dishes. At some point, she thought she heard the words "Burn the papers!"

Was this perhaps the call that Maurice admitted receiving? Massu put a trace on it, and by the end of March, he would have confirmation that the call from the Parisian bistro had in fact been to Maurice Petiot. Vic stood by her statement that the man who borrowed the telephone was Dr. Petiot.

Detectives now wanted to speak with the previous owners of the establishment, Louis and Emilie Bézayrie, who had operated the bistro from 1935 to December 1943, when they moved to a new location, on rue de la Jonquière in the 17th arrondissement.

Louis Bézayrie had known Petiot since September or October 1940. His wife Emilie was then pregnant, and as her doctor had been taken prisoner by the Germans, she had consulted Petiot on a recommendation from a friend. He had assisted at the birth of their son, and, as the baby was often sick, she continued to see him regularly. Petiot also was a customer at the bistro, sometimes buying coal in bulk (many bistros during the Occupation supplemented their income by selling coal). Bézayrie had not seen him for some time, he said, and he had not sold him coal since September 1942, when he arrived with his cart and purchased about three hundred kilos.

The owners of the café had more information for the detectives. In fact, Louis Bézayrie would provide a lead that might well have resulted in an early apprehension of the suspect, had investigators pursued it. He suggested that the detectives question "old man Redouté," a house-painter in his mid-fifties who often shared a drink with the physician. The French police later defended this failure to investigate on the extraordinary grounds that they believed Redouté was the man's first name and could not locate him.

Petiot had indeed been hiding with Georges Redouté in his small apartment at 83 rue du Faubourg Saint-Denis. The exact date of his arrival was never determined, but it was early in the manhunt. Redouté would later claim that it was March 25, 1944; Petiot would say it was the twelfth or thirteenth. The police would never clarify his first movements before he arrived at Redouté's apartment, suitcases in hand, claiming to be a member of the Resistance on the run from the Gestapo.

Redouté, of course, knew about the murder allegations, as they had been plastered in every Parisian newspaper. But he believed Petiot's tales of fighting the Germans and agreed to allow him to stay in his apartment. The murder suspect slept on a mattress on the floor of Redouté's dining room.

During the day, Petiot tended to remain inside reading newspapers, working crossword puzzles, and listening to clandestine BBC radio broadcasts. He continued to devour police novels, and created special dice for making a range of probability calculations, something that would soon absorb his attention. Generally he refused to let anyone inside the apartment. The concierge, Henriette Kraeber, later recalled the difficulty of convincing him that a man sent around to fix a leak was actually a plumber. Redouté's guest, she said, "only went out for food and books." Petiot, "a convincing talker," would spend many evenings regaling his host with stories of his alleged Resistance activities.

He was also growing a beard and often wearing dark glasses to disguise his profile, raising the question of whether the *L'Oeuvre* journalist who believed he had seen Petiot on a Parisian métro quay in late March had not in fact come across the suspect.

=

AFTER hours of searching rue Le Sueur or reading police reports, Massu would often enjoy a brisk walk, even if it was only to a nearby bistro. Along the way, he tried to imagine how Petiot murdered his victims, disposed of the bodies, and evaded detection for so long in the middle of Paris. He started thinking of various possible poisons. If only, he mused, the people he passed by at the secondhand bookstalls on the quays could read his thoughts.

For a homicide detective, however, Massu believed that "a single small piece of uncovered evidence is better than a thousand ideas," and he would often simply leave his office with the urge to visit the site, or, as he put it, "speak to the walls." On the way there, he frequently encountered sightseers pleading to be shown inside the town house. Most of them, he believed, would probably pass out after five minutes.

His son, Bernard, would continue to follow him to the crime scene. "He had youth, I had experience," the commissaire said, and the clash of the two perspectives would often lead to valuable results. Bernard had another quality that his father admired: When it came to finding answers, he was as "impatient as a young dog." All of this would be crucial to the task of reconstructing the ways the killer lured victims to the house for a horrific odyssey that somehow involved the triangular room, the dissection table, the basement furnace, and the lime pit.

On one visit to rue Le Sueur with his secretary, Canitrot; his deputy, Battut; Dr. Paul; the examining magistrate, Georges Berry; and several other inspectors, Massu drove up past a crowd of about one hundred spectators on the sidewalk. The first stop was the pit, which was still ghastly, despite the fact that the gravediggers had already sifted through the remains and the firefighters, on Massu's instructions, had aired out the surrounding coach house. Indeed, the forensic team had now scraped the bottom of the pit and retrieved the last lime-coated "debris of bones and bundles of muscles."

Massu showed the inspectors the triangular room, or "torture chamber," as the press had dubbed it. The wallpaper had been peeled and the thick walls had been examined for other decoys or secret rooms. Massu said that he knew the macabre room better than his own bedroom. Except, of course, the commissaire still did not fully understand its significance.

To demonstrate the Lumvisor viewer, named after the German company that manufactured it, Massu asked his secretary to stand near a pair of iron hooks in the "field of vision" and then went to the adjacent room to take a look. The hole was above his height, but when he stood on the electric heater, which was placed directly underneath, he could look into the lens. His eyes fell right on the face of his secretary. When he checked the range of the device, the view did not shift more than a few centimeters either way. Massu imagined the victim, incapacitated, perhaps drugged, and then hanging there, suspended by the hooks, while the doctor watched every move of the victim's face in magnified perspective.

One magistrate asked Massu how Petiot killed his victims. The commissaire explained that the police had found no trace of blood in the room, and the forensic experts had thus far found no evidence either of stabbing, shooting, or strangling. Massu was inclined to think of poison, injected perhaps in the guise of being anesthesia or medicine. But with the lack of viscera for examination, toxicologists had found no trace of poison. Was there perhaps another method that Petiot used that eluded detection? Massu was still, as he put it, "reduced to hypotheses."

Another official asked about the last moments of life, where the survival instinct took control, resulting in a final, desperate fight for existence. But again, the triangular room showed no signs of struggle. The group, no strangers to horror, turned silent on yet another mystery in the case.

Asked about the events after the murder, Massu explained that Petiot probably took the victim's body across the courtyard to the basement. The high walls he had constructed would have shielded him from the view of his neighbors. At the kitchen workstation in the basement, he probably scalped and disinterred the corpse. He used the two large and deep sinks, joined by a slender draining table that was stained a dark red or brownish tint. The entire setup, which rested against the tiled wall, was certainly large enough for this work. Water could flow across the draining board and then into the second sink, where a side container was placed. The drain under the larger, higher sink, police had discovered, led directly to the sewer.

At one point during the visit, Dr. Paul approached the commissaire, grinning, his hand extended. Massu knew that the forensic expert often added a few details in person that he did not insert into his report. Sure enough, Paul had some news. "It's like two years ago," he said. Paul was referring to a period between May 1942 and January 1943 when a number of arms, legs, torsos, and other body parts had been fished out of the Seine or dropped in parcels around town.

The first of these packages had been found on May 7, 1942, when a trunk, tied with a rope, had been hauled out of the Seine under a bridge near a canal at Saint-Ouen. It contained a body of a male approximately forty-five to fifty years old without head, hands, or feet. The head had been removed, the police report detailed, "at the level of the neck, with a sharp cutting instrument, just short of the shoulders." The hands had been cut off at the wrist, or the radioulnar carpal joint, the feet just below the shin, at the tibiotarsal joint. Apart from the dismemberment, there was no scar, fracture, or "trace of violence." The body was never identified.

There would be many other horrific finds over the next eight months: July 2 at Neuilly, just outside the 16th arrondissement; August 6 at Asnières, northwest of the city center; August 10 at Saint-Denis, north of the center; August 19 again at Asnières; and so on. On August 22, 1942, investigators found a trunk on the northwest outskirts of Paris, at Courbevoie, containing two human hands without skin or fingertips, two feet without toenails, the skin of two legs including the heel, and three scalps, the first with reddish-blond hair, the second almost black, and the third gray. There was also a chest wall, a left ear with part of the skin of the face, the point of a nose without any cartilage, a penis with two testicles in a lacerated scrotum, and an entire face mask, with the point of a nose, mouth, lips, and both ears. Four other mutilated fragments of human bodies could not be identified.

Bodies and body parts continued to emerge from the Seine in bulging trunks tied shut with ropes. In each find, the decapitation and dismemberment had been expertly administered, the perpetrator wielding his scalpel like "a man of the lecture hall." What's more, each one was treated in a strikingly similar way.

As far as authorities could tell from the recovered body parts, the hair was shaved, the eyebrows were removed, and the face mask peeled away in a single smooth cut. Even the fingerprints on the severed hands had been meticulously filed off or dosed with acid. Everything was done with such skill and precision that Dr. Paul had more than once feared that someone on his own staff had been committing the murders.

But Dr. Paul saw something else in the dissection and dismemberment. He explained:

> *We forensic scientists are in the habit, in a dissection, of not passing our scalpel on the table of operation when we stop in the middle of our work, but instead stick it in the thigh of the cadaver.*

He had found such marks on the first find of human remains in May 1942 and then on many others pulled from the Seine—four thighs alone, for example, on October 4, 1942. He had seen those marks again in the "shreds of flesh" sent over to him from the lime pit. He suspected that this was the work of the same man, a well-trained physician who was also remarkably talented at covering his tracks.

While the police looked around rue Le Sueur, a number of reporters had joined the crowd outside the town house, swarming, Massu thought, like "a storm cloud of mosquitoes." They could not wait to question the commissaire. How many victims were there in the case? Were there really fifty murders, as some newspapers were now reporting? What other accomplices, if any, were involved, and what had been decided about Madame Petiot? Could the commissaire confirm that the murderer was scalping his victims and decorating his basement with a sinister ring of skulls?

Did Petiot really have a folio copy of the Marquis de Sade with a cover made of human skin? What about the rumor that the killer, before finishing off the victim, donned a frightening rubber mask? The reporters, eager for any tidbit of information, virtually blocked Massu's path to the car. The commissaire felt like he was throwing crumbs to pigeons outside Notre Dame.

"Is it tomorrow, then, that you will arrest the doctor?" one reporter asked Massu. Where was Petiot, and why had he still not been found? The press, impatient for more details, was exerting a considerable amount of pressure on the Brigade Criminelle. Paris was devouring the tale of horror in the heart of this chic neighborhood.

German authorities, by contrast, were being surprisingly aloof. After the initial order to arrest Petiot, the Gestapo had not yet obstructed, facilitated, or otherwise directly interfered in the search. It turned out, however, that a suboffice of the Gestapo had quite a file on Marcel Petiot. On March 15, 1944, this dossier was forwarded to Commissaire Massu.

12.

THE GESTAPO FILE

HE SAID TO ME THAT HE WOULD SOON BE SHOT AND THAT,
IN THIS CASE, HE ONLY REGRETTED ONE THING:
HE HAD NOT DONE ENOUGH.

—Renée Guschinow, describing a conversation with Marcel Petiot

THE Gestapo had certainly known Marcel Petiot. As Massu now learned to his astonishment, the German secret police had suspected him of operating a secret organization that helped Jews, downed Allied pilots, and deserting German soldiers escape Occupied Paris. According to one of the estimated twenty thousand Parisian informers, this clandestine organization was headquartered in a beauty salon at 25 rue des Mathurins, a street known for its many theaters and brothels, located just around the corner from the grand department stores Galeries Lafayette and Printemps, on the Boulevard Haussmann.

The hair salon, decorated in the faded elegance of a previous era, was run by Raoul Fourrier, a short, stocky sixty-one-year-old hairdresser and wigmaker. He was assisted by his friend, the fifty-six-year-old makeup artist and former cabaret performer Edmond Marcel Pintard, who had acted under the stage name Francinet and played small roles in a number of silent and early talkie films. Pintard's task in the organization was to frequent bars, bistros, cafés, and nightclubs, looking for people interested in leaving Nazi-occupied Paris. Once he had established contact, he would refer potential clients to the hair salon, where details of passage would be arranged.

Both Fourrier and Pintard were believed to be serving under Marcel Petiot, who, to Massu's further surprise, had actually been arrested by the Gestapo and held in prison for almost eight months. The German file detailed the campaign that the secret police had waged in the spring of 1943 to capture Petiot, the rumored Resistance leader and enemy of the Third Reich.

One branch of the Gestapo was particularly involved in the pursuit: IV B-4. In the Nazi bureaucracy of terror, the Gestapo was Department IV of the SS Reich Security Main Office (Reichssicherheitshauptsamt). Section B dealt with "sects" and subsection 4 with Jewish Affairs. Since March 1942, Gestapo IV B-4 had worked in every stage of the Nazis' "Final Solution": arresting Jews, seizing their property, and deporting them to death camps in the east. The office in Paris, like all other branches in Occupied Europe, answered to Adolf Eichmann in Berlin.

A commissioner in the bureau, Dr. Robert Jodkum, a solidly built man in his late fifties with a crew cut, thick glasses, and pale blue eyes, was anxious to obey. As former secretary and interpreter for SS Hauptsturmführer Theo Dannecker, the resident Nazi "Jewish expert" in Paris, Jodkum now served under Dannecker's successor, SS Obersturmführer Heinz Röthke. Although also nominally under Sturmbannführer Loperz, Jodkum was effectively in charge of this anti-Jewish service.

Jodkum, a former pork butcher, was one of the rare civilians to obtain such prominence in the Reich Security Main Office, which had been established in 1939 to bring together the seven departments of the SS under one security office. Jodkum was, moreover, under pressure for his alleged leniency on the Jewish question. Apparently he decided to prove himself with an energetic pursuit of Petiot's rumored escape organization, believed to be engaged in the "contraband of persons."

Jodkum's plan was not simply to storm the hair salon and start arresting people. Instead he decided to send in a plant, or *mouton* (literally a sheep or stool pigeon), who would pose as a man desperate to leave Paris and seeking the organization's services. That way, the Gestapo could infiltrate the organization, learn its procedures, and then, at the opportune moment, seize its ringleaders, intermediaries, files, and assets. Plotting carefully, Jodkum selected Yvan Dreyfus for this role. Dreyfus was a thirty-five-year-old former silk merchant from a Jewish

Alsatian family who had come to Jodkum's attention due to an unfortunate turn of events.

Back in 1939, when the war began, Dreyfus was working in the United States, where he had previously studied engineering. His friends, concerned about the danger to him as a Jew, urged him to stay there in safety. Dreyfus had resisted. "I am a Frenchman," he said, unable to abandon his country in a time of need. He returned home to France and enlisted in the army. He arrived just before the German Occupation.

After the army was demobilized, Dreyfus found that the silk business had been decimated, and he turned to selling radios and electronic equipment in Lyon. In early 1943, wanting to join de Gaulle's Free French Army in London, Dreyfus decided to hire a *passeur*, or guide, to lead him and four of his cousins out of Occupied France. But they were betrayed and the men were captured at Montpellier, imprisoned at Nîmes, and eventually sent to Compiègne, a notorious transit stop on the way to the Nazi death camps at Dachau and Buchenwald.

Hearing of his arrest, the Dreyfus family of course wanted to buy his release, if it was at all possible, and sure enough, a French lawyer with the right connections appeared. This was Jean Guélin, a former Lyon attorney and mayor of a small commune in Deux-Sèvres, until he lost his position for black market dealings. Now in Paris, Guélin operated a lucrative purchasing agency that sold scrap iron to Occupation authorities. He also engaged in a number of other ventures, including directing the Théâtre des Nouveautés, not far from Fourrier's hair salon, and also for the last five months, with his colleague Marcel Dequeker, the Théâtre Édouard VII. Both Guélin's restaurant, Zardas on rue de Sèze, and his apartment on rue de Longchamp had been confiscated from Jewish victims.

Well informed of the wealth of the Dreyfus family, Guélin approached the Gestapo commissioner with a proposal to release the prisoner. A ransom, Guélin added, could be split three ways between Jodkum, the Third Reich, and himself.

Such ransoming of individual Jews was on the increase in both Occupied France and Europe. Six months earlier, Heinrich Himmler had (with Adolf Hitler's support) allowed IV B-4 offices to free certain people deemed a low "security risk" in exchange for a fee. Some offices in Europe had drawn up lists of rich Jews to ransom, such as the Frielingsdorfs Liste of the Netherlands' IV B-4. At least four hundred individual Jews purchased their freedom in that country alone, raising a total of 35 million Swiss francs. The money was in part used to finance Third Reich operations as well as line the pockets of Nazi officials who brokered the deals.

Jodkum accepted the proposal to sell Dreyfus's release, but added the stipulation that the prisoner had to perform a service and infiltrate the escape route. From previous surveillance, the Gestapo knew that the underground organization could easily be contacted in the cafés and bars of the 9th and 10th arrondissements. Getting accepted, however, was more difficult. The organization was believed to take many safety precautions, including rigorous background checks, conducted allegedly by a French police officer, and a number of interviews, to ensure that a potential client posed no security threat.

If the applicant gained admission, the time and date of the departure would be set at a later meeting at an undisclosed location. The traveler would usually be notified three or four days in advance. At the time of the rendezvous, a member of the escape organization would meet the client and escort him or her to a secret hideaway, thought by Gestapo informers to be a "hotel or a doctor's office." All ties with family and friends were at this point severed. Departure was believed to take place about every three weeks.

Charges were typically assessed at various stages of the journey to freedom: an initial payment of 50,000 francs, an additional fee of 400 francs for each night in the organization hotel before departure, and another 90,000 francs for the false papers that were handed over at the railway station. (The fees, actually, differed depending on the person.) All the client's money and jewels were entrusted to the escape organization for safekeeping until the client reached the Spanish border. The organization under scrutiny was believed to send its clients to Irun, a Basque border town in Gipuzkoa (Spanish: Guipúzcoa), and then farther by train, to a port in Portugal, where a neutral ship took them to South America. Clients arrived with diplomatic papers identifying them as commercial agents of the Republic of Argentina.

One Gestapo report summed up the organization: "The management of this underground railroad for the escape of persons from under German control must be assumed to be found or sought out among France's leaders or upper classes." It enjoyed the support of a foreign embassy, and the organization was, the report concluded, "remarkably efficient."

TO secure the prisoner's release from the concentration camp, Dreyfus's wife Paulette was forced to pay a ransom, which included 100,000 francs just to open the dossier and a series of other fees to cover "unexpected costs" along the way that eventually surpassed 4 million francs. Yvan Dreyfus was then coerced into signing two important documents.

The first guaranteed that he would inform German authorities of all the information gained about the clandestine organization; the second required him to swear an oath that he would never act in any way against the Third Reich. Paulette Dreyfus, who had been led to believe that the ransom would purchase her husband's unconditional freedom, was horrified. Guélin reassured her that it was a mere formality designed to satisfy Gestapo bureaucracy. He then asked for another 700,000 francs.

Yvan Dreyfus, a staunch patriot, was at the mercy of his captors. Signing the papers thrust in front of him by the men in brown leather jackets was the only way to leave the concentration camp. His cousins, moreover, were still held by the Germans, and his wife had been lured into Paris from Lyon to complete the negotiations. The German negotiators had made it clear to Dreyfus that any failure to cooperate would be construed as an act of hostility toward the Third Reich.

On April 9, 1943, Dreyfus signed the papers, and, shortly afterward, his wife paid the final installment of the fee at the Madeleine métro station. Dreyfus was released and the couple went to dinner to celebrate.

Guélin also tagged along. On May 18, 1943, two Gestapo agents demanded that Dreyfus fulfill his end of the bargain.

By this time, Guélin had already made arrangements for Dreyfus to meet the purported leader of the escape organization, "Dr. Eugène." He accompanied Dreyfus to the rendezvous, which was indeed a hairdresser's salon on rue des Mathurins. Guélin described the evening:

> *We climbed a dirty, dark staircase, and passed through a succession of rooms in the hair salon, until we came to the one where Monsieur Fourrier was . . . Dreyfus asked him if he could obtain a passport for him, and Fourrier escorted him into a neighboring room, where in the shadow between the curtains, I saw a rather tall man who spoke with them.*

Dreyfus was informed that this was the first of several meetings because the organization needed to verify his credentials and evaluate his application. For the next interview, he was instructed to bring ten photographs for the false passports and papers: five full-face and five profile. He was also asked to pack his valuables in two suitcases. The fee was 200,000 francs.

After the background checks and the interviews, which were counted as numerous in the Gestapo report, though in reality there were probably no more than two or three, Dreyfus was selected to leave Paris on May 20, 1943. He was told to arrive at the salon on that day, and he would then be taken to a secret location to receive vaccinations and await departure. Gestapo agents planned to follow him, catching the members of the organization in the act of accepting payment. Once this was accomplished, one Gestapo report noted, they could search the headquarters, identify the people who furnished the false papers, and, of course, seize the organization's assets, which were assumed to consist of "many millions of francs."

At the appointed time, Dreyfus made the connection with Dr. Eugène, and the two men left the hair salon headed toward the Place de la Concorde. Somewhere on the Champs-Élysées, likely inside the métro station, they managed to elude the Gestapo agents and disappear. Dr. Eugène was evidently quick on his feet. Had Dreyfus, convinced of the doctor's services to the Resistance, tipped him off about the trap?

Jodkum, furious at the failure, prepared to infiltrate the organization a second time. An agent quickly secured a meeting for four days later. But before that occurred, another German organization intervened.

U NBEKNOWNST to Jodkum, a separate subsection of the Gestapo had also been investigating the alleged escape organization. Parallel organizations with similar and indeed rival aims were notorious in the Third Reich, but this only partly explains the duplication. Jodkum had investigated the agency for its rumored assistance to Jews hoping to escape Occupied Paris. The second organization, suboffice IV E-3, which dealt with military security and counterintelligence, was concerned because of its alleged help to German soldiers who preferred to desert, rather than risk a transfer to the Eastern Front in the war against the Soviet Union.

The leader of IV E-3 was Hauptsturmführer Dr. Friedrich Berger. Like Jodkum, Berger had also recruited a *mouton* to infiltrate the group, Agent VM-X (V-Mann "X"), or Charles Beretta, a small man who looked more like a university professor than the hardened black market racketeer he was, who had been released from prison camp in 1940. Beretta worked as a tailor when he met Dr. Berger and, seduced by payment and privileges, began to cooperate with him. By January 1943, Beretta had been placed in charge of some lucrative purchasing agencies on behalf of the occupying power.

So while Jodkum's team prepared for a second strike at the underground escape network, Berger sent Beretta into the hair salon, posing as a prisoner of war on temporary leave who feared being sent to a German work camp and wanted desperately to flee abroad. He also told Fourrier that his wife was held at Drancy and he wanted to raise enough money to buy her release. He pleaded for last-minute inclusion in the escape party.

After passing the series of interviews and background checks, Beretta was taken into a back room of the salon. Like Dreyfus, he handed over the ten photographs for his false papers. He saw his forged passport, or something purporting to be it—"the doctor showed it, but did not let me take it and study it closely," he said. Beretta was asked to bring two suitcases and a blanket. He submitted a diagram showing a layout of the premises.

Although he had not learned the identity of the doctor, Beretta described him as a man approximately "thirty-five to thirty-eight years old, height about 175 cm [5'7" to 5'8"], brown hair, thin, clean-shaven, wearing a navy blue and white striped suit. Nervous. He has the habit of rubbing his hands constantly."

Beretta played the part of an aspiring fugitive, feigning financial distress and negotiating the fee of 100,000 francs down to 60,000. He paid an initial 10,000 and promised the last 50,000 the following day. When he showed up to complete the transaction, he handed over the first 45,000, all supplied by the Gestapo with serial numbers duly noted. He delivered the remaining 5,000 in a telephone booth outside Café de la Renaissance, near métro Strasbourg-Saint-Denis. At this point, the hairdresser said that Beretta would leave Paris in a party of eight. He claimed to have a list of names in a book in his pocket.

On May 21, 1943, Beretta arrived at the hair salon for his scheduled departure. Fourrier and the makeup artist Pintard were there, but not Dr. Eugène. Berger sensed that the agency's leader might have become suspicious, perhaps even had been tipped off about the raid. He ordered his Gestapo men to pounce. Agents exiting black Citroëns dashed into the salon and threw the men to the ground as they accepted payment.

When Jodkum learned of this arrest, he was livid. He would have preferred to watch the organization longer to discover its inner workings, not just its recruiters, who were easy enough to identify and arrest. Jodkum wanted the more shadowy agents who guided clients across the frontier, the officials who helped with the false paperwork, and, of course, the leader of the organization himself and the reputed treasure, all of which he feared would now be harder to seize. He blamed Berger's panicked arrest for spoiling his opportunity. As a higher authority, Jodkum pulled rank and seized control of the interrogations.

The prisoners were handed over to Jodkum, with apologies. The hairstylist and makeup artist at first denied everything, but as questioning soon turned brutal, both men admitted working for a well-connected physician known as Dr. Eugène. He smuggled clients out of Occupied France across the mountains into the Free Zone, or abroad, passing through Andorra and then Spain, where they were put on a ship to Argentina. He also obtained false passports and other required travel documents for his clients. The doctor, they confessed, lived at 66 rue Caumartin.

W AS Marcel Petiot really Dr. Eugène, the man the Gestapo suspected of helping desperate people escape Occupied Paris? What implications, if any, did the Gestapo file have for discovering the identity of the remains at rue Le Sueur? And what had happened to Yvan Dreyfus?

By six o'clock on May 21, 1943, three hours after the arrest of the hairdresser and makeup artist, the Gestapo had stormed Marcel Petiot's apartment and hauled him off to their headquarters in the imposing former French Ministry of Interior, at 11 rue Saussaies. They also arrested his old friend, René Nézondet, who had just arrived with theater tickets for the night's performance of Champi's musical comedy *Ah, la Belle Epoque!* at Théâtre Bobino.

Gestapo headquarters was an intimidating place even to its own officers. Former member Hans Gisevius described the atmosphere that prevailed in Berlin—and the tension could certainly apply to the office in Paris:

> *[It was] a den of murderers. . . . We did not even dare step ten or twenty feet across the hall to wash our hands without telephoning a colleague beforehand and informing him of our intention to embark on so perilous an expedition.*

His colleague, Arthur Nebe, entered and exited the building using the back staircases, "with his hand always resting on the cocked pistol in his pocket."

Dragged past the armed guards, Petiot was taken to a room on the fourth floor for questioning. He would later claim that the Gestapo had beaten him savagely at one point after his arrest, every hour throughout the night. The first few days—"three days and two nights," as he put it—Petiot was shuttled between this building and other offices, including a branch of the military espionage and counterespionage organization, Abwehr, at 101 Avenue Henri-Martin.

Petiot suffered a series of brutal interrogations. As he described it, they drilled and filed his teeth, and put his head in a vise ("skull crushing"), causing him to spit blood for days and suffer excruciating cases of vertigo for a long time afterward. He was also given "the bath," the technique of stripping a prisoner naked and then submerging him, head-first, with arms and feet bound in chains, into icy water until he fell unconscious, at which point he was revived and the torture repeated. He was eventually dressed and sent in his soaking wet clothes to shiver away in a cold cell.

Sometimes prisoners faced other savage treatment, such as crushing or twisting of the testicles, or electric currents running through the hands, feet, and ears, with one end attached to the rectum and the other to the penis. There is no evidence that Petiot received either of the latter, but these served, along with the lash, the whip, the bath, and the vise, in the arsenal of interrogation methods used in Gestapo offices in France and elsewhere in Occupied Europe. It was called "running a prisoner through the dance."

Petiot was interned at Fresnes Prison, a white stone structure seven miles outside of Paris that was at that time the largest prison in France and indeed the continent. It was also a notorious holding place for Resistants, captured British agents, and other enemies of the Third Reich. Petiot was detained in cell 440 on the fourth floor of the first division.

The cells in the long corridors were small, with a chair, a table, and an iron cot chained to the wall and covered by a straw mattress often infested with fleas or other bugs. Near the table were an open toilet and a single brass faucet. Graffiti was sometimes scratched or penciled into the walls, offering a glimpse into the spirit of the prisoners—many of them marshaling their resources in expectation of the next interrogation.

In cell 44 of the Second Division, American Sergeant H. Hilliard scrawled his name, the date "June 1943," and the words "God bless America." Guy Gauthier (alias André Nantais) of the Resistance network Franc-Tireurs et Partisans (FTP), locked in cell 205 of the Second Division, wrote, "Live Free or Die Fighting. France Free Yourself." Cell 147 noted the death of "Mazera Dédé, innocent victim of the Gestapo," while someone in cell 34 had drawn a heart with a pierced arrow and the letters R and L. He added not "*Vive de Gaulle,*" but "*Vive le fin de la guerre.*"

Like many other people arrested together, Marcel Petiot and René Nézondet had been separated upon arrival. Eight days later, Nézondet saw his friend again when both men stood outside the main entrance at Fresnes awaiting transfer from their cells for further questioning at Gestapo headquarters. Petiot was, Nézondet said, a pitiful sight. Handcuffed and chained at his ankles, Petiot "seemed to have great difficulty moving. He stood slightly stooped and patted his head constantly with a wet handkerchief."

What, in the end, did Petiot admit to his interrogators? According to his confession, which he had been forced to sign, Petiot was not the main leader of the escape organization. He claimed to work for a patient in his medical practice named Robert Martinetti, or the "Martinetti Organization."

Petiot had begun this work, he told his interrogators, one day in November 1941 when the alleged Martinetti informed him of the escape route to South America and asked if any of his clients wanted to use it. Months later, Petiot asked one of his patients, the hairdresser Charles Fourrier (his name was actually Raoul Fourrier), who in turn agreed to send him people wanting to leave Paris. Petiot met the potential clients at the rendezvous, usually at or near Place de la Concorde, such as outside the entrance to the métro at rue de Rivoli or, alternatively, in front of the station at Saint-Augustin. From here, he claimed to take them to Martinetti. The charge was at first 25,000 francs, though it later increased to 50,000 or higher, depending on the case.

Departures had begun in late 1942, Petiot said, pleading ignorance of most of the details about the organization, its escape route, and its hideaways. "All I knew, and all I was supposed to know, was Martinetti and delivering the travelers to him," Petiot declared. Explaining why he was questioning Dreyfus if he were only a cog in the machine as he claimed, Petiot said that he had become skeptical of many people that Fourrier brought to him. He had taken it upon himself to examine candidates for their suitability.

"I never saw any of the persons turned over to Martinetti again," Petiot said. He did not know how to contact the boss, who, he claimed, always instigated communications by visiting his office or calling him. This professed ignorance must have sounded suspicious to the Gestapo, but the files revealed no further elaboration.

As one cell mate, a British-trained Resistance fighter named Lieutenant Richard Héritier, later claimed, he had no doubt that Petiot was a member of a network active in the French Resistance. He was moreover shocked at the brazen disrespect Petiot showed the guards. He acted as if he simply did not care what happened to him. Curiously, however, Petiot was never deported, executed, or made a hostage to be shot in reprisal for an attack on German soldiers. In fact, on January 13, 1944, Petiot was removed from his cold, damp cell and released. Less than two months later, the bodies were discovered on his property at rue Le Sueur.

The file in front of Massu was silent on the mystery of his release. Was it because, as Jodkum later implied, the Gestapo had concluded that Petiot was a complete lunatic? Did the Gestapo manage, as it sometimes did, to "turn" prisoner Petiot and have him work for them? Would that explain the sense of invulnerability he seemed to feel as he repeatedly insulted the Germans? Had he, as Petiot himself later claimed, proved so stubborn that the Gestapo chiefs had calculated that they would learn more if they released him and tracked his activities?

The French police would later find out, thanks to Germaine Barré, an agent in the British Secret Intelligence Service (SIS), that Jodkum had offered Petiot his freedom in return for 100,000 francs. Having heard the conversation herself, while awaiting her own interrogation, she recalled that Petiot had declined, claiming that he suffered from cancer of the stomach and did not care whether they released him or not. Jodkum then called Petiot's brother, Maurice, who promptly paid the ransom.

But this testimony begs the question why the Gestapo would release Petiot in the first place, particularly at such a relatively cheap price. Did Petiot benefit from protection? If so, who or what was looking after him, and why? The Gestapo file was certainly helping Massu learn about the case, but at the same time, it raised many questions about the murder suspect, the identity of the bodies found on his property, and of course the motives of the crimes.

On March 15, 1944, with Gestapo file in hand, Massu ordered the arrest of the hairdresser Raoul Fourrier and makeup artist Edmond Pintard. Later that same day, as Massu was trying to make sense of the murky and increasingly puzzling case, a middle-aged man contacted the police after reading in the newspapers about the discovery on rue Le Sueur.

13.

POSTCARDS FROM THE
OTHER SIDE

SOMETIMES I AM UNABLE TO PREVENT MYSELF FROM
QUIVERING WHEN I IMAGINE THE SCENES THAT HAVE BEEN
WITNESSED AT THE HOUSE ON RUE LE SUEUR.

—Commissaire Massu

JEAN Gouedo, the man who appeared in Massu's offices, owned a leather and fur shop across the street from Marcel Petiot's rue Caumartin apartment. He had purchased the store in 1941 from his friend and former partner, Joachim Guschinow, then a forty-two-year-old Polish-born Jew who had been frightened by a number of developments in Occupied Paris. Gouedo had no need to explain why Guschinow had lived in fear.

On September 27, 1940, a new law had forced Guschinow, like all Jewish store owners, to display the bilingual black-and-yellow sign identifying his business as Jewish: JÜDISCHES GESCHÄFT and ENTERPRISE JUIVE. The following month, Guschinow became one of 7,737 Jewish shop owners and 3,456 co-owners in the Department of the Seine who were forced to sell their businesses to a non-Jew. The German Occupation was making a tragic mockery of France's tradition of tolerance, which had long attracted immigrants like Guschinow to the country.

In early May 1941, the Préfecture de Police used the recent German-ordered census, identifying the almost 150,000 Jews in Paris, and required the 6,494 foreign Jewish males of Polish, Austrian, and Czech nationality between the ages of eighteen and sixty to report to one of five locations on the fourteenth of the month. The 3,747 who obeyed were promptly deported to the concentration camps of Pithiviers and Beaune-la-Rolande. Most of them would later die at Auschwitz.

Three months later, at the next roundup, the French police sealed off an area of the 11th arrondissement, north and east of the Place Bastille, with a large population of foreign-born Jews, and began seizing men between the ages of eighteen and fifty. They forcibly removed them from home, work, the métro station, and the streets. The 2,894 arrested in the initial sweep, however, were not sufficient, according to German authorities. Follow-up operations raised the number to 4,232, all of whom were sent to the new concentration camp Drancy, three miles away, in an old unfinished housing project. On the night of October 2–3, Gestapo-organized riots burned six Parisian synagogues and destroyed a seventh with explosives. Everywhere, it seemed, Nazi persecution was increasing in frequency and intensity. Each day, Guschinow feared arrest.

As Gouedo explained to the commissaire, Guschinow had told him that his medical doctor, Marcel Petiot, claimed to know a way out of the country. It was not easy, the physician had warned, but it was certainly possible. For a fee of 25,000 francs, an underground escape network would smuggle him over the mountains into Spain or alternatively across the line of demarcation into the unoccupied zone, where he would board a ship at Marseille for Argentina. All travel documents, including forged identity papers, false passports, and phony entry and exit visas, would be provided.

Guschinow was supposed to maintain complete silence about the secret organization, but, in his excitement, he confided to his colleague— a fortunate circumstance that would help the investigation. Despite his misgivings about the risks of such an enterprise, Gouedo had agreed to help his friend prepare for departure, and he now told Massu what he knew. The instructions had been minutely detailed. No pictures or identifying papers of any sort were to be carried; any initials or marks on articles of clothing or any item on his person had to be removed. After all, it was worthless, the physician had reportedly said, to purchase a false identity, only to carry evidence that contradicted or cast doubt on it. The fee was to defray the costs for the *passeurs,* the stay in a string of remote hideouts, the voyage across the Atlantic, and the bribes of corrupt officials along the way.

Instructed to bring one or at most two suitcases of personal belongings, Guschinow had sewn two five-hundred-dollar bills in US currency into the shoulders of his tweed coat and concealed another sum in a secret compartment of one of his suitcases. In total, he carried about 500,000 francs, along with a fortune in gold, silver, diamonds, and other family heirlooms, which included an estimated 500,000 to 700,000 francs in jewels alone. He also brought along several fur coats to start a new furrier shop in Buenos Aires.

Hearing the extraordinary story, Massu called in Guschinow's wife, Renée, for an interview, which took place on March 21, 1944. A small blond woman in her early forties, Madame Guschinow confirmed Gouedo's account in many respects and elaborated on other details as well. On January 2, 1942, the night of departure, she accompanied her husband to the L'Étoile, perhaps farther. It was dark and they were trying not to be seen. Guschinow had been told to come alone.

It was striking that Renée's husband had been told the location of the rendezvous—rue Pergolèse, which intersects rue Le Sueur. In every other case that the police would discover, all of which came later chronologically, the physician would never again reveal the address in advance. Had he perhaps learned to be more reserved with this information? At this point, too, there was no mention of the name Dr. Eugène, though of course Petiot had no need to use a pseudonym with Guschinow, who, as his patient, already knew his identity.

As Madame Guschinow continued relating what she knew about the enterprise, Massu learned that her husband had been referred to one of Petiot's colleagues, a specialist in tropical diseases who would make some "necessary injections," presumably vaccinations. Guschinow was asked to pack a special suntan lotion, two blankets, and selected valuables in no more than two suitcases. That evening, Joachim and Renée

Guschinow dined together, walked around the Arc de Triomphe area, and then kissed good-bye, never to see each other again.

In March 1942, two months after her husband's departure, Renée was worried that she had not heard from him. She visited the doctor, who was said to be the only acceptable way to contact a client abroad. Petiot assured her that her husband was doing well. After traveling through Marseille and Casablanca, he had reached Buenos Aires. Petiot showed her a postcard that he said he had received from Guschinow: "I have arrived. I got sick during the crossing but I am completely healed. You can come." That was all it said, or at least that was what Petiot claimed it said. The letter had been written in code. There was no obvious date, stamp, addressee, or signature. It seemed to be written in Renée's husband's handwriting.

Two other postcards and letters purportedly from Guschinow appeared that spring, written on stationery bearing the name of the "Alvear Palace Hotel, Buenos Aires," where Petiot claimed that Renée's husband was living. In these communications, Guschinow never elaborated other than to say that, after nearly losing his mind at the initial departure and breaking down in tears, his voyage had been comfortable and he had arrived safely. His business was thriving, and above all, he wanted his wife to join him.

Once, on her insistence, Petiot allowed Renée Guschinow to retain the card from her husband, on the condition that she later tear it up. She had complied, she told Massu. In the last message, Guschinow demanded that his wife immediately depart, threatening to cut off ties unless she consented. Petiot seconded the urgency of the request, advising her to "sell all [her] belongings and carry as much money as possible."

MARCEL Petiot had purchased the property on rue Le Sueur from the Princess Marie Colloredo-Mansfeld in May of 1941 for 495,000 francs. He paid 373,000 down, covering the remainder with annual payments of 17,500. The building was put in the name of his son, who became the ninth owner since its construction in 1834. On August 11, 1941, Petiot took possession of the town house, and within six weeks, he began making renovations.

The construction company, Laborderie et Minaud, had made a number of improvements to the property. In addition to pouring a concrete foundation in the garage, the masons had built a high outer wall in gypsum around the courtyard and constructed an inner wall in one of the buildings, which created the triangular room. They then surrounded this new space with a wall consisting of twenty-two centimeters (8.6 inches) of solid brick. A viewer was installed, a double door was inserted, and eight iron hooks were added. In the kitchen, they had also installed a concrete sink and, he claimed, plugged some holes in the basement that gave access to the sewer. The renovation work was completed in October 1941—two months before the disappearance of the first known victim, Joachim Guschinow.

Jean Minaud, one of the owners of the firm, said that he had never visited the site or inspected the work. It was a small project compared to his company's usual ventures. He had delegated everything to two brothers, Louis and Gaston Dethève. When Massu asked to speak with them, Minaud told him that Louis had died two years before in an air raid. Gaston, however, was available, and on March 23, 1944, he accompanied the commissaire to rue Le Sueur, where he would point out the work in detail. He also removed the Lumvisor lens from the wall for examination.

As Dethève explained, Petiot had told them that he planned to open a clinic and mental institution after the war. The newly constructed triangular room would house an "electric transformer." Petiot wanted the walls reinforced to drown out the sounds, so as not to disturb the neighbors and also to protect against the dangers of radiation. "With electrotherapy," he had allegedly told the Dethève brothers, "you cannot be too careful." Petiot had also explained the insertion of the viewing lens into the wall as a device to monitor the progress of his machine. The courtyard addition, which was built on top of a wall already several stories high, would protect his patients from the prying eyes of his neighbors, not to mention shield them from the peach pits that he claimed children liked to throw into his yard. As for the hooks in the triangular room, Dr. Petiot had not explained their purpose.

WITH news of the "murder factory" on rue Le Sueur splashed on the front pages of all the major Parisian papers, a number of people approached police headquarters with stories about the suspect. One of the more useful tips came from Roland Albert Porchon, a thirty-two-year-old former deliverer of wine who had made a small fortune during the years of the Occupation. He owned, among other things, a trucking company near la porte de Sainte-Cloud and a restaurant on rue du Faubourg Poissonière, which had been "Aryanized." A large man with short dark hair and a thick neck that the French then described as Germanic, Porchon had many friends on the police force and in the criminal underworld.

Like Gouedo, Porchon claimed knowledge of the clandestine escape agency. In March 1943, Porchon had suggested it to a friend, René Marie, and his wife, Marcelle. After the usual round of background checks and interviews, the couple had been accepted by the organization. The cost was to be 45,000 francs, the fee clearly varying depending on many factors, not least being the desperation of the potential client to leave and his or her ability to pay. Porchon, who operated a secondhand furniture business on the side, had offered to buy the couple's furniture for a lump sum of 220,000 francs. The couple, in the end, had not left with the agency.

But there was more to Porchon's testimony. After the news on rue Le Sueur first broke, Porchon had panicked. Realizing that he had sent over a couple to the doctor and fearing that police might find their names, as well as his own, at rue Le Sueur, Porchon had tried to cover up the incident. He confessed to Massu that he had gone to the Maries, and told them, in no uncertain terms, to avoid speaking with the police.

And if the police came to them, they should deny everything. Porchon, busy with his own concerns, did not need any additional hassles from the authorities.

In the course of the conversation, Porchon also mentioned a name that Massu and his inspectors kept encountering: René Nézondet. He was, they already knew, a friend of Marcel Petiot, and he had also been arrested when the Gestapo arrived at the physician's home. They were in prison together until Nézondet's release in June 1943. After twenty years of friendship dating back to their bachelor days in Villeneuve-sur-Yonne, Nézondet had served, in Porchon's words, as Petiot's "right arm."

Nézondet had approached Porchon once with a proposal from Dr. Petiot to sell a large stock of alcohol. Porchon, tempted, picked up the phone and called a friend in a purchasing agency that sold goods in bulk to the German Occupation authorities. He was not interested. Nézondet came with many other proposals, which Porchon said he had not taken seriously.

On one such occasion in 1943, Nézondet had come to him with an idea of launching a new, German-sanctioned radio station that would operate in Paris. While they discussed the proposition, Nézondet related some gossip about Dr. Marcel Petiot, calling him "the King of the Gangsters." Then, Nézondet added mysteriously, "I would never have believed he could ever commit murder!"

According to Porchon, when he challenged this statement, Nézondet told him that he had entered a basement somewhere in town—he did not say where—and seen "sixteen corpses stretched out." Porchon was still skeptical, he said, but Nézondet replied that he had seen the corpses himself. "They were completely black," he added. "They must have died by injection or some poison."

Nézondet then allegedly told Porchon why he thought Petiot had killed his victims: "I suppose he asked them for money to pass them into the Free Zone and instead of helping them escape, he killed them." Nézondet swore Porchon to silence, assuring him that he would report the murders to the police himself as soon as the war ended.

As if that were not disturbing enough, Massu now learned that this was apparently not the first time Porchon had reported Petiot's suspected murders to the police. On August 2, 1943, Porchon had contacted a friend, Commissaire Lucien Doulet, then a forty-two-year-old director of the police économique at the quai de Gesvres, which investigated financial crime, and told him about a rumor circulating in the underworld about "a Parisian doctor who, under the pretext of passing young people out of the country, asked them for sums of money between 50,000 and 75,000 francs, and then did away with them after payment." This doctor, Porchon added, disposed of the remains "by burying them in the courtyard of his building."

Doulet had told him to report the news to the Police Judiciaire, which Porchon did. "He didn't seem to take the matter seriously," Porchon said. The police officer in question, Massu learned, was an inspector on his own Brigade Criminelle: René Bouygues. When the commissaire interviewed him on August 19, Assistant Inspector Principal Bouygues admitted knowing Porchon for five years and praised him as a valued police informer. But he denied ever hearing anything about Petiot or any murders. He later changed his mind, saying that he had "forgotten about it."

That Inspector Bouygues would attempt to make this excuse for not pursuing the allegation illustrates the sheer disregard for human life during the German Occupation—a time when many people simply disappeared without explanation. Porchon's testimony also underlined the extent to which the police department, even when tipped off about possible murder, neglected to investigate. Was this an example of incompetence, an overwhelmed police force, or yet another sign that perhaps someone was protecting Marcel Petiot?

It was at this time that Massu learned that the rumors of a stranger arriving at and departing from the crime scene at rue Le Sueur on the night of March 11 were true. Patrolmen Teyssier and Fillion, the policemen who spoke with the man, had always denied it, persisting in their stance even after fireman Corporal Boudringhin gave his testimony on March 16, describing the visitor in detail.

Teyssier admitted that there had been many curious people outside the town house, but he said none had been allowed to enter. He flat-out denied the claims of the fire chief. "At no point," Teyssier said, "have I seen Dr. Petiot on the premises." Fillion supported Teyssier, but the evidence was mounting. Robert Bouquin, one of the first arrivals to rue Le Sueur, also saw the stranger, as did Maurice Choquat, who had arrived that night about 7:45.

On March 18, 1944, Patrolmen Teyssier and Fillion reversed themselves. A man claiming to be "the brother of the owner," Fillion confessed, had approached him and entered the building with his permission. He explained this lapse of judgment by the fact that he had been shocked and overwhelmed by the "staggering spectacle and the unbreathable air from the smell of rotting cadavers burning in the stove." Teyssier also now acknowledged seeing the stranger. After his return from calling headquarters for reinforcement, Teyssier noticed this unknown man standing under the vault of the carriage entrance with Fire Chief Boudringhin and Fillion, the latter looking uncomfortable. The man had remained three or four minutes, Fillion said, and then left, profiting from the general chaos. "At that moment," Fillion added, "I was far from thinking that this man was the killer."

For this negligence of duty, as well as their repeated lies, Patrolmen Teyssier and Fillion were removed from their positions and ordered to appear before the Germans at the Pépinière Armory. Both men fled, fearing severe reprisals. Teyssier, a thirty-nine-year-old member of a Resistance group inside the police—l'Honneur de la police—escaped by jumping out of a window at the armory.

14.

DESTINATION ARGENTINA

IF THE AMOUNT OF DOUGH EDITH DONATED FOR ALL THESE
GOOD CAUSES IS ANY INDICATION, SMUGGLING PEOPLE
ACROSS THE BORDER WAS A GREAT WAY TO MAKE A LIVING.

—Simone Berteaut, on her sister Edith Piaf

ON the evening of March 19, 1944, Pablo Picasso's play *Le Désir attrapé par la queue* (Desire Caught by the Tail) was performed in private at his friends Michel and Zette Leiris's fifth-floor apartment on the Quai des Grands-Augustins. It was a dark surrealist farce that featured a star-studded cast: Jean-Paul Sartre, Simone de Beauvoir, and Picasso's former lover Dora Maar. Albert Camus narrated, describing the largely imaginary sets—that is, except for a large black box that served alternatively as a bed, a bathtub, and a coffin.

Picasso had written the play three years earlier, beginning, as he recorded in a notebook, on the evening of January 14, 1941, and, in the tradition of surrealist automatic writing, finishing it three days later. Reminiscent of 1920s avant-garde theater, the play revolved around deprivation and indulgence, or more specifically hunger and sex. Michel Leiris, who had selected the cast, played the lead role of Big Foot. Sartre was The Round End; Raymond Queneau, The Onion; and Jacques-Laurent Bost, Silence. Simone de Beauvoir played The Cousin, while publisher Jean Aubier was The Curtains.

When Gertrude Stein had read the script, she suggested that Picasso stick to painting. But the photographer Gyula Halász, better known as Brassaï, after his native Transylvanian village of Brassó, thought otherwise. He praised Picasso's virtuosity, comparing the composition style to a "verbal trance [that] gave free rein to dreams, obsessions, unavowed desires, comical connections between ideas and words, everyday banalities, the absurd." This play, he added, displayed the painter's "humor and inexhaustible spirit of invention . . . in their pure state."

The audience, filled with painters, writers, playwrights, surrealists, and even Argentine millionaires, seemed to agree. They applauded loudly and congratulated Picasso on his success. Afterward, the cast and audience retired for a celebration, fueled by wine and desserts, including a chocolate cake brought by the Argentines.

As the play ended at about eleven, just before that night's curfew, Leiris had invited the cast and several friends to stay the night. They sang, listened to jazz records, and admired Sartre playing the piano. Camus and the host acted out various scenes, enhanced in part with wine served warm with cinnamon. The party ended at five in the morning. Simone de Beauvoir was overjoyed: "A year before we would never have dreamed of gathering together like this and having a noisy, frivolous party that went on for hours."

This was the first of the fiestas, as Michel Leiris dubbed them, that would take place in the spring of 1944. Beauvoir described another one not long afterward, at surrealist Georges Bataille's house in the Cour de Rohan:

> *We constituted a sort of carnival with its mountebanks, its confidence men, its clowns, and its parades. Dora Marr used to mime a bullfighting act; Sartre conducted an orchestra from the bottom of a cupboard; Limbour carved up a ham as though he were a cannibal: Queneau and Bataille fought a duel with bottles instead of swords; Camus and Lemarchend played military marches on saucepan lids, while those who knew how to sing, sang. So did those who didn't. We had pantomimes, comedies, diatribes, parodies, monologues, and confessions: the flow of improvisations never dried up, and they were always greeted with enthusiastic applause. We put on records and danced; some of us . . . very well; others less expertly.*

Beauvoir, looking back, remembered being "filled with the joy of living. I regained my old conviction that life can and ought to be a real pleasure."

ON March 19, Commissaire Massu began questioning the hairdresser Raoul Fourrier and the makeup artist Edmond Pintard individually about their involvement in the alleged escape organization.

Raoul Fourrier, a short man with white hair in a black beret, was brought into the commissaire's office on the third floor first. Slumped into an armchair, Fourrier appeared nervous, cautious, and highly distrustful. He spoke in a low voice, as his eyelids fluttered and his fingers clutched the armrest. When the subject of Petiot was broached, Massu noted that the sweat beaded on Fourrier's forehead and then disappeared into the wrinkles of his thick neck.

After an early silence, Fourrier told Massu that he had been a patient at Petiot's clinic on rue Caumartin for seven years, and it was there that the doctor first alluded to the escape organization. The time, he believed, was May 1941, because they had been discussing the case of some unfortunate young cyclists who had been punished for crossing the line of demarcation. Petiot had then let it be understood that he knew how to pass Frenchmen into the unoccupied zone and then into South America. It was a dangerous operation that could be infiltrated at any time by the Gestapo. He kept a packed suitcase ready in case he should ever have to leave in a hurry.

Perhaps Fourrier, with his contacts at the hair salon, knew some people who would want to take advantage of this escape opportunity. Fourrier was surprised by this question, he said, claiming that he had always tried to avoid any action that would bring him into conflict with the authorities. But, as Fourrier put it, "the doctor is a charming man, seductive even." He convinced the hairstylist that he was an active member of the Resistance helping fellow patriots escape "the vengeance of the Germans."

At the same time, Petiot promised Fourrier a "nice commission." Defensively, Fourrier told the commissaire that he had hesitated at the thought of his own personal gain. He was after all a patriotic French-man. Massu, unconvinced, returned to the subject of the organization. Fourrier freely admitted that he had agreed to help Petiot find recruits, and he sought out the assistance of his old friend, Edmond Pintard, who had many more contacts throughout the Parisian demimonde.

Fourrier told Massu of the client Charles Beretta, a safe choice since this man was already known from the Gestapo file. Since being released by the Germans in January 1944, Fourrier said that Petiot had twice tried to recruit him. When he refused, Petiot became angry and blamed Fourrier for causing their arrests by recommending Beretta.

After a short break in the interrogation, Massu asked about other people Fourrier had referred to Dr. Petiot. One of the first clients, he said, was known in the underworld as "Jo the Boxer," "Iron Arm Jo," "Jo la Ric," or "Jo Jo." A handsome, dark-haired thirty-something man with a broken nose and prominent scars under his chin, "Monsieur Jo," as Fourrier called him, often dressed in a flashy style, with baggy, high-waisted, and tight-cuffed pegged trousers, and a long, loose coat with wide lapels and padded shoulders. He had been recruited by Pin-tard at a small bar on rue de l'Echiquier, in the heart of a notorious pros-titution district along rue du Faubourg Saint-Denis.

Fourrier later picked him out from a series of police photographs. His real name was Joseph Réocreux, and he was, as Massu put it, "no choirboy." Jo the Boxer had a long criminal record that ranged from robbery to procurement, with several terms in prison, from Lyon to Saint-Julien-en-Genevois in the Haute-Savoie on the Swiss border. He had four or five warrants out for his arrest, but there was a more press-ing reason why he wanted to leave France.

Jo the Boxer had fallen out with the leader of one of the most vio-lent and notorious criminal gangs in Occupied Paris: Henri Lafont (real name Henri Chamberlin). Alias "Henri Normand," "Monsieur Henri," or "The Boss," the forty-two-year-old Lafont ran the group known informally as La Carlingue or the French Gestapo. The official name was Active Group Hesse, after a German SS officer under Helmut Knochen who'd looked after its foundation. Lafont's men would not only engage in the usual racketeering and run bars, restaurants, and nightclubs; they would also kidnap, rob, ransom, and torture "enemies of the Third Reich"—and indeed they would often be rewarded by German authorities for their attacks. Lafont would ride through Paris in his white Bentley, always the latest model and usually with a mistress at his side. He seemed to prefer aristocrats and dancers.

In his palatial office on the second floor of 93 rue Lauriston, which was filled with the dahlias and rare orchids that he obsessively collected, Lafont ruled over a brutal and increasingly profitable criminal empire. He had an extensive network of agents and informers who kept him updated about affairs. Lafont insisted on order and discipline, demanding that his men remain *régulier* with him, that is, showing at all times, as one former member of the gang put it, "discretion, efficiency, team spirit, and a strict regard for instructions." Jo the Boxer had broken this rule. He was donning a Gestapo uniform and, on his own initiative, committing a string of burglaries, thereby defrauding both the Third Reich and his own organization. Punishments in the cellar of Lafont's gray stone building were more feared in the underworld than the tortures of the Gestapo.

As Fourrier described the events for Massu, Edmond Pintard had arranged for Jo to meet with Marcel Petiot at Café Mollard near Gare Saint-Lazare. Over a few glasses of brandy, they discussed Jo's departure from Occupied Paris. Despite agreed protocol, however, Jo had not come alone. He brought along François Albertini, or "François the Corsican," a thirty-four-year-old pimp from Vescovato Corsica with a prominent scar on his face. They were joined by two women, both prostitutes and mistresses: Lucienne or Claudia Chamoux (Lola, Lili, or Lulu), the older of the two and described as "dark-haired and elegant," and Annette Basset, "Annette Petit," "La Poute," or "Little Bedbug," a twenty-one-year-old from Lyon.

Petiot, known to his clients only as "Dr. Eugène," refused to send four people at once on the escape route. He called the challenge, Fourrier recalled, "difficult, even impossible," and insisted that the gang depart the country in two groups. As Jo had become suspicious of the doctor, apparently made uneasy by the look in Petiot's eyes, which he told a friend "gave him the chills," François the Corsican went first, accompanied by Jo's girlfriend Claudia. The gangsters switched women, most likely to keep each other honest. Fourrier could not recall the exact time of the departure, though Jo and Annette had probably left at the end of October 1942.

But when the time for his departure neared, Jo the Boxer still had doubts. Pintard had tried to cheat him, he sensed, as indeed he had, arbitrarily doubling the departure fee and hoping to pocket the difference. Petiot, on hearing of these shenanigans, exploded, saying that this was a patriotic organization, not a commercial one, and threatened to end his working relationship with Pintard. This show of anger, however, had not removed Jo's suspicions about the physician. And when news of François and Lulu's arrival in South America proved slow to arrive, the gangster became more distrustful and restless.

At some point that autumn (neither Fourrier nor Pintard could recall the exact time), Petiot had produced a card or letter, purportedly written by François, relaying news of their arrival in Argentina. Pintard took it to the reluctant client, who then agreed to depart. Jo arrived, as planned, at Café Mollard, near Gare Saint-Lazare, with not one, but two women, Annette and a prostitute, whose name Fourrier could not recall. Rumors in bars referred to her as "Yoyo" or "Yvonne." She was never identified.

Although Petiot usually balked at taking more than one or two people at a time, he agreed on this occasion, likely inspired by the fact that Jo could not be allowed back on the streets with the inside knowledge he had gained about the organization. He may also have been persuaded that the gangster carried a sizable fortune, which indeed he did: an estimated 1.4 million francs, some sewn into the shoulder of his suit, and an array of other valuables, such as signet rings, a gold watch, and gold, concealed in the heels of his shoe. Annette also wore a great deal of jewelry, not least a large emerald ring studded with diamonds. It was believed that the three planned to start a brothel in the new world.

From his window Fourrier watched them leave, headed in the direction of rue Tronchet. He never saw Jo, Annette, "Mademoiselle X," François, or any of the gangsters and their mistresses afterward. Weeks after the departure, Pintard saw Petiot wearing Jo's gaudy gold watch. It had been a gift, the doctor said.

"Really, did you not doubt what happened to the people you sent to Dr. Petiot?" Massu asked.

"Not at all," Fourrier said, claiming that he had always believed that the physician was sending people to freedom. Massu, after the interview, felt a sudden need for a shower.

DESPITE the commissaire's skepticism, Fourrier was not necessarily lying. Clandestine escape agencies were rampant in Occupied Paris, and several of them were run by doctors. There was, for instance, the network Vengeance, founded by Dr. Victor Dupont of the Red Cross and Dr. François Wetterwald, which worked to help Allied pilots evade capture and cross into Spain and Portugal with General Charles de Gaulle's London-based intelligence service, Bureau Central de Renseignement et d'Action (BCRA). Another doctor, Sumner Jackson, the Maine-born head surgeon at the American Hospital in Paris, at Neuilly, concealed Allied pilots as patients in his hospital.

Many of the escape networks of the French Resistance worked with Allied intelligence organizations. Britain's Special Operations Executive (SOE), founded in the summer of 1940, after the Fall of France, with the famous charge by Winston Churchill to "set Europe ablaze," had established Section DF to focus on helping downed Allied pilots and other agents trapped behind enemy lines evade capture. At the time of Fourrier's interview, Section DF was smuggling Allied soldiers out of France at an average rate of one agent a day.

British Military Intelligence Section 9 (MI 9), founded and led by Norman Crockatt, focused on helping British prisoners escape from enemy prisoner-of-war camps. This remarkable organization was later joined by the American Escape and Evasion Section MIS-X of the Military Intelligence Department and another staff branch called P/ W & X.

All of these Allied organizations and the French Resistance groups made important contributions, not least in saving men from gruesome torture, helping preserve Allied secrets, and also facilitating the return of experienced soldiers for later missions in the war against the Third Reich.

But not all evasion networks concentrated on military personnel, and several were known to specialize in helping Jews leave the country. Between the time of Petiot's arrest by the Gestapo in May 1943 and the end of the Occupation, the Zionist Armée juive, for instance, would help at least 313 Jews cross through the Pyrenees into Andorra and then on to Barcelona. Two hundred and seventy-two of them continued on to Palestine. Other organizations had further specialized, such as the Éclaireurs israélites de France (EIF or Jewish Scouts of France) and the Oeuvre de secours aux enfants, a Jewish children's welfare organization, both of whom rescued children from the Nazis.

Virtually every claim Fourrier made about Petiot's supposed organization conformed to well-known features of genuine evasion networks. One of the most common paths out of the country was indeed through Marseille or over the rugged Pyrenees mountains. Smugglers had long used the narrow, steep shepherd trails, as had refugees fleeing the Franco regime at the end of the Spanish Civil War. The German seizure of the unoccupied zone in November 1942, however, had forced *passeurs* to seek out more difficult, higher altitude crossings amid fog, grueling winds, and the risk of avalanche and snowstorm as late as May, not to mention the more active border patrols with trained dogs.

There was the emphasis on departing in groups of two, or at most three, as Petiot had told Fourrier. The town house at 21 rue Le Sueur, with its private courtyard surrounded by high walls, was moreover better suited for shielding escapees than many of the attics, cellars, churches, and other safe houses used by Resistance groups. As for the hair salon, some Resistance organizations were indeed known to use them as fronts, a good choice, actually, for a clandestine business that relied on personal contacts, word-of-mouth publicity, and inconspicuous arrivals and departures. Agent Rose or Andrée Peel (née Virot), who helped save more than one hundred downed British and American pilots in Brest, was only one example of a Resistant who worked out of a beauty parlor.

Argentina would not have been an unlikely destination either. For one thing, the South American country had long welcomed immigrants. With the immense pampas, a rich grassy plain sweeping westward to the Andes Mountains, and a flourishing beef industry, Argentina had enjoyed a rising prosperity but often lacked a sufficient labor force to exploit its resources fully. The capital, Buenos Aires, had grown sevenfold since the turn of the century, making it the third-largest city in the western hemisphere, behind New York and Chicago. Cosmopolitan residents of Buenos Aires called themselves *porteños,* or "the people of the port."

The welcoming of foreigners was not only central to Argentine history; it was also written into its constitution. "The federal government shall promote European immigration," Clause XXV stated, giving specific responsibility to its House of Representatives and granting each arrival full equality, with the option of becoming a citizen after only two years. Later legislation had offered additional incentives. The Immigration and Colonization Law of 1876, for example, promised arrivals a free five-day stay in a government hostel, assistance in obtaining employment, and if necessary, free travel to the job in the hinterland. The government would eventually help defer costs of the voyage and grant the first hundred people of each convoy one hundred hectares of land.

During the Great Depression, however, the government began to restrict immigration. In fact, the influx of illicit Argentine papers onto the black market in Occupied Paris was an unintended consequence of a series of new rules and regulations issued in Buenos Aires. In July 1938, a confidential act known as Directive 11 required Argentine consuls to "deny visas, even tourist and transit visas, to all persons that could be considered to be abandoning or to have abandoned their country of origin as undesirables or having been expelled, whatever the motive for their expulsion." The target clearly was Jews fleeing persecution. Many other decrees followed. Jewish emigration to Argentina was halved within a year, and continued to drop. As the future vice president Vicente Solano Lima put it, "We don't want the ghetto here."

As the difficulty of legally entering Argentina increased, officials in Argentine consulates around Europe seized an opportunity to profit. In Milan, the Argentine consulate was notorious for selling immigration documentation. "What price for an Argentine visa today?" was a question often heard outside its offices, recalled Eugenia Lustig, the Italian Jewish physician. The Argentine consulate in Hamburg was known to sell visas to Jews for approximately 5,000 Reichsmarks. An Argentine consul in Barcelona, Miguel Alfredo Molina, confiscated passports from Argentine citizens to resell for 35,000 pesetas each. Closer to Petiot, the Argentine ambassador in Paris, Miguel Ángel Cárcano, was also cashing in on the opportunity. Before his recall at the beginning of the Occupation, he was believed to have made one million dollars from selling Argentine visas to Jews.

This was sordid business. At the same time, it illustrates painful moral ambiguities at the heart of the Second World War. As the historian and grandson of a wartime Argentine consul, Uki Goñi, asked, which was worse: selling visas that allowed hunted Jews to flee Nazi tyranny, or remain "uncorrupted" and refuse to issue any immigration documents at all?

So when Petiot said that his escape organization had access to someone inside an Argentine embassy, it would not have sounded preposterous. But that, of course, is not the same thing as saying that he actually had the documents, or that they would have managed to secure their entry into that country. At the time Petiot claimed to have such power, Argentine diplomatic papers, both real and forged, were losing their value. Immigration was tightening against legal and illegal entries, even before the military coup of June 4, 1943, would restrict it to a trickle.

EDMOND Pintard, the tall, garrulous, extroverted fifty-six-year-old makeup artist and former vaudeville performer, stepped into

Massu's office on March 20, 1944. The commissaire later remembered how poorly the interrogation had begun, and how arrogant the detainee had been.

"Monsieur le commissaire," Pintard said, with an exaggerated self-confidence. "Do you know who I am?"

"Yes. Edmond Pintard, theatrical makeup artist currently threatened with an indictment of complicity for . . . crimes."

"Me, an accomplice of crimes, the Great Francinet? Yes, I mean the Great Francinet, known by all the directors of music halls of Paris, a specialist in songs for weddings and banquets. My name, Monsieur le Commissaire, was on the advertising columns in letters *this large*," demonstrating by stretching out his hands, his fingers stained yellow by tobacco. "And if I am a makeup artist today, it is because I chose to retire at the height of my glory."

"How much were you paid to be the recruiter of Dr. Petiot?"

"You dare . . ."

"I dare say that if you continue to tell me about your life, I am going to get angry. We are not at the theater here." Massu pointed to the files on his desk, detailing the "innocent men and women who have been murdered by the careful attention of your friend Petiot. Murdered and perhaps tortured, before being cut up into bits and thrown into a lime pit. You have never smelled human flesh burning, have you?

"I asked you how much Petiot paid you," Massu repeated. "I don't believe that I heard your answer."

Pintard would eventually say that, despite recruiting for the escape organization for about two and a half years, he had only been paid twice. The first time was 6,000 francs, and the second 12,500 francs. His friend, Fourrier, had paid him directly out of his own commission. Pintard had only met Petiot once or twice, he added, and dealt through Fourrier, whom he had known for almost twenty years. Like the hairdresser, Pintard said that he did not know of the town house at 21 rue Le Sueur until he read about it in the newspapers.

"Did you solicit in bars?"

"Yes, sometimes."

"And the other times?"

"People began to know me in the neighborhood. They came to me."

When asked what exactly Petiot had promised his clients, Pintard explained that it was a safe passage to South America and official papers that proclaimed them commercial agents of a republic there. Like Fourrier, Pintard claimed to have believed that Dr. Eugène was a hero, a patriot, and a "great Resistant." As for his own responsibility, he said he thought he was only "doing [his] duty helping other Frenchmen escape their enemies."

At the end of the questioning, Pintard paused at the door. Massu asked if he wanted to say anything.

"Monsieur le Commissaire, if you would kindly ask the photographers to give me some peace. Everyone who knows me . . . I am ashamed."

"I am unable to do anything. They are doing their job."

Pintard opened the door, exiting to the blinding light of magnesium flashbulbs.

15.

WAR IN THE SHADOWS

A WORLD WHERE THERE IS NO MORE ROOM FOR
HUMAN BEINGS, FOR JOY, FOR ACTIVE LEISURE,
IS A WORLD WHICH MUST DIE.

—Albert Camus

AT the time Fourrier and Pintard began recruiting clients to escape
Occupied Paris, Nazi Germany looked almost invincible. The
swastika flew over capitals across the continent: Berlin, Vienna,
Prague, Warsaw, Copenhagen, Oslo, Amsterdam, Brussels, Paris, and
after April 1941, Belgrade, Sofia, and Athens. London, many believed,
would be next, fulfilling Marshal Philippe Pétain's prediction that Britain would soon be a corpse.

On June 18, 1940, General Charles de Gaulle had entered the London BBC studios and issued a powerful appeal to his countrymen: "The
cause of France is not lost." All French officers, soldiers, and workers
should join him at once in the continued struggle, he said. "Whatever
happens, the flame of French Resistance must not and shall not die."

Few people in France actually heard that landmark broadcast; fewer
still had answered the call. In fact, no prominent military officer, politician, or businessman had signed up to de Gaulle's cause, except for the
governor general of Indochina, Georges Catroux, and, almost one year
later, the forty-one-year-old left-wing prefect of the département of
Eure-et-Loire, Jean Moulin. Most of de Gaulle's earliest supporters were
Bretons, estimated in July 1940 to represent some two-thirds of his small
army of seven thousand patriots.

After the conquest of France, the Nazis had tightened their grip over the occupied zone, pouncing on any sign of unrest. When morale hit new lows in the winter of 1940–1941, as temperatures fell below freezing for a record seventy times, which was fifty more than average, the Resistance gained few additional recruits. By the spring of 1941, when Petiot first told Fourrier about his supposed organization, all of Paris and its surrounding region could have produced fifty fighters, as Charles Tillion recalled with some exaggeration, "capable of using any weapons at all."

Resistance to the German Occupation in Paris had, of course, lagged behind resistance in cities in the south, like Lyon, Toulouse, and Marseille. There were, after all, some thirty thousand to forty thousand Nazi troops stationed in Gross-Paris, not to mention the Gestapo, SD, and French affiliates who patrolled the streets, forcing opposition to the regime, at first, to take symbolic forms.

On November 11, 1940, Armistice Day, several thousand Parisian students, waving the illegal tricolor and singing the banned "*La Marseillaise*," marched down the Avenue des Champs-Élysées to the Étoile, where they placed a wreath on the Tomb of the Unknown Soldier. The French police, wielding batons, tried to control the crowds. The Nazi occupying authorities then took over, attacking with rifle butts and eventually opening fire. Rumors swirled of a massacre. Although there were no known deaths, more than one hundred people had been arrested and many people injured when German authorities fired on the demonstrators.

Early acts of defiance in Paris took place in many subtle ways. When newsreels were shown in cinemas, for instance, the portrayal of German victories or images of the Führer sparked such spasms of coughing that they forced the owners to keep on the lights. In February 1941, Liliane Schroeder reported how her mother was nearly arrested for powdering her nose during a newsreel. Similarly, Parisians expressed their opposition to the Occupation by wearing particular colors on certain days, like black ribbons and black ties on the first anniversary of the German conquest, or red, blue, and white on Bastille Day 1941, which led to some 488 arrests.

Churchillian "V" signs of victory gradually adorned walls and pavements around Paris, the French police counting a thousand such markings on April 7, 1941. Anti-German slogans were scrawled on walls, official German posters were slashed, and handwritten stickers denouncing the Occupation were pasted around town, four hundred of them, for instance, found by the police in one week in January 1941. Students liked to creep up behind a German truck at a traffic light and pin to it a small typewritten sticker that carried the words "Vive de Gaulle."

French protests, however, soon took a different turn. On the morning of August 21, 1941, a twenty-two year-old French communist named Pierre-Félix Georges (code name "Fredo" or "Fabien," later "Colonel Fabien") killed a German naval cadet, Alphonse Moser, as he boarded a train at the Barbès-Rochechouart métro station. The Nazis responded ruthlessly. Kommandant von Gross-Paris, General Ernst Schaumburg, announced a new policy of creating a pool of "hostages" from all Frenchmen arrested or taken into custody and then choosing a number of them for execution "corresponding to the gravity of the case." Six hostages were shot in reprisal for the murder of Moser.

But the severity of the punishment did not deter further attacks. The day after the announcement, two German officers were killed at Lille and then two more the following day in the Nord. This pattern was repeated throughout the autumn of 1941. An officer was gunned down at a métro station ticket window, a soldier knifed exiting a brothel; incendiaries, stolen from the Nazi depot, were tossed into a German hotel. A hand grenade was lobbed at a Nazi canteen; a bomb exploded at a German bookstore on the Place de la Sorbonne. Trains were derailed, cables were cut, and fuses in factories sabotaged. In December of that year alone, the German army estimated that there had been some 221 attacks against officers, soldiers, and property.

Resistance groups were now on the rise in Paris and elsewhere, especially after the Red Army repulsed the Nazi invasion and began to pursue the Wehrmacht on the Eastern Front. Inside France, a new German policy further swelled the ranks of Resistance. In February 1943, the Germans implemented the hated STO (*Service du travail obligatoire*), which required all Frenchmen aged twenty-one to twenty-three to serve two years of compulsory labor in Germany. By the end of the war, some 650,000 Frenchmen would be sent to the involuntary work program in war-related industries. To avoid this fate, young men fled to the countryside, leading to the spontaneous creation of bands of *maquis,* named after the Corsican word for thick scrubland and soon carrying connotations of a bandit or outlaw.

From remote bases in hills or mountains, many of the emerging "armies of the shadows" engaged in sabotage and attacks on German and Vichy authorities, ranging from disruption of railways to guerrilla-style raids. As they needed food and funds to survive, not to mention strike German targets, some gangs raided farms, robbed shops, and attacked people suspected of collaborating or profiteering on the black market. Some *maquis* became popular legends, like L'Hermine in the Drôme with his black cape and coat of arms. Other Frenchmen denounced them as criminals masquerading under a noble cause.

The STO was extended several times in 1943 and 1944, eventually making all men aged eighteen to sixty and childless women eighteen to forty-five liable to forced labor. As the number of defaulters increased dramatically in 1943 and 1944, and many law-abiding citizens came to their aid against this law widely regarded as arbitrary and unjust, the Germans threatened harsher punishment for evasion. "All close male relatives, brothers-in-law, cousins over age of 18 will be shot; all women similarly related will be sentenced to hard labor." Children under the age of seventeen would be packed away to an "approved school." The brutality and exploitation at the heart of the Occupation was evident to an increasing number of Frenchmen.

By the time Petiot was locked up in the Gestapo prison, the Resistance had gradually moved beyond individual acts of opposition and sabotage to become, as the socialist Jean Texcier put it, "a good occupation for the occupied." Resistance newspapers and pamphlets all over Paris sounded the call to action. Albert Camus, who joined the editorial staff of *Combat* in the autumn of 1943, put it this way only days after the discovery of Petiot's crime in March 1944: "Total war has been unleashed, and it calls for total resistance. You must resist because it does concern you, and there is only one France, not two." Sympathizers, he warned, would be punished just as active Resistants. Now was the time to act.

A S the story of Petiot's "murder house" broke, Albert Camus was holding rehearsals for his first play, *Malentendu* (The Misunderstanding). The plot revolved around owners of a hotel who recruited, entertained, and then robbed and killed their guests—a Petiot-esque project that would debut in June, ironically at the Théâtre des Mathurins, just across the street from Fourrier's hair salon.

The piece was in fact inspired nine years before when Camus read a short item in the Associated Press about a young man who returned home to Yugoslavia only to be killed by his mother. Camus added the element of the disguised return and the twist that the family had, in his absence, transformed the hotel into a profitable slaughterhouse. Camus set the story instead in the distant Bohemian town of České Budějovice (Czech Budweis), which he had visited eight years before. His new lover, the actress Maria Casarès, played the sister.

Camus was coming to terms with his new life in Paris. At first, he had found the occupied city a dismal gray, like its pigeons and statues, and a stark contrast to the sun, sea, and shimmer of his native Algeria. He missed his favorite café, which was decorated with a guillotine and a skeleton and had a flamboyant manager who wandered the establishment with a dildo in his hand. And Camus also missed his wife, Francine, though he continued to have love affairs.

For a time, Camus had considered taking advantage of an escape agency to cross into Spain and then return to Algeria. He certainly had experience with clandestine departures. Before coming to France, Camus had helped men and women pass into Morocco with the hope of joining de Gaulle in London. Camus, however, soon abandoned the idea of leaving Paris, no matter how appalling the impact of the German

Occupation was on intellectual life—Henri Jeanson compared it to living in a "madhouse run by the lunatics." Camus instead concentrated on his work, which in the spring of 1944 also included writing at night on his new novel, *The Plague,* which would be set in a city overrun by rats.

As Camus put the final touches on his play about the murderous hotel owners, Jean-Paul Sartre was preparing for the opening of his *No Exit,* a one-act play that would debut on May 27, 1944, at the Théâtre du Vieux-Colombier. The story took place, appropriately enough for the Occupation, in hell. Sartre had first picked Camus to direct and play the lead male role of Garcin. The rehearsals, which had begun at Christmas 1943 at Camus's or Simone de Beauvoir's apartment, were suspended in February, when the actor playing the lead female role, Olga Barbezat, was arrested by the Gestapo and imprisoned at Fresnes. At this point, either Camus backed out of his commitment or Sartre decided to replace him. The result was the same. *No Exit* was staged with an established director and a professional cast.

The German-controlled press lambasted the play for its "immoralism," but Sartre's *No Exit* would prove to be a major success, particularly with the young. "Hell is other people" was the line most cited. Sartre later explained that he only meant that people judge themselves with criteria given by other people, and therefore, if and when relations sour, humanity falls into a state of "total dependence" resembling hell. Sartre's popularity soared. After this piece, he became, in the words of Jean Paulhan, "the spiritual leader of thousands of young people." The scholar Guillaume Hanoteau agreed. Looking back at the postwar flourishing of Parisian intellectual life, Hanoteau credited Sartre's *No Exit* with inaugurating the "golden age of Saint-Germain-des-Prés."

The Wehrmacht, the Luftwaffe, the Kriegsmarine, the SS, and other elite Nazi officers and selected collaborators, meanwhile, were enjoying their own day in the sun. It was a sumptuous world far removed from the privations of everyday life replete with shortages and regular power outages. The officers were also avoiding the carnage of the Eastern Front: sipping champagne in the silk-lined suites of the Crillon or at the Ritz, dining by candlelight under the chandeliers of Palais du Luxembourg; and of course enjoying the fashionable soirees at the German embassy hosted by its Francophile ambassador, Otto Abetz. The spectacle of his social events prompted Céline to dub him King Otto I.

Germany's waning fortunes in war, if anything, strengthened the desire of its officers and soldiers to enjoy Paris. German officers were regular visitors to the cabarets and brothels. Madame Fabianne Jamet (real name Georgette Pélagie) remembered them at hers, One Two Two, with fondness: handsome young SS men showing perfect manners; Wehrmacht soldiers shouting "Heil Hitler" as they raised their champagne glasses; Luftwaffe pilots coming in for a last drink and fling before embarking on a bombing mission in the Battle of Britain. She recalled the latter passing around a tube of a stimulant designed to increase their concentration and confidence to face the Spitfires and anti-aircraft guns, and confessed that she started using the drug herself.

The French criminal gangs, on the other hand, were "horrible creatures." The gangsters in their fashionable jackets bulging with concealed weapons would lounge around downstairs with their women, "emptying magnum after magnum and boasting to one another about their exploits." Worse, they were unpredictable and often unruly, like the hooligan who got drunk and started juggling hand grenades. These "vile, disgusting thugs," Jamet added, "threw their money about on champagne and girls as though there was no tomorrow."

16.

THE ATTIC

I CANNOT SAY WHO I AM. STILL YOU KNOW ME.
EVERYONE KNOWS ME. IF I WERE TO TELL YOU MY NAME,
YOU WOULD BE TERRIFIED.

—Marcel Petiot to FFI Lieutenant André Rolet

DETERMINED to catch the killer, Commissaire Massu was dreaming of the moment he would place the handcuffs on Marcel Petiot. He would show the suspect to his seat near the window overlooking the green square below, offer him a cigarette, and then launch into what he called "the most passionate interrogation of [his] entire career." By the end of this battle of wits, he would be able to put together the many loose pieces of the puzzle and ensure that cruelty, malice, and deviousness on such a horrific scale would not go unpunished.

But far from being close to a resolution, the case seemed only to be expanding. After François the Corsican and Jo the Boxer had "passed" to the new world, as it was called, news of the escape organization had circulated around rue de l'Echiquier and the many cafés, bars, and other hot spots of Faubourg Saint-Martin. Soon Pintard was approached by several of Jo's associates, including the notorious gangster Adrien Estébétéguy, known as "Adrien the Basque," "The Cold Hand," or "The Right Hand." A forty-five-year-old from Bayonne, Adrien had worked much of southwestern France, particularly Toulouse, racking up some eight prison sentences and seven current warrants for arrest, not to mention a string of assault charges over the years, four of them recently, against French policemen.

Packing two standard automatics, which he was said to draw at the slightest dispute in a poker game, Adrien had a reputation as a tough guy with a biting wit and a penchant for fine clothes. He particularly liked new suits, this at a time when one on the black market cost the equivalent of the annual salary of a ticket collector on the métro.

By early 1943, Adrien the Basque had many reasons for wanting to leave France. As part of his work with the Devisenschützkommando, an outfit that tracked down people selling currency and gold illegally, a highly profitable enterprise virtually annexed by Henri Lafont's criminal gang, Adrien was accused of reselling for personal profit some of the gold he seized and then turning in an inferior gilt substitute. He was apparently making significant omissions in his reports of confiscated goods.

Some of the unreported profits probably also came from his work with Kurt von Behr of the Einsatzstab Reichsleiter Rosenberg (ERR) office, which was removing art and cultural property from "ownerless" Jewish homes. Adrien was involved in particular in the *Möbel Aktion,* or "Furniture Operation," that involved retrieving furnishings in apartments where Jews had been deported, and then sending the loot to newly formed German administrations in the east. Later, after the Allied bombing of Cologne on the night of May 30, 1942, ERR authorities changed the stated mission, claiming that the seized property would be used to compensate German victims of the air raids. By the end of the Nazi Occupation, some thirty-eight thousand apartments in Paris alone would be looted by this organization.

Adrien the Basque was guilty of yet other omissions. Like Jo the Boxer, he had been using his German security identity card (a *Sicherheitsdienst,* or SD, card) and Gestapo uniform to impersonate a policeman and commit a number of robberies. This kind of crime, unfortunately, was on the rise. Approximately one thousand cases of false Gestapo agents were known, many of them targeting the most exposed residents with the least recourse, such as foreign-born Jews or small-time black marketers believed to have hidden away cash. Profits could be substantial. And Lafont was not one to tolerate being defrauded, or insulted, by men in his gang.

Adrien needed to leave Paris in a hurry, but he did not want to travel alone. He recruited one of his subordinates to join him: Joseph Didioni Sidissé Piereschi, known variously as Zé, Dionisi, or Joseph the Marseillais. This surprisingly handsome man, with a scar two inches long and one inch wide running from the base of his nose to his left cheek, came from a similar background. He had been imprisoned at age eighteen for his first murder. During World War I, he deserted twice and progressed to other crimes, such as stealing military supplies and selling arms on the black market. By the fall of 1940, he had been released from the Marseille prison by the Germans, and he soon began running a series of brothels for German soldiers.

As with Jo and François before them, Adrien and Zé brought along their mistresses. Adrien's was Gisèle Charlotte Rossmy, a petite brunette, aged thirty-four, who had worked as a typist and performed on stage as "Gine Volna." Zé sported Joséphine, or Paulette, Grippay, "La Chinoise," a star from an exclusive brothel in Marseille and a recent arrival in Paris. Planning to open a new brothel in South America, they were believed to have carried some 800,000 francs in cash.

The gangsters again traded lovers to ensure honesty. On the last Sunday of March 1943, Adrien left with Paulette; a few days later, Zé followed with Gisèle. The group used a sign for communicating their safe arrival in Argentina: they took a 100-franc note, drew a flaming sun on it, and ripped it into two, each group taking a half. Adrien and Paulette would send their piece back through the organization to prove that they had arrived in South America. Not long after their departure, Petiot handed Fourrier the half note. "My men got them through," he said.

In March 1944, Massu's detectives found the other half of the note in a drawer at Petiot's office on rue Caumartin.

PETIOT'S closest friend, the forty-nine-year-old René Nézondet, was now brought into custody. Tall and slender, with his dark hair slicked back over his high forehead, Nézondet had known Petiot longer and arguably more intimately than anyone else outside his family.

As Massu already knew, Petiot and Nézondet had often dined to-gether in their bachelor days in Yonne. They had been arrested together, twenty years later, by the Gestapo. In between, Nézondet had left his position as a clerk after injuring his arm. He started breeding trout and growing watercress at a ranch outside of Villeneuve-sur-Yonne. He also operated a restaurant and entertainment center, La Fontaine-Rouge. The Petiots liked to attend his Saturday night dances, invariably on Georgette's urging. Marcel Petiot hated dancing.

By 1936, after the end of his first marriage and losing his investment in a fire, Nézondet had moved to Paris and begun working as a concierge for *Le Figaro*. He had started to see Petiot again after consulting him for a throat condition that developed in the First World War. Nézondet was also in a new relationship with a nurse at Hôpital Cochin named Aimée Lesage, and they soon began to dine often with the Petiots. The Nazi Occupation, however, prompted *Le Figaro* to move to Lyon; Nézondet followed, only to be sacked shortly afterward for his alleged black mar-ket dealings. In 1942, he had returned to Paris and reconnected a third time with Petiot. It was his old friend who helped him obtain a job with the father of one of Petiot's patients, Victor Braun, who ran a pharma-ceutical company that sold many supplies to the German army.

An inspector observing Nézondet told Massu beforehand that he would probably prove a difficult interviewee, likely to tense up at the least provocation and force the commissaire to have to draw out each monosyllabic reply. Massu, thus warned, began slowly. He walked behind the suspect without saying a word. He stood there, still silent, at his cabinet, pretending to search through papers. Nézondet remained tense. His raised shoulders, Massu noted, had not moved.

The inspector was right about Nézondet's lack of candor. When Massu asked if he liked his friend Petiot, Nézondet did not answer. When he asked about his line of work, Nézondet was evasive. Massu, tiring of the charade, pressed a button and told the secretary who entered the room to watch the witness. He went for a drink at a nearby bistro on the place de Dauphine. Nézondet was left, as he put it, "to simmer."

An hour and a half later, when he returned, Massu asked Nézondet again about his relationship with Dr. Petiot. This time, Nézondet spoke of his friend's love of art, furniture, and deal making. For instance, sometime last spring, Petiot had asked him to offer his boss the opportunity to buy "1000 to 2000 bottles of cognac," which he in turn could sell to the German army. Braun had declined because the military had stopped making bulk purchases of alcohol. What an interesting proposition from a so-called member of the Resistance.

Massu then asked Nézondet about the claims of the trucking company owner and secondhand furniture dealer Roland Porchon—namely, that he had seen sixteen bodies at rue Le Sueur. Nézondet dismissed this allegation with a laugh. It was outrageous, he said. He had not seen any bodies personally; Porchon must have been mistaken. He had merely reported what someone else had told him. Who was that? Nézondet stalled and hedged, before finally admitting that the source of the information was Maurice Petiot. On March 22, after many evasions and denials, he said that he would now tell the truth.

In late 1943, either November or December, Nézondet began, he met Maurice Petiot at the Hôtel Alicot to negotiate the purchase of radio equipment. Petiot arrived an hour late and nervous unlike any time Nézondet could remember. He looked as "white as a sheet," Nézondet said.

"I have just come from my brother's house," Maurice allegedly told him. "There's enough there to have us all shot."

"Enough what? Hidden weapons? A secret radio transmitter?"

"I wish that's all it was. The journeys [to South America] begin and end at the rue Le Sueur."

At this time, with Petiot still held in prison by the Germans, Maurice had also discovered "a pit full of bodies and quicklime—all of them were naked, with hair and eyebrows shaved off." A book was found nearby, containing the names and addresses of all the victims, along with the dates and other notes about the executions. He found a syringe, a hypodermic needle, poison, and many bodies. "There must have been fifty to sixty victims." Maurice also allegedly found a great deal of clothing, including suits, dresses, and German military uniforms.

Nézondet had been astonished, he told Massu, claiming that it was not possible, that "it's a nightmare!" But Maurice's demeanor seemed to confirm the horrors. Nézondet noted how his hands quivered as he related his discovery.

What's more, according to Nézondet, Maurice Petiot proceeded to describe the means of execution as some sort of distance-operated syringe. The victim, locked in the triangular room, would eventually press a button in the wall, which activated the lethal device. A miniature needle hidden inside the button pricked the finger with poison. That way, Petiot had not technically killed his victims; they had done it to themselves.

"Why did you not inform the police?" Massu asked. "It's your duty." The Law of 25 October 1941 had established the legal obligation to denounce a crime or the intent to commit a crime. The failure to comply carried a penalty of three months to five years in prison.

"I know that well," Nézondet said. "But Marcel Petiot was my best friend. I also thought of his wife and his son."

Commissaire Massu asked how much Georgette Petiot knew of her husband's activities. After a slight hesitation, Nézondet said that she knew everything because, as he feared for her safety, he had told her "the horrible truth" himself. In early January 1944, a few weeks after his meeting with Maurice Petiot, he had invited Georgette and Gérard Petiot to dinner at his apartment at 15 rue Pauly. They had discussed her husband, who she was sure would soon be released by the Germans, as indeed he was. Nézondet waited until the two of them were away from the teenager. As Nézondet put it, she "fainted, or almost fainted three times and threatened to commit suicide."

Georgette Petiot would later confirm that the events that evening were substantially true as Nézondet described them. She added, however, that she had not believed a word of his story. He seemed to be lying. In addition, Nézondet had suggested that she should divorce her murderous husband and the two of them have an affair, and this, she told Massu, further convinced her that he had made up everything to seduce her. (Nézondet countered unconvincingly that he only said she needed to have an affair, though not necessarily with him.)

Maurice had been furious at him, Nézondet said, for telling Georgette about the dead bodies. The last he heard, Maurice was trying to figure out what to do about them, and also find a truck to haul away the many suitcases he'd found at his brother's property.

Since that initial conversation at the Hôtel Alicot, Nézondet said that he had lived in mortal fear of his former friend. Not long after the physician's release from the Germans, which Nézondet said had astonished him, Marcel Petiot invited him to rue Le Sueur. He politely declined, but when the physician, with his charm, refused to take no for an answer, Nézondet had relented. It was his lover, Aimée Lesage, who put a stop to the meeting, insisting that he never go to rue Le Sueur alone. She was certain, she believed, that she had saved his life.

THE French police continued to question neighbors of the reclusive physician. Augusta Debarre, a thirty-nine-year-old woman who lived on the third floor of 22 rue Le Sueur, had some information for the detectives. About nine or nine thirty one night the previous summer, Debarre had seen an old truck, probably a Ford, parked outside Dr. Petiot's building across the street, and a couple of men had loaded a number of suitcases into it.

Other neighbors had witnessed the same event. Andrée Marçais, the thirty-four-year-old woman in No. 22 whose husband had made the first call to the police about the smoke, remembered that the vehicle was gray, and there were two or three men piling luggage into the truck. Yvonne Staeffen on the fifth floor believed that one of the men was the stranger who came regularly on the bicycle. "With my daughter," Staeffen said, "we have amused ourselves by counting the suitcases." They reached forty-seven, but they had not started from the beginning.

It was the eyewitness account of Angèle Lalanne of 26 rue Le Sueur that brought the police one crucial step closer to finding the truck. She reported seeing a sign on the old vehicle: TRANSPORTS AVENUE DAU-MESNIL. Massu now had something tangible to pursue.

An investigation into the transport companies and garages on the two-mile-long avenue, however, did not immediately turn up any valuable information. At one point, the detectives stopped by the Hôtel Alicot and struck up a conversation with a group of truckers. One of them, Emile Henri Pintrand, remembered that the man in the police photograph, Maurice Petiot, had approached him the previous summer about a delivery. Pintrand had declined because he was already busy that day. His friend, Leopold Sturlèse, had accepted.

But when Sturlèse arrived at the rendezvous at the Hôtel Alicot as planned, he learned that Maurice had hired someone else and the delivery had already been made. After a wild-goose chase to find this person, the inspectors discovered that the driver of the truck had been Maurice Lion of the Manjeard Company.

Lion verified that he and Maurice had loaded a number of suitcases onto his gray Renault truck and driven them to Gare de Lyon. A quick visit to the baggage office at that station revealed that, on May 26, 1943, train number 2001 had carried three separate shipments of a total of forty-five suitcases, weighing 683 kilograms, to the nearby town of Courson-les-Carrières:

Group No. 18	11 suitcases	160 kilograms
Group No. 235	18 suitcases	280 kilograms
Group No. 436	16 suitcases	243 kilograms

All of these suitcases were signed for by Albert Neuhausen, the man both Monique and Maurice Petiot had claimed slept in their property in Auxerre. Neuhausen immediately became a key figure in the ongoing investigation.

On March 30, 1944, when the police came to search his electronics shop in Courson-les-Carrières, he was not there. His wife, Simone-Andrée, however, admitted knowing about the suitcases. Maurice had brought them to the house the previous summer, claiming that they belonged to his brother, who had been arrested by the Germans. The arrest had happened just five days before. Had Maurice moved the suitcases to avoid seizure by the Gestapo?

Madame Neuhausen promptly escorted Massu, Inspector Battut, and a couple other detectives up to the attic, which was filled with suitcases stacked neatly in rows. Some were made of leather, a few still in dustcovers or carrying labels such as GRAND HOTEL AMSTERDAM; others were plain, even plywood, like many made during the Occupation. Several of the suitcases still carried baggage tickets from Gare de Lyon.

There were, in fact, forty-nine pieces of luggage in Neuhausen's attic. Thirty-seven of these were from the shipment from Gare de Lyon; the other twelve were not previously known. There were a few trunks, which were so heavy that they could not be carried down the steps and had to be lowered by rope through the dormer window. The suitcases were placed on the police truck for delivery to the station. Half of the village, Massu said, seemed to be standing outside watching.

As rain poured down, police cars brought what Massu called "the most tragic cargo" to the headquarters at 36 quai des Orfèvres.

Reporters, sensing a scoop, descended on the building. As cameras popped, Massu, umbrella in hand, helped unload the suitcases. Rain splashed on the evidence, threatening to rub off the ink of the luggage tags. Five inspectors carried the trunks up to the third floor, which, as Massu put it, soon looked like a hotel lobby, while his office resembled a luggage room in a train station.

The contents of the suitcases would prove remarkable. Inside, in no apparent order, were a total of 79 dresses, 26 skirts, 42 blouses, 48 scarves, 52 nightgowns, 46 pairs of panties, 14 dressing gowns, 13 negligées, 77 pairs of gloves, 35 belts, 25 handbags, 26 hats (women's), 10 pairs of boots, 6 jackets, 5 fur coats, 3 mink stoles, and 311 handkerchiefs. There were also 115 men's shirts, 104 cuffs, 82 pairs of socks, 66 pairs of shoes, 29 men's suits, 14 overcoats, 4 pairs of slippers, and 3 pairs of swimming trunks, in addition to an assortment of towels, tablecloths, sheets, pillowcases, pajamas, nightshirts, raincoats, eyeglasses, handbags, hairnets, hatpins, nail files, cigarette cases, and bus tickets. In short, there were 1,760 items in the inventory.

Analysis of the contents of these suitcases, Massu hoped, would provide clues to catch the killer and evidence to prosecute him afterward. It might also, with a great deal of time and perseverance, help identify the many victims and perhaps even answer the most difficult question of all: namely, the motives for the grisly murders.

17.

FRUSTRATION

IF SHE HAD COMMITTED SUICIDE, IT IS VERY LIKELY THAT
[HER] BODY WOULD HAVE BEEN FOUND.

—Commissaire Massu

ALBERT Neuhausen was found on March 31, 1944, at the Hôtel Alicot. When detectives questioned him, Neuhausen reaffirmed that he was only holding the suitcases for his friend Maurice Petiot, who had done many favors for his family, including giving them a loan to buy their house. Neuhausen said that he had never looked through the suitcases, claiming no curiosity whatsoever about their origins or contents. A detective asked if this had changed after he read the newspaper accounts of the events at rue Le Sueur.

"I do not read the newspapers," Neuhausen said. "I have never heard anyone speaking about it." He claimed only to have learned of the discovery of the crime while staying at the Hôtel Alicot on a business trip.

The search of Neuhausen's property had, however, uncovered a number of items that had clearly been removed from the suitcases. In the bedroom of their sixteen-year-old son, Christian, was a man's wardrobe, including a suit and an overcoat. In Albert and Simone's bedroom were a number of other personal items that police believed had been unpacked from the suitcases.

Confronted with the evidence, Neuhausen no longer denied opening and taking a few things from the trunks. Around March 27, he said, he and his wife had gone to the attic and looked through "three or four" suitcases that were not locked. He had also used one of the suitcases for a trip to Paris, reasoning, "Now that Dr. Petiot is in flight, I can just as well take something. He will never come to reclaim it."

Neuhausen had other information for the police. About two or three months after the arrival of the suitcases, Maurice Petiot had come to the house. Neuhausen escorted him to the attic and returned to work. He did not know if Maurice had opened or rummaged through the suitcases, or if he carried anything away. Another time, Maurice had brought Georgette Petiot to his attic. Again, he claimed that he did not know if they opened or removed anything, as he had left them alone and he had not seen them leave. His wife, Simone, on the other hand, did. She told the police that they had taken two suitcases.

In light of the discovered luggage in Neuhausen's attic, the Brigade Criminelle made another search at 21 rue Le Sueur. The haul, this time, was smaller: a white shell necklace, a pearl necklace in earthenware, a toothbrush in a white-and-red case with the words EXTRA HARD on it, and a framed portrait of socialist leader and former prime minister Léon Blum. Among other things, there were also a thermos, a pipe, a tube of Vaseline, a Gillette razor, soap from Marseille, a Vienna newspaper dated October 26, 1942, and a shoehorn inscribed with the name HÔTEL EUROPA, DRESDEN.

They also found two suitcases—a brown one full of pieces of paper, including a calling card for "Dr. Marcel Petiot, Faculty of Medicine," and a black one that contained a gray hat designed by the Parisian hatter Berteil and bore the initials P.B. Detectives also found a jacket soiled with lime, and a copy of the journal *Le Crapouillot* of May 1938, with an article entitled "Crime and the Instinctive Perversions." The police did not know what to make of this collection, particularly as it was not clear which items had belonged to Dr. Petiot and which had belonged to the bodies in his basement.

By late March, detectives had found Marcel and Georgette Petiot's former maid, Geneviève Cuny, who was living about two hundred miles southwest of Paris. Cuny was at the cloister of Notre Dame de Charité in Angers, where she was in the process of becoming a nun.

As Cuny told Chief Inspector Battut, she had worked for Dr. Petiot for almost two years—and these two years, tantalizingly, corresponded to the height of the suspected reign of terror. She had started in October 1941, the same month that Petiot began making his renovations to the newly purchased 21 rue Le Sueur. She left in August 1943, a few months after the disappearance of his last known victim, Yvan Dreyfus.

Cuny's job consisted of receiving patients and cleaning the rooms, all of them except the kitchen, which Georgette did. "During my time with Dr. Petiot," Cuny said, "I have never noticed anything unusual." She did say that, on occasion, Petiot brought home a variety of gentlemen's clothes, and he and Georgette had gone through them on the kitchen table.

"Yes," she said, "Dr. Petiot often presented his wife with lavish gifts." She remembered "jewels, rings, precious stones, a pearl necklace." Asked if she knew anything about an escape agency, Cuny said that she did not. If Petiot operated one, she added, it was not to her knowledge.

ANOTHER person in the Petiot family drawing attention in the press was sixteen-year-old Gérard. While he enjoyed good grades and popularity in school, some people thought that the media scrutiny would no doubt take its toll. One friend predicted Gérard would eventually change his name; another feared that he might commit suicide. His uncle Maurice, it was believed, was trying to arrange for him to attend a different school, a Jesuit academy in Joigny, where he would be shielded from questions from his classmates.

On March 30, 1944, Inspectors Cloiseau and Hernis interviewed the teenager in Auxerre. As usual, the detectives began by establishing his background. After living his first five years at Villeneuve-sur-Yonne, Gérard had moved with his family to Paris in 1933. Initially, he lived six months with his grandfather, Georgette Petiot's father, in Seignelay. He soon returned to Paris, where he enrolled at the Lycée Condorcet, where Jean-Paul Sartre lectured.

In 1939, as war loomed, the Petiots sent Gérard to the countryside.

Over the next few months, he would move often, living first again with his grandfather, then with a great-uncle, and eventually with Maurice. As the feared bombardments and aerial gas attacks failed to materialize, Gérard had returned to Paris in April 1940. Two months later, however, the Germans were approaching the capital. Dr. Petiot obtained a car and drove Gérard back to his grandfather. Georgette had remained in Paris.

Gérard would have one more stint in Paris, living at rue Caumartin and studying at the Lycée Condorcet. This stay ended three years later, when the Gestapo arrested his father. Georgette sent him to live in safer Auxerre, with Maurice and Monique. The last time he saw his father, Gérard said, was at Mardi Gras, when he visited his parents at rue Caumartin for almost a week.

Had he ever been to rue Le Sueur?

Yes, Gérard said. "I went there three different times with my father at about two-week intervals." Although he did not remember the exact date, he believed that it was not long after the purchase. The house was then empty, except for some kitchen utensils that Dr. Petiot told him had belonged to the actress Cécile Sorel.

As for March 11, 1944, Gérard had been at school until about half past twelve, when he ate lunch with Maurice at rue du Pont. At five thirty that evening, he went to a Spanish lesson and then returned home for dinner with Monique and the two children. At nine fifteen or so, he remembered, Neuhausen arrived at the house, as he often did. Gérard also remembered a telephone call that night.

He and Maurice had been playing a game of chess. When the phone rang, Maurice left the room to answer it. Gérard then went to the kitchen with Monique. Several minutes later, when Maurice returned, "he did not say who had called or what it concerned, at least in my presence." Maurice and Gérard then returned to their game of chess.

BACK at the Quai des Orfèvres, Massu was examining the contents of the suitcases for clues to identify possible victims. He was looking first at the labels on the clothing, such as where they were made, bought, or perhaps laundered, or any other distinguishing feature, such as age, condition, and nature of the material, including any stain, mark, or initial that had not quite been removed.

As the commissaire was learning, the search was exasperating to say the least. On one hand, the accumulation of evidence—the butchered bodies in the basement, the human remains in the lime pit, and the personal items in the suitcases—suggested that Dr. Petiot's enterprise was far larger than previously imagined. But who were these victims, and how could he identify them among the many thousands who had disappeared—thirty-three thousand Jews alone in the eleven-week period following July 17, 1942?

"You would phone a friend one day," Jean-Paul Sartre recalled, "and the telephone would ring and ring in the empty apartment; you would ring the doorbell and he would not come to the door; if the concierge broke in, you would find two chairs drawn up together in the hallway with German cigarette ends between the legs." Jews, Communists, members of the Resistance—anyone denounced as an enemy of the Third Reich—was at risk of a sudden arrest and deportation.

As the story of Dr. Petiot broke, desperate people with missing family members or friends increasingly contacted the police to ask if their loved ones might have been another one of his victims. Sometimes the distressed person, hoping to learn a relative's fate, however horrific, acknowledged that they did not know of any connection with the murder suspect. Other times they could establish reason to believe that there had been a relationship, but the police struggled to prove that Petiot was in fact responsible for their loved one's disappearance. The case of Denise Bartholomeus Hotin vividly illustrates the uncertainties that bedeviled investigators.

After reading about the murders in the newspapers, Charles Bartholomeus informed the police about his daughter Denise, or "Nelly," who had been missing since June 1942. At the time of her disappearance, she was a twenty-seven-year-old former employee and model for Lancel, the luxury leather goods and accessories store on the place de l'Opéra. In

June 1941, she had married Jean Hotin and moved onto his family's farm near the village of La Neuville-Garnier in the Seine-et-Oise, where Jean's father served as mayor. The former husband, Bartholomeus suggested, should be helpful for the investigation.

Denise and Jean had not known each other for a long time before their marriage. They had met only the previous December, when Jean, on a trip to Paris, saw her selling handbags and was struck by her beauty. Denise had followed him to the village but soon became unhappy, struggling to adjust to life on the farm, quarreling often with her in-laws. She began to miss her family, friends, and old social life in the city.

Not long after their wedding, Denise discovered that she was a few months pregnant. Jean's father, fifty-seven-year-old Henri Hotin, fearing for their reputation, apparently pressed for the couple to have an abortion. Later that year Denise traveled to Paris to see a midwife in the Saint-Lazare district, named Madame Mallard, to be treated for "pneumonia," but many in the town believed that she secretly carried funds from the mayor to pay for an operation.

Mayor Hotin would deny knowing she was pregnant, let alone ordering an abortion or paying for it. He said Denise's trip was a mystery. Jean's mother, Pauline, also denied knowing anything about any medical procedure and only said that if Denise went to Paris, it was "on her own initiative." But Jean, as one police report put it, freely admitted what his parents tried hard to deny.

One year to the date after their wedding, as the town was still gossiping over the unhappy couple, Denise went back to Paris to obtain a certification declaring that she had not had an abortion. Wearing a yellow orange dress and matching bodice, she left on June 5, 1942. It was supposed to be a short trip, with Denise returning the same evening. She didn't take any luggage.

Two days later, an enigmatic letter from Paris arrived at the Hotin farm saying that Denise could not return home and never had a "miscarriage" because, she emphasized, in a text replete with underlined and fully capitalized words, she was "<u>never pregnant.</u>" She had done

"NOTHING wrong" and promised to return home soon. By the end of June, another letter arrived from Paris, this one for Denise's husband. It was shorter:

> *I am very sad about being away* from you. *I can't come home. I don't know when I will be able to. I am so sad. I embrace you tenderly, and I love you.*

Asked about his response, Jean said that he had first been surprised, but then assumed that his wife had decided to remain in Paris a little longer with her family. He was not sure if she had been to see Dr. Petiot, he said, but he knew for certain that she had consulted him in July 1941. Hotin's attempts to find her had been in vain.

Denise's family was worried and suspicious, certain that she would never leave her husband like that. They asked the Hotins for information, only to be told that she was not on their farm and they did not know her whereabouts, but everything was fine. Denise's family remained unconvinced.

Curiously, her husband, Jean, was already not only in a new relationship, but also engaged to be remarried. He had filed for divorce from Denise on the grounds that she had deserted him. His father was pleased with the new match. Indeed, having observed the prominent family over the last year, many residents in the community were convinced that the Hotins were glad to be done with Denise. Some people saw her disappearance as all too convenient, and whispered that Jean might have murdered her. Why, after all, did he not report her missing to the police?

Hotin's search for his wife, moreover, was not inspired. In January 1943, six months after her disappearance, he had finally gone to Paris, spoken with the midwife, and learned that she had referred Denise to Dr. Petiot. Had Hotin seen him? detectives asked, in his questioning on March 25, 1944. No, Hotin had to answer: "It was half past four when I arrived. I went upstairs and saw on the plate: 'The doctor receives from five o'clock to seven o'clock.' I did not dare to ring the bell." He couldn't wait, he added, because his train back to La Neuville-Granier was soon departing. That was the end of his search for his wife.

Now, if Jean Hotin's claims were true, then Denise would have visited Petiot in the first week of June, a difficult time, when he was already under investigation for two separate cases of selling narcotics, not to mention the two mysterious disappearances of witnesses, Van Bever and Khaït. Would he really have risked another disappearance, when any one of them, if proved, could end his career and send him to prison? This is not impossible; Petiot liked to toy with danger, as Massu would soon learn. He certainly did not lack confidence in his ability to escape punishment either, with or without protection.

Of course, it is possible that Madame Mallard did send Denise to Petiot; even if Parisian midwives rarely made such referrals in the early 1940s, they would do so when an operation went wrong or threatened to endanger the life of the patient. Perhaps the doctor had seen her and attempted an operation, only to have it result in a complication, or a dangerous infection from the unhygienic conditions that often surrounded black-market abortions. To avoid exposure to what was then a capital offense, Petiot had perhaps tried to cover the trail of his botched operation. There is, however, no evidence supporting this hypothesis.

The police kept reaching dead ends in this investigation. Jean Hotin's claims that he visited Mallard—and the story of her referring Denise to Petiot—could not be verified because, by April 1944, Mallard was dead. She died that same month of natural causes. Mallard's daughter, Gilberte Mouron, could not confirm the incident either, admitting only that she believed that she had heard Petiot's name mentioned before. As for the office hours Jean Hotin cited, they did not match the ones Petiot kept at the time. No evidence tracing the disappearance of Denise to Dr. Petiot was ever found, and in fact, the police could not prove that she had visited the doctor, or that she was even dead. Still, the name Denise Hotin was added to the list of the doctor's murder victims.

18.

NINE MORE

IF YOU START ASKING QUESTIONS ABOUT EVERYONE WHO
DIES, YOU'RE GOING TO BE A VERY BUSY MAN.

—Marcel Petiot, attributing the words to Dr. Paul

AFTER Paulette Grippay's black satin dress, Massu now made a
second connection between the testimonies of witnesses and
the contents of the suitcases found at rue Le Sueur and in
Neuhausen's attic. This was the collection of Sulka silk shirts with the
monogrammed initials "A.E.," which were identified as belonging to
Adrien the Basque Estébétéguy. Confirmation came from a tall, stocky
man who arrived at the quai des Orfèvres in a new white Bentley: Henri
Lafont.

Lafont was undoubtedly one of the most powerful men in Occupied
Paris. This was an unexpected position for a former small-time crook
who could not read or write. Abandoned by his mother at age thirteen,
immediately after the death of his father, Lafont had eked out an existence on the street, stealing café chairs for resale, writing bad checks,
and drifting in and out of reform schools and detention centers. His first
prison sentence, begun May 15, 1919, was for theft. Ten more incarcer-
ations would follow by 1934, for similar charges, totaling about eight
years in prison.

By then, too, Lafont had worked briefly in a number of jobs: errand
boy, dockworker, mechanic, car dealer, and chauffeur. He enlisted for
two years in the Thirty-ninth Régiment des Tirailleurs Algériens and,
later, after finishing his military service, gained work under his alias,
"Henri Normand," as manager of a canteen for the Préfecture de Police.

He had the chance to meet and befriend many policemen. In 1939, with war on the horizon, Lafont tried to reenlist with the army. His application was refused because of his criminal record. His many experiences, both on the street and in prison, however, would bear fruit during the Occupation.

Indeed it was during a prison stay that Lafont met a man who would later introduce him to the German authorities: Max Stocklin, a tall, cultured Swiss national who had been arrested in the late 1930s for his work as an informer for the German military intelligence service, the Abwehr. When the Germans arrived in France in June 1940, Stocklin's espionage contacts released him, and he soon recruited Lafont into the Abwehr's champagne-swilling set then settling into the Hôtel Lutétia at 45 Boulevard Raspail in preparation for its tasks of arresting French Resistants.

By the end of June 1940, Lafont was placed in charge of a new Abwehr creation called a *Dienstelle*, or purchasing bureau, known informally as an "Otto agency" after the Abwehr's Hermann "Otto" Brandl, who helped establish them. These agencies bought objects in bulk, using funds provided by the French according to the Armistice, and then sold them to Occupation authorities, thereby facilitating the German exploitation of the French economy and, in the process, greatly enriching agency leaders. Lafont's bureau, located on rue Tiquetonne, was responsible for buying food and later clothing, furniture, and objects of gold.

Within two weeks, Lafont had established a second branch of his purchasing agency on rue Cadet, in the seized former headquarters of the Freemasons. This one would concentrate on Jewish property. Other offices opened, including a large one on rue du Faubourg Saint-Antoine that focused on the purchasing of wheat, butter, and livestock of Normandy. His profits soared. Beyond that, as with the other Otto agencies, Lafont was making contact with a diversity of Frenchmen, from bankers and lawyers to art experts and black market dealers. Many of these people would later prove helpful as his own star rose in Occupied Paris.

Lafont's real break came that same summer when he succeeded in infiltrating a Resistance cell that had eluded the Abwehr for six months.

With the help of his underworld contacts, Lafont found the group's leader, a Belgian named Lambrecht, in Bordeaux, in a matter of days. Then, too, with his underworld methods, including a propensity to crack a whip in a man's face and repeat "you will talk" in his surprisingly falsetto voice, Lafont managed to learn the names of the entire organization. The Germans then arrested some six hundred Resistance fighters in Paris as well as in Brussels, Amsterdam, Berlin, and other parts of the continent.

The leader of the Abwehr in France, Colonel Friedrich Rudolph, an old-fashioned Prussian officer and First World War veteran, was impressed with the resourceful new hire, though he was also appalled by his vicious methods. The German leader agreed to continue employing Lafont "on condition that he does not have to see him." The Abwehr headquarters in Berlin cabled congratulations to the Paris office for its success, and Lafont's supervisors hosted a celebration in his honor, culminating with a visit to the brothel One Two Two.

The Abwehr had found Lafont useful indeed. In August 1940, with the approval of a high-ranking Abwehr officer, Captain Wilhelm Radecke, Lafont had been allowed into Fresnes prison to recruit criminals for the expansion of his gang. One of the first of the twenty-seven men Lafont handpicked was Alexandre Villaplane, the captain of the French national soccer team that won the first World Cup in 1930, defeating Mexico 4–1. Villaplane had fallen on hard times in the Depression and resorted to rigging horse races. Another man he selected was Adrien the Basque, whose Sulka shirts he now identified.

The most famous member of the gang was Pierre Bonny, a former police detective who had once been praised as the most talented policeman in the country. This was, of course, an exaggeration. In 1935, one year after helping solve the notorious Stavisky Affair, a financial scandal that nearly caused the collapse of the republic, Bonny's own police career ended in a charge of corruption and a three-year prison sentence. After his release, Bonny scraped by operating a fledgling private detective agency that mainly shadowed unfaithful spouses. A short, wiry man with a dark mustache, Bonny brought a rigor and meticulousness, not to mention an administrative skill, to Lafont's gang when he joined in 1942.

During this time, Lafont became a naturalized German citizen and also joined the SS, thereby switching his allegiance from the Abwehr to new patrons in the Gestapo. Lafont continued soliciting tips, following up on denunciations, tracking down hidden gold and currency supplies, and infiltrating Resistance groups. As the Allied bombing raids increased in 1943, Lafont would also hunt downed parachutists, airmen, and arms caches. No one knows how many people Lafont's gang tortured and killed, or how much profit was earned from these activities. Lafont's power would grow beyond his wildest imagination.

By May 1941, Lafont's gang had moved from old headquarters on avenue Pierre-1er-de-Serbie to 93 rue Lauriston. At his highly sought after Saturday night dinners here, elite Nazi officials, SS men, industrialists, press barons, artists, film stars, and high-society women and men gathered over the finest delicacies available in Occupied Paris. In the cellars below, meanwhile, French Resistants and other enemies of the Third Reich were brutally tortured.

There were many questions that Massu would have liked to ask Lafont. For one thing, one of Adrien the Basque's brothers, Emile Estébétéguy, and a member of the gang had claimed that Lafont had decided to punish Adrien by sending him to Marcel Petiot, knowing that the "escape agency" was actually a death factory. Was this possibly true, and if so, was there a connection between Lafont and Petiot? At the moment, Massu could not simply confront the gangster. As German police number 10 474R, Lafont was untouchable.

A PROMISING new lead about other possible Petiot victims, meanwhile, came from an anonymous letter of late March 1944 to Massu's office. It described a family of Jewish refugees from the Netherlands who arrived in Paris in September 1942, only to attempt to leave a couple of months later with the help of a physician who promised them passage to South America.

There was nothing in this letter, Massu acknowledged, that could not have been fabricated based on information published in the newspapers. But the details had a ring of authenticity. The doctor had emphasized precaution and vigilance: not speaking to anyone about the organization, reliance on last-minute calls supplying details of the rendezvous, and of course, the careful instructions to bring along personal valuables in two suitcases.

The author had only referred to the victims by their initials and age: Madame W (about age sixty-three), her son Maurice W (about thirty-six), and his wife L.W. (about forty-six). Wanting to pursue this lead further, the commissaire released the information to the newspapers, asking for anyone with knowledge of the letter to contact him. He promised to protect the identity of the letter writer.

A few days later, a woman walked into his office claiming to be the sender. Given her knowledge of the letter's contents, which had been closely guarded, Massu was convinced that he had the right person. Her name was Ilse Gang. She now provided the police with additional details of the missing family. "Madame W" was Rachel Wolff (born Rachel Marx), sixty-year-old widow of Salomon, or Sally, Wolff, once owner of the lumber company Incona C.V. Her son, "Maurice W," was thirty-six-year-old Moses Maurice Israel Wolff, and L.W. was his wife, Lina Braun Wolff, a forty-seven-year-old divorcée from Breslau with a son by her first marriage in Tel Aviv. Lina was one of Gang's oldest friends. Originally living in Königsberg, Germany, the Wolff family had fled to Paris when Adolf Hitler had come to power. In 1936, they had moved again, to Amsterdam.

But Amsterdam had not proved the safe haven it had historically been. After the Nazis conquered the Netherlands in the spring of 1940 and tightened their grip with racial laws in June 1942, German occupying authorities had proceeded to wage a campaign of terror against the Dutch Jewish community. The concentration of Jews in Amsterdam, coupled with the relative lack of hiding places, made the Nazi house raids, roundups, and ultimately the deportation of Jewish men, women, and children to extermination camps the worst in Western Europe.

Seventy-eight percent of the 140,000 Jews in the Netherlands would be deported, compared, for example, to twenty-five percent in France.

As for the Wolffs, their family business had been seized by the Nazis. They sold what remained of their onetime wealth at a fraction of its value and, in July 1942, fled for their lives.

To escape Nazi detection, they adopted the name Wolters. The family had been helped in their escape, first into Belgium by several people, including a customs official who hid them safely in a convent near Charleville. A lawyer in Rocroi, Maître René Iung, had also assisted them in their flight and overlooked the money they carried (about 300,000 francs), which, being illegal in the Nazi-occupied country, was subject to confiscation.

When the Wolff family reached Paris in early September 1942 with their last name again changed, this time to Walbert or Valbert, they moved into the Hôtel Helvetia on rue Tourneux. They stayed a few days before moving on to the Hôtel du Danube on rue Jacob in the Latin Quarter. They would soon move again because, in October 1942, German authorities seized this building as well.

Gang had looked without success for a more stable apartment for the family. Eventually her friend, Dr. Rachel Gingold, a Romanian dentist at 21 rue Cambon, suggested that she contact one of her patients, a Romanian-born Jewish woman who would soon command much attention from the police, the press, and the public. This was Rudolphina Kahan, or "Eryane," a cosmopolitan woman with dyed strawberry blond hair, who spoke a handful of languages, including Italian, German, French, and Romanian and, as one journalist put it, looked like "a spy on the Orient Express." Finding this woman seemed a lucky break.

In the story that later emerged, Kahan not only found the Wolffs a room in her apartment building at 10 rue Pasquier, but also told them about Dr. Eugène, who helped people leave Occupied Paris. She knew of his operation because she, too, she said, hoped to flee. A meeting was arranged with the help of Kahan's doctor and likely lover, Dr. Louis-Théophile Saint-Pierre, who in turn put her in touch with one of his patients, a pimp who worked several Montmartre bars, known variously as Robert or Henri le Marseillais (real name Henri Guintrand). This man introduced her to the actor and agency intermediary Edmond Pintard.

At a café in the Place de la Madeleine, Pintard met Kahan and then led her to a nearby hair salon. Dr. Eugène arrived ten minutes later and offered to take all three members of the Wolff family, making an exception to his rule of two at a time, probably because of the age of the mother-in-law. When he learned the price that Pintard had quoted (and arbitrarily doubled), he berated the makeup artist, threatening to end their working relationship. Apparently charmed by Kahan, the physician tried to recruit her for his organization. "We always need a woman like you," he reportedly told her, offering her a commission for helping people escape and a promise, in turn, to arrange her journey later out of Occupied Paris.

The following day, Dr. Eugène met with the Wolff family in a room at Kahan's apartment building. After a pleasant conversation about the arts, over tea, the Wolffs had been impressed with the physician, who had seemed, in the words of their lawyer, Jacques Bernays, "a man of vast culture and fine sentiments, whose magnanimity and character fully explained his devotion to the noble cause of clandestine passages." Dr. Eugène told them to bring no papers, clothing, or anything that would reveal their identity. Valuables were to be packed in two suitcases or sewn inside their clothing. Maurice Wolff concealed a number of diamonds and other jewels in the shoulders of his jacket. The stakes were high. A single mistake would mean, the doctor said, "twelve bullets in my carcass" and "perhaps worse" for them.

In late December 1942, an old horse-drawn carriage pulled up to the entrance to Kahan's building. The driver, an old man with an old-fashioned top hat and baggy winter coat a few sizes too large, put the Wolffs' suitcases on the cart and opened the door for them. The carriage headed toward Place St. Augustine and then on to rue Boetie, Champs-Élysées, and L'Étoile. After turning onto Avenue Foch and then onto a side street, it stopped at the carriage entrance to No. 21 rue

Le Sueur. The Wolffs entered the mansion, hoping to depart for South America.

Within two weeks, three additional couples who had recently arrived in Paris would follow the Wolffs, seeking the help of Dr. Eugène: Gilbert Basch (alias Baston), a twenty-eight-year-old former cosmetics executive in Amsterdam, and his twenty-four-year-old wife, Marie-Anne Servais Basch; Marie-Anne's parents, Chaïm Schonker, another perfume executive, and his wife Franciska Ehrenreich Schonker, who lived in Nice (aliases included Stevens and Eemens); and Marie-Anne's sister, Ludwika Holländer Arnsberg and her husband, Ludwig Israel Arnsberg (alias Schepers and Anspach). By January 1943, there had been at least nine people, using about a dozen pseudonyms, sent by Kahan to Dr. Eugène. All of them were wealthy Jews. None of them would be seen or heard from again.

Not long after helping the Wolffs, Ilse Gang told Massu, a woman with reddish-blond hair wearing dark sunglasses came by her apartment to inform her of the Wolff family's safe arrival in South America and asked her if she wanted to follow them through the escape network. She had declined.

19.

THE LIST

ALWAYS THE SAME PROCEDURE, ALWAYS THE SAME MEANS.

—Pierre Dupin, avocat général

WHO was this woman who sent Dr. Petiot nine Jews in fifteen days at the end of 1942 and early 1943? An anonymous letter to Commissaire Massu from Auxerre, dated March 26, 1944, claimed that she, "doctoress Iriane," worked as a recruiter arranging passage out of Paris for a commission and, moreover, earned twice the rate for every woman she recruited.

Massu sent detectives to question Kahan. But when they arrived at her apartment on the fourth floor at 10 rue Pasquier, which runs into the rue des Mathurins where Raoul Fourrier had his hair salon, Kahan was nowhere to be found.

A number of her neighbors spoke to the police, but insight into her possible motives remained elusive. Arriving in Paris in 1927, Kahan had worked at various times as a masseuse, a singer, and then as a medical assistant. Some thought that she seemed poor; others believed that she was a bohemian enjoying a comfortable lifestyle with money deriving from an unknown source.

Louise Nicholas, who had known her since she sang in cabarets in Montmartre, told the police that Kahan had a close friend in the German army. Actually, this man, thirty-seven-year-old Herbert Welsing, was a junior officer in the Luftwaffe. When he was interviewed in April 1944, Welsing had little to say, other than to claim that he did not know that Kahan was Jewish or involved in any clandestine organization.

Kahan's landlady, Fernande Goux, had met her in the spring of 1942 at the nearby Georgette Bar. Within months, Kahan had moved into a small two-room apartment on the sixth floor of her building, though she soon exchanged this for a larger flat on the fourth floor. It was about March 20, 1944, Goux said, that Kahan had abruptly moved out of her building.

No one would admit knowing where she went. No one, either, would acknowledge hearing anything to suggest that Kahan had worked for an escape organization; the penalty for this illegal activity, after all, could be death. The trail for the moment went cold.

On April 12, Massu and Battut drafted a list of probable victims of Dr. Petiot. There were now seventeen:

1. Joachim Guschinow
2. Jean-Marc Van Bever
3. Marthe Fortin (Khaït)
4. Denise Hotin
5. Annette Basset, or "Annette Petit"
6. Joseph Réocreux, "Jo the Boxer"
7. Lina Braun (Wolff)
8. Rachel Marx (Wolff)
9. Maurice Wolff
10. Charles Lombard
11. Joséphine Grippay
12. Adrien Estébétéguy, "The Basque"
13. Gisèle Rossmy
14. Joseph Piereschi, "Zé"
15. Yvan Dreyfus
16. Claudia Chamoux
17. François Albertini, "The Corsican"

Charles Lombard, number ten on this list, was actually soon removed. A thirty-nine-year-old gangster notorious for committing robberies as an impersonated police officer, Lombard had disappeared in March 1943. His wife, Marie, feared that he had, like his friend Adrien the Basque, contacted Dr. Petiot in an attempt to leave for Buenos Aires. But police soon learned that Lombard was alive and well, flourishing in the criminal underworld. He would surface in Turin after the war, apparently trying to find a ship to flee to South America.

Three of the victims sent by Kahan, the members of the Wolff family, had been added to the list. The police had found their names in a suitcase from Neuhausen's attic. Within a month, Kahan's other six recruits would be added as well. A number of invoices from the company Wagons-lits Cook had been found in the suitcases, bearing the names, or rather the aliases, of the Schonker and Arnsberg families. The list of probable victims was now at twenty-two.

B Y May 1944, the rapid movements on the Eastern and Southern fronts dominated the front pages. After conquering the Crimean peninsula in a six-day campaign, seizing 24,000 prisoners, and inflicting some 110,000 casualties, the Soviet Red Army thrust forward into Romania, consolidating its hold over the strategic plateau that held Europe's largest oil supply, which was desperately needed by the Third Reich. Only 140 miles away, some 448 U.S. Flying Fortresses and Liberators of the Fifteenth Army Air Force pounded the oil fields at Ploesti and then Bucharest itself. Everywhere, it seemed, the Nazis were engaging in what the controlled press called "strategic retreats."

While the Allies marched up the Italian peninsula, seizing Rome and Mussolini, anxious and hopeful Parisians speculated about the long-expected Allied attack on Occupied Europe. Winston Churchill would call this undertaking "the most difficult and complicated operation that has ever taken place." On the early morning of June 6, at 0630, H-hour of D-Day, or *J-Jour* to the French, the massive Allied armada of some 175,000 troops, 11,000 planes, and more than 5,000 vessels swarmed over the rough English Channel in what would be the largest seaborne invasion in history.

One week and thousands of casualties later, as the Allies fought through the bocage of Normandy, with its thick hedges and sunken lanes protected by three elite SS Panzer divisions, Adolf Hitler unleashed a new "wonder" weapon: the long-range, pilotless, and jet-powered V-1 flying bomb, to wreak vengeance on the city of London. Carrying a one-ton warhead and moving at a speed of 700 km an hour, which was faster than any Allied plane or anti-aircraft gun, the V-1 "Hell Hound" or "Fire Dragon" would, by end of summer, kill 6,184 people and destroy 75,000 buildings. The war, it was clear, would not be over any-time soon.

Nor, it seemed, would the search for Marcel Petiot. Reported sight-ings continued around Paris and its surrounding area for weeks. On June 24, 1944, a man showed up at police headquarters with a strange tale. He introduced himself as Charles Rolland, a former cinema film projector operator who had briefly served the French army in Tunisia. He claimed to know Petiot well.

Seven years earlier, Rolland related, he first met the murder suspect. It was in Marseille, when a prostitute named Solange approached him and asked if he wanted to make a quick 100 francs. All he had to do was have sex with her while one of her rich clients looked on. Rolland, struggling financially, accepted the offer. The man who paid to watch was Marcel Petiot.

After this incident, which culminated with the three of them engag-ing in a ménage à trois, Rolland further alleged, Petiot recruited him to sell drugs in Marseille. The two men would meet at the Cintra-Bodega Bar in the Old Port, where Rolland would receive the cocaine and then proceed to sell it at the American Bar on the Canebière. Then, after finding a customer, Rolland would hide the narcotics in a tank above a certain toilet in the men's room. At the appointed time, the customer arrived, picked up the packet, and handed the money to Petiot as he entered the bathroom.

Petiot in Marseille? Yes, Rolland said that he stayed at a hotel on rue Panier, and their partnership had continued until early January 1938, when Rolland volunteered for the Fifteenth Infantry Regiment and sailed to Tunisia. The following year, when he was discharged for "physical incapacity," Rolland decided to come to Paris and reconnect with his rich friend. Rolland allegedly resumed the business of selling cocaine for Petiot, working the Café de la Paix and the Dupont-Bastille bar in the Opéra district.

Although he was eventually arrested in late 1940 on an unrelated charge, Rolland said he saw Petiot two other times. The first was in January 1943, when he stopped by unannounced at his house at 22 or 21 [*sic*] rue Le Sueur. Petiot, he said, appeared anxious. "He seemed in a strange condition and did not want me to stay." The physician declined to renew their working relationship, handed Rolland 500 francs, and sent him away, claiming that he expected clients at any minute. Rolland said the room smelled heavily of chloroform.

The second time was a fortuitous meeting at the end of the following month, at the Cintra-Bodega in Marseille. The doctor was allegedly more welcoming. He told Rolland of his latest invention, a powerful new aphrodisiac that he claimed to have tested on more than sixty women. Then, when Rolland said he needed some important papers to join the P.P.F., Parti Populaire Français, a pro-Nazi collaborationist outfit, Petiot helped him obtain false certificates. Petiot also decided to join the military-political organization under a fake name, "Marcel Sigrand," and the two of them often met near the beach at Les Catalans or in the Old Port. Later Rolland heard that Petiot had been seen that spring in Pont-Saint-Esprit in southern France, wearing a Nazi uniform and hunting down French Resistants.

These claims were extraordinary, and indeed far-fetched. For one thing, when Rolland claimed to have worked with the doctor in Marseille, Massu knew for a fact that Petiot was in Paris practicing medicine and running his false escape organization. He was not in Pont-Saint-Esprit then either, as he was convincing Adrien the Basque and other gangsters that he could help them leave Paris. Even more damaging to his credibility, Rolland had made several errors in his testimony.

Petiot's house was not located, as he said, "on the corner" of rue Le Sueur. He did not live on rue Le Sueur or own the building in 1939 or 1940, when Rolland claimed to have visited him at that location. Rolland also incorrectly identified the address as the 15th arrondissement, and other descriptions also proved inaccurate. Petiot did not have only one floor, as Rolland claimed, but the entire building, and there was no concierge there either. Rolland's tale seemed wrong on so many points as to be dismissed outright as worthless.

When he was later criticized for spending so much time speaking with Rolland, Massu explained that he had to follow a lead, no matter how outrageous it might first sound. Indeed, Rolland's testimony illustrated the degree to which many false rumors about Petiot flourished in the demimonde and were soon picked up by many newspapers.

On July 26, 1944, the *New York Times* announced, "The Greatest Bluebeard of all time was reported from Paris to have been discovered at last." Petiot was identified as a member of a French division of the Waffen SS, an elite Charlemagne unit of fanatical Nazi supporters. Three weeks later, Leonard Lyons noted in the *Washington Post* that civilians leaving France confirmed that Petiot, an Iron Cross recipient, had joined the SS. The French, the columnist added, blamed the police for missing the obvious.

But what, in the summer of 1944, was obvious about the Petiot case? Did Rolland come to help the police catch Petiot or mislead them, or did he have some other motive? Was he simply a deluded or grossly misinformed attention-seeker? Who, if anyone, sent him? When the police, and later the media, wanted Rolland for additional interviews, he was never found. The question of the peculiar informant became more charged because this outrageous and largely false tale would soon play a key role in helping the police unravel the mystery of Petiot's disappearance.

20.

APOCALYPTIC WEEKS

THIS WAS THE DAY THE WAR SHOULD HAVE ENDED.

—Irwin Shaw

DESPITE the international media coverage, the Petiot Affair drew increasingly less attention that summer in French newspapers. This was not just because the landing in Normandy overshadowed its coverage; nor was it simply a reminder of how cold the police trail had become. By May 1944, it looked unlikely that Petiot would be found alive, and many police officers feared he was already dead. But there was another cause for the dramatic decline in media attention.

Although evidence is elusive and the files were long ago purged, there is reason to believe that the German Occupation authorities intervened to stop the police investigation. Georges Suard, chauffeur for the commissaire of police at the Sûreté National, M. Béranger, heard about German obstruction in late April 1944. His source was the head of the French police himself. In an interview with Commissaire Louis Poirier on October 9, 1945, Suard revealed that, when he had been driving his boss, then an associate under Vichy Ambassador Fernand de Brinon, he was told that the French police would never find Marcel Petiot as long as the Germans occupied Paris.

Béranger, he added, "told me that he had been present at a meeting when a German figure gave the order to de Brinon to quash the affair from the French police point of view." The German leader was not identified. Neither Béranger nor de Brinon would ever admit to interfering with the Petiot investigation. After the Liberation, when both men stood trial for collaboration with the enemy, it is not surprising that they would deny taking any action that blocked the arrest of the suspected serial killer.

The time Suard first heard of the German intervention—late April—moreover coincides with a sudden media silence on the Petiot case. Immediately before that, the press speculated on his whereabouts, ending with a noticeable spike in stories of witnesses reporting that the physician had been captured or found dead. On April 21, the Nazi Transocean News Agency asserted that Spanish authorities had arrested Petiot after "a vain flight across the French frontier into Spain" and handed the fugitive over to the police at Bordeaux.

Interestingly, Commissaire Massu always denied that the Germans had hindered his investigation, claiming only that the French police had to file daily reports on the affair and never received any reaction to them whatsoever. But Massu was not privy to decisions made in the upper echelons of the Occupation authorities. Count Fernand de Brinon, Vichy's ambassador to the occupied zone, answered to the German authorities and gave orders to the prefect of police, Amédée Bussière, who was, in turn, Massu's supervisor. Not surprisingly, too, Massu carefully denied German interference but not French.

But why would Occupation authorities want to block the investigation? There was still no obvious answer. Likely, though, the ramifications would strike at the heart of the messy, complicated Petiot case, and any unraveling of the mystery would indeed, as the chauffeur said, have to wait until after the Germans left Paris.

B Y late July 1944, Allied armies had finally broken through Nazi defenses in the bocage of northwestern France. Caen had fallen not after one day, as planned, but fourteen, and then the Allies conquered a pile of ruins. As Montgomery's Twenty-first Army continued moving slowly, methodically eastward from Caen, Patton's Third Army was nearing the Seine, just southeast of the capital. The question for the Allies was whether to head straight for Paris to liberate the city or race to the Rhine with the hopes of reaching Berlin as soon as possible.

At the forward post of the Supreme Headquarters Allied Expeditionary Forces (SHAEF), then located about two miles inland from the Normandy beachhead at Granville, on the Cotentin Peninsula, General Dwight D. Eisenhower wanted to postpone the Liberation of Paris. The top priority, in his assessment, was defeating the Nazis. Paris, by contrast, fulfilled no overall strategic or tactical objective. Besides, the German army had comparatively few troops in the capital; the Allies could always liberate it later. Eisenhower did not want to provoke unnecessary street fighting, potentially wreaking untold destruction and creating a Stalingrad on the Seine. Never mind the logistical nightmare of supplying the minimum four thousand tons of material daily to feed and fuel a city of two million people, when dwindling supplies of gasoline could be marshaled for a direct attack on Germany.

Charles de Gaulle disagreed. In addition to disarming the launching sites for Hitler's V-1 flying bombs in northern France, de Gaulle called Paris "the key to France" and pressed for an immediate seizure of the capital for enormous symbolic and humanitarian reasons. There were also political realities. Continued Nazi occupation, he believed, would only play into the hands of his Communist rivals. He already feared that they were plotting an insurrection to seize power themselves.

While he sent representatives to plead his case with Eisenhower, de Gaulle ordered General Pierre Koenig, his chief of staff and the leader of the irregular army of the Resistance, the Forces françaises de l'intérieur (French Forces of the Interior, or FFI), to prevent a revolt from occurring in the city without his consent. The task was difficult. De Gaulle wanted an insurrection, but he did not want to give the Communists a chance to exploit it for their own purposes. He then ordered Philippe de Hauteclocque, better known by his nom de guerre, General Jacques Leclerc, of the French Second Armored Division, under the authority of the US Third Army, to head for Paris. Leclerc was instructed to disobey Patton and Eisenhower if necessary.

Some nine hundred miles away, at the Wolf's Lair, then Nazi field headquarters in an East Prussian forest, Adolf Hitler had other plans for the city. "Paris must not fall into the hands of the enemy, or, if it does, he must find there nothing but a field of ruins," Secret memo Nr. 772989/44, of August 23, 1944, informed the commanding general of Greater Paris. To carry out this destruction, Hitler had appointed Dietrich Von Choltitz, a forty-nine-year-old general who was notorious for his hardness, experience, and not least, his ability to follow difficult directives without question. It was Von Choltitz who had given the order in May 1940 to firebomb the inner city of Rotterdam, and then in July 1942, he oversaw the massive destruction in the siege of Sevastopol.

Von Choltitz had arrived in Paris on August 7 to replace General Karl von Stülpnagel, who had been implicated in the failed plot to assassinate Hitler on July 20, 1944. Stülpnagel had in fact arrested the entire SS in Paris. But when word arrived that the Führer had survived, Stülpnagel was recalled to Berlin. Instead of following orders, he hopped into a black Horsch, drove to his old battlefield at Verdun, and tried to blow his brains out. Blinded but still alive, he was captured by German soldiers. Stülpnagel was brought back to Plötzensee Prison in Berlin, where he hanged himself.

While Allied armies succeeded on the fifteenth with a second major landing near Saint-Tropez in southern France, the Gestapo struck at police headquarters, attempting to seize its weapons. The French police rebelled. Under the leadership of several Resistance groups inside the police, particularly the Front national de la police, L'Honneur de la police, and Police et patrie, the police refused to hand over their weapons, and then to patrol the streets—a shutdown that was part of a widening breakdown of city services. Workers in the métro, the railway, the post office, and the Bank of France were also on strike. Electricity, gas, and many other services no longer worked. Then, as Paris threatened to erupt, the police seized the prefecture.

At this time, General de Gaulle was still in Algiers, trying to arrange a flight back to the continent and growing more desperate by the minute. First, the American B-17 that had promised him a flight suffered repeated delays, most recently to fix its landing gear. Then, on August 19, General de Gaulle boarded the Lodestar Lockheed plane *France* and flew north. The Royal Air Force escort that was supposed to meet him over the Channel was not there. Running low on fuel, the general had to make a decision. The pilot believed that there was perhaps enough fuel to reach France, but it was not certain. The general ordered the pilot to proceed.

The plane landed at a little airfield near Saint-Lô with about two minutes of fuel to spare. Having left as an obscure brigadier general, de Gaulle returned as the leader of the Free French. There was no fanfare. He was welcomed by three people.

That same morning, de Gaulle learned, just as he had feared, that rival Communists had launched an insurrection. Colonel Rol, the nom de guerre of Henri Tanguy, was orchestrating the revolt from his headquarters some ninety feet belowground, in the cellars of the Paris Department of Water and Sewers. This secret location was linked to a maze of catacombs, the old stone quarries, nineteenth-century sewers, and almost the entire Parisian métro system. Rol planned to use this network for quick, decisive acts that would culminate in the seizure of key government buildings. The Communists would then, de Gaulle feared, use the uncertainty of the Nazi retreat to consolidate their control of the postwar world. Alternatively, the Germans would quash the rebellion with a savage massacre.

Meanwhile, at a banquet in the Palais du Luxembourg, with many high-ranking Nazi Wehrmacht, Luftwaffe, Kriegsmarine, and other Occupation authorities in attendance, the Luftwaffe commander in chief, Hugo Sperrle, stood and raised his glass: "To this city of Paris where the flag of Germany shall fly for a thousand years."

The next morning, General Von Choltitz received a phone call from Generaloberst Alfred Jodl at the Wolf's Lair. Adolf Hitler demanded to know why no buildings had yet been destroyed.

—

LIKE "sparkling torpedoes," as the satirist paper *Le Crapouillot* put it, limousines and black Citroëns were speeding away from the hotels in central Paris. Inside the automobiles, former administrators and "purple-faced generals, accompanied by elegant blonde women, looked as if they are off to some fashionable resort." Administrators of lesser rank, left behind, burned files and packed away loot.

Mines were continuing to be laid around the capital, in accordance with Hitler's wishes to leave no building of cultural significance standing. German tanks maneuvered into the place de la Concorde, which gave a commanding presence over the long, straight, and wide boulevards that spread out from the square. Panzers did the same at the Palais du Luxembourg and the École Militaire near the Eiffel Tower. At Place Saint-Michel, they had established a crossfire that would soon be called "the crossroads of death."

Bands of Resistance fighters took to the side streets and dark alleys, or moved behind the barricades to rally supporters. With forces estimated by one leader at fifteen thousand, the FFI had few weapons, perhaps enough for two thousand, though many of these were old rifles hidden since 1940 or arms that had survived Allied parachute drops and evaded Nazi detection. One group of young Communists, taking the dearth of weapons into their own hands, used women to lure German soldiers around Pigalle into back alleys, where Resistance comrades waited to pounce on them and steal their weapons.

Men in cars painted with the Cross of Lorraine patrolled, with two gunmen in the front, like republicans in the Spanish Civil War. At the Sorbonne, Professor Frédéric Joliot-Curie, winner of the Nobel Prize in physics, made Molotov cocktails, borrowing green champagne bottles from cellars as well as bottles from the laboratory where his wife's parents, Marie and Pierre Curie, had discovered radium. Other Resistants continued to fire stray shots at German sentries or seize goods. One man even sneaked outside the German embassy on rue de Lille and stole the German ambassador's convertible.

Police, on strike, still refused to patrol the streets—probably the first time in Parisian history that police and rebels fought on the same side. As fighting spread sporadically across the capital, a German tank fired radio-guided incendiary shells into the Grand Palais. Inside, the Swedish entrepreneur Jean Houcke had been planning a lavish production to coincide with the Liberation. It was to be the largest circus in Europe, complete with exotic animals, trapeze acrobats, and even a clown impersonating Adolf Hitler. Houcke, in shock, sobbed as his investment burned to the ground.

More intense fighting occurred near police headquarters, which had barricades outside as high as the statue of Joan of Arc. The prefecture was now flying the tricolor, its first appearance atop a major city building since the Occupation. The weapons and ammunition of the Resistance were running low. German tiger tanks approached with Frenchmen "roped to the turret of each tank" as human shields.

Barricades were hastily erected elsewhere in the city, particularly in working-class and Communist strongholds of the north, east, and southeast. Communist Party leaders in the Resistance were calling for a full revolution, shouting the old battle cry of the Commune: "*Tous Aux Barricades.*" Resistants moved into position behind barricades assembled from overturned cars, rails from bombed railroad tracks, and wood from chopped-down trees and reinforced with other city facilities, from park benches to pissoirs. Another popular cry—"*Chacun son Boche!*"— instructed everyone to "get his own German."

D E GAULLE'S representative, Major Roger Gallois, had in the meantime presented the case for immediate Allied entrance to Paris to the chief intelligence officer of the Twelfth Army Group under General Omar N. Bradley. The information was passed along. Eisenhower, after first rejecting de Gaulle's arguments, changed his mind. "What the hell, Brad," he said, "I guess we'll have to go in." That evening, August 22, just south of Argentan, General Leclerc's Second Armored Division was ordered to march to Paris.

General de Gaulle had stressed to Leclerc the importance of arriving quickly, before the Communist uprising gathered momentum and perhaps even succeeded in seizing the reins of power. But there was another reason for hurrying into the capital. General Bradley received a message from Swedish Consul Raoul Nordling, who was mediating on behalf of Von Choltitz, that the German general was under great pressure to start the destruction of Paris.

"We can't take any chances on that general changing his mind, and knocking hell out of the city," Bradley told his aide, General Edwin Sibert, and ordered Lt. Gen. Courtney Hicks Hodges to move. After all, even if Von Choltitz held firm, he might very well be replaced by a general determined to follow orders. Another thing Bradley knew from intelligence reports: German Panzer Divisions Twenty-six and Twenty-seven were on the way to Paris, and if they arrived in time, Von Choltitz would have no choice but to obey orders and fight.

Von Choltitz was trying to stall with his anxious German superiors, hoping that the Swedish consul would manage to convince the Allies to act. He assured the Germans that he planned to dynamite the Arc de Triomphe, detonate the Eiffel Tower, and ignite the gold-domed Les Invalides. Seven tons of TNT were already under the Palais du Luxembourg, and another five tons of mines and munitions were secured under the former home of the Kriegsmarine on the Place de la Concorde. "The Grand Palais," Von Choltitz reported, "you'll be happy to know is in flames."

Later that day, CBS News broadcast to the world that "Paris has been liberated." Wanting to be the first to announce the news, reporter Charles Collingwood had prepackaged a general statement and sent it along to London to be ready at the moment the city was liberated. Military censors, unable to listen to the "experimental tape," simply passed it on London, where radio authorities guessed it was cleared. That was at least the official story of how newspapers all over the world carried Collingwood's premature account of the Liberation. Paris, in the meantime, was near catastrophe.

=

I N his march across northern France, Leclerc was encountering heavy rains, deep mud, and resilient Nazi attacks. The American Fourth Infantry, by contrast, did not meet many retreating or resisting forces. For them, the race to the capital consisted mostly of streams of people lining the streets and cheering wildly. Major S.L.A. Marshall of the US Army Military History section recalled having sixty-seven bottles of champagne thrust into his jeep by the time they reached Les Invalides. Private First Class Charley Haley of the Twelfth Regiment credited one of his friends with kissing about a thousand women. Sergeant Donald Flannagan compared the joyous reception to Charles Lindbergh's triumphant parade up Broadway after his famous oceanic flight.

In his bunker at the Wolf's Lair, Hitler flew into a rage. Had the Panzers not arrived yet? Where were Von Choltitz's promised detonations? Then, famously, Hitler turned to Generaloberst Jodl and asked, "Is Paris burning?" He ordered the Luftwaffe to strike and V-1 and V-2 rockets to rain down on the capital.

On the evening of August 24, some 150 troops entered the Porte de Gentilly and rode past stunned Parisians to the Hôtel de Ville on the rue de Rivoli. Parisians on the street eventually realized that the men in the Sherman tanks and "olive drab jeeps" were not Germans or Americans. The Cross of Lorraine identified them instead as Free French. Leclerc's men had arrived.

The next morning, as children played in the Tuileries and boats sailed on the Seine, the main army of Leclerc arrived and fighting grew intense. FFI soldiers, with white armbands over their biceps, hustled from doorway to doorway to avoid sniper fire. The École Militaire and Les Invalides saw much action. The foreign office on Quai d'Orsay caught fire. Leclerc thought some seventy-six men were killed, with another two hundred wounded. Leaders of the FFI estimated that they lost a thousand, with another six hundred citizens. Estimates for Germans vary, probably between two thousand and twenty-five hundred, with perhaps as many as sixteen thousand prisoners.

On August 24, the fourteen-ton bell of Notre Dame rang for the first time in four long years. Other churches followed suit. Camus, working on the Resistance paper *Combat,* wrote that day, "The greatness of man lies in the decision to be stronger than his condition."

Taken prisoner the following day, Von Choltitz signed the surrender document in a billiard room of the prefecture. During the ceremony, the Communist leader Colonel Rol burst into the room uninvited and demanded that he sign the paper as well. After a spirited debate, Leclerc agreed. Rol signed his name, putting it above Leclerc's. At ten o'clock, the Nazi swastika was lowered from the Eiffel Tower and replaced by a huge Tricolor. Raymond Sarniguet, the fireman who had been forced to take down the French flag on June 13, 1940, climbed the 1,671 steps to the top, beating competitors, to raise it once again over the city.

That evening, crowds milled in front of the Hôtel de Ville in expectation of General de Gaulle's speech. Shots were still being fired sporadically from windows and rooftops around the city. De Gaulle stepped onto the balcony and proceeded not to proclaim the republic, because, as he put it, it had never ceased to exist. France was not beginning, but continuing. "Paris," he shouted, "Paris abused, Paris broken, Paris martyred, but Paris liberated"—liberated, he added, "by itself, its people, with the help of the armies of France, with the help and support of the whole of France, that is to say of the France which fights, that is to say of the real France, of eternal France." There was no mention of the Allies.

The following morning, Saturday, August 26, 1944, the Feast of Saint-Louis, patron saint of France, de Gaulle paraded down the Champs-Élysées and Paris erupted into a monumental victory celebration—and one of the most unforgettable days in its history. Four bitter dark years ended in the uncorking of champagne bottles, the waving of tricolors, and singing of "La Marseillaise." "I was drunk with emotion, drowning in happiness," the future historian Gilles Perrault recalled. Crowds cheered madly. Journalist Ernie Pyle, swept up in the excitement, described the scene as "the loveliest, brightest story of our time." After 1,553 nights of Occupation, Paris was once again the City of Light.

21.

"P.S. DESTROY ALL
MY LETTERS"

I HAVE NEVER SEEN MY HUSBAND SUFFER FROM MENTAL
TROUBLES. I HAVE SEEN HIM SAD AND PENSIVE SOMETIMES,
BUT I ATTRIBUTED THIS STATE TO THE CARES AND FATIGUES
OF HIS PROFESSION. IN ANY CASE, HE HAS NEVER SHOWN
ANY VIOLENCE IN MY PRESENCE OR IN HIS CIRCLES.

—Georgette Petiot, 1936

EARLIER that summer, the French police had begun to release some of Petiot's suspected accomplices. Fourrier and Pintard were freed on July 4, 1944, for lack of evidence, followed by Simone Neuhausen and Roland Porchon. On September 30, 1944, Georgette Petiot was "provisionally released." Maurice Petiot, René Nézondet, and Albert Neuhausen remained in custody.

The police were still trying to identify Dr. Petiot's likely victims. Massu, a firm believer in the managed use of the press to aid an investigation, had released a reasonably detailed list of selected items from the suitcases, hoping that anyone with information would come forward.

It was a description of two articles of clothing that caught Marguerite Braunberger's attention when she read the paper at her home at 207 rue du Faubourg Saint-Denis. The first was a man's dark blue shirt with white pinstripes, size 40 collar, made by David at 32 Avenue de l'Opéra; the other was a gray felt hat monogrammed with the initials "P.B." and fashioned by A. Berteil on rue du Quartre-Septembre. Braunberger's husband, the sixty-six-year-old physician Dr. Paul-Léon Braunberger, had worn a shirt and hat of that description the day that he disappeared.

At eight thirty on the morning of June 20, 1942, Dr. Braunberger had received a phone call about a patient in distress somewhere on rue Duret in the 16th arrondissement. The caller refused to provide details of the ailment, the name of the person, or even his exact address. He asked the doctor to meet him at eleven o'clock that morning at the L'Étoile métro station.

Such secrecy was not unusual. The Nazis were exerting tremendous pressure on Jewish residents in the occupied zone, who, since the previous month, were now forced to wear a yellow star, about the size of the palm of a hand, sewn onto the breast of their outer clothing. Jews, more than ever, were now at risk of being arrested on the street. The Germans had demanded that French authorities deport a quota of one hundred thousand for the first eight months of 1942.

Braunberger appeared to recognize the caller. He left the apartment on foot, carrying only a small medical bag. Thirty minutes after the time for the rendezvous at the métro station, a special delivery letter arrived at the house of one of Braunberger's patients, an insurance agent named Raymond Vallée who lived at 20 rue Condorcet. The letter purported to be from Dr. Braunberger, and it was on his stationery.

"I was almost arrested but managed to escape," the writer of the letter related. "Tell my wife that I am not coming home, and that she should pack her most valuable possessions in two suitcases and prepare to leave for the Free Zone and then abroad." Details would be forthcoming. In the meantime, Vallée was instructed not to say a word to anyone, other than to inform Braunberger's patients that he had fallen ill on a visit in the suburbs and could not offer any medical services.

Confused at receiving such a letter from his doctor, Vallée took it to Marguerite Braunberger, who soon received two letters of her own. In the first one, dated June 22, she was told the same story of her husband's near arrest and escape, and she was warned to be careful, as she was surely being watched. She should, moreover, write to inform their friends that they were soon leaving Paris, but under no circumstances was she to talk to anyone. Her husband would write soon with further instructions. Like the letter to Vallée, this one was written on

Braunberger's stationery and appeared to be in his handwriting, if hurried, shaky, and somewhat distorted. Both letters were stamped at the post office on rue de La Boétie, not far from the L'Étoile métro station.

The following day, June 23, a second letter arrived at Madame Braunberger's, this time on plain paper, informing her that her husband would be limiting future communication given his "fear [that] my letters will be read." He told her to be courageous, obey his friend Vallée's instructions, and prepare for her departure. "P.S. Destroy all my letters," he concluded. Both of these letters were addressed in an odd manner, the first to "*ma chère amie*" (my dear friend) and the second "*ma chérie*" (my darling), terms of affection Dr. Braunberger never used. He called his wife "*Ma chère Maggi.*"

Everything seemed so peculiar, so disturbing. Marguerite Braunberger knew that her husband was under enormous pressure. Not only did he fear arrest, but a new law was about to remove his right, as a Jew, to practice medicine. But he would not leave her that way, without the slightest hint of planning and certainly not without a good-bye. And he would never confuse her pet name.

Why, too, of all his family, friends, and patients, would he choose to write to Raymond Vallée, a man whom he did not know well and, moreover, never really liked? The two families had met socially because Marguerite Braunberger was a close friend of Raymonde's wife, Paulette, and the women had insisted on it.

As they tried to figure out what was happening, Vallée received another letter on June 24, with a stranger request:

My dear friend,
I know that your cousin, the doctor, bought a house near the Bois de Boulogne in which he does not intend to live until after the war. Would you do me the service of making arrangements with him to have all my furniture and property moved to his house? I am counting on your help. Please have this done within forty-eight hours. Thank you.

Vallée was certain that he had never mentioned such a house to Braunberger and could not understand how he could have known about it. As for his "cousin the doctor," Vallée had no such relative. His wife's cousin, on the other hand, was married to Marcel Petiot.

The Vallées, the Braunbergers, and the Petiots had met one evening before the disappearance. Madame Braunberger could barely remember the occasion some thirteen years before, calling it "a baptism or first communion of the Vallée child." There in the Vallée salon, Dr. Braunberger and Dr. Petiot had discussed many things, from cancer treatments to antique furniture.

After the party, Braunberger had told his wife that Dr. Petiot was "either a genius or a madman." Was this meeting why Vallée was selected to receive the letters? He was the only person known at that time who could be traced back to both Petiot and Braunberger. (Actually, there was another connection that the police had not yet found: one of Braunberger's patients was the makeup artist Edmond Pintard.)

This was admittedly an odd case. Unlike the other disappearances, Braunberger was not about to testify against Petiot and he carried no jewels or fortune with him; the killer would have earned little from such an enterprise. Perhaps this explains the requests for transporting the physician's property.

About one in the afternoon on June 30, the Braunbergers received an anonymous telephone call. When the nurse at the doctor's practice, Marie-Cécile Callède, answered, a man on the line immediately launched into the details of Braunberger's fate: "I'm going to give you news of the doctor. I guided him through to the Free Zone but he went a little nuts. In the métro, he already began to act strange and at the border he nearly caused our arrest. Let Madame take care of herself as best she can. I will not guide her through. I have been too poorly paid." All of this was spoken as if it were being read from a sheet of paper.

Asked about Braunberger's health and whereabouts, the man said that he was on his way to Spain and Portugal. The nurse pressed for details and tried to coax the caller over to the apartment with the offer of a reward, but he refused. He said only that he had another letter, which he was supposed to deliver but preferred to put in the mail. He didn't say anything else, other than mention that Braunberger's brother, Marcel, would be well advised to leave Paris too.

The letter arrived the following day, sent from the post office at quai Valmy, not far from the Braunbergers' apartment. Using the same, if incorrect, pet name for Dr. Braunberger's wife, it was a short, undated note on ordinary white paper instructing Madame Braunberger to "follow the person who brings you this letter." He promised that they would meet soon and wished her "all my love," again using unusual phrases and signing the letter, uncharacteristically, with his title, Dr. Paul Braunberger.

Madame Braunberger had not heard anything else, either by letter or telephone. But, on July 3, a young man in a Nazi uniform identifying himself as "German Police" visited her building and inquired about a doctor who had previously served as a medical captain in the First World War and now owned a private practice. The concierge said no one fitting that description lived there, which, given Braunberger's recent disappearance, was technically not incorrect. The man left. She never learned the purpose of the visit.

The police never determined if this was in fact a real German soldier or another imposter. At any rate, whatever the purpose of the visit, Madame Braunberger did not immediately report her husband's disappearance. The timing of the visit was curious, coming, as it did, just one month after Petiot escaped damage from the narcotics cases with no more than a token fine.

Reporting the case of Dr. Braunberger to the authorities would not have done a lot of good anyway. Jews in Occupied Paris had no formal legal recourse, and Madame Braunberger certainly could not count on any sympathy from authorities. She had kept quiet for another three months, when finally, on September 25, 1942, at the maid's insistence, she reported her husband's disappearance to the police station at Saint-Vincent-de-Paul. At that point, she felt she had nothing to lose. The police officer on duty filed a report. The case was closed on January 9, 1943, on the tragically incorrect grounds that Braunberger had returned home.

22.

AT SAINT-MANDÉ-TOURELLE STATION

WHEN YOU KNOW WHERE THE APPLE IS PICKED, IT IS
ENOUGH TO WAIT FOR IT TO FALL FROM THE TREE.

—Commissaire Lucien Pinault

"THE Mad Butcher was no Nazi propaganda myth," United Press foreign correspondent Dudley Ann Harmon wrote on August 31, 1944. He was "a swarthy, sinister-looking [man] with the sadistic features of a Krafft-Ebing nightmare and the cleverness of a scientist." The Liberation of Paris had finally put to rest the rumor that Petiot was a Gestapo fabrication. As one policeman remarked, he wished the murderer had been a myth: "He is only too real. We have identified 54 victims, and heaven only knows how many more there are."

Paris-Soir was also estimating that the total number of victims was probably about fifty. Parisians, however, continued to attribute new murders to the serial killer. One anonymous letter accused Petiot of slitting the throat of a twenty-nine-year-old Italian woman named Laetitia Toureaux on a train on May 16, 1937—the first murder on the French métro. Another suggested that he planted the bomb that killed socialist minister of the interior Max Dormoy in late July 1941, and a third one claimed that he killed Carlo and Nello Rosselli, two anti-fascist Italian refugees, near Bagnoles-de-l'Orne, receiving payment of one hundred semiautomatic guns from Benito Mussolini. Each of these allegations was far-fetched, and the murders showed few, if any, of the characteristics that the police ascribed to the assassin of rue Le Sueur. A more likely suspect, in every one of these cases, would later emerge: a French fascist group, CSAR (Secret Committee of Revolutionary Action), known informally as La Cagoule, or the "hooded ones."

As Paris was transforming itself again in the autumn of 1944, the French police were still no closer to finding Petiot. Perhaps he had fled to Germany with retreating Nazis, as many people believed, the *New York Times* reported. Other newspapers, like *La patrie*, suspected that Petiot had remained in Paris. Sightings of the murder suspect were again on the rise.

Possibly to lure Petiot out of hiding, the French police handed over the dubious tale of Charles Rolland to the young journalist and Resistance fighter Jacques Yonnet. On September 19, 1944, Yonnet published an article in *Résistance*, one of the many underground papers that had emerged as popular dailies in post-Liberation Paris. After opening with a disclaimer that he could not vouch for the truth of the allegations, Yonnet proceeded to outline Rolland's deposition in vivid detail. He titled the article: "Petiot, Soldier of the Reich."

A few days later, there was a dramatic breakthrough in the investigation. A long, handwritten response signed by someone claiming to be Marcel Petiot arrived at the newspaper's offices, forwarded by attorney René Floriot. To verify its authenticity, the police obtained a sample of the physician's handwriting and asked leading graphologist Professor Edouard de Rougemont to study the two specimens. The letter, he concluded, was genuine, and Petiot's full rebuttal was published on October 18, 1944.

"Dear Mr. Editor," Petiot began. "All accused persons should be considered innocent until proven guilty. . . . Because of law and justice I have the right to defend myself and to ask you to print my answer." Indignant and scornful of the article's many errors, Petiot accused the police of inventing the absurd so-called Charles Rolland and then having the "sick imagination" to attribute such worthless claims to him.

As a longtime member of the Resistance, Petiot said, he had fought valiantly against the Nazis, only to be arrested, tortured by the Gestapo, and imprisoned for almost eight months. Many high-ranking members of the Resistance, including some now holding "public office," he said, were trying to find a way to reveal the truth about his patriotic activities without exposing themselves to danger. Petiot outlined his alleged services to the Resistance, which had for so long been slandered by the German-controlled press.

His code name, Petiot admitted, was Dr. Eugène, and his code number was 46. He claimed to have served in the secret Resistance network called "Fly-Tox," which had concentrated on attacking the Organization Todt and stealing secrets from German industry. With no less bravado, Petiot next discussed his "liquidations," as he called them, insisting that they were always "Germans and collaborators and Gestapo agents." It was outrageous, he said, to call him a soldier of the Reich. The letter concluded:

The author of these lines, far from having committed dishonorable acts, far from having forgiven his torturers and still further from having helped them, adopted a new pseudonym immediately after his release from the German prison [January 1944]. He has also retaken his place with the Resistance with [another] new pseudonym and asked for a more active role in order to avenge the hundreds and thousands of Frenchmen killed and tortured by the Nazis. He always remained in contact with his friends, and fought for the Liberation to the best of his abilities, despite the dangers that his action has caused him. He still contributes as much as possible to the Liberation, and apologizes if he cannot take the time to follow the polemic more closely.

Still using the third person to describe his actions, Petiot concluded: "Having lost everything except his life, he is risking even that under a false name, scarcely hoping that tongues and pens now freed from their shackles will tell a truth so easy to guess, and forget the clumsy kraut lies that require only two *sous* of French common sense to see through."

Understandably, the police were thrilled by this response. Not only did this letter confirm that Petiot was still alive—and many detectives had feared that the reports of his death might prove true—but it also provided many clues to his whereabouts. Petiot, in rushing to defend himself, had aided them far more than he realized.

In addition to admitting his identity as Dr. Eugène and claiming a specific code number, which could be verified, Petiot had volunteered that he was in fact working in the Resistance under a different name and provided them with no less than eight pages of his handwriting to discover his alias. He had not bothered to type his response or to ask his lawyer to do it for him. The envelope's postmark showed that the letter had been mailed in Paris; the speed of Petiot's rebuttal suggested that he might well still be in the capital.

At this point, many people helped track down the serial killer. An editor of *Résistance*, Louis Jean Finot, released Petiot's letter and the police circulated it throughout the FFI. All indications suggested that Petiot was probably masquerading as a doctor, which would make sense as a cover for someone with his background, and so the search focused on physicians in the Resistance. Colonel Rol, leader of the FFI in Paris, secured samples of handwriting that resembled the letter in question.

Among a number of people assisting the investigation was Captain Henri-Jean Valeri, originally from the commune of Villepinte in Seine-et-Oise and the leader of an FFI counterespionage unit in charge of rooting out traitors and "collabos." A slender man in his late forties, with dark brown hair and a thick mustache and beard, Valeri served as investigations officer for the intelligence organization G2 in the First Infantry Regiment of the FFI, stationed in the armory of Reuilly. Valeri had considerable skill and experience, and his quick promotion to captain—even for a time that saw many quick promotions—proved his zeal. Police investigators were more optimistic about the case than they had been in months, but they were quickly running out of time.

AFTER the Liberation, Frenchmen began the long and difficult process of coming to terms with the dark years of the Occupation. The first priority in the reckoning was to remove collaborators from positions of power. Sometimes this was done through the legal system in the High Court newly created to judge cases of treason, or "intelligence with the enemy." Other times, it was action taken by people themselves in the form of lynchings, summary executions, or a wide range of vigilante-style punishments. Women accused of sleeping with the Germans, the so-called "horizontal collaboration," in particular, were punished by the wrath of mobs.

An estimated ten to twenty thousand women would have their heads shaved, be stripped naked or semi-naked, and then marched through the streets, sometimes with swastikas tarred or tattooed on their breasts or with signs around their necks bearing the words "I whored with the Germans." Some of them, being new mothers, carried babies in their arms. German authorities estimated that fifty to seventy-five thousand children had been born to German fathers and French mothers in the Occupation. A recent study by Jean-Paul Picaper and Ludwig Norz, *Enfants Maudits* (2004), raised the figure to about two hundred thousand.

The violent purging was more common in the south of France, where tensions between Resistance and Militia were more severe, and many places were liberated by the French Resistance rather than the Allies. But no town of any size was immune. In all, about 310,000 cases involving some 350,000 people charged with "intelligence with the enemy" were brought to court. About 60 percent of the cases were dismissed for lack of evidence. Of the 125,000 that went to trial, approximately 100,000 resulted in convictions, though almost half of them (49,723) received the verdict "national indignity," which bore no prison sentence or fine. About 20 percent of the trials ended with a prison sentence (25,901), with another 13,339 sentenced to forced work. Officially, 7,055 people received death sentences, though the vast majority of these were not carried out.

Estimates for the number of summary executions with no attempt to use the legal system have dropped significantly. In the immediate aftermath of the Liberation, historians believed that there were anywhere from 30,000 to 100,000 slayings. More recent studies have estimated the total figure at perhaps 8,000 to 9,000. At any rate, the euphoria of liberation was giving way to the bitter controversies of retribution. Veteran intelligence agent Roger Wybot compared the atmosphere surrounding the search for collabos that autumn to the "stock market in a moment of madness."

Some Frenchmen believed that the exuberance in purging suspected collaborators was undermining the shaky foundations of the country's unity. François Mauriac was one of many people who urged caution, appealing for reconciliation, not revenge, as France's new leaders confronted the challenges of rebuilding the country. Others, like Albert Camus at *Combat,* pressed to take the purges further, punishing the criminals for cruelties they committed—the author of *The Stranger* had not yet reached his famous opposition to the death penalty. Captain Henri Valeri, working on the Petiot case, agreed with Camus, pushing his men at the Reuilly armory to show no mercy tracking down collaborators and rooting them out of power. France, he said, was using eyebrow tweezers, when the proper instrument should be a shovel.

O N the morning of October 31, 1944, a man in khaki uniform with a kepi, an FFI armband, dark glasses, and a thick beard stepped onto the platform of the Saint-Mandé-Tourelle railway station. At 10:45, as he punched his ticket, a stranger walked up to him and asked the time. Then, with this distraction, the stranger kicked him in the groin and three other men jumped on him. The man in khaki was carried out of the railway station, blindfolded, and gagged, with his hands cuffed and feet bound. After seven months and twenty days eluding arrest, Marcel Petiot had been captured.

Escorted back to the Reuilly armory, Petiot was forced to remove his FFI armband and uniform, so that he would "no longer sully the honor of the French army." The murder suspect carried a loaded 6.35 revolver, 31,780 francs in cash, and a large number of false identity papers and blank documents for search warrants, orders, and arrests. A Communist Party card, identification number no. 268004, only eight days old, was found in his possession, along with a membership card (No. 29 097) for the Communist organization of the France-U.S.S.R. Friendship Committee. Petiot also had a number of ration cards under various names, including one for a little boy named René, whose last name had been smudged and replaced. At this time it was not known who the child was, though police would soon have a good idea.

Given the amount of coverage that the murders initially received, it might seem that with his arrest Marcel Petiot would again dominate the news. This was not the case. Although reports would regularly appear both in French and international media, many of the former underground newspapers did not care for the topic. It was embarrassing, to say the least, to have this man claim the cause of the Resistance, as he would do with fervor, and his story would certainly raise many unwelcome questions. The Petiot case, moreover, had been sensationalized so much in the captive press, to distract from the harsh realities of the Occupation, that it alienated editors who once worked on Resistance papers.

Albert Camus's paper, *Combat,* exemplified the trend when its editors reported Petiot's arrest and then proclaimed their reluctance to cover the monstrous tale: "We believe we have fulfilled our journalistic obligations by relaying this news without commentary. We will do the same each day, but we refuse to glorify an affair which is repugnant from so many points of view." This reaction—if understandable in the charged circumstances of the autumn of 1944—was unfortunate. Without a full investigation, many questions about the case would remain no closer to resolution.

The man who actually arrested Petiot, Captain Simonin, was himself a recent recruit to the Resistance—one of approximately ten thousand agents who then belonged to the emerging intelligence service answering to the War Ministry and known as the DGER (Direction Générale des Etudes et Recherches). Actually, Simonin was not his real name, and he was not authorized by French police to make the arrest. He was later identified as a thirty-one-year-old former police officer named Henri Soutif, who had served as the *commissaire des renseignements généraux* of Quimper in northern France, collaborated closely with the Occupation authorities, and ordered the arrest, torture, and deportation of many Frenchmen.

Simonin's arrest had come at a propitious time. Among the papers in Petiot's possession was an order for the suspect, under one of his several aliases, to transfer to DGER offices in Saigon. Was Petiot hoping to escape to French Indochina, where he would serve in the Medical Corps of the intelligence service? This was at least one of his options. Petiot's date of departure was apparently set for November 2, 1944.

In perhaps the biggest surprise, Captain Henri Valeri and Marcel Petiot turned out to be the same person. In typically bold style, Petiot had posed as Valeri and maneuvered into a position inside Reuilly to help authorities find the killer of rue Le Sueur. At one point during his investigation, he even gained a meeting to discuss the case with the *procureur de la république*, who later said he had been impressed by Valeri's thoroughness, energy, and command of the facts of the case.

"It's unbelievable," Valeri's secretary, Cécile Dylma, said to Inspectors Lucien Pinault and Émile Casanova, about learning the identity of her boss. "He's a man so sweet, so calm. Captain Valeri has never shown a single act of anger towards us." At the same time, she acknowledged that he declined most invitations and generally kept quiet about his private life. "To think that I have been alone with him in his office for a month," Dylma said, "it makes me shudder."

Commissaire Massu would not have the satisfaction of arresting Petiot. In the purges that followed the end of the Occupation, which soon escalated to involve the removal of twelve hundred officers from the police department, Massu had been arrested on August 20, 1944. He was accused of four specific charges of collaboration with the enemy, which included furnishing information to the Occupation authorities that led to the execution of patriots, working cordially and "dining on several occasions" with the German liaison to the Police Judiciaire, and deporting a Jewish woman and two girls who had been arrested for a misdemeanor. His enemies pounced. The commissaire was taken away to Fresnes.

One of the documents that Petiot carried at the time of his arrest was an elaborate accusation against Commissaire Massu. The former head of the Brigade Criminelle, Petiot-Valeri wrote, should be suspended not just from his duties at the quai des Orfèvres, but more important, in the name of justice, from "the end of a rope." Petiot's job of punishing "collaborators" had put him in a frightening position to destroy anyone who could expose his past. How far could Petiot have gone in wiping the slate clean if he had not succumbed to his vanity and written an editorial to the Parisian newspaper? And, one wonders, how far did he go?

In December 1944, the disgraced and depressed former commissaire, recipient of the Légion d'honneur, slit his wrists in an obvious suicide attempt. Rushed to Hôtel-Dieu, Massu recovered and eventually returned to face an official collaboration tribunal, which on April 20, 1945, cleared him of all charges, for lack of evidence. There was not a single "anti-national act with which one could reproach Massu," Arthur Airaud, president of the Commission d'épuration at the Préfecture de Police, declared. That same day, Massu was freed from Fresnes, just over one year and three months after Marcel Petiot had walked out of the same building.

"A good colleague," Massu said, "profited from the circumstances to settle in my chair at the head of the Brigade Criminelle." Massu would return to the police force to serve with distinction. On his retirement in 1947, he went to work in security at the American Embassy in Paris.

Eleven years later, Massu appeared in a French television documentary together with his old friend, the bestselling mystery writer Georges Simenon. The two of them reminisced about how they first met over a glass of red wine at Les Trois Marches. Simenon described how, for inspiration, he had "haunted the Palais de Justice, the Place de Dauphine, [and] the little corner cafes." He elaborated:

> *I took all my models from right here. I watched them at work, and I picked up their habits. Maigret is a little of Chief Inspector Massu, a little of Chief Inspector Guillaume [Massu's former supervisor].*

Commissaire Massu lives on today in Simenon's gruff, earthy fictional detective Jules Amédée François Maigret.

23.

INTERROGATIONS

AN INDIVIDUAL WITHOUT SCRUPLES AND DEVOID OF
ALL MORAL SENSIBILITY.

—Dr. Claude, Dr. Laignel-Lavastine, and
Dr. Génil Perrin on Marcel Petiot

AS Captain Simonin later revealed, he had discovered Marcel Petiot's exact whereabouts thanks to a tip from one of Petiot-Valeri's subordinates at the Reuilly armory. FFI Corporal Jean-Richard Salvage told him that the suspect was staying in an apartment owned by his mother at 22 rue Paul-Bert. Simonin had investigated the lead. Sure enough, Petiot left the building every morning, took the métro at Saint-Mandé-Tourelle station, and exited at Reuilly-Diderot for a quick walk to the armory.

After making the arrest, Simonin did not immediately hand Petiot over to the police. Instead, he decided to question him about his activities. From the beginning, Petiot took on a brash, condescending tone, claiming to be, as Simonin put it, "a hero of the Resistance." He bandied about the terminology of the Communist Party, blasting the "hirelings of the capitalists" and "mercenaries in the service of the Americans." He spoke vaguely about only "obeying orders" and implied that his comrades in "the party" would not hesitate to free him.

According to Simonin's account of the interrogation, which eventually ended up in the files of the Paris police, Petiot elaborated on his many alleged services for the Resistance. He identified himself as an investigations officer and captain in the First Infantry Regiment of the FFI based at Reuilly. Later Simonin would say that he believed

Petiot had chosen to apply to this particular armory because of the prominence of several Communist leaders there, including Commandant Raffy, a former ranking member of the Resistance group FTP (Franc-Tireurs et Partisans), who would serve as Petiot's supervisor at Reuilly. It is also significant that Reuilly—so recently evacuated by the Germans—was also taking a lead in forming the tribunals to purge former collaborators.

Petiot denied that he had revealed his real name when he arrived at the armory in September 1944 looking for a commission. He presented himself, he said, as Dr. Wetterwald, who in turn used the alias Dr. Valeri. Simonin later said that he was positive that Petiot was lying. Petiot would only admit that he believed that Raffy's own boss, the head of the First Infantry Regiment, Colonel Ruaux, knew his true identity. In time, Petiot added, other people at the armory learned about his past. He defended them by pointing out that they had not put much credence in the wild slanders of the German press.

After discussing his medical practice, which he said earned 500,000 francs a year, an ironic boast perhaps for an avowed Communist, Petiot told Simonin that he had begun working for the Resistance in 1941. He had used his work as a physician to "demoralize German officer patients who came to consult me." He made contact with a Resistance organization based on rue Cambon, to send him French workers who had returned ill or wounded from their work in Germany. These Frenchmen, Petiot said, often provided "very interesting intelligence," which he readily passed on to the Allies.

Petiot mentioned specifically informing the American consulate in Paris about a secret German weapon, based on the principle of the boomerang, that was being developed just over forty miles southwest of Berlin. He identified his contact at the consulate as a man named Thompson. The American consul was Tyler Thompson, but he would later deny having any contact with the suspect. As for how Petiot could have known his name, Thompson had a theory. At the beginning of the Occupation, when he served as third secretary, Thompson had signed more than one thousand red certificates to be placed on American-owned buildings and businesses all over Paris, declaring them inviolable according to international law.

By late 1941, Petiot had allegedly made many more contacts in the Resistance. He claimed to be working with a group of anti-Franco Spaniards in the outlying district of Levallois and receiving training from a man from London who organized Resistance in Franche-Comté. Who was this British agent? Petiot said that he never knew his name, or even his code name. He did mention working with a man called "Cumulo," who operated the Resistance group Arc-en-Ciel, which in turn served under Pierre Brossolette in Charles de Gaulle's intelligence service, the BCRA.

There were already many allegations to investigate, and authorities would pursue them, but Petiot was not done talking. As in the letter to *Résistance*, Petiot described how he had worked for a supposed Resistance group, "Fly-Tox," that specialized in tracking down and executing informers, or *mouchards*, a slang term derived from the French word for fly (*mouche*). The name "Fly-Tox," Petiot later said, had been inspired by a commercial fly-killer product because, like the pesticide, his men liquidated *mouchards*.

When Simonin asked Petiot to provide names "and all the information in your possession" about members of his alleged group, Petiot replied calmly that his organization was well known and it was unnecessary to provide further details. He did, however, elaborate on Fly-Tox's methods of operation.

Members of his organization staked out the offices of the Gestapo on rue des Saussaies. Any civilian who left the premises was followed. The Fly-Tox Resistant, posing as a member of the German secret police, waited until the target went to a secluded spot and then seized him. If the latter protested that he worked for the Germans, he had, as Petiot later put it, "convicted himself." The suspect was then thrown into a truck. Interrogations took place at his property on rue Le Sueur, which he had used since his purchase earlier that year to store his antiques and "the bulk of his fortune."

The suspected collaborator—"once we acquired the certainty of his guilt"—would be executed by revolver or a secret weapon that Petiot claimed to have invented, which could fire in silence up to one hundred feet with deadly accuracy. The bodies were then dumped in the forests of either Marly-le-Roi or Saint-Cloud. Petiot claimed to have killed sixty-three people this way. As for the exact place his group disposed of the bodies, he said that he could not remember. He did not know the names of his victims either, as he had not recorded them and often could not determine with any certainty if his men knew a suspect's true identity. "We only knew that they were enemies who had to disappear."

In December 1941, when the United States entered the war, Petiot claimed to have offered the design of his secret weapon to the American consulate (and this was also when he first adopted the pseudonym Dr. Eugène). By this time, Fly-Tox was supposedly managing a clandestine organization that helped Frenchmen escape Occupied Paris. False papers were obtained from a man close to Lucien Romier, Vichy minister of state, and another person known as "Desaix," or more probably "De C," who served the embassy of the Argentine Republic. A police commissaire based in the 7th arrondissement of Lyon further helped Petiot's clients cross the border. The identification documents allowed Frenchmen to cross into Spain, then Portugal, and from there, reach safety in Argentina.

All this work as a Resistant, Petiot said, led to his arrest, imprisonment, and torture by the Gestapo. Then, after his release, Petiot realized that he was under close surveillance by the Gestapo, and still shaken by his prison ordeal, he retreated to Auxerre to recuperate. He returned to rue Le Sueur for the first time in early February 1944. It was then that he discovered that his building had been filled with bodies.

A FTER this unofficial interrogation, Captain Simonin handed Petiot over to the Police Judiciaire. The following day, Simonin would himself be brought before an official purge tribunal that examined cases of suspected collaboration. It was a five-minute hearing. Receiving a guilty verdict, Simonin was ousted from his position in intelligence. He disappeared. Years later, when he reemerged, he was convinced that his punishment had emanated from a certain faction that sought revenge for his arrest of Marcel Petiot.

Petiot, in the meantime, was met at the Police Judiciaire by Lucien Pinault, Commissaire Massu's successor, and Ferdinand Gollety, the *juge d'instruction*, the examining magistrate, who, in French law, conducts pretrial questioning, summons the witnesses, and compiles the dossier. Then, if he finds sufficient reason, the *juge d'instruction* forwards the evidence to the public prosecutor to draw up the indictment. Gollety, a short man from Boulogne-sur-Mer, on the northern coast, was regarded as a rational, no-nonsense magistrate with a scrupulous regard for detail. He was also a thirty-two-year-old official in his first posting.

The defendant was, at this point, required only to declare his identity, not make a statement. Petiot made one anyway:

> *My conscience does not reproach me in the least. I am proud of what I did as a patriot. If I have not obeyed all civil laws, I have obeyed the laws of war. Otherwise, the occupation imposed certain precautions on me. Among my comrades in combat, fifty knew my true identity. It required only one of fifty to denounce me, and one did.*

Petiot also retained as his legal counsel a rising star in the world of criminal defense, the forty-one-year-old Sorbonne-trained Maître René Edmond Floriot. "A demon for detail," Floriot had already defended Petiot in the two narcotics cases of 1942. Petiot had first seen Floriot's talents firsthand in 1937, when the attorney successfully defended one of his patients, Magda Fontages, for attempted murder of the French ambassador to Italy, Count Charles de Chambrun. Fontages was also known for seducing many powerful men, including Benito Mussolini, who at the height of passion liked to rip off her black silk scarf and pretend to strangle her.

Pretrial questioning would be an elaborate process that would ultimately last fourteen months. It would not begin for another thirty-six hours, however, as it was already late in the evening of the 31st and November 1 was a public holiday. Petiot was taken to cell 7 of Sector 7 of Prison de la Santé, a large gray building constructed in 1867 in the 14th arrondissement. Petiot would join many suspected collaborators, Gestapo agents, black market profiteers, and other people who were accused of benefiting from the German Occupation. Petiot's sector was reserved for prisoners on death row.

"I have been a member of the Resistance since the Germans first arrived in Paris," Petiot said in his first official interrogation on November 2, 1944. He would repeat many of the claims he had made to Captain Simonin, but also add a few details. He had issued false certificates of disability to help Frenchmen avoid deportation to Germany and other requisitions or demands from Occupation authorities. He told of using his secret weapon twice, fatally wounding a German motorcyclist on rue Saint-Honoré and another soldier on rue La Fayette. He said that the Americans had declined to adopt his invention, and that was a mistake. "A five-ton truck," Petiot said, "could have carried enough of the gadgets to liquidate the million Germans trampling France under their jackboots."

Petiot refused to provide more detail about this supposedly deadly weapon. There was still too much uncertainty, he argued, and the Germans might return at any time and use it against his country. However unlikely this may have sounded, this belief was actually common in some circles, particularly in rural southern France. Many people feared that former collaborators were hiding in the countryside and planning to sabotage the Liberation with hopes of installing another German-friendly authoritarian regime. When a handful of former collaborators were uncovered in December 1944 after in fact secretly returning to France, probably as part of the Nazi Ardennes offensive, the unlikely rumor would gain more credence.

Then, in his blunt fashion, Petiot gave another reason for his reticence to describe his invention: His interrogators were "too uncultivated in scientific matters to be able to understand."

When Gollety mentioned that Petiot would be well advised to reconsider, given that he was likely facing twenty-four counts of murder, Petiot countered unexpectedly that the *juge d'instruction* was ill-informed. He had killed sixty-three people. But these, he emphasized, were *not* the bodies at his house. The people he killed had been buried in the forest.

Upon his release from prison, Petiot explained to Gollety, he had been eager to avenge himself. He tried to contact his colleagues in Fly-Tox, but the organization had been vanquished, and its members who had not been imprisoned or executed had fled. It was difficult to reconnect with any of his remaining comrades because everyone used code names and they had all been changed. At the same time, Petiot had hesitated in finding his colleagues because he knew that the Gestapo often released prisoners in order to track their activities. He was certain that he was being watched and followed, and he did not want to put his fellow Resistants in harm's way.

Petiot also related how, since being tortured by the Gestapo, he had suffered terrible headaches and increased bouts of anxiety. He felt sick upon his release from prison and needed to relax. In the end, he decided to visit his brother in Auxerre. He only returned to his apartment in Paris on or around February 8, 1944. What he found had immensely disturbed him.

Not only had the Germans stolen much of his medical equipment, including an ultraviolet machine, an infrared machine, and many other items that he had hoped to use in his clinic after the war, but Petiot found the house itself "in a great disorder, furniture knocked over or broken, cupboards disemboweled." The old manure pit, which he had sealed long before to keep out the rats, had been uncovered and filled with various missing items from his property, including tools, smaller instruments, a portable electrical heater, and two large cushions from the waiting room. Also in the pit were a number of corpses.

"The bodies were fresh," Petiot said, suggesting that they were put into the pit while he was in jail. The skin was still red and the heads were heavy, indicating that the brain had not yet disappeared, and this, Petiot explained, happened "very quickly during putrefaction." The stench in the courtyard, the pile of bodies, and the bones in the basement—"I was absolutely bewildered and panic-stricken," Petiot said.

He first believed that the bodies had been concealed there by members of Fly-Tox who must have panicked. Later, after contacting a few members in secret, he said, he changed his opinion. It was the Germans who had dumped the bodies on his property. Petiot never explained how he would have connected with his fellow Resistants when, as he had just said, the surviving members had all changed names and he had not tried to find them for fear of exposing them to the Gestapo.

As for the bodies, Petiot said that he could not just load them into the truck and haul them away, as he claimed to have done to dispose of traitors earlier. The vehicle, at that moment, needed repairs, and although he was a decent mechanic who could have fixed the job himself, he was reluctant to attract undue attention. This was why he had ordered four hundred kilos of quicklime from Auxerre.

But once he obtained the material, he found the method slow and only partially helpful in disposing of the bodies. Fearing a Gestapo raid at any moment, two of his colleagues suggested that they burn the bodies. The colleagues, of course, were not identified.

To speed the process, the men hacked the cadavers into bits and fed the boiler, which was, Petiot said, the first time it had been used since he bought the building. He did not know anything about the bodies lacking hair, eyebrows, and facial masks. He suspected that it was either a lie or an effect of the lime. The hair might also have fallen out when they tried to move the corpses.

BEING a patriot and a Resistance fighter, however, was not Petiot's only possible defense. In the hands of his attorney, René Floriot, there was another strategy that prosecutors would have to consider.

At the end of the First World War, Petiot was known to have been incarcerated in a number of mental institutions. He had been discharged from the army with 100 percent mental incapacity, though this had later been reduced to 50 percent. He had received disability payments from the state, and continued to do so during the time he was elected mayor, built his medical practice, and even during the period when he stood accused of turning his property on rue Le Sueur into a slaughterhouse.

What's more, Petiot's stays in asylums had not stopped immediately after the First World War. As late as 1936, he had again been interned. The circumstances would be relevant should Petiot or his lawyer plead insanity, which, according to Article 64 of the Penal Code, could make him not legally responsible for his actions.

On April 4, 1936, Petiot, then a thirty-nine-year-old doctor with a thriving Parisian medical practice, had been browsing among a display of books outside the Joseph Gibert Bookshop at 26 Boulevard Saint-Michel. About twelve thirty p.m., as he turned and walked away, a store employee, René Cotteret, caught up with him and pointed to a book under the doctor's arm. It was an old, worn copy of a treatise on electricity and mechanics, Etienne Pacoret's *Aide-mémoire formulaire de l'électricité, de la mecanique et de l'électro-mécanique.*

Petiot, appearing surprised, claimed that he had not realized he had taken the book. He showed his identification papers, as requested, and offered to pay the full price of twenty-five francs. The man refused. He took the doctor by the arm and proceeded to escort him to the police station. Petiot lost his temper. According to the police report, he seized the employee by the throat, began to strangle him, and threatened to "bash his face in." Moments later, as Cotteret fell to the ground, Petiot ran away in the direction of the Odéon métro station.

Later that day, when an officer telephoned his apartment, a man answered and said that Petiot was not at home and had been out of town for several weeks. When two policemen knocked on his door, however, Petiot calmly opened it and received the summons for questioning at the St. Michel police station on April 6. On that date, Petiot arrived one hour late. His eyes were red, his face was puffed, and it appeared that he had been crying. He looked confused. When the officer began to ask about the shoplifting incident, Petiot handed him a letter that he said would explain everything.

According to this document, Petiot had been exhausted and consumed by his latest inventions, including work on a pump to massage the intestines and cure chronic constipation, as well as a perpetual-motion machine that he claimed to have nearly perfected. He had been so absorbed in his inventions that he had not realized that he still held the book when he walked away from the shop. He had never planned to buy the book, let alone steal it. He already knew its contents.

Petiot disputed the assault charge. As for his refusal to follow Cotteret to the police station, he reminded them that he had committed no crime and claimed that his family was waiting for him and he was already late when he stopped at the bookstore. He had cooperated with the detective, he emphasized, even giving his name: "If I hadn't given it, you never would have found me."

Surprised by the physician's behavior, both at the bookstore and at the station, the police commissaire ordered a psychiatric examination. During the session, held at St. Antoine Hospital, the performing psychiatrist, Dr. Michel Ceillier, thought Petiot seemed nervous, depressed, and highly unstable. He struggled to answer basic questions and could not state the title of his medical thesis. He "wept convulsively" and, in answering questions, spoke incoherently, except when he discussed his inventions, which Ceillier believed were pure imagination.

Petiot appeared to suffer from "mental debility," including "psychic disturbance, fits of depression, and delirium of invention." He showed a "deep distate for everything, especially life." He was, in short, given his profession as physician, "dangerous to himself and others"—the criteria used for placing someone in a mental institution (Law of 1838). So, on the basis of this report, dated July 22, 1936, Petiot was not held responsible for shoplifting and assault. The psychiatrist recommended that Petiot be interned in a mental hospital, forcibly if necessary.

Typically, in these circumstances, a patient would be institutionalized in a state asylum, but Petiot was granted a private hospital, as his wife had requested on his behalf: the Maison de Santé d'Ivry, just outside Paris. The head psychiatrist, Dr. Achille Delmas, supervised the cure himself. Delmas had a reputation for being very lenient and client-friendly—he would also care for surrealist poet Antonin Artaud and

James Joyce's daughter, Lucia, who came to the institution for schizo-phrenia during Petiot's stay. The physician arrived on August 1, 1936.

As Petiot's dossier, number 363 831, revealed, Dr. Delmas diag-nosed the new patient as "cyclothymic," that is, suffering from a mild manic-depressive psychosis. He noted that Petiot alternated between depression and hyperactive excitation. In depression, he experienced anxiety, insomnia, and *taedium vitae*, with an overwhelming need "to justify his past acts," and in excitement, a tendency to overwork, "attempting a variety of simultaneous tasks, inventive spirit, intellectual exaltation, and excessive scientific preoccupations."

Not long after he entered the sanatorium, thereby removing the criminal charge, Petiot started petitioning for his release. Eighteen days after his admission, Dr. Joseph Rogues de Fursac described Petiot as "calm, lucid, and non-delirious." Whatever mental troubles had ailed him were no longer present. On August 25, 1936, Delmas supported this diagnosis, pronouncing Petiot cured. The patient was, he wrote, in "a state of mental equilibrium that would permit one to conceive of lifting his internment and facilitating his imminent discharge." No immediate action was taken. Marcel and Georgette Petiot began writing letters to officials asking for support for his release.

"I am absolutely sane in mind," Dr. Petiot wrote on August 19, 1936, to the procureur de la république "I have a very honorable profes-sional past and I enjoy the esteem of everyone."

In the end, the court chose a panel of three distinguished psychi-atrists to examine the case and issue a recommendation: Dr. Georges Paul Génil Perrin, the author of *The Prevention and Cure of Nervous and Mental Disorders,* who was joined by Drs. Paul-Marie Maxime Laignel-Lavastine and Henri Claude, author of *Medico-Legal Psychia-try.* Petiot did not like the choice at all. The first doctor, he said, was crazy; the second was just "a couch man" who, he implied, took liberties with his female patients, and the third had been plucked out of obscu-rity. The committee finished its examination of Petiot and submitted its findings on December 19, 1936.

While appearing "amoral and unbalanced," Petiot was found to be "free from delirium, hallucinations, mental confusion, intellectual disability, and pathological excitation or depression." He, in short, "presented no psychopathic trouble susceptible to justify a prolongation of his internment" and should be released from custody, which was done on February 20, 1937.

Inside the report was a warning that "in the event of a future criminal indictment," Petiot's stay in a mental institution "should not weigh excessively in the deliberations." This internment, in other words, did not mean that he was insane, and Petiot should be held responsible for his actions.

But would this testimony be strong enough in case of an insanity plea now? As of November 1944, Petiot had convinced some psychiatrists that it was necessary to confine him in an asylum; others had concluded that he had cynically exploited French law to mimic symptoms of a troubled mind. The debate was far from over.

24.

BEATING CHANCE?

BESIDES, I NEVER HEARD OF A DOCTOR-SURGEON-MAYOR-
MURDERER IN FACT OR FICTION, MUCH LESS ONE WHO
WAS ALSO A SPY, OR INTELLIGENCE INFORMER, WRITER,
CARTOONIST, ANTIQUE EXPERT, MATHEMATICIAN, OR
WHO CALMLY CLAIMED POSSIBLY A HUNDRED AND FIFTY
VICTIMS . . . HE HAD LOST COUNT.

—Dr. Albert Paul

IN Cell 7 of Sector 7 of the Prison de la Santé, Petiot was confined in a space, nine feet by twelve feet, with little more than a bed, a couple of blankets, a water faucet, a chair, and a small table chained to the floor. He read, dabbled in poetry, and doodled, handing over some of his sketches to one of the armed guards who were posted outside his cell twenty-four hours a day. He also sewed, knitted, embroidered, and smoked heavily, earning the nickname "Cigarette Butt."

When one prisoner shared some cigarettes, Petiot thanked him with some lines of his own poetry. The piece was an obvious parody of a work that circulated through French prisons that autumn, by the writer Robert Brasillach, then imprisoned for collaboration, but it ended in Petiot's own style:

> It would be marvelous to see a town in arms,
> Crying "Get the bastards!" or, without the least alarm
> Sacking the palace of justice. But more than that,
> Skinning this one and then that one,

1. The townhouse at 21 rue Le Sueur. After Dr. Petiot purchased it from Princess Marie Colloredo-Mansfeld, neighbors began to note peculiar sights, sounds, and smells coming from the building.

2. Courtyard of the townhouse. The door of the brick building led to Dr. Petiot's office, and beyond that, his death chamber.

3. The basement stove where human bodies were found burning on March 11, 1944.

4. The kitchen workstation where the bodies were dismembered.

5. Commissaire Georges-Victor Massu, head of the Brigade Criminelle, told his son, Bernard, that they were confronting "the most dreadful criminal plot that I have ever seen."

6. Entrance to the lime pit at rue Le Sueur.

7. Rope and pulley found over the pit.

8. Gravediggers from Passy Cemetery were hired to sift through the debris for human remains.

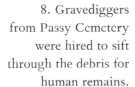

9. Remains of the victims were carried away for examination at the Institut médico-légal.

10. The photographs of Georgette and Marcel Petiot used
in the warrant for their arrest on March 13, 1944. The third
photograph is of young Dr. Petiot.

11. "THE MYSTERIOUS CHARNEL-HOUSE OF RUE LE SUEUR."
The occupied press was quick to speculate on Petiot's relationship with
drug addicts, prostitutes, and "terrorists" in the Resistance.

12. Crowd outside Petiot's residence at 66 rue Caumartin.
Paris would soon be engulfed in "Petiot Mania."

13. Georgette Petiot is carried away after her apprehension by the police.

14. The arrest of Dr. Petiot's younger brother, Maurice.

15. Black satin dress found at 21 rue Le Sueur. The garment was still scented with perfume.

16. Forty-nine suitcases belonging to victims arrive at 36 Quai des Orfèvres.

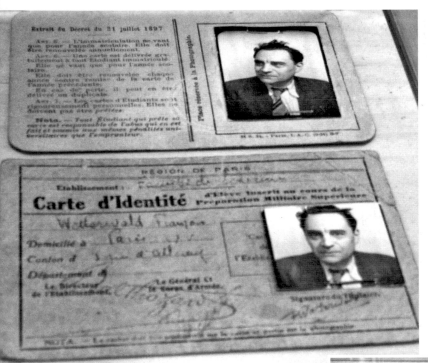

17. He did not steal identities, Petiot said; he only borrowed them.

18. Police believed that this viewer, found in the wall, was used to watch victims suffer in the death chamber.

19. In court, Petiot put on a show, and the trial soon became a circus.

20. Petiot liked to sketch and doodle in his prison cell as well as at the trial. This drawing was made in prison.

21. This is a page from the manuscript Petiot wrote in prison. "Man," Petiot wrote, "has been created to play, to challenge chance, to make love, and to struggle. But he has lost the rules, and, at the same time, something of the taste for the game."

So that it would be beautiful to see them die a slow death,
And to see, for ten years, ten skins of judges put up
for sale.

A prisoner across the hall, however, suggested that it was not the judges who should be skinned. "If Petiot is condemned as he deserves," the man screamed, "he will be carved up in slices like a sausage."

Another prisoner, who later spoke with a reporter for *France-Soir*, described Petiot as "very cultivated, very intelligent. He has sound judgment, he holds forth intelligently on his favorite authors: Voltaire, Beaumarchais, Anatole France. He detests deeply his [medical] colleague Céline, whom he holds for a madman, and whose scatological prose he loathes." Petiot was also credited with devising a way of communicating with fellow prisoners by slipping messages inside pieces of bread, and keeping abreast of the news. On April 12, 1945, Petiot reportedly announced the death of Franklin D. Roosevelt to his guard, who had not yet heard the news.

Petiot did not have a great deal of contact with other prisoners. Nézondet, held in a different cell as an alleged accomplice, claimed to have bribed guards to speak with Petiot on walks in the garden. "I never saw the least emotion on his face," Nézondet said. "He gave the impression that he could not care less what happened to him."

A few days after arriving at La Santé, Petiot had shaved off his mustache and dark beard and begun work on a manuscript that would serve as his primary occupation in prison. It was a bizarre book. Rather than directly addressing the murder charges he faced, Petiot concentrated on offering tips on how to defeat the odds in games of chance, from poker to the lottery, roulette to the races. Still, the work, with its many columns of calculations, astrological symbols, and often surreal ramblings, provides insight into his state of mind.

Human beings—described as animated "meatballs"—roamed a world that had degenerated into "a concert of bitterness."

Not a single one of all creation is content with its fate. The stone is sad thinking of the oak that grows in the sun. The oak is sad thinking of the animals that run in the shade of the forest. The animal is sad thinking of the eagle that ascends the blue sky. And man is sad because he cannot understand why he has been placed here, and he knows all his imperfections.

"This is a serious book that I am writing to amuse myself," Petiot wrote in a small, clear, and unadorned cursive. "By reading it seriously, you will amuse yourself and certainly gain something." He dedicated the manuscript: "To you who have given me this leisure . . ." The research, he wrote, was undertaken by "Doctor EUGENE, ex-Chief of the Resistance Group FLY-TOX." The columns of numbers were under the supervision of Captain Valeri. The errors in the book should be ascribed to Dr. Marcel Petiot. The title of his 360-page work was to be *Le Hasard vaincu,* or "Beating Chance."

Chance as commonly understood, Petiot argued, was really an illusion. "There is no chance," but only "probabilities that submit to special laws." All of these could be discovered with reason and application because, as he put it, "there is no effect without cause, and all effects result from a certain number of causes," which are often multiple and complicated. But once a person discovers those laws, he or she can control them and apply them with profit. Petiot promised to guide the reader through this uncharted territory, this "virgin forest bristling with calculus." The attempt to play games and master "chance" reveals a great deal about the murder suspect—Petiot the gambler and risk-taker who prided himself on overcoming opposition, regardless of the odds, the obstacles, or evidently any moral scruples.

Authorities, in the meantime, continued looking for the identity of his alleged victims. On November 10, 1944, any person who had a member of the family or a friend disappear between January 1, 1942, and March 11, 1944, was invited to the quai des Orfèvres to look through a collection of clothing, household goods, and other personal items believed to have belonged to Petiot's victims.

Fifty-three suitcases would be on display, including the forty-nine found last spring in Neuhausen's attic in Courson-les-Carrières. The remaining four bags consisted of items discovered in closets at rue Le Sueur, or at Neuhausen's house. These included three blouses, thirteen dresses, fourteen nightgowns, sixteen girdles, and twenty-four pairs of panties. One journalist referred to this macabre exhibition as the "Petiot Exposition at the Gallery Orfèvres."

Like many Parisians that autumn, Petiot followed with interest the high-profile chase and eventual arrest of Henri Lafont and Pierre Bonny. On November 30, thanks to a tip from a former member of the French Gestapo who had hidden inside the Resistance, Lafont and Bonny were found on a Burgundian farm outside Bazoches. This hideout was suspected of serving as the center of a network to help former Gestapo men and informants escape the country. The police barged in on this embryonic "French Odessa," captured the men, along with a stash of five to ten million in francs and jewels, a fraction of the treasure they had looted during the Occupation.

On December 12, 1944, less than two weeks after the arrest, the jury reached its verdict. Both Lafont and Bonny, as well as five of their men, were guilty and would be executed by firing squad on December 27, 1944. Petiot said sarcastically that these traitors had been "honorably" executed while he would likely be sent to the guillotine for doing the same thing as French justice: punishing traitors.

THE new commissaire, Lucien Pinault, was questioning some of Petiot-Valeri's closest FFI colleagues at the armory. One of them, Jean Emile Fernand Duchesne, recalled that Valeri had arrived at the end of September or early October. Valeri was, Duchesne said, "very esteemed" for his work, and he rose quickly. As far as he knew, the authorities did not know his real identity. The general consensus was that "he had belonged to a group called Fly-Tox and he had killed many Germans."

Duchesne admitted, however, that he had eventually come to

suspect that Valeri was Dr. Petiot, and he believed that one or two other people shared his opinion. At one point, Valeri told him that he had "participated in the murder, or rather execution of 63 people, including a boxer, whom he himself had killed with a revolver."

Yvonne Salvage, the owner of the five-room apartment where the murder suspect stayed at the time of his arrest, told police that she had no idea of her guest's real identity. She had loaned the apartment to this man as a favor to her son Jean, who had approached her with the request at the end of October. It would only be a few days, he had said. All she knew, Salvage added, was that his name was Dr. Valeri. Police now wanted to question her son, but he had taken flight.

If Petiot had stayed in the Salvage apartment for only a few days, there was someone else who had sheltered him for months. This was Georges Redouté, a fifty-five-year-old Belgian housepainter who lived on the fourth floor at 83 rue du Faubourg Saint-Denis. On November 4, 1944, police began to question this man.

About nine o'clock one evening in late March, probably the twenty-fifth, Redouté was returning home from work when he found his friend and physician, Marcel Petiot, wearing a large gray overcoat, a brown suit, a beige fedora, and a pair of dark horn-rimmed glasses. He also carried two small suitcases and a third, larger one. Dr. Petiot immediately launched into a discussion of the newspaper accounts of rue Le Sueur. "The cadavers," he said, "are the cadavers of Germans that I executed myself."

At that point, Redouté had known Petiot for almost three years, having met him when the physician came to treat the wife of a friend, bistro owner Louis Bézayrie. Petiot appealed to their past friendship. "You know that I was incarcerated for eight months by the Germans for clandestine passages. I am still sought by the German police. Perhaps you can put me up for a few days?"

Redouté had accepted, bringing a hungry, tired, and apparently broke fugitive to his small apartment. He gave him a bowl of soup and a piece of bread. The next day, Redouté asked for more details about rue Le Sueur. Petiot repeated his answers, adding that he had hidden parachutists, retrieved weapons dropped by British planes, and dispersed them to the Resistance fighters in the countryside.

"I should tell you," Redouté said, "Dr. Petiot was not very talkative and did not always respond to my questions." On one occasion, he said that the bodies burned in his basement should have been removed by a truck, but it had broken down and his colleagues had decided to "make the cadavers disappear by burning them." He did not name these comrades. As for the triangular room with the iron hooks and viewing lens, Petiot dismissed it as mere nonsense.

In May, Redouté's twenty-one-year-old daughter, Marguerite Durez, also moved into the apartment. Redouté had introduced his male guest as Captain Henri Valeri, a member of the Resistance on the run from the Gestapo. By this time, Dr. Petiot had grown a beard, and he continued to wear dark glasses, at least outside the apartment. Durez remembered her father calling him a "Corsican" and did not ask any questions, though she noticed that he often wore the same clothes and his shoes were in poor repair.

Did Dr. Petiot appear to be working for the Resistance?

"During the time that I sheltered him," Redouté said, "he never gave the impression that he was engaged in any clandestine action." He rarely left the apartment, and then, almost never at night. And for someone who claimed to be a leader of Fly-Tox, Petiot received surprisingly few visitors. Petiot was, the housepainter said, "always alone."

This was not completely true. Speaking with Marguerite Durez, police learned that there had been one visitor: Redouté's friend and bistro owner Emilie Bézayrie. Detectives would soon question her, but first they searched Redouté's apartment.

In the dining room where Petiot slept was "a drum with German colors with two drumsticks and a third one with rubber at the end." Petiot had called this a trophy from the battle of Paris, Redouté said. Police also found two bicycle license plates and two books, Joseph E. Mills's novel *L'Enigma du Maillet—Scotland Yard* and a yearbook of the *Comite de forces françaises 1933–1934*. In a drawer in Durez's room was a notebook entitled "Thoughts," which Redouté said had belonged to his daughter. Police also found forty-seven wooden dice. Dr. Petiot used these, Redouté said, to play a "game of poker."

On November 6, 1944, police questioned Emilie Bézayrie about her contact with Petiot during his months in hiding. She had learned of his whereabouts at her bistro thanks to her friend Redouté. It was only a couple of visits, she said, and always as consultations for her three-and-a-half-year-old son. They never spoke of rue Le Sueur. "I was convinced at that moment that he was innocent of the accusations made by the newspapers." Bézayrie would later admit that they had in fact spoken of "the war, the Germans, and perhaps the police hunt of which he was the object." But she insisted that she carried no message from Georgette or anyone else.

A S pretrial questioning continued, Petiot's version of the events of March 11 differed substantially from the police record. After the telephone call to his apartment, Petiot said that he had biked over to the building immediately, arriving in about twelve minutes, not thirty minutes. The police and firefighters had concocted the story of his late arrival to cover for their hasty decision to break into his building.

Petiot denied that he had ever posed as his brother. He identified himself, he said, as a Resistance fighter who had just been released from the Gestapo prison. At this point, he had wanted to wait on the arrival of the police chief, but the patrolman at the site had been a "true patriot" and advised him to leave because he did not know how closely allied his boss was with the Nazis. The patrolman promised to cover for him. He also instructed him to call the police the following morning and ask for "Monsieur Wilhelm or William." Joseph Teyssier's middle name was William.

When Petiot complied, he said that he was told that the Germans were interested in his case and he should disappear. Petiot took the advice. He stayed that night with an unidentified friend, before his Fly-Tox comrades took him to Redouté's apartment. Petiot spent the next five months there, not far from the home of the alleged victim

Dr. Paul Braunberger and the bars and cafés where Edmond Pintard recruited for the escape organization.

The Nazi-controlled press had seized on the story, slandering him with a barrage of lies and sensationalism. Compromised, Petiot no longer received important missions with the Resistance. Dr. Eugène was relegated to the background. Under his new code name, "Special 21," Petiot labored among a series of mundane duties largely confined to writing tracts and administrative drudgery. He was bored and frustrated beyond belief.

It was the Liberation that saved Paris—and also, Petiot said, himself. August 1944 had been thrilling, as the capital rose up against the Nazis. After emerging from hiding, Petiot claimed to have participated in the battle, collecting a number of souvenirs, such as German hand grenades, a gun from a fallen Resistance comrade, and, as police had already discovered, a drum from the place de la République. In early September, he went to a number of Resistance offices, hoping to renew his contacts with Pierre Brossolette of de Gaulle's BCRA, then called the DGER. Brossolette could explain his Resistance work at rue Le Sueur, help him obtain the release of his wife and brother from captivity, and find him continued employment in intelligence.

It was this desire to serve the country, Petiot said, that forced him to assume the false identity Dr. François Wetterwald, alias of Captain Henri Valeri. As a thirty-three-year-old, he'd hoped to see more action than he did as a forty-seven-year-old, as his Valeri papers described him. He also told his FFI colleagues that he had to adopt the false identity to escape former Gestapo agents, Nazi informers, and other enemies who wanted to punish him for his services to the Resistance.

If Petiot had committed so many patriotic services for the Resistance, Gollety asked, why did he not simply tell the police his story after the Liberation? Petiot said that the accusations made against him by the "German press" were so "manifestly false" that he could not imagine anyone believing them. Besides, he said, "I did not go to the police because the police had not yet been purged of collaborators, and I was more useful to France continuing the fight than discussing my personal affairs."

Gollety, no surprise, sometimes suffered migraine headaches during the pretrial questioning. On one such occasion, when he looked particularly disturbed, Floriot reminded him that there was a doctor present. Petiot, laughing, offered to give his interrogator an injection.

A S Gollety could not evaluate the merits of Petiot's claims to have served the Resistance on his own, he summoned two consultants, Lieutenants Jacques Yonnet and Albert Brouard of the military security organization Direction Générale des Etudes et Recherches (DGER). Both men, well-versed in the culture and traditions of the underground, would question Petiot at length about his activities.

Lieutenant Jacques Yonnet was the author of the *Résistance* article about Petiot that helped uncover his whereabouts. A twenty-nine-year-old who had been wounded by a German grenade and captured at Boult-sur-Suippe in June 1940, Yonnet had escaped and returned to Paris, where he taught in a vocational college, collected material for a history of the city of Paris that he hoped to write, and hung out with a smart bohemian set with radical leanings. Yonnet had begun using the alias "Ybarne," which he had borrowed from a priest who had died in his prisoner-of-war camp.

Joining the Resistance in 1943, Yonnet had operated a clandestine radio and mapping service. One of his main tasks was helping London coordinate bombing raids against sites most likely to harm German interests and yet result in the fewest French casualties. Yonnet had expanded his role, recruiting and personally hiding a downed Allied pilot in his apartment on the Left Bank. His associate, Albert Brouard (Brette), a forty-three-year-old former police inspector who joined the Resistance in May 1942, had helped Allied pilots escape to Spain.

Neither Yonnet nor Brouard had heard of Fly-Tox. When they asked him for names of colleagues, Petiot refused to answer. That would have been an understandable position under the Occupation, when the lives of his comrades and their families were at stake. But now, after the Liberation, this stance seemed peculiar at best. Even when Yonnet and

Brouard promised complete confidentiality, Petiot scoffed at their guarantees. He would not—or could not—name a single person from his organization.

The names he did mention, however, raised many questions. When Petiot had said that Pierre Brossolette could attest to his activities, that man could not confirm anything because he had been dead for seven months. On March 22, 1944, after his arrest by the Gestapo, Brossolette had jumped from a sixth-floor window on avenue Foch rather than risk betraying fellow Resistants under torture. Another Resistant Petiot mentioned was "Cumulo" of the Arc-en-Ciel (Rainbow) network. Jean-Marie Charbonneaux ("Cumuleau") had among other things worked in the information section of Arc-en-Ciel, concentrating on industrial and military intelligence and establishing a network to help Allied aviators evade capture.

Petiot said that he provided security for this man and had even served as a double. This was an odd statement, given that the twenty-five-year-old Charbonneaux was almost half his age and did not look like him. Petiot also said that he eliminated traitors who attempted to infiltrate Charbonneaux's organization, though this claim also did not hold up under scrutiny. Charbonneaux could not confirm Petiot's assertions, either, because he, too, was dead. In October 1943, while fleeing the attack of the feared Belgian torturer who used the false name Christian Masuy (inventor of the bath torture method), Charbonneaux was shot in the thigh. He staggered to a nearby building at 4 rue Francisque Sarcey, where he made his way up to the fifth floor and attempted to escape via the roof or gutter. Masuy and his men pursued. Charbonneaux jumped, nearly bringing Masuy with him.

Petiot never elaborated on the unnamed man from London who had supposedly trained him, or provide any details on the training he had allegedly received. He only said it had helped him invent his own simple, cheap, and highly effective plastic explosive that consisted of a couple of bottles filled with gasoline and sulfuric acid. Once they were hidden on a Nazi supply train, the bottles—separated by a cork and suspended from the ceiling by a string—would knock and ignite, creating a powerful explosion. Petiot also claimed that this man from London introduced him to a Resistance network, Agir (Action).

As Yonnet and Brouard knew, this was another legitimate organization with major achievements. Established by Michel Hollard, a French businessman with the gas engine company Maison Gazogène Autobloc, Agir had recruited many railway stationmasters, hotel owners, dockyard foremen, and other patriots to inform on German military positions and troop movements. With more than one hundred agents at its height, Agir had uncovered the exact placement of coastal batteries, departure schedules for ships, and even plans for a new torpedo powered by hydrogen peroxide. Agir's most dramatic coup, however, was identifying one hundred V-1 launching sites in northern France and even swiping the blueprint for the inclined platform from the overcoat pocket of a German engineer while he read the newspaper in the bathroom. This information would spare London much grief in the rocket attacks. Eisenhower later suggested that this piece of intelligence had helped ensure that D-Day invasion plans were not postponed, if not derailed.

No one in Agir, however, seemed to know anything about Marcel Petiot or his alleged Resistance activities. Indeed, Petiot's answers to Yonnet's and Brouard's questions were curiously uneven. Sometimes he seemed to show an intimate knowledge of the Resistance; other times he garbled the most basic facts. As for Petiot's alleged code number, "46," Yonnet and Brouard said that a ludicrously low number was unknown in the history of the Resistance. Who gave it to you? they asked. Petiot's answer—that he no longer remembered—was a serious error. Members of the Resistance were trained to give the standard response: "A guy who did nothing but that."

25.

THE KNELLERS

WHILE WE DEBATE, THE DIE IS CAST.

—Jean-Paul Sartre

A S Gollety assembled the Petiot dossier, Albert Camus gave Jean-Paul Sartre an extraordinary opportunity. The United States State Department was looking for eight French journalists and former members of the Resistance to take a seven-week tour of the country, all expenses paid. Camus asked if Sartre was interested in representing *Combat*. "Shit! I'll run over there," Sartre said, accepting the offer. Simone de Beauvoir later said that she had never seen him so happy.

On January 11, 1945, Sartre departed on a twenty-four-hour flight with three stops in a nonpressurized DC-8 military plane. It was his first trip outside Europe. He would write thirty-two articles, published in *Combat* and *Le Figaro*, detailing his experiences in a place he had earlier equated with the future: skyscrapers, jazz, movies. In Manhattan, Sartre would dine with Antoine de Saint-Exupéry's widow, Consuelo, in her apartment overlooking the East River, which had been decorated for Greta Garbo. Her husband, the author of the previous year's *The Little Prince*, had disappeared on a reconnaissance flight over Corsican waters on July 31, 1944. Sartre met W. H. Auden, attended a private screening of *Citizen Kane*, and sought out the jazz he'd long loved, including a performance by Charlie Parker on Fifty-Second Street.

Leaving behind the despair of post-Liberation Paris, mired in shortages, continued rationing, and the ever-present threat of being denounced as a collaborator, Sartre was flown coast to coast and shuttled between stops in a limousine. He attended a Washington, D.C., cocktail party hosted by Walter Lippmann, toured a Hollywood studio, flew over the Grand Canyon by plane, talked with trade union leaders in Chicago, interviewed farmers in the Midwest, and in the South experienced the deep social and racial divisions that permeated the "land of freedom and equality." On March 9, he was treated to an evening at the White House. President Franklin D. Roosevelt told him about how much he loved France, how he had biked throughout the country as a boy, and showed him his collection of miniature donkeys, which, Sartre noted for his French readers, was the symbol of his Democratic Party.

But the most significant event for Sartre that year occurred back in Paris. On October 29, 1945, five months after his fortieth birthday and his decision to quit teaching to pursue a full-time writing career, Sartre delivered a public lecture entitled "Existentialism Is a Humanism." The former teacher came out to a crowd of two or three hundred people, with no notes, his hands in his pockets, and defined the philosophic system soon to be inseparable from his public persona. Existentialism, he said, was "that doctrine which makes human life possible."

War and its atrocities had spread disillusionment. Sartre's philosophy was already sometimes cited as emblematic of the anguish and despair that gripped the postwar world. Despite what both his conservative and Communist critics said, Sartre would present his philosophy instead as a "doctrine based on optimism and action":

> *Existentialism defines man by his actions; it tells him that hope lies only in action, and that the only thing that allows man to live is action; Man commits himself to his life, and thereby draws his image, beyond which there is nothing. We are alone without excuses. This is what I mean when I say that man is condemned to be free.*

Maurice Nadeau titled his article in *Combat* about the talk: "Too Many Attend Sartre Lecture. Heat, Fainting Spells, Police. Lawrence of Arabia an Existentialist."

Others were less impressed. A reporter for *Samedi Soir* wrote that Sartre might be a hero to "the hairy adolescents of Saint-Germain-des-Prés," but for more discerning readers, he was a "murderer," stealing his ideas from German philosophers such as Edmund Husserl and Martin Heidegger, and crowning his bastardized philosophy with a "barbaric name" that no one understood and yet "everybody speaks of it over tea." For sheer promotional talent, Sartre had surpassed everyone since P. T. Barnum.

But this review, like the positive one in *Combat* and other papers, also helped spread Sartre's name and awareness of his philosophy beyond the cafés of Saint-Germain-des-Prés. Other Parisians began to seek out Sartre's works, including the monumental treatise he published two years before that had been ignored, *Being and Nothingness*. Existentialism was on its way to becoming what the historian Ronald Aronson called the first postwar media craze.

THE last French Occupation media craze, meanwhile, was nowhere near subsiding. As the capital prepared for its first Christmas in four years without German soldiers, a certain Parisian aristocrat was celebrating a midnight supper with a masked ball with the theme of Marcel Petiot. A journalist asked the hostess if a ball based on a mass murderer was appropriate. Yes, she said, she and her friends also needed their fun.

While Yonnet and Brouard investigated Petiot's alleged Resistance activities, Gollety appointed a team of psychiatrists to examine the suspect's mental health. The committee consisted of three men: Dr. Paul Gouriou, director of the Psychiatric Hospital of Villejuif, who had examined Petiot at Villeneuve-sur-Yonne when he was accused of stealing oil cans and concluded that he was insane; Dr. Georges Paul Génil Perrin, of the Henri Rouselle Center at Sainte-Anne's Neurological Hospital, in contrast, found Petiot only a "constitutional delinquent" who exploited legal loopholes by emulating well-known symptoms. The third member, Dr. Georges Heuyer, a leading specialist in pediatric neuropsychiatry and juvenile delinquency, had not previously rendered an opinion on the suspect.

In the first psychiatric evaluation, conducted in late December 1944, the doctors probed into similar territory covered by Judge Gollety and the DGER lieutenants. Petiot, however, showed more arrogance and disdain for his medical colleagues. He emphasized that rue Le Sueur had served as a center of Resistance activity, with Fly-Tox helping Frenchmen escape from German camps, liquidate his country's enemies, and fetch arms caches dropped by Allied planes. "At one time," he boasted about his property, "there were over sixteen hundred pounds of arms hidden there!"

It was simply impossible for him, Petiot said, to liquidate dangerous collaborator gangsters like Jo the Boxer and Adrien the Basque by himself. This was the work of an organization, not one man, let alone a medical doctor. "You forget it was I who was imprisoned and tortured by the Germans at Fresnes for eight months, then the bastards framed me with the bodies they stuffed into my house."

The doctors asked about the enormous wealth Petiot had accumulated, reported by the media at the time to include "over fifty properties worth millions" and a fortune worth, according to one police estimate, approximately 200 to 250 million francs.

"I did not acquire my fortune from my alleged victims," Petiot said. "I made five hundred thousand francs per year from my medical practice. I spent hardly one hundred thousand per year. My wife is very frugal and my servants very cheap. Then my secondhand and my antique business brought me profits." Petiot mentioned an oriental rug that he purchased for 17,000 francs and then sold later that same day for 60,000. He also claimed to have profited from his real estate investments, though of course such methods did not explain how he could have purchased the property in the first place.

But the question, it was soon clear, was not only the source of his fortune, or even its amount; it was also its fate. Petiot's answers then and later were never satisfactory. The interrogators, ill-prepared to deal with his financial situation, did not at this time probe further. Instead Petiot took the offensive, noting that he had joined the Resistance, "ready to make any sacrifice," and now he found himself being "labeled both a murderer and a-monster."

After the interview and physical exam, which showed Petiot to be in good health except for slow reflexes and a cholesterol spot in his left eye, the doctors evaluated his mental state. They were impressed by his intelligence—undoubtedly highly intelligent, with a solid understanding of psychology and forensic medicine, and well read in the literature of mental disorders. At the same time, they could find no sign of mental instability, noting only that he appeared "completely amoral." Most important for the upcoming trial, the committee concluded that Petiot should be held responsible for his actions.

On May 3, 1945, the military security team Yonnet and Brouard also submitted the conclusions of their six-month investigation. It was a scathing verdict.

> *[Petiot's] hesitations, his contradictions, his glaring ignorance of the structure of a Resistance network for which he pretends to have worked, the numerous improbabilities in his declarations, his systematic habit of mentioning only Resistance comrades who are either dead (Cumulo, Brossolette) or who cannot be found (the members of Fly-Tox) lead one to believe that Petiot was not at any time in serious contact with any Resistance organization whatsoever.*

WHEN it came to stealing the identity of Dr. François Wetterwald, Petiot's methods had been brutally simple. On September 11, 1944, he had shown up at the apartment of sixty-eight-year-old Marthe Wetterwald, whose son was held at the concentration camp of Mauthausen. Petiot claimed to be a representative of the International Red Cross responsible for negotiating the release of French prisoners still held in Germany. He wanted to help her son.

To facilitate his efforts, Petiot asked to inspect his identity papers. Overjoyed, Madame Wetterwald complied. When some of her son's military documents, including his army paybook, were not handy,

Petiot asked her to find them. Two days later, he returned as planned and began leafing through the items. When Madame Wetterwald left the room, he slipped some important documents into his pocket, and then later used them to obtain his false identification cards. Madame Wetterwald's son would remain at the concentration camp until the Allies liberated it in May 1945.

The real François Wetterwald was not only a physician, he was also a prominent member of the Resistance. He was a leader of the group Vengeance, which collected information, sabotaged German sites in preparation for D-Day, and conducted other raids, most notably stealing German cars and uniforms, the latter often grabbed in the changing rooms of swimming pools. Among its many other activities, Vengeance operated an evasion network that helped Allied soldiers leave Occupied France.

Assuming Wetterwald's identity proved to be advantageous. Petiot gained instant credibility as a Resistance fighter, and he had not been shy to exploit it.

B EFORE the pretrial questioning ended, three last victims would be added to the official total. In the fall of 1945, the French Ministry of Justice received a letter from an American Jew living in La Paz, Bolivia, named Siegfried Lent. The letter was originally addressed to the Jewish Deportees Service of the American Joint Distribution Committee of New York, and in it Lent asked for any information about his relatives, Kurt Kneller, his wife Margareth (Greta) Lent Kneller, and their son René, who had lived in Paris during the Occupation. It was known that this family tried to escape with the services of a doctor, but they had been missing since the summer of 1942.

Kneller, a forty-one-year-old electrician, had then served as codirector of Cristal Radio, a company that distributed radio and home appliances from its plant on rue Saint-Lazare. He also served as a technical consultant to other companies, including a battery manufacturer. Kneller and his wife had left their native Germany in June 1933, six months after the rise of Adolf Hitler. He sought French citizenship and, on the outbreak of war, volunteered for the French Foreign Legion, serving until his release in September 1940, following the armistice.

When the police tried to track down the landlady of their two-room apartment at 4 avenue du Général-Balfourier in the 16th arrondissement, they found that she no longer lived there. One of their neighbors, thirty-two-year-old Christiane Roart, however, proved to be a wealth of information.

The Knellers, she told Inspector Louis Poirier, had considered leaving Paris for some time, given the growing dangers the city now posed for its Jewish community. Kurt Kneller, a patriot who identified strongly with his new French homeland, wanted to remain in Paris, but he changed his mind on July 16, 1942, a date that came to be known as "Black Thursday."

Alone in the third-floor apartment with René, Greta Kneller happened to see the arrival of French police from her window. Instinctively, she realized the danger. She grabbed René and rushed upstairs to hide with Roart.

This visit was part of the *grand rafle,* or "the great raid," when, over the course of forty-eight hours, some 12,884 Jewish men, women, and children were seized by French police, marched into the city's green-and-white buses, and then crammed into the sports stadium Vélodrome d'Hiver to await deportation to one of several concentration camps. Had the Knellers been at home that day, they would have had to face an eight-day ordeal in the hot, cramped arena, without access to adequate food, water, or basic sanitary facilities. After the stadium and a concentration camp, they would most likely have been herded onto freight cars on the way to Auschwitz.

Realizing that the authorities would likely return, the Knellers decided to find another place to live. Leaving young René temporarily with Roart, his godmother, the couple sought shelter with another family friend, Klara Noé, who lived nearby, at 19 rue Erlanger. On the following day, Friday, July 17, Kurt Kneller told his friend Ernest Jorin, a man who had invested in his firm and served as René's godfather, that they had found someone who would help them escape Nazi-occupied Paris. It was his doctor. They were instructed to pack their valuables into suitcases, which would be picked up by him personally that night. Petiot asked for the usual passport photographs and recommended a photography studio on Boulevard Saint-Martin.

As Jorin later told police, he had been skeptical of the so-called escape organization. When he expressed his doubts to Kneller, the latter had shrugged them aside, saying, "I know, this appears suspect to me too, but what else can I do?" Kneller was desperate.

On the evening of July 17, the Knellers' doctor arrived with a cart and horse-drawn cab driven by an elderly gentleman, matching the description given in the Wolff case. They loaded the luggage, two large and four or five small suitcases, onto the cart. The doctor said that he would return shortly for the furniture—suggesting again that, as in the Braunberger case, he was attempting to make even larger profits.

Roart was struck by how forcefully the doctor insisted on having all the apartment furniture handed over to him. He even threatened not to cross the Knellers into the unoccupied zone unless she complied. Kurt and Greta were not there to approve the transfer of property, as they had already moved, as instructed, into Noé's apartment to await the doctor's next communication. Reluctantly Roart and the concierge had agreed to the demands, handing out the bed linen first and promising the rest at a later date. The doctor, she remembered, had played with young René on his knee, but the boy did not want anything to do with him.

The doctor had orchestrated the departure to the smallest detail. He would arrive at Noé's apartment that night, take Kurt Kneller first, and then return the following day for Greta and René. They would all be taken separately to the same location, believed to be a resting home, where they would receive false identification papers and a series of vaccinations and inoculations. The family looked forward to being reunited in time for their departure to the new world.

After this alleged escape from Paris, many of the Knellers' friends and relatives began receiving postcards. Roart received one about fifteen days later, as did Noé and Jorin, the latter in particular perhaps because he was believed to have kept some of the Kneller jewelry and other valuables. Each communication told essentially the same story. The Knellers had succeeded in "crossing over" and were doing well, though the journey had been difficult and Kurt had fallen ill. The letters and postcards ended, as in the Braunberger case, with the plea to destroy them.

There were other peculiarities. Madame Kneller signed each communication "Marguerite," though friends knew she had retained the Germanic spelling of her name Margareth and always preferred the shortened form of "Greta." The handwriting was more angular and strained than usual. Still, the letters seemed to have silenced any concern that something was amiss. They also likely served another purpose. As in the Braunberger case, the postcards would serve as recruiting tools for future clients.

When Christiane Roart was interviewed at the police station, she picked out Petiot immediately from a series of mug shots. She thought that the handwriting in the postcard matched the sample of a prescription signed by Dr. Petiot that the police provided. Moreover, when she looked through the suitcases, which she had packed for the family, she believed that the men's shirts monogrammed with the faint initials "K.K." (which someone had attempted to remove) had belonged to Kurt Kneller.

Other items in Petiot's suitcases would be traced to this family, including a woman's black coat, a woman's bathrobe, and a number of kitchen and other towels monogrammed with their initials. Roart also recognized a pair of striped pink silk pajamas, though she could not say for certain that they had belonged to young René. The pants bottoms of a second pair of pajamas, however, seemed to be his, because, she remembered, it had been made from one of his father's shirts. The boy's name, age, and birth date matched one of the ration cards that Petiot carried at the time of his arrest.

The Knellers were never seen again in Paris or Argentina. On August 8, 1942, three weeks after their disappearance, workers on a barge on the Seine near Asnières reported discovering a bag wedged in some bushes. Inside were the mutilated remains of a young boy, approximately eight or nine years old, and the head, femurs, pelvis, and arms with the shoulder blades and clavicles of a woman between the age of forty and forty-five. Three days later, a man's head was found in the river. The remains have never been identified, but the Knellers were added to the list of victims.

O N October 30, 1945, almost one year to the date after his arrest, Petiot suddenly refused to answer any questions. There had been ample time, he concluded, for the *juge d'instruction* to conduct his investigation and ask any question that he deemed relevant. Petiot was drawing the line. He would henceforth save his answers for the trial.

Gollety tried to prod him, but he would not relent. Sometimes the dossier reads like a farce, as seen, for example, in the interrogation on November 3, 1945.

"On what date did you buy the property on rue Le Sueur?" Gollety asked.

"I have decided that I will no longer answer any questions, except in public."

"For what purpose?" Gollety asked, returning to the question of his purchase of the house.

"Write 'ditto' and things will move along more quickly."

Gollety would arrive with a long list of questions, including a forty-eight-page compilation on December 28, 1945, and Petiot would simply refuse to answer any of them.

The following month, in accordance with French criminal law, Gollety sent the Chamber of Accusations a bulging dossier that weighed approximately fifty kilos. There was enough evidence, it was concluded, to warrant sending the Petiot case to trial.

As for the alleged accomplices, including Georgette Petiot, Maurice Petiot, René Nézondet, Albert and Simone Neuhausen, Raoul Fourrier, Edmond Pintard, Roland Porchon, and Eryane Kahan, it was now officially decided that all charges would be dropped. There was simply not enough evidence to prosecute them. "Yet it is certain that, if justice can do nothing against them," the future prosecution assistant Maître Michel Elissalde said, "the name that they bear and the sad reputation which affects them personally may already serve as a constant source of shame, at least if Petiot's amoral insensitivity has not triumphed over them."

The state was going to concentrate on Marcel Petiot. The number of victims was set at twenty-seven, and the file was turned over to the *procureur général* to draw up the formal *acte d'accusation*.

26.

THE PETIOT CIRCUS

THOSE OF YOU WHO WISH TO AMUSE YOURSELVES SHOULD
GET OUT OF HERE AND GO TO THE THEATER.

—Marcel Leser

ON the crisp spring morning of March 18, 1946, some four hundred spectators and one hundred journalists packed the Cour d'assises of the Palais de Justice on the Île de la Cité. Everyone was eager to see the man accused of killing twenty-seven people, chopping them into pieces, flushing their inner organs into the sewer, and then disposing of the other remains in his lime pit or burning them in his basement stove. All the while, he amassed a fortune. This was expected to be, the *Washington Post* reported, "the most sensational criminal trial in modern French history."

As at the opening of a new play, actors, film stars, and ladies of high society, wearing turbans or fashionable small feathered hats, flocked to the courtroom, jostling for any empty seat or a place to stand. Many other Parisians, brandishing binoculars or opera glasses, came in anticipation of the thrilling denouement of the macabre affair. The air reeked of perfume. Outside, street vendors hawked souvenirs in an atmosphere increasingly resembling a carnival.

The evidence for the prosecution, lining the entire back wall of the courtroom, weighed more than one ton. All the parcels, trunks, suitcases, and baggage, it was noted, gave the courtroom the appearance of a train station. There were also glass containers of other items found at rue Le Sueur, ranging from an umbrella to the wheel of a bicycle.

At the center of the long high table would sit the president of the tribunal, fifty-seven-year-old Marcel Leser, in a long scarlet robe trimmed with ermine. He would preside over the trial and, in accordance with French criminal law, conduct the *interrogatoire*, or preliminary questioning, himself. At his side were two magistrates who would be asked to take part in the deliberations of the jury and even vote on the verdict. This practice was supposed to ensure legal expertise in the debate, though it also meant that the state could exert considerable influence on the outcome. A jury in 1946 had only seven members, and two-thirds majority sufficed to reach a verdict. All jurors were, by law, male.

To the immediate right of the magistrates sat the chief prosecuting attorney, Avocat Général Pierre Dupin, a thin, balding man with gray hair. He had only been appointed to the case six weeks before, when a number of higher-ranking prosecutors declined and his predecessor abruptly resigned. His assistant, thirty-year-old deputy Maître Michel Elissalde, had spent his honeymoon cramming for the trial, covering the floors of his apartment wall to wall with the documents and regaling his new wife with arguments about the case.

At a right angle to the prosecution was the defense, led by the celebrated forty-four-year-old Maître René Floriot in black robe and white cravat. Floriot wore his trademark round tortoiseshell glasses. His hair was short, cut to the top of his ears, slicked back over his forehead, and parted to the left. Four young attorneys assisted him: Eugène Ayache, Paul Cousin, Pierre Jacquet, and Charles Libman. Each one, apportioned a fourth of the dossier, had devoted the last eighteen months to preparing the case. As their hairstyles were similar to their superior's, they were soon dubbed the "Floriot boys."

There were also nine civil attorneys participating in the proceedings—in French law, families of victims may hire lawyers to represent them during the criminal trial and, like the prosecutor, cross-examine witnesses and the defendant. The Khaït, Braunberger, Guschinow, Kneller, Wolff, Basch, and Dreyfus families had all hired representation, as had the families of Paulette Grippay and Gisèle Rossmy. The most prominent of the civil parties was Maître Pierre Véron, a highly decorated Resistance fighter who represented the Khaït and Dreyfus families. Paulette Dreyfus had hired another attorney as well: her brother-in-law, Maître Pierre-Léon Rein.

At 1:50 p.m., a small door in the back reserved for the defendant opened and in walked Dr. Petiot, wearing a gray overcoat atop his blue-gray suit with lavender pinstripes and a purple bow tie. He was not restrained in handcuffs, as he had asked that they be removed just moments before. Security was tight. Two Gardes Mobiles, each wielding a tommy gun, accompanied the defendant into the prisoner's box, which was located at a raised level right behind his defense attorney. Other helmeted guards stood at attention around and outside the room.

Petiot smiled to the jury and audience. One journalist thought he looked like an actor, an artist, or a pianist; another quipped that he looked like the "devil's poet." Petiot's black "piercing eyes" gave even the hardened forensic expert Professor René Piédelièvre the chills.

Aware that he was the center of attention, Petiot took off his overcoat, folded it gently, and placed it on top of the dossier beside him. Then, evidently not finding his effort satisfactory, he unfolded his coat and proceeded to refold it a second time more meticulously. He straightened the knot of his bow tie. The crowd watched his every move. The show was just beginning.

Cameras popped and flashed a dazzling light. The defendant first raised his hands to shield his face, before relenting and turning his favorite profile to the photographers. "Gentlemen, please," Petiot eventually said, when he had had enough. He scanned the crowded room looking for his wife, son, and brother, all of whom, of course, were in attendance, as were three widows and the few surviving family members of his alleged victims.

The clerk of the court read out the *acte d'accusation*, or indictment, charging Marcel Petiot with twenty-seven counts of "willful homicide . . . committed with premeditation and malice aforethought, for the purpose of preparing, facilitating or affecting the fraudulent appropriation of clothing, personal items, identity papers, and a portion of the fortune of the above-mentioned victim." The statement ran to more than twenty closely typed pages.

Of the victims, there were fifteen Jews; nine gangsters, prostitutes, and other people wanted by the police, the Gestapo, or both; and three people who had no known connection with the escape agency: Jean-Marc Van Bever, Marthe Khaït, and Denise Hotin. One victim was unidentified, described as a young woman who'd disappeared in late 1942 or early 1943. This was the second woman who had accompanied Jo the Boxer in an attempted departure from Occupied Paris.

During the indictment, rather dull, monotonous, and hardly audible for most people in the packed room, many of the attendees watched the defendant closely. Although stooped over or propped up on an elbow leaning onto the ledge of the prisoner's box, Petiot had a formal bearing that still somehow looked dignified. He had the high forehead of an intellectual, with prominent cheekbones and thin lips "like the edge or blade of a knife." His hair was thinning, and, for many, like Kenneth Campbell of the *New York Times*, he looked younger than expected. Perhaps the most commonly noted feature was his hands. They were those not of a doctor or a surgeon, but rather, it was said, of a strangler or a butcher. The press was clearly not going to change its tune in painting a portrait of a killer, regardless of the fact that he had not yet been convicted and faced a trial with his life at stake.

Petiot, acting like the star in his own film, listened to the indictment, already looking bored. He brushed his hair back from his forehead with one hand and then the other. The dark circles under his eyes reminded the writer Jean Galtier-Boissière of the makeup applied to sleepwalker Cesare in the German expressionist film *The Cabinet of Dr. Caligari*. The defendant gazed out into the distance, sometimes fixing his "famous hypnotic stare," as one journalist recalled, on a specific member of the audience. At other times, he looked down, concentrating on his doodling in the margins of his own copy of the indictment. The drawings, it was later discovered, were caricatures of the prosecutors, and not poorly done either.

During the roll call of the witnesses enlisted to testify in the trial, which included about ninety people, Floriot raised his first question: "What about Colonel Dewavrin?" This was a key official in the

Resistance, the chief of the DGER, the military intelligence and counterintelligence organ of the Free French. Petiot had identified him in his
pretrial interviews as someone who could vouch for his activities in the
Resistance. Leser answered that the witness was "on a mission."

"I am anxious to know the duration of this mission," Floriot said.

"That's my thought as well," Dupin, the prosecutor, said.

At a quarter after three, after the hour-and-a-half *acte d'accusation*
seemed to drag on interminably, Président Marcel Leser opened with
the *interrogatoire,* a detailed examination of the charges that included a
brief biography of the accused. In French law, a defendant's past record
plays a more important role for the prosecution than in Anglo-Saxon
countries. In addition, the president of the court questions the defendant
and may, if he chooses, comment on the answers as well. The accused
may challenge witnesses or the prosecuting attorney, even in the middle of a testimony, and indeed failure to allow such a question may be
grounds for a mistrial. Any of the lawyers—prosecution, defense, or
civil attorney—may intervene at any time as well. To an outsider, a
French trial might seem somewhat disordered; the Petiot case would
look like pure chaos.

Indeed, in recounting the introductory overview of Petiot's life,
Leser had only gotten to the defendant's work as a student at the University of Paris, which he called "mediocre," when Petiot interrupted:
"I did however get 'very good' on my thesis. I should be modest about
these things."

"You enjoyed a lot of popularity as a doctor. You were quite
seductive."

"Thank you."

"Don't mention it," Leser answered spontaneously, prompting
laughter. Leser then reminded the court of other crimes that Petiot had
been accused of committing as a young man. He mentioned a woman
who leased Petiot his first house in Villeneuve-sur-Yonne and claimed
that he had stolen furniture, including an antique stove, which he had
tried to replace with a replica.

"She told everyone that she was having sexual intercourse with me," Petiot said. "I declined this honor. She lied."

Leser asked about Petiot's former maid and suspected lover, Louisette Delaveau, who had disappeared in 1926.

"My first murder," Petiot said sarcastically. "I assume of course that you have a witness."

Pierre Scize of *Le Figaro* noted that Petiot had good fortune in drawing Leser for his trial. The president would be accused of being too lenient with the defendant. Jean Galtier-Boissière thought that Leser seemed like a plump, jovial St. Antony on the bench. In Leser's defense, it was early in his career and he had no experience with witnesses as brazen as Petiot, or trials as high profile as this one. Leser simply pressed ahead in his biographical introduction, noting the suspected thefts of oil, gasoline, and tires and, one example that the press would particularly seize on, a supposed Christmas Eve theft of a cross from a cemetery.

"That was a story spread by all the bigots and hypocrites in the country." The cross, Petiot said, "disappeared two hundred years ago. There must be a statute of limitations, isn't there, Monsieur le Président?"

"But you were convicted for tapping electricity?"

"Yes, I was convicted," Petiot said, "but that does not prove that I was guilty." The audience roared in approval.

"Next you are going to tell me the whole dossier is false."

"No, I would not say that. Only eight-tenths of it is false."

The prosecutor, Dupin, apparently uneasy about how the *interrogatoire* had opened, intervened. At this point, Petiot lost his temper in a startling outburst of anger. "Stop!" he shouted, glaring at the prosecutor and clenching his hand into a fist. "Would you please be so kind as to allow me to finish?"

Leser reprimanded him. "I forbid you to speak in that tone."

"All right," Petiot said, described as waving off the president with the back of his hand. "But I don't care to be treated like a criminal. And I ask the gentlemen of the jury, who will be the referees of this battle, to note all the lies in the dossier."

After recounting the scandals of Petiot's career as mayor in Villeneuve-sur-Yonne, with frequent interruptions, Leser discussed his Parisian medical practice. He noted the leaflet Petiot handed out announcing his arrival, which boasted his ability to cure everything from appendicitis to pain in childbirth. Leser, unimpressed, called it "the prospectus of a quack!"

"Thank you for the advertising," Petiot said, "but I would ask you to keep your opinions to yourself."

Floriot objected. "The first requirement of a court is to be impartial. I request that you withdraw the epithet 'quack.' "

"I never said that," Leser replied, before agreeing to retract the statement. He next questioned Petiot about his substantial wealth, particularly the contrast between his "astronomical salary" and the paltry sums he declared on his tax returns.

"Oh, astronomical," Petiot said, again with sarcasm, adding that his 300 to 500 thousand francs a year hardly qualified as astronomical. When Leser pointed out that Petiot had only claimed 25,000 francs in income, the defendant said he was observing a long-standing medical tradition: "When a surgeon earns eight or ten million a year, he declares a hundred thousand francs. That proves that I am a Frenchman. I didn't want to seem like some kind of sucker."

At this point, some members of the audience laughed, and others applauded. The audience was indeed having a taste of Petiot's wit, a hint of the verbal sparring to come, and a preview of the many difficulties the *président* would face in a trial already on the verge of slipping out of control.

AS Leser continued his preliminary examination, he turned to the charges of shoplifting against Petiot at the Joseph Gibert Bookshop in April 1936. The defendant denied stealing anything. It was raining, he said. "I was engrossed in my invention. I consulted the book, and then I put it under my arm by distraction." When Leser asked which invention, Petiot launched into a monologue about his device to cure chronic intestinal problems and claimed that "everyone with a fancy for invention is suspected of being crazy."

"But it was you who pretended to be insane every time you had trouble with the law."

"No one ever knows if he is crazy or not," Petiot said. "You can only be crazy by comparison."

Turning to the subject of rue Le Sueur, Leser recounted the defendant's history with the building and began to describe its features. When he made it to the triangular room with its false door, fake alarms, iron hooks, and one-way viewing lens, Petiot interrupted. "Nothing is simpler," he said. This was going to be the room of his clinic that would house his radiotherapy equipment. The bell did not work because he had not yet installed the electrical wires. The "false door" was mere decoration, with the wood chosen for its ability to protect against humidity. As for the viewer, what good was it when it was "obstructed by wallpaper"? The small room had been exaggerated beyond recognition by the lies of the Nazi press. "You understand me, don't you?"

Petiot also repeated his assertion that the bodies found in his house had been planted there by Germans while he was imprisoned as a Resistance fighter at Fresnes. Before drawing this conclusion, the defendant admitted that he had first blamed his Fly-Tox colleagues for dumping the dead bodies of Germans and traitors on his property.

"But what comrades?" Dupin asked. "What are their names?"

"I will not deliver the names of the comrades of my group because they are not guilty, no more than I am anyway. Some of them offered to testify here for me, but I didn't want them to do so because these men deserve the Croix de la Libération for eliminating thirty *Boches* and you would put them in handcuffs."

"Let them come, and I will give them the Cross. I promise you."

"No, no. I will not give you their names so long as the purge [of collaborators] is incomplete, and people are still free who swore an oath to Pétain."

As several eyewitnesses described it, Leser then threw his arms into the air and claimed that he had never seen anything like this.

"Don't lift your arms to the sky, Monsieur le Président," Petiot said.
"I'll lift my arms to the sky if I want!"

"Then you'll have reason to lift them even higher in a little while."

Clearly Petiot was scoring points with a public that looked back on the discredited Vichy regime with extreme distaste. Leser moved the conversation on to Petiot's assertion of having joined the Resistance from the very beginning and noted that "there was no Resistance at that time." At this unpopular position, the audience booed.

"No organized Resistance, I mean." Leser retreated, asking Petiot to elaborate on his purported invention of a secret weapon.

The defendant refused, claiming that it was not appropriate to discuss it as the *Boches* might use it against Allied troops stationed in Germany. He then repeated his claims of having killed German soldiers with his weapon, mentioning hitting a man on a horse in the Bois de Boulogne. After a heckler suggested that they call the horse to the stand, Petiot spoke of his Resistance group, its work with the Arc-de-Ciel network, and its relationship with the same unnamed English special operations officer who supposedly trained Resistance fighters in the Franche-Comté. He told how he and his comrades in the Fly-Tox organization blew up German trains in the Chevreuse Valley.

When Leser ordered a short recess, many members of the audience refused to budge from their seats. Some ate sandwiches in the courtroom; others ventured out only after ensuring their seat was saved and returned with a copy of Petiot's book, *Le Hasard vaincu*, which was being sold in the street outside the Palais de Justice. Often in intermissions throughout the trial, Petiot would leave his box and sign copies.

After the break, the attorney representing the Khaït and Dreyfus families, Maître Pierre Véron, began to question Petiot on his alleged Resistance activities. Tall, broad-shouldered, with close-cropped hair and a *Legion d'honneur* pinned on his gown, the thirty-six-year-old Véron was well qualified for this task. A Resistance fighter himself, Véron had detonated many bridges, as he helped protect the right flank of Patton's army while it approached Paris in the summer of 1944. One film producer working for the U.S. Army and in attendance at the trial said that Véron was one of three people in the room who could play himself in a Hollywood production. The other two were Leser and Petiot.

Véron opened with a simple question about a subject Petiot claimed expertise in: "What are plastic explosives?"

Petiot stammered, appeared ruffled, and, some thought, reddened with embarrassment. Véron charged ahead as if his suspicions of Petiot's ignorance were confirmed: "How do you carry plastic explosives? How do you prime them? How do you detonate them?"

"Is this an entrance exam for the École Polytechnique?" Floriot asked, coming to Petiot's defense.

"An exam for the École Polytechnique? Certainly not. This is an examination on the Resistance, and it didn't take long to show that your client is an imposter," Véron said. "I am now certain that this man, this so-called great Resistant, has never seen plastic explosives and does not know what they are."

"You did not let me finish," Petiot said, trying to overcome the poor impression he had made by his answers. Véron kept the focus on technical matters of the explosions that a Resistance fighter should know. In the midst of continuing his account of a German potato-masher grenade with wooden handle, Petiot suddenly exploded at the attorney: "You defender of Jews and traitors!"

With boos and hisses from the gallery and many shouts from hecklers, Leser pounded the gavel. The ruckus continued. At six thirty that evening, the court adjourned.

"Why?" Petiot asked. "I'm not the least bit tired."

27.

"NOT IN DANGER OF DEATH"

I ACTED WITH A SPORTING SPIRIT.

—Marcel Petiot

MAKING front-page headlines in most Parisian newspapers, the Petiot trial evoked passionate debate, and opinions of the defendant were by no means all negative. Letters of support poured in for the accused murderer. The prosecutor, for one, was appalled, particularly with the Petiot fan mail and what he called the "hundreds of marriage proposals" from "neurotic, deranged women."

As the second day of the trial opened on another spring morning, an even larger crowd angled for a seat or, more realistically, a place to stand in the packed courtroom. An unknown number of spectators had slipped inside sporting dubious press badges. Street vendors were selling not only Petiot's book, but also the small yellow tickets signed by Président Leser that granted admission to the trial. Lessons from the wartime black market were in full display around the Palais de Justice.

When Petiot arrived in the prisoner's box, he found that it was already occupied. A young woman in a red dress sat there, apparently pleased with her luck of finding the last empty seat. Petiot, with no small charm, kissed her hand and insisted that she keep her place, noting that his honor as a gentleman would be offended if she refused. The audience appreciated the wit.

Leser opened the proceedings by returning to the central question of Petiot's work with the Resistance, asking how he recruited members for his alleged Fly-Tox network and how exactly it worked. Petiot explained that he used the auction house on rue Drouot as a recruiting center—a good answer since there would be no lack of witnesses who could vouch for his regular attendance on its premises. Ignoring the part of the question about the selection of members, Petiot elaborated on the method of liquidation, or execution, as he insisted on calling the acts.

"It is very simple," he said. "I have detected them by the following way: by approaching them and challenging them by saying: 'German Police.' By the way they reacted, we were informed." Many of the suspects protested that they, too, worked for the police. In that case, Petiot continued, "we shoved them in a truck and left, under the protection of men armed with submachine guns. We took them either to rue Le Sueur or the woods, and there, after an interrogation, our conviction being confirmed, we slaughtered them."

"How did you get rid of the bodies?" Dupin asked.

"We buried them. It was the safest [thing to do]." The audience, weaned on press accounts of rue Le Sueur, was surprised. There was no mention of a basement stove or lime pit.

"You told the police your executions were at 21 rue Le Sueur," Dupin said. "Now you speak about a truck."

"Yes," Petiot said. His Fly-Tox men killed "traitors" in the forest, but if they were for any reason under pressure, they went to rue Le Sueur. "All this may seem unbelievable, Mr. President. We lacked neither a certain courage nor a certain nerve."

"Did you take part personally in these executions?"

"No."

Gasps of surprise were again heard in the gallery.

"Yet you have acknowledged that before."

"The day of my arrest, I was questioned by someone no one has ever been able to find, a captain of the DGER. I had handcuffs on my wrists, and signed what was desired."

Floriot filled in some details for the jurors, taking advantage of news that had only emerged a few days before, thanks to an investigative piece by Jacques Yonnet in *Résistance*. "My client was arrested by that famous Captain Simonin of the DGER. Where is he? He was served with papers along with Colonel Dewavrin." Now, addressing Leser,

Floriot asked, "Why don't you have him appear—as Simonin, or under his real name, Soutif, police inspector of Quimper and Gestapo collaborator, responsible for the execution of a score of French Resistants!"

Véron interrupted, asking again about specific people Petiot had killed.

After his initial refusal, Petiot agreed to give one name, with Floriot's approval: Adrien Estébéteguy, or "Adrien the Basque." Véron pressed the defendant for details, only to receive another outburst from him: "Shut up, you defender of Jews." Petiot then accused the lawyer of "searching for dramatic effect."

"No," Véron answered, "but I won't allow you to soil the Resistance with your lies!" This response drew loud applause.

"You're a double agent!" Petiot shouted, leaning forward, his knuckles white from gripping the edge of the box.

"If you don't take that back immediately, I'll break your face!" Clenching his fist, Véron started toward Petiot. The audience loved it. Had a lawyer and a defendant ever come to blows in the Palais de Justice? The trial had just opened for the day, but some journalists already had their lead-ins for the morning paper. Leser pounded the gavel, demanding silence and threatening to call a recess. Someone looked at Petiot's lawyer, Floriot, who, remarkably, appeared to be asleep. The Petiot trial was threatening to become a farce.

Président Leser returned to the question of victims of the so-called escape network he'd raised before the interruption.

The first victim, Petiot said, was Jo the Boxer, though by the prosecution tally, it was actually Joachim Guschinow. The defendant described Jo as having "a head like a pimp, or if you like, a police inspector." Such physiognomy would "make sure he was stopped at the border" and that was why Petiot's group insisted on solid documentation for voyagers.

Petiot was again asked for specific names of people who helped furnish the false papers.

"I would like very much to be able to tell you," the defendant said. "Unfortunately, I no longer remember." He put his head in his hands and remarked that he had a bad memory for names. Moments later, as if the truth suddenly occurred to him, Petiot said that, although he did not want to promote inexactitudes, he seemed to recall that his group obtained its false documents with the help of "an employee in the embassy of Argentina at Vichy." Petiot was still claiming to be a small part of the larger organization who did not know all the details of its operations.

He was asked about Lucien Romier, a Vichy administrator who had an assistant who Petiot claimed helped with false documentation to enable transit into the unoccupied zone. This time, Petiot only said that this "minister of Pétain" was no Resistant, and he had never worked with him.

"What are the names of the people who actually helped escapees across the border?"

"Oh, you know, they changed names fairly often."

"We also know that you did too," one of the civil parties, Pierre-Léon Rein, said to Petiot, loud enough for some members of the audience to hear.

"Some names, some names," Véron demanded.

"At [Chalon-sur-Saône], there was a man named Robert. At Nevers, there was a German who later committed suicide. At Orléans you met a man with a black beard at the train station café." He mentioned something vague about a countess on horseback with a property near the line of demarcation. When this line of questioning did not progress, veering instead into the realm of a "cloak and dagger novel," as trial observer Claude Bertin put it, Maître Véron turned to Petiot's arrest in May 1943 and his nearly eight-month imprisonment by the Gestapo.

"It was the famous Jodkum who took charge of me," the defendant explained. " 'Ah, you're Dr. Eugène!' he said, and then he had my head crushed, suspended me by my jaw, filed my teeth, put me in the bath of frozen water, and other things. I will not go into the details. In short, the usual 'fantasies.' " Petiot followed with a monologue about how he did not ask for any thanks and people were naturally ungrateful, especially forgetful of "the sufferings of heroes." He started to cry.

The courtroom was silent, as if dumbstruck by the defendant's sudden change of emotion.

Leser asked Petiot about his mysterious release from the Gestapo in January 1944.

Petiot said only that his brother bought his freedom for 100,000 francs. Unfortunately, Petiot was not pressed to explain why the Germans would have agreed to free him at such a low price. The prosecution lost another opportunity to cast doubt on Petiot's defense that he worked for the Resistance.

"What about the bodies at the rue Le Sueur?" Leser asked.

"I found a large pointed heap of them when I went there. I was very annoyed. I didn't want that sort of thing about my house."

"Is that why you asked your brother for quicklime?"

"Oh no! The lime was for exterminating roaches." One journalist noticed that family members of victims winced. Petiot continued, noting that as his colleagues could not haul away the bodies, he had decided to use the lime, and then, as that did not work well, they tried the stove, which he had already lit to destroy a mite-infested rug.

Instead of pressing Petiot about the contradictions in his statement about why he obtained the lime, Dupin asked Petiot yet again to identify his colleagues.

"You know well that I am not going to give them to you," Petiot replied and shrugged, "because you would just indict them for complicity."

"I have given you my guarantee that I will not arrest them."

"I know that tune. You do not arrest them, but your buddy does."

Dupin told Petiot that he could help himself by citing names.

"All right, I'll give them to you—as soon as I'm acquitted."

"Do you think that you will be acquitted?"

"I should hope so. I've never had the least doubt. Besides, it is not you who will judge me. It is the gentlemen of the jury, and I have more confidence in them." The audience was relishing the give-and-take thrusts of the exchange. *L'Aurore* used this quote as a headline the following morning: I AM NOT IN DANGER OF DEATH.

=

WHEN the court reconvened after the recess, the crowd was even larger, prompting Petiot to complain that he did not have anywhere to lay his overcoat. The questioning turned to the first of the twenty-seven alleged victims, Marthe Khaït, the mother of a young patient, Raymonde Baudet, who disappeared in March 1942 before her planned testimony in the narcotics trial against the physician.

Véron not only represented this family as civil attorney, but he had previously served as Baudet's lawyer in the drug case. Ironically, it was Petiot who had recommended Véron to the Khaït family—and it was Marthe Khaït's disappearance that had first awakened his suspicions about the physician.

Petiot naturally dismissed Baudet's allegations that he had murdered her mother. "You know how it is. Drug addicts lie and cheat."

"Madame Khaït embarrassed you," Véron said, cutting to the heart of the issue. "Since the narcotics affair was discovered, you feared to be viewed as guilty. Summoned to justice, you risked being removed from the medical establishment." The letters of Khaït, he added, resembled those of another patient who disappeared, Van Bever.

"You have a great deal of talent," Petiot said. "I congratulate you. I shall have to send you more clients."

"It is less dangerous for you to send me clients than for me to send them to you." The audience laughed at the riposte.

Leser asked the defendant why he decided to help Khaït's daughter Raymonde Baudet.

"It's rather simple. She was a very lovely girl."

"Not at all. Raymonde Baudet was rather commonplace," Véron said.

"You knew her too late."

As the discussion rambled on, threatening to move even further away from the main topic, Véron tried to show that Petiot's actions were steeped in fear that he would lose his medical license for drug trafficking.

"Mlle. Baudet," Floriot interjected, "attempted to obtain heroin with the aid of a prescription of Dr. Petiot, which was rubbed out with a corrector and then rewritten. Where is Petiot's responsibility for her actions?"

"I have said that Madame Khaït was a threat to you," Véron said, turning to the defendant. "You have done away with her."

"Pure invention. Your delirious imagination will play bad tricks on you. Madame Khaït often expressed the desire to escape to the unoccupied zone."

"She had so little intention to leave that she did not even bring her ration cards, and left her laundry on the stove."

Khaït's husband, Floriot objected, had confirmed that she had long expressed the desire to leave for the unoccupied zone, and there was no documentation about the washing on the stove. As the two dueled, with the prosecuting advocate-general jumping in to support Véron, Petiot was relegated to the background. "What about me?" he asked. "Am I just a walk-on in this show?"

"What, are you bored?" Véron asked. Petiot reportedly yelled and kicked the box in response.

Leser adjourned the court at a quarter to six that evening. Some newspapers reported that Petiot had stumbled, falling into contradictions, showing ignorance about the Resistance, and generally losing credibility with his highly selective memory. By other tallies, he was winning over the inept prosecution, who appeared to be outmatched. Dupin's limited exposure to the enormous dossier was showing.

At the end of the day, David Perlman of the *New York Herald Tribune* managed to interview two of the jurors—a shocking feat only surpassed when he succeeded in questioning Président Leser himself. In an article entitled "Paris Bluebeard called 'Demon' by Two Jurors," Leser was quoted as calling Petiot "a demon, an unbelievable demon. He is a terrifying monster. He is an appalling murderer." Another juror called him intelligent, mad, and guilty, adding that "the guillotine is too swift for such a monster."

Jurors—and even the *président* of the tribunal—speaking about the defendant like this in the middle of a trial to the international press? Floriot now had grounds for a mistrial.

28.

TWO TO ONE

AFTER the two jurors cited in the international edition of the *New York Herald Tribune* were replaced, Président Leser opened on Wednesday, March 20, 1946, by declaring that, in contrast to previous days, he would not allow matters to get out of hand. The trial was already behind schedule. From now on, he would keep it on course and preserve an atmosphere of "calm and dignity."

One problem with the president's new strategy was that rushing through the proceedings sometimes caused a sloppy treatment of the material that left many questions unanswered, or even unasked. This was not in the interest of the prosecution, let alone justice, and the defense would have many opportunities to exploit the newfangled urgency.

No surprise, the rapid progress through the twenty-seven murder cases prohibited the audience—and worse, the jury—from fully appreciating the tragedy of each disappearance. The trial was ironically, as several journalists noted, making it harder to sympathize with the plight of the victims. Indeed the last five years of world war had desensitized many people who had lived through the Holocaust, the ferocious fire-bombing raids, and an array of horrors that left between fifty and sixty million people dead. One of the trial's low points was when Dupin protested that "human life is sacred" and the audience laughed.

After a short questioning about the disappearance of Van Bever, which prompted Petiot to launch into digressions on the young man's drug abuse and sex life, Dupin turned to the Guschinow case. Petiot admitted accepting the Polish furrier as a client in his escape organization, but denied that he had murdered him. He testified to helping him flee Paris, referring him to Robert Martinetti, "the expert in clandestine passages across the Spanish border."

Petiot told the court how he met Martinetti, claiming to treat him for "an affliction I don't care to name," a tactic that the physician often used to discourage further questions about his relationship with alleged associates or victims.

"Where is Guschinow now?"

"In South America."

"Explain to us why no one has found him."

"You are forgetting that Argentina is a German colony. A Polish man is not going to draw attention to himself there."

Floriot asked if the prosecution had searched for Guschinow, because he did not see any evidence in the dossier of investigators being sent to South America.

Dupin replied that the *juge d'instruction* had investigated.

The dossier, Floriot objected, only contained evidence that Madame Guschinow had written to two people in Argentina asking if they knew her husband's whereabouts; of course they did not, the defense counsel added, "any more than you have seen ninety-nine percent of the people in Paris."

Petiot interrupted with his assertion that he had received three letters or cards from Guschinow in Buenos Aires, written on the stationery of the Alvear Palace Hotel. The defendant rambled on about the light blue color of the paper and how people in South America open letters from the side, not the top.

When Leser asked if he had been paid for arranging Guschinow's departure, Petiot answered no, before correcting himself and explaining that he had asked the furrier for ermine for his wife. Guschinow had instead given him five sable coats, which he later learned were rare and worth 100,000 francs. The expensive furs found on Petiot's property were, in other words, gifts in appreciation of his services. Petiot seemed to be holding back a sob as he related the value of the alleged present.

The civil attorney representing Guschinow's widow, Maître Jacques Archevêque, asked about the false passport and papers. They were impeccable, Petiot said, "as if requested by Hitler himself."

"Why did you advise Guschinow to remove all his initials from his laundry?"

"It's elementary . . . that is, provided that you served in the Resistance."

"I know the Resistance better than you do," Dupin interrupted.

"Perhaps, but not from the same end [of the gun]."

As Petiot scored again with the audience, Archêveque tried to put the physician back on the defensive by demanding that he identify the members of his group.

"Again?" Petiot asked, launching into a lengthy monologue about how the prosecution and civil attorneys were making a mockery of French justice and causing the French people to look like buffoons. This was typical of the proceedings on the day Leser said he would take control of the trial.

THE cases of the nine gangsters and prostitutes were in a different category because Petiot did not deny killing them. In fact, he admitted to "executing" them and used this fact to support his overall defense, namely that he worked for the French Resistance and only liquidated traitors and collaborators who served the Gestapo.

"Jo the Boxer wanted to leave for Argentina with a woman and a friend," Petiot explained. "He handed Fourrier twenty-five thousand francs per person. The first to travel was François the Corsican, and he wanted to leave with a woman. The scene took place behind the Madeleine." Ten members of Fly-Tox, he said, "played the German police trick," referring to their tactic of impersonating the Gestapo. François the Corsican then supposedly confessed to working for Lafont and the French Gestapo on rue Lauriston. "Hence, the execution."

Leser asked Petiot for details.

"My, you have sadistic tastes!" Petiot said, in a faux-scandalized, if delighted, tone that amused the audience. Claiming not to have been present, Petiot said that he only knew that the gangster's head had been smashed with a bludgeon made from a rubber pipe filled with lead, sand, and the spokes of a bicycle.

According to Petiot, Jo the Boxer made an "awful scene." He had tried to excuse his behavior by claiming to be a poor man who had gone astray, and then allegedly offered Fly-Tox 400,000 francs to spare his life. He also vowed to betray Lafont. Jo and the two women who accompanied him, Annette and the unidentified woman, were shoved into the truck. Along the way, one of the women took out a revolver and "gave us some heat." All three were buried at Vincennes.

Adrien the Basque, on the other hand, had resisted arrest. "We had to stick a gun in his kidneys to force him into the truck." Later, at rue Le Sueur, the gangster pulled a dagger and stabbed one of his men near the liver. Adrien was executed. "It was true butchery." Petiot asked the *président* to show the court the photograph of the notorious tough guy he was proud to have killed.

Dupin acknowledged that the gangsters had worked for the Gestapo, but asked why Petiot had to kill the women. His answer provoked gasps of horror: "What would you want us to do with them?"

Realizing how his answer had been understood, Petiot elaborated: "They were mistresses of Gestapo agents. They would have denounced us."

"What gave you the right to judge and execute people?"

"If there had been a *procureur de la République* at the time, we would gladly have let him take the job. It was not a very pleasant one."

Floriot intervened on his client's behalf. Three of the men worked for the Gestapo, he reminded, and the fourth, Zé, operated a brothel for German officers. "Why, then, would they want to leave France?"

"It is very simple," Dupin said. "They were sought by the police."

"Do you really believe that a member of the Gestapo would be afraid of the French police?"

"I respect human life in any case, Maître."

"Do you respect the life of a member of the Gestapo?"

This was a delicate subject. In the awkward silence, Leser asked Petiot how much money he had made by killing these gangsters and prostitutes. Petiot said that his group did not work for material gain and did not receive a sou. This was another contradiction, which, in the rush, was not rigorously pursued.

Adrien the Basque had sewn 1 million francs into the shoulder pads of his suit, Dupin said, and his fellow gangsters carried another 3 or 4 million, not to mention the fees they paid for the alleged journey to Argentina.

Président Leser agreed to open the suitcase to see if Adrien's jackets had in fact been ripped or altered in any way. As the clerk of the court, Wilmès, tried to remove the suitcase, the towering stack of evidence started to sway. Leser called for an immediate recess. Wilmès later admitted that he had feared that the suitcases might fall on him.

Petiot suggested that the guards remain in the room to prevent any theft. Turning to Floriot, he joked that if the court did in fact find a million francs, would he receive ten percent?

WHEN the court reconvened, the clerk opened seal number 54, a yellow suitcase with black leather corners that contained the clothes and personal belongings of Adrien the Basque. A musty odor escaped the old suitcase, as the usher rummaged through its contents looking for the gangster's suit. When he found the jacket in question, Petiot snatched it and displayed it for the court, triumphantly pointing out that the garment was intact. Petiot grabbed another one. "Same thing," he said, "not unsealed, very sure of that."

Once again, instead of trying to poke holes in the defense, Dupin retreated, this time moving on to what should have been more solid ground. "The Wolffs were Jews who fled the German repression. They were one hundred percent Resistants."

"They were Germans," Petiot said. "They came from Berlin."

"That's false," the Wolff family lawyer, Maître Jacques Bernays, interjected. "The Wolffs left Holland on June 12, 1942, and I have obtained a number of witnesses that prove that they lived in fear of reprisals from the Gestapo."

Floriot countered with a police report written by Inspector Battut that documented the Wolffs' arrival in France with a passport issued in Berlin identifying them as "refugees." Jews who feared for their lives because of state-sanctioned terror, Floriot added, rarely applied to that government for a passport. In Paris, they "hid in a hotel requisitioned by the Germans."

"They hid themselves the way I did when I was newly married," Petiot said. "I pulled the sheets over my head and said to my wife, 'Try to find me.' "

In the ensuing laughter, Dupin neglected to call out Floriot for omitting one important fact: The Wolffs' passport was not issued in 1942, as it appeared in the discussion, but nine years before.

Petiot admitted to killing the Wolffs, as well as the Jewish couple that followed them, Gilbert and Marie-Anne Basch. They were a similar case, Petiot said, and therefore received the same fate.

"What about the Schonkers, the parents of [Marie-Anne] Basch?"

Petiot mocked the prosecutor. "I don't know anything about them, but if it makes you happy, you can put them on my account. They came from the same bunch, and if I had met them I would have killed them."

All of these Jewish families, Petiot added, had been sent to him by Eryane Kahan, whom the defense would present as a German agent trying to infiltrate Petiot's Resistance organization.

"Why didn't you kill Eryane Kahan, then, if you knew she was collaborating with the Germans?"

Petiot wanted her to send him more traitors. "If Kahan had sent me a hundred, like the Wolffs and the Baschs, I would have killed all one hundred. Then, Kahan would have been the hundred-and-first."

The press, now keeping score of the trial like a soccer match, generally handed the victory to Petiot. The prosecution was failing even to establish that Jews fleeing Nazi persecution were not Gestapo agents.

Petiot had had a good day indeed. After three days, he was winning by most accounts two to one.

At the end of the session, when two elegant women left the courtroom, one turned to the other and said that she had "never been more amused." Overhearing the comment, a thin man in a shabby suit shouted at the women and attacked. He was, it was later learned, an Auschwitz survivor who had lost almost his entire family in Nazi death camps.

29.

INSIDE MURDER HOUSE

I AM ONE OF THOSE VICIOUS PEOPLE WHOM WORK AMUSES.

—Marcel Petiot

ON Thursday, March 21, 1946, the first official day of spring, the trial continued with the wrap-up of the *président's interrogatoire* and ended with the calling of the first witnesses. There were as usual many heated debates and lengthy digressions, including Petiot's story of a Nazi attempt to capture a Resistant, who had parachuted into the farmlands outside Lyon, by mobilizing a force of "four hundred prostitutes." Leser repeatedly interrupted, insisting that Petiot stay on subject.

Very little new information emerged this day. Petiot at one point said that he had handed over Yvan Dreyfus to his so-called chief, Robert Martinetti, near the Place de la Concorde and watched the two men walk away in the direction of the Naval Ministry. This statement contradicted his previous account, namely that he left Dreyfus with his comrades at rue Le Sueur, but the prosecution again failed to force him to explain the discrepancy.

Petiot was instead allowed to tell the court how he had stood up to his Gestapo interrogators in prison. When they questioned him about Dreyfus, for instance, Petiot boasted of his answer: "If he's a Jew, what difference does it make to you that he disappeared? If he's an informer, you'll soon find another. I was risking my neck, Monsieur le Président, but I was having a lot of fun."

When Leser asked about Petiot's brother's concern for the fate of Yvan Dreyfus, Petiot admitted that Maurice had been a client and friend of the Dreyfus family, and he had tried to convince Yvan's father to intervene on his behalf. This was not followed to any significant conclusion, and the jury never heard Nézondet's allegation that Maurice claimed to have seen Dreyfus's body in June 1943 on top of the pile of cadavers at his brother's basement.

Before the jury had time to appreciate the tragedy of this disappearance, Floriot declared for the court that a Gestapo file from 1943 confirmed that Dreyfus had served as "an informer of the Gestapo." As a result, Floriot said, "there is no need to feel sorry over the fate of Yvan Dreyfus."

Président Leser, the advocate-general Dupin, and the Dreyfus family attorney, Maître Véron, all objected to this statement. Véron questioned the accuracy of the file, reminding the court of Dreyfus's patriotic record: how he had returned to France in 1939 to fight the Germans, only to be arrested when he tried to escape to England and join de Gaulle.

"Dreyfus was a traitor four times over: a traitor to his race, a traitor to his religion, a traitor to his country, and a traitor . . . ," Petiot began, before Leser, Véron, and Dupin all again protested loudly. The correspondent for the *Sydney Morning Herald* described the scene in the courtroom: "Petiot ranted, roared, stamped his feet and waved his fists to the accompaniment of quarrels among counsel as fights broke out in the public gallery."

As tensions remained high, Leser turned to the Kneller case, the last discovery before the investigation officially closed in the fall of 1945. Would Petiot really claim that Kneller, a veteran of the French Foreign Legion, was a collaborator? Was his seven-year-old son, René, also a collaborator?

Kurt Kneller was his patient, Petiot said, adopting his usual tactic of pointing out that "professional secrecy" precluded him from revealing the nature of his ailment. This argument was wearing thin, and as for his professional secrecy, that had not stopped him in other instances.

Petiot then boasted of how much he had allegedly helped the Kneller family. He had secured them false identities, one Alsatian, the other

Belgian, and advised them to carry two bottles of cognac to give the guides who would escort them across the border. He had even loaned the family money to buy railway tickets to Orléans for the first part of the journey. Given these services, and the fact that the Knellers still owed him 2,000 francs for previous medical treatment, Petiot had asked the family to leave their furniture with him as collateral.

Asked about the lack of communication from the Kneller family describing their safe arrival and establishment of a new home, Petiot said that they were ungrateful. This answer, however, did not address the question of why the Knellers had not contacted other family members.

Leser asked about the child.

"Yes," Petiot said, "he was a delightful boy."

" 'Was' is the operative word," Dupin said, noting that his pajamas were found at rue Le Sueur.

Floriot instructed his client not to respond.

"Those must be the pajamas that the kid slept in the last night," Petiot answered anyway. Calm as usual, he proceeded to explain that the family did not want to begin their journey with "dirty laundry," especially when it bore their initials. He always instructed his clients not to carry any identification papers and to remove anything from their personal belongings that might cast doubt on the forged documents. As for the pajamas, Petiot asked, "Why would I have kept them?"

Dupin stood and, as if he were finally about to trap Petiot as many expected, said that Petiot's defense was "collapsing." But he offered no major revelation or rebuttal. He only noted that Petiot refused to answer any question about the Kneller family.

"That's false," the defendant replied, claiming that he had answered many questions on the subject and only stopped when "they wanted to make me sign a list of answers to 362 questions that had not been asked." To dramatic effect, he added, "I do not know if it is the habit of the justice to use such manners."

Floriot tried to silence his client by shouting over him. Petiot was correct, he said. The prosecution had never provided him with any list of "what was allegedly found in the suitcases."

At this point, Dupin interrupted, disputing the claim: "The *juge d'instruction* showed him the inventory several times. Petiot refused to answer."

"Why do you only say such inexactitudes? Petiot never saw that inventory. Show me the interrogation in the dossier. . . . If you can provide me with that, I'll immediately stop practicing law."

Elissalde whispered something to Dupin, who then said that the *juge d'instruction,* Ferdinand Golletty, had confirmed that morning that Petiot had seen the inventory several times.

"Well, then call him to the stand."

No one, Petiot repeated, had shown him the list or the suitcases. "You could have put anything in those suitcases."

Petiot had a point. Strictly speaking, he was correct when he stated that the police did not provide him with a list of contents—they had *offered,* but he had refused on the grounds that the police had never shown him the suitcases themselves, let alone opened them to reveal the contents. The seals on the suitcases, moreover, had been placed on them at a later date and removed several times without his or his attorney's presence. The contents had been handled by many investigators and even been exhibited to the public. Under the circumstances, Petiot had refused to sign any statement. Leser must have realized this, as he immediately called for a recess to evaluate the situation. The inventory of the suitcases was not discussed again.

THE first witnesses of the trial took the stand later that afternoon. The most effective one was Lucien Pinault, Massu's successor and the commissaire in charge at the time of Petiot's arrest. A broad-shouldered, heavily perspiring man who had, in the words of Pierre Bénard of *France-Soir,* the "face of a kindly boxer," Pinault testified that he had conducted extensive interviews with Resistance fighters, and not a single one had known or recognized Dr. Petiot or his alias Dr. Eugène. The police officers who gave evidence after him, however, added little new information.

Day five opened on a rainy Friday, March 22. Professor Charles Sannié, the director of the Identité Judiciaire, Legal and Police Identification, at the Natural History Museum in Paris, described the physical evidence uncovered at Petiot's town house. Jury and journalists alike listened intently, at least for the first part of the presentation. Many were restless because later that afternoon, the entire court would pack up, file into a long procession of cars outside the Palais de Justice, and reconvene at 21 rue Le Sueur. The "Circus Petiot" was going on tour.

René Floriot had proposed the temporary change of locale to demonstrate to the jury how much the police had distorted and exaggerated the claims about Petiot's building, which, the defense maintained, was to be converted after the war into a medical clinic. True, Petiot had also used the property temporarily for his antiques business and for the headquarters of his Resistance organization, but it was hardly an "execution chamber," as the newspapers during the Occupation reported and then embellished to distract a war-ridden city from its woes.

Before Professor Sannié could finish his testimony, several journalists left the courtroom, hoping to beat competitors to the remarkable photo opportunity of capturing the man accused of being France's most deadly serial killer arriving at the scene of the crime. Rue Le Sueur was already filling up with spectators. Parisian newspapers had reported the day's trip, complete with maps of the "chamber of horrors" in the middle of the elegant 16th arrondissement.

Rue Le Sueur had been blocked off from traffic, and Petiot's building roped off from pedestrians. Two hundred policemen, using wooden barricades, would try to hold back the curious spectators pushing their way forward to a better view. Other people looked out from balconies or upper-story windows, or took their conversations about the "murder house" with its death pit and triangular chamber to nearby cafés and bistros.

Just before two p.m., as the rain continued to fall, Président Leser, the magistrates, Floriot, Dupin, and all the attorneys, assistants, and members of the jury descended the monumental front steps outside the Palais de Justice and filed into the fifteen cars waiting outside. An escort of police motorcyclists led the procession from Place Dauphine over the Pont-Neuf to the Quai du Louvre, the Quai des Tuileries, and then the Place de la Concorde. Avoiding the busy Champs-Élysées, the chauffeurs maneuvered through a number of streets on the Right Bank unil they reached the Étoile, Avenue Foch, and finally rue Le Sueur.

At the town house, a handcuffed Marcel Petiot stepped out of the black limousine, the fifth one in the procession, wearing his tweed overcoat with collar turned upward in the slight drizzle and smiling to the photographers. Two plainclothes police officers, with the brims of their felt hats turned down, were at his side, escorting him to the building. Taunts and jeers were heard from the crowd.

Président Leser, raising his hand, called the reassembled court to Petiot's office. Judge, jury, prosecution, defense, civil parties, and the many relatives and spectators followed Professor Sannié into the room. No one, however, had thought to reconnect the electricity, and so the court met in the house of horrors by candlelight. "Truly enlightened justice," Petiot quipped.

With the defendant appearing perfectly at ease, Sannié walked the members of the court through rooms of the mansion filled with what a *Time* correspondent described as "a strange conglomeration of expensive Louis XVI furniture, human bones, and 600 volumes of murder mysteries." Pierre Scize of *Le Figaro* described the dilapidated building with knocked-over furniture and ripped-open divans as having "the leprous walls, the décor of a shady office, and the mezzanine of an abortionist drug trafficker." Debris threatened to soil clothes. One person slipped on rat excrement. Many people thought that they could still smell human rot.

The court essentially retraced an alleged victim's path. The triangular room was too small for everyone to fit in at once, and so they broke up into groups. When Leser, Dupin, Floriot, Sannié, Petiot, and a couple of jurors entered, the candle went out, and no one had a match to relight it. After an uncomfortable moment in the dark, a policeman finally arrived with a flashlight. One thing, however, was missing: the Lumvisor viewer that Petiot allegedly used to spy on his victims.

"Where is the viewer?" Floriot asked.

"I don't know," Sannié said.

"This is unbelievable," Floriot said, criticizing the prosecution for its handling of evidence under official seal.

"I would have preferred that the viewer had been here," Petiot said, because he wanted to explain its function. Turning to a specific juror, who seemed frightened at being addressed, Petiot offered to describe the lens. It was not a periscope, he said, but "a sort of telescope" that allowed him to see a certain part of the room from the outside: "Precisely where Monsieur le Président is now standing." The device would help him monitor his radiotherapy equipment, which he had planned to install in the room.

One of the jurors asked, if Petiot intended to use this viewer for medical purposes, why he covered the lens with wallpaper? Petiot explained that he had wanted to wallpaper the room but one of the workers had covered the lens by mistake. Another juror wondered if this small room could be used as a cell.

Petiot denied that with sarcasm, saying that it was impossible to detain anyone in here, let alone kill them in "this little hole." He turned to Président Leser: "Would you tell me how you would go about killing someone here?"

A member of the jury pointed out that a murder can take place in smaller places, like the truck Petiot claimed that his Fly-Tox organization used.

"Oh, obviously you can kill anywhere," Petiot said, losing his temper. He had admitted executing people, so what difference did it make where he killed them? "Stories like this are going to make us look like idiots to the rest of the world."

Yet the walls were thick enough to drown out any cries for help, it had been noted. Petiot explained the thick, soundproof walls as a protection against the radiation of his X-ray machines—he could not use lead, of course, as it was a very difficult substance to obtain during the war. No one asked why he did not wait for better materials, as he claimed he was not going to use the clinic anyway until after the war.

At times, during the visit, Petiot looked pale. Once or twice, losing his balance, he was forced to grab on to a nearby rail or on to Floriot's arm. After exiting into the courtyard and into the garage, Petiot again nearly stumbled. This time, he was standing at the edge of the lime pit. Several journalists witnessing the scene reported that Petiot had finally come to grips with the sheer magnitude of his crimes. Another one believed that he was mocking the tragedy.

It is more likely, however, that Petiot was suffering giddiness from a poor diet. As the Swiss journalist Edmond Dubois discovered, the defendant had barely eaten all day, or indeed the last five days, since the trial began. He had been picked up at prison before breakfast and returned to his cell after dinner. He had been subsisting on little more than a small bowl of soup and a slice of bread.

At this point, it was time to enter the basement. Professor Sannié continued explaining, like a tour guide, what they had found, pointing out its location and describing its state. "It is here at the bottom of these steps that I discovered pieces of cadavers," he said. "Next to the two furnaces you see there was half a human body, split in the middle. In the larger furnace were human remains burning and sizzling with human juices and blood oozing out from the heat."

Sannié also mentioned the bag, outside the landing, that contained "half a corpse."

Petiot interrupted, asking the expert to confirm that it was a German army mail sack.

Sannié thought it was a cement bag.

"This sack is under seal, isn't it?" Floriot asked.

Sannié did not answer.

"This is truly incredible."

There were certainly risks in moving the courtroom to this location, and many irregularities emerged, any one of which could cause a mistrial. In addition to the growing list of missing or misplaced evidence, the door to Petiot's town house had remained open; when someone tried to close it, Leser refused. It was a public trial, he said, not wanting to open a loophole for the defense. Yet, because he had insisted on the openness, the crowds eventually managed to swarm past the roped barriers and the police officers. Robert Cusin of *L'Aurore* compared the rush of spectators to a rugby scrum.

Several members of the public roamed the building virtually at will. "Do you want to see the boiler?" an elderly couple was overheard asking their granddaughter. A reporter was inspecting the stove closely enough with his flashlight to spot the hairs scorched into the grate. Another journalist witnessed members of the public urinating in a corner.

Souvenirs were snatched, like an ashtray from Petiot's office, medical brochures, and review journals, some of them with the physician's notes in the margins. Someone walked away with Petiot's copy of Céline's *Bagatelles pour un massacre;* another person with an early edition of Pascal. One man was seen rushing out of the building carrying a stack of Petiot's criminal novels and treatises. More disturbingly, papers were flung out of office windows. Leser's son was said to have uncovered a tibia. Prosecution lawyers were even photographed that day holding what one astonished reporter identified as "human shin bones in their hands." Some of the many alleged bones were likely chunks of quicklime left over from the retrieval of the remains from the pit.

Just after four o'clock that afternoon, as the expedition wound its way back to the front of the building, certain members of the audience started shouting, "Death to the assassin!" As for the jurors, the trip to 21 rue Le Sueur had not delivered the wave of sympathy that Floriot and Petiot had hoped. The so-called future clinic of the doctor had not seemed innocent, but rather more grim and horrific than ever.

30.

BLACK FINGERNAILS

THESE INJECTIONS, PETIOT SAID, WOULD RENDER US
INVISIBLE TO THE EYES OF THE WORLD.

—Michel Cadoret de l'Epinguen

PROFESSOR Sannié took the stand again in the short late-afternoon session at the Palais de Justice. Maître Jacques Bernays, the civil attorney representing the Wolff family, asked him about Petiot's statement that he had planned to put medical machinery in the triangular room. "It is absurd and ridiculous," Sannié answered. He could not squeeze an examination table into the small room, let alone bulky machinery.

Petiot protested that, while the room was small and he had used it to question traitors captured by his group, it had not served as a torture chamber. Nothing he said, however, addressed Sannié's point that medical equipment for his so-called clinic simply would not fit into the room. Floriot came to his client's assistance, reminding the court that there was no evidence whatsoever to support the hypothesis that the triangular room was a torture chamber or prison cell. There was not even a sign of a struggle or any attempt to escape its confines, as surely would be the case if the room had been used as the prosecution claimed.

"Did you find any of Petiot's fingerprints on any of the objects taken from rue Le Sueur?" Floriot asked.

"No, we did not find any of his fingerprints."

It was an astonishing revelation. Not only were Petiot's fingerprints lacking, but Sannié further testified that the ones found on-site remained unidentified.

Georges Massu, then serving as commissaire of Grandes Carrières in the 18th arrondissement, followed Sannié to the stand, his left hand and wrist still healing from his suicide attempt. After the tour of rue Le Sueur, his testimony proved anticlimactic. Floriot hounded him about the missing bag that had been found at rue Le Sueur with half a body inside. Massu thought it had been a potato sack. Floriot and Petiot both said it was actually a German mailbag, with the implication that it was the Germans who brought the bodies to rue Le Sueur.

When Floriot asked where the bag was now, Massu said that he thought it was with the Identité Judiciaire. The commissaire added little new substance to the trial, prompting several journalists to criticize him for testimony that seemed vague, imprecise, and even contradictory. "Why do these civil servants, nine times out of ten, cut such pathetic figures?" asked Pierre Scize of *Le Figaro*. The least difficulty, he added, "sends them hiding behind each other."

Massu would later defend himself against these charges. Although he had not succeeded in arresting Petiot, he had identified the murderer, uncovered the evidence to bring him to trial, apprehended several accomplices, and identified a number of Petiot's alleged victims. It was his team that had established the basic parameters of the case. Massu was proud of his work, he said, even if he never had the chance to interrogate Petiot, as he had long wanted.

On Saturday, March 23, the trial resumed at one o'clock in the afternoon, drawing probably the largest crowd yet. Newspaper accounts of the court's relocation to rue Le Sueur had evoked more curiosity and attracted even more members of high society. Rainier, the heir to the Principality of Monaco, and Laure, the wife of the provisional president of France, Félix Gouin, were among those who came *à la Petiot* as if it were the theater. The duke of Windsor, it was said, had written Leser to ask permission to attend the trial.

Just before the *président* opened the proceedings, a man fainted and the ushers struggled in the packed room to remove him to safety. After the delay, Commissaire Massu's assistant, Inspector Marius Battut, took the stand, carrying a stack of notes. He had handled many of the details of the investigation, including the discovery of the suitcases in

Courson-les-Carrières and the identification of many victims. The inspector was able to hold his ground.

When asked if the Wolffs and the Basches had served as Gestapo informers, Battut was adamant: "I can assert the contrary under oath."

After a heated exchange that ended with Floriot forcing Battut to admit that Dreyfus had been working for the Gestapo, Floriot asked the witness if the suitcases the police found were ever shown to the victims' families.

"To my knowledge, no."

"Why not?"

"Maître, you are forgetting that we were under the Occupation." It was difficult to imagine Nazi authorities making an effort to help families of Jews, criminals, or other people who had tried to escape.

Floriot asked about Lafont's visit to Massu and the identification of the silk shirts that had belonged to Petiot's now acknowledged victim, Adrien Estébétéguy. "I am not well informed on that matter," Battut said. He knew that Lafont was interested in the fate of some of his men who had posed as German police and committed a number of robberies. All of them went missing, he said, except for "a man named Lombard, who did not disappear."

"Are you sure?" Petiot asked, the tone and timing of his question making some wonder if this man should be considered victim number 28 in the docket.

Despite the impression Petiot's comments made, this man was not his victim. Charles Lombard, or "Paul the Beautiful," had fled France, where he was wanted for charges of "intelligence with the enemy."

"Your investigation was conducted very hastily, Inspector," Floriot said.

"I did not have a dozen secretaries to prepare my work, maître," Battut said, glancing over at the defense counsel, who was supported by the "Floriot boys" and a number of other assistants who had joined them that day. The audience appreciated the remark.

"Yet you have a dozen inspectors who work under your orders," Floriot said.

"Would you like to inform us," Petiot interjected, "of how many patriots you arrested and sent to the Germans to be shot?"

Inspector Battut glared at the defendant.

"Of course," Petiot answered for the officer. "There were too many to count."

"Who is the criminal here?" Véron asked.

In rapid succession, three other police inspectors were called to the stand that afternoon to testify that the investigation could find no confirmation of Petiot's claims of being a Resistance fighter. A Resistant, Captain Henri Boris, also confirmed that the group Fly-Tox was "completely unknown to Fighting France." Petiot countered by arguing that his group was independent of the mainstream Resistance forces based in London.

After Jean Hotin's unimpressive testimony, which added little to the trial except comic relief, Captain Urbain Gouraud, formerly of the Villeneuve-sur-Yonne police department, called Petiot "an adventurer without scruple" and boasted of issuing him seven tickets. He also testified about his long-held suspicions that Petiot had killed his earlier lover, Louisette Delaveau.

Floriot then pointed out a problem with the witness's testimony: "Before he accused Petiot, do you know how many other people he knew were guilty? . . . Nine, gentlemen, nine. If they had not closed the case, he would have accused the entire town."

At the end of the first week of the trial, the police investigation appeared botched, hastily conducted, and riddled with many errors and omissions. The prosecution, likewise, looked lost in the thirty-kilo dossier. Swiss journalist Edmond Dubois summed up the strange dichotomy: While "the Parisian newspapers continue to treat Petiot as a monster and publish his sniggering photograph with the menacing eyes, the conversations that take place in the corridors [of the Palais de Justice] during the intermissions of the trial far from reflect that unanimity."

=

A FTER a welcome rest on Sunday, the trial resumed on day seven, Monday, March 25. First to take the stand was the widow Renée Guschinow, a small blond woman dressed in black mourning veils who looked young and thin—"thin as an umbrella," one journalist put it. With quivering voice, she retraced the reasoning behind her husband's decision to leave Paris and how Dr. Petiot had invited him to rue Le Sueur to discuss his escape to Argentina.

Guschinow's attorney, Maître Archevêque, turned to Petiot and asked why he took his client to rue Le Sueur if he was a patient at rue Caumartin.

Petiot replied that he could not organize flights where his wife lived, his housekeeper worked, and medical practice flourished. The physician added with sarcasm that he would like to invite the court to his apartment, but he would have to give the matter some thought because of the mess everyone made at rue Le Sueur.

"You are very intelligent," Archevêque said.

"You know, Maître, intelligence is only relative."

Archevêque asked about the injections Petiot had allegedly administered, wondering why they would be necessary for a clandestine journey to Argentina.

"That's totally idiotic," Petiot said. The Australian INS correspondent for the trial remarked that Petiot seemed again to turn angry. "There were certainly no health regulations for admittance to Argentina. Everyone who thinks, like you, that I gave injections has just read the newspapers."

Madame Guschinow testified that her husband told her that Petiot would take care of all the details and he was not concerned, except for the injections.

"Nonsense!" Petiot interrupted. "I gave him injections for a year. Why would he be worried?" He accused her of making up the story based on an article she read in *Paris-Soir*.

Leser warned Petiot to choose his words wisely. The witness was testifying under oath.

"No, that is just what she is not doing," Petiot said.

Leser, grabbing the edge of the table, lunged forward in anger at the defendant for this latest defiance. Petiot, however, was correct. The witness had not been sworn in; as a party to a civil suit, she was not legally required to take an oath.

Maître Archevêque asked about the handwriting in the postcards and letters, which appeared shaky and more strained than usual. He was leading into his theory that Petiot had kept Guschinow as hostage for three days, forcing him to write letters to his wife.

"It's normal," Petiot said, brushing aside the irregularities in the script. "He was a sick man on the point of making a long journey." Petiot then challenged the witness, her attorney, and the prosecution to produce a single piece of Guschinow's clothing or jewelry found at his apartment.

"But a suitcase that he purchased was found there," Dupin said.

"I'm the one who told you that," Petiot said. The suitcase had been left behind, he added, because it was too heavy for the upcoming journey. "You do not cross three frontiers with a weight like that. I then suggested to Guschinow that he should exchange that suitcase for a smaller bag."

Madame Guschinow recounted how she went to Paris every month to ask Petiot about her husband. Each time, the physician told her that his business was thriving in Buenos Aires, and suggested that she sell her belongings and join him. Other than the first communication written in code, Petiot would not show her any of the letters, because he claimed that they contained confidential information about his organization and he had destroyed them.

Petiot accused her again of lying and of wanting to remain in Paris because she had a new lover. Floriot agreed, suggesting that she had memorized her testimony and repeated certain phrases verbatim. Several people began speaking at once.

After order was restored, Floriot wanted to know why Guschinow did not join her husband.

"My health, my business," she began, before Petiot again interrupted.

"She had found a younger lover."

"But you had confidence in Dr. Petiot?" Floriot asked.

"Yes, I had confidence in him."

"You said during the investigation that you didn't leave because you didn't have faith in the doctor."

Petiot asked if she knew about her husband's condition and the injections he received for his treatment. The way he said the words made it clear that Guschinow had caught a venereal disease. Leser did not like the way the questioning was proceeding. There were many witnesses scheduled to appear, he said, and asked Guschinow to stand down. Otherwise, he added, the trial might drag on until July.

After Guschinow's former associate Jean Gouedo testified about the fortune that his friend had carried and that the furs in Petiot's possession were certainly not gifts, Floriot went on the attack. He wanted to know if a court-appointed commission had been sent to Buenos Aires to look for Guschinow.

When Dupin dodged the question, Floriot insisted that the prosecution had had ample opportunity to investigate Guschinow's whereabouts and neglected this simple means of verification. He was relentless. Leser said that the court should "send a telegram."

"No one is dead or missing," Floriot started, before members of the audience laughed and he realized how the words sounded.

"No one is dead or missing *in the Guschinow case,*" Floriot corrected himself. "Let's first make these confirmations in Argentina."

O NE of the more interesting witnesses in the trial took the stand that day. Michel Cadoret de l'Epinguen, a thirty-three-year-old interior designer, was one of the few known people who had attempted to escape through Dr. Eugène but, after gaining admission, backed out. He had left Paris with his wife and son by another underground route in July 1943. When the family returned to the capital after the Liberation, they found that they had been listed among Petiot's victims. Cadoret de l'Epinguen had a valuable perspective indeed.

The witness explained that he had been referred to Petiot through

Robert Malfet, a chauffeur who had been arrested after the Liberation with more than 300,000 francs and a fortune of jewels in his possession, in addition to fur coats, clothes that did not match his size, and a collection of fifty-five newspaper articles about the Petiot case.

Malfet, the witness said, had spoken of the process ahead, including the acquisition of false papers, the stay in a town house belonging to the organization, and the necessity of injections to enter Argentina. These injections, Petiot said, would "render us invisible to the eyes of the world."

Petiot scoffed. "The mad doctor with his syringe. It was a dark and rainy night. The wind howled under the eaves and rattled the windowpanes of the oak-paneled library."

Leser admonished him. "Petiot, please."

Cadoret and his wife, a psychiatrist, had been skeptical of the need for papers and injections, and more than a little concerned about Petiot's knowledge of drugs like peyote. Petiot himself seemed to be under the influence, as did the woman Cadoret called "his secretary, Eryane." There was only one Eryane close to Petiot in 1943: Eryane Kahan, the alleged recruiter who herself would soon take the stand.

In December 1944, Cadoret had told the police that he and his wife had met with Kahan. On their way to the hair salon, the three of them passed a number of German soldiers, who, worryingly, saluted Kahan and exchanged a few words in German with her. The Cadorets had also been concerned about Petiot's vague responses and the inability to get a straight answer from him about the place of departure and the place of arrival in Argentina. What particularly disturbed them, however, was something else: "He had black stains under his fingernails, which we found unusual for a doctor." Petiot laughed again.

The witness testified that they had also been surprised that a supposed member of the Resistance operating a philanthropic organization would charge a fee of 50,000 francs for passage out of the country.

Wasn't the charge, Petiot asked, at first 90,000?

Cadoret did not remember.

"It's very important," Petiot said. "That's what saved your life!"

At these words, members of the audience shrieked in horror. Petiot tried to clarify his meaning, claiming that he asked such a high fee to discover if the witness was a real candidate for departure. The Cadorets' refusal showed that they were not Gestapo informers and so he had reimbursed them for their expenses.

Floriot wanted to underscore this point. Who had backed out first? Cadoret admitted that he contacted Eryane Kahan to decline, but she immediately announced that Petiot would have no further dealings with him and his family.

The defense counsel had scored again, but the question remained why Petiot would, all of a sudden, refuse a client who passed his test for not working for the Gestapo. Wasn't he claiming to be operating an escape organization, and if not, what did this new admission mean for his assertion that he had helped other clients reach South America? The questions were unfortunately not addressed.

"Will we have the pleasure and honor of seeing Madame Cadoret this afternoon?" Petiot asked, as the witness left the stand.

The next man to testify was Joseph Scarella, a maître d'hôtel at the Café Weber, and a Petiot patient who had, in fact, with his physician's help, escaped deportation to Germany. Petiot had written a false certificate claiming that Scarella suffered from syphilis. Scarella also told how he had wanted to flee because there was not much work for a master chef in Occupied Paris who did not want to serve the Germans. When he approached Petiot about departure, Scarella said, he was told to bring 100,000 francs and some jewels as a precaution because it sometimes took a lot of time before people found work.

Why didn't the Scarellas attempt to leave with Petiot's escape organization? He was prepared to depart, the witness said, but his wife had refused.

By the time Scarella left the stand, it was already a quarter after five in the afternoon and the witnesses scheduled to testify next had left the courtroom. Leser adjourned the court. It had been another long day in a trial that only seemed to become more sensational and controversial, and no closer to resolution.

31.

"A TASTE FOR EVIL"

THE COLDEST FISH AND THE MOST BRILLIANT CRIMINAL,
YET THE MOST CONVINCING TALKER THAT I EVER MET IN MY
LONG CAREER IN THE FIELDS OF CRIME AND MEDICINE.

—Dr. Paul on Marcel Petiot

O N Tuesday, March 26, the courtroom was again packed beyond capacity in what was arguably the largest audience yet. This was the highly anticipated session devoted to expert witnesses, including the main attraction, the celebrated forensic scientist Dr. Albert Paul. He would make jury and audience alike, as *Le Pays* put it, "grit its teeth," but his testimony would not be as shocking or as pivotal as it had been in the Landru case.

Wearing a gray tweed suit with a white handkerchief in his left breast pocket, Paul described how the murderer had scalped his victims and removed the facial mask with a single cut, making a circular incision from the chin to the hairline. He then proceeded to dismember the body. Despite the detailed study of the remains, however, there were many fundamental questions that Paul and his forensic team could not answer. Wisely, Dupin, the prosecutor, decided to introduce the uncertainties before the defense could exploit them.

Paul explained that they found three main types of human remains: cadavers more or less intact, burned and broken fragments, and debris in "one hundred bony pieces." The latter included four collarbones, ten shoulder blades, seven humerus bones (upper arm from shoulder to elbow), and five ulna and four radius bones (forearm). There were three complete sternums, a fourth sternum without an appendix, and one extension of the sternum known as a xiphoid process. The forensic team had also uncovered one complete pelvis, eight ilia (the largest bone in the pelvis), and seven sacrums (the triangular bone at the spine, pelvic cavity, and hips), as well as two kneecaps, two femora (thighbone), five tibias (shinbone), and two fibulas (calf bone). There were two "globular skulls," both with an attached mandible, or lower jaw, and a number of scalps, in red, blond, brown, and almost black hair.

All the bones at rue Le Sueur were human. Only two bodies, however, were found complete, both "very mummified." One was a man approximately forty to fifty years of age with an estimated height of five-foot-three. The other was of a woman, twenty-five to thirty, just under five-foot-six.

"How many bodies were there in all?" Dupin asked.

"We were able to conclude that the number of victims was a minimum of ten, but the vast amounts of hair recovered suggested a much greater number."

Floriot asked if any white hair had been found on the premises of rue Le Sueur. "No, not a scrap," Paul answered. This was significant because one of Petiot's alleged victims, Dr. Braunberger, had white hair, and another one, Joachim Guschinow, had some white strands.

"Were you able to determine the age and gender of the victims?"

"Five were men, five women," Paul said. The tallest victim was a male with a height of 1.78 meters (5'10") and the shortest, a female of 1.50 (4'11"). The height was estimated based on measuring the humerus, radius, cubitus, and tibia bones. As for the ages of the victims, Paul testified that they ranged from twenty-five to fifty. The youngest was a female and the oldest a male; in fact, the male victims tended to be significantly older than the female and also, as his report put it, "robust." It was difficult to add more specifics because the quicklime had devoured the bodies for too long a period before the discovery.

"What was the date of the murders?"

"We can say that these are old cadavers, but we cannot specify further because the level of putrefaction is such that we cannot determine the exact date when the subject was killed. In effect, the debris was in such a state of decomposition that the toxicology examination failed to provide definite conclusions."

"What was the cause of death?"

Paul admitted that his team could not establish that either. "Not a single bullet wound or fracture of the skull. That leaves the possibility of asphyxiation, stabbing, strangling, and poison. There's no way to tell. Could it have been an injection? Perhaps, but I am not in the habit of reveling in hypotheses." Looking at the dissections, each cut beginning, as far as he could tell, in the same spot on the spine, the limbs, or the face, Paul believed that it must have been the work of someone highly skilled in anatomy, almost certainly a physician.

"Didn't you make statements about similar, dismembered bodies that were found in the Seine in 1942?" Dupin asked.

"Yes," Paul said, noting that for a period of eight months, between May 1942 and January 1943, the Seine had been "stuffed" with bodies and body parts in small parcels that had been fished out at a frightening rate. At that time, he further stated, "I shared my fears with a colleague that 'it must be a doctor who did this and I am afraid that it might be one of my students.' "

As he had earlier told Commissaire Massu, Paul was struck in particular by the scalpel marks on the thighs of the cadavers, both of the victims on rue Le Sueur as well as those retrieved from the Seine. He explained that, when he changed instruments or took a break during an autopsy or dissection, he had the habit of not laying the scalpel on the table. Instead, he would stick it in the right thigh or arm of a subject "like a dressmaker sticks a pin in a pincushion." This was a safe way to prevent injury and contamination. "Well, the bodies that I scrutinized have precisely these punctures of the scalpel."

Floriot intervened, pointing out that Marcel Petiot had received only "mediocre" in his dissection course in medical school.

"That astonishes me," Paul said. "In any case, it is regrettable because he dissects very well."

"Pardon me," Floriot said. "You should say, 'The dissector dissects very well.' "

Two other forensic experts, Dr. René Piédelièvre of the Institut médico-légal and Professor Henri Griffon of the Toxicological Laboratory at the Préfecture de Police, were scheduled to appear on the stand that afternoon. Like Paul, Piédelièvre praised Petiot's skill with the scalpel. Later in his memoirs, he went further, calling Petiot simply his "colleague." At the trial, he offered no earth-shattering revelation. The bodies were simply too "putrefied and damaged by the quicklime" to draw many conclusions, including the time of death.

Petiot, who appeared to be taking notes, asked the witness if they could not have used a method based on insect larvae.

"Yes, the diptera and coleoptera lay eggs on corpses. By measuring the size of the larvae and examining their tracks as they burrow through the flesh, one can arrive at a fairly accurate estimation. In this case, the lime and fire had destroyed the traces of the insects."

"Yes, you know these things better than me, as I am not a forensic scientist," Petiot mumbled. "Diptera and coleoptera . . . hmmm. This is fascinating. Could you tell me more about it?" When Piédelièvre responded that the subject did not pertain to the case, Petiot agreed and invited himself over after the trial to discuss the matter further.

Professor Griffon then testified that he had not found any evidence of poison. But "that does not mean that there wasn't any," he added, noting that the small triangular room was well suited to serving as a gas chamber.

"But there was a gap of over two centimeters under the door," Floriot objected.

"It would have been easy to close it," Griffon said, suggesting a simple rug.

"That's only a hypothesis. Can you produce this rug?"

"If it were gas, then what kind of gas?" Dupin asked.

"Almost any one you would like, except perhaps lighting gas because we found no trace of equipment." Griffon then reminded the court that Petiot's apartment on rue Caumartin contained "a pharmaceutical arsenal of uncommon size" with an "abnormally high proportion of narcotics."

"They were used for painless deliveries," Petiot said.

"Did you find a single poison at rue Caumartin?" Floriot asked.

"Morphine."

"Morphine is not a poison."

"That depends upon the dose."

"Did you find any morphine at rue Le Sueur?"

"No."

"I see," Floriot said. "No poison at rue Le Sueur. No way to block the opening in this famous gas chamber of yours. Nothing at all? Thank you very much."

The psychiatrists who had examined Petiot came next, including Dr. Georges Paul Génil Perrin, who had noted Petiot's attempts to pretend he was insane to escape punishment.

"I have examined Petiot from a mental point of view," Génil Perrin said, "and found him endowed with a lively intelligence and a remarkable gift for repartee . . . ," a statement that drew laughter from members of the audience and prompted Dupin to note that he had observed this quality himself even without psychiatric training. Génil Perrin then testified about Petiot's troubled or "arrested moral development," before concluding, as in his previous report, that the defendant was "fully responsible for his acts."

Another psychiatrist, Dr. Paul Gouriou, testified that Petiot was not "a monster or a madman," but rather "perverse, amoral, a scamp and a simulator. In times of trouble, he has attempted to avoid prosecution by faking insanity." Petiot's "lack of moral education," he added, "has allowed him to develop a taste for evil."

Floriot objected that the doctor's patients found him quite the opposite.

"I know of doctors whose mental disequilibrium is expressed by an increased devotion to their patients."

"Did he pretend to be insane with you?" Floriot asked.

"No, he lied about many points, but not that."

"You concluded that Petiot completed his studies in a 'mysterious' fashion. Do you know his examination results?"

"I saw his grades. He had 'mediocre' in dissection," Gouriou said to laughter in the courtroom. "His thesis received the grade '*très bien*,' but that is done easily. A thesis can be bought if desired. At any rate, it is based on books and does not give an indication of the personal worth of a physician."

Floriot pointed out that the witness was making insinuations without proof. He then asked the expert if, in his examination of Petiot's relatives, he found anything unusual about his sister. After a slight hesitation, Gouriou said, "She is in good health."

"Sorry, but Petiot does not have a sister."

The courtroom erupted in laughter, prompting Leser to call for a recess.

THE trial recommenced with the prominent graphologist Professor Edouard de Rougemont, who was asked to testify about the handwriting of the letters supposedly sent by Van Bever, Khaït, Braunberger, and Hotin. In each case, Rougemont believed the letters were genuine, though the text was in disagreement with the actual sentiments of the writer. Rougemont detected a high degree of stress, probably even dictation under duress or the influence of drugs.

Floriot asked if the scholar could really draw these conclusions based only on looking at the handwriting. When Rougemont answered yes, Floriot scribbled something on his pad, ripped off the sheet, and handed it to the expert. Would he mind informing the court if Floriot believed what he had written? Rougemont read the paper and then refused to say anything. Floriot had written: "Monsieur de Rougemont is a great scholar who never makes a mistake."

"If we had asked Petiot to write out his story and Monsieur de Rougemont to read it, we could have dispensed with this whole trial," Floriot said, to another round of laughter in the courtroom.

Colonel André Dewavrin, director of the DGER intelligence service under General de Gaulle, was scheduled to testify. When the bailiff called his name, however, another man stood and announced that he represented Dewavrin. Président Leser was often criticized during the

trial for his relaxed courtroom, but he was not going to accept a spokes-
man for a witness. Floriot also objected, claiming that the defense was
counting on Colonel Dewavrin's testimony, because as de Gaulle's chief
of intelligence, he could officially confirm Petiot's work as a Resistance
fighter.

Instead, a witness with much greater potential for damaging Petiot
took the stand, Jacques Yonnet, who had published the article "Petiot,
Soldier of the Third Reich," which had played an important role in the
capture of the physician. Yonnet had also investigated Petiot's claims to
have fought Germans and their collaborators, and drafted his summary
for the court, which had concluded that Petiot had no Resistance credentials whatsoever.

Asked by Floriot about the newspaper article, Yonnet admitted that
the piece was based on a copy of a report that he claimed later to find out
had contained many falsehoods. He had published the article with the
caveat that he could not vouch for all the allegations. As for the investigation, which Floriot criticized for its lack of objectivity, Yonnet stood
by its results.

Petiot could not have known any of the people he mentioned, such
as Brossolette, Cumuleau, or the other members of Arc-en-Ciel. Yonnet and his colleague Brouard could not find a single person who had
heard of his so-called Fly-Tox organization, which moreover was not
included on the files of Fighting France that were housed at 76 Avenue
Henri-Martin. Fly-Tox, Yonnet concluded, had not existed other than in
Petiot's imagination.

Despite Yonnet's sweeping claim, the files of the Brigade Criminelle
show that several people had in fact heard of Fly-Tox, including the
widows of Brossolette and Cumuleau. Still, no evidence of the group's
existence has ever been made public, and, if Fly-Tox existed, did Petiot
really belong to it, or did he just exploit it for his own purposes?

It is unfortunate that Dewavrin did not appear at the Petiot trial. He
could have helped clear up the matter of Petiot's Resistance credentials,
or lack thereof. Instead, his absence only raised questions. Dewavrin
did not refer to the episode in his memoirs and never spoke of it, at least

publicly, except for one time. On that occasion, he gave a terse rejection of Petiot: "Organized Resistance has never, for any reason whatsoever, had dealings with Dr. Petiot."

Véron asked the defendant to elaborate on his claim of killing sixty-three people, thirty-three collaborators and thirty German soldiers. Beginning with the latter, Véron wanted to know how specifically Petiot had killed them. Petiot said vaguely that many of them had been his patients. Véron countered that Petiot was not authorized to treat German citizens.

"I refuse to tell you," Petiot said. "I did not work to earn a stripe or a decoration. When there are invaders, there are always avengers."

Véron persisted in his demands.

"I do not have to explain murders that I am not accused of committing. When I have been acquitted, you can indict me for the thirty *Boches* that I have taken down," Petiot said, his usual bluster likely strengthened by his belief that the trial was swinging in his favor. Actually, several reporters in the room agreed with him. Headlines the next day noted that Petiot's conviction looked doubtful.

Véron asked Petiot about his relationship to the Gestapo. Why did they not react to his so-called killings of German soldiers, and more important, once they had arrested him, why did they release him from prison? This was an important question that deserved more attention. Civilians arrested for helping evaders could expect no mercy from the Gestapo.

"Obviously," Yonnet said, "this man should have been shot."

"Monsieur Ibarne," Petiot said, using Yonnet's Resistance alias, "I saw you somewhere that you would not like me to mention."

"On the contrary, I demand that you say it, because I am sure that I have never seen you."

Petiot, who did not say a word, sat there beaming with a smirk that suggested that he held some valuable inside knowledge. Yonnet demanded that he answer.

"Do you not play tennis at the Racing Club?" Petiot asked, suggesting that Yonnet was affiliated with an institution requisitioned by the

Germans and favored by many elite French collaborators. No, Yonnet said, he did not play tennis and had never been to that club. Petiot made no rebuttal.

Yonnet's DGER colleague, Lieutenant Brouard, next testified that Petiot could not pick out Cumuleau in a group of photographs. Moreover, he reiterated the results of their investigation, which included no fewer than twenty-five instances where Petiot's testimony contradicted basic facts about the Resistance. By the time Leser adjourned the court at seven that evening, these last two prosecution witnesses had dealt harsh blows to Petiot's credibility.

32.

THE HAIRDRESSER, THE
MAKEUP ARTIST, AND
THE ADVENTURESS

PEOPLE WANT TO PORTRAY ME AS A PROCURER, PEOPLE
WANT TO PORTRAY ME AS AN ACCOMPLICE; WORSE, THEY
WANT TO PORTRAY ME AS AN AGENT OF THE GESTAPO.
THEY'VE CALLED ME A LOOSE WOMAN. I'VE BEEN CALLED
EVERYTHING. THEY'VE RUINED ME, AND NOW THEY
WANT TO DESTROY ME.

—Eryane Kahan

THE ninth day of the trial, March 27, the prosecution called
Petiot's alleged accomplices to the stand, including the hairdresser Raoul Fourrier, the makeup artist Edmond Pintard,
Marcel's brother Maurice, and his old friend René Nézondet. The witnesses certainly had a wealth of relevant information, but the challenge
for both prosecution and defense was ferreting it out and making sense
of testimony that often obscured more than it revealed.

When a guarded and taciturn Fourrier took the stand, Président
Leser returned to the question of his motives for bringing clients to
Petiot. Fourrier would not admit to anything other than that he had
helped what he believed was a patriotic organization. His confidence in
the integrity of the group was confirmed, he said, when the Gestapo
arrested Petiot and held him in prison for almost eight months.

Asked about the disappearance of the gangsters and their mistresses,

Fourrier said that he did not know that the men would bring the women with them. No, he had not asked many questions, because Petiot told him that the matter was confidential. He emphasized how little he in fact knew of the organization and that it was actually his colleague, Edmond Pintard, who went looking for travelers.

Pintard admitted scouring the bars and cafés of Montmartre for potential clients, generally soliciting by speaking "neither of business nor politics, but of everything and nothing." He confessed to recruiting all nine of the gangsters and their girlfriends. Like Fourrier, he seemed to believe that he was only helping people escape Nazi oppression.

At one point, Pintard testified that Fourrier showed him a letter or note from Jo the Boxer confirming his arrival in Buenos Aires. Petiot smirked and then, almost off the cuff, admitted that he had imitated Jo's handwriting and forged the note. This was a surprising confession, coming out, as it did, after the handwriting expert had concluded that other similar surviving letters were genuine. Petiot was apparently enjoying the sensation of showing up an authority, even one whose testimony might be said to work in his favor.

Marcel Petiot's oldest friend, René Nézondet, took the stand. His testimony—if not much more enlightening—was more damaging to the defendant. Just as he had told the Gestapo following his arrest with Petiot in May 1943, Nézondet said that he did not know anything at that time about Petiot's activities. It was in prison, he said, that he learned that the physician conducted "clandestine passages" and expected the Germans to shoot him. It was after his own release from prison, Nézondet said, that he learned what Petiot was really doing to his clients.

The realization had come in a conversation with Maurice Petiot. "The journeys begin and end at rue Le Sueur," Petiot had allegedly told him, before describing the "many suitcases, postdated letters, syringes, a formula for poison, and some bodies" that he found on the property. When Nézondet expressed his shock, calling the doctor a "monster," the younger Petiot had defended his brother as "a sick man" who needed treatment and insisted that Nézondet keep quiet about the information. Otherwise, he said, everyone would be shot.

Nézondet's date for this conversation with Maurice, July 1943, differed from the time of December 1943 that he had indicated to the police. Still, this was the most harmful testimony to Petiot that day, coming from a source close to the defendant. At the same time, Nézondet related how Maurice told him about finding several German uniforms at rue Le Sueur, though the question remained open whether this would ultimately help or hurt Petiot. Would this testimony, for instance, support his claim that he posed as a German policeman to arrest traitors, or did it perhaps indicate that the defendant had much closer ties to the Nazis than hitherto revealed?

When Maurice Petiot took the stand, he flat-out denied Nézondet's statements. He spoke softly and with considerable difficulty; he was then suffering from the late stages of throat cancer. Petiot admitted seeing German uniforms at his brother's property, but, he emphasized, he had never seen any bodies, poisons, syringes, or, in fact, anything disturbing. Certainly, he never said those things Nézondet claimed. Nézondet was simply carried away by his imagination.

Maître Charles Henry, the attorney representing the family of Paulette Grippay, asked the witness about the uniforms. "Were you not surprised to find all those clothes, particularly the German uniforms, as you stated?"

"No, I concluded that my brother had killed soldiers of the Wehrmacht."

"And what conclusion did you draw from the presence of the civilian clothes?"

"None."

Maurice Petiot would not, under any circumstances, provide testimony to hurt his brother, even if it came to the detriment of his own credibility. He admitted to delivering the lime to rue Le Sueur, as Marcel had asked, but maintained that the purpose was to whitewash the façade. He also admitted moving the suitcases to Courson-les-Carrières, claiming that he did not want them to fall into the hands of the Germans. Their origins and contents, he added, were never revealed to him. Maurice's loyalty to his brother was clear. As he left the stand, he was observed giving a quick smile to Marcel. The defendant looked down, or away.

The next witnesses were no more helpful in unraveling the complicated affair. Both René Nézondet's girlfriend, Aimée Lesage, and her friend, Marie Turpault, confirmed that Nézondet had told them about the bodies Maurice Petiot had found at rue Le Sueur. Lesage added that Georgette Petiot knew about them as well because Nézondet had told her in Aimée's presence. As a nurse, Lesage was also convinced that Madame Petiot's fainting bouts were contrived. Georgette Petiot, she believed, knew all along what her husband was doing.

The defense would dismiss this testimony as simply a witness protecting her boyfriend. The prosecution had not found any credible evidence, Floriot emphasized, to suggest that Georgette Petiot had any reason to doubt that her husband worked for the Resistance. Besides, despite the claims made on the stand that afternoon, no German uniforms were found in the suitcases, the basement closets of rue Le Sueur, or at any of Petiot's other properties around the capital.

"The longer this trial goes," Petiot said at this point, "the more confusing it becomes."

"Voilà," Leser said, to the amusement of the audience.

THE testimony of suspected recruiters and accomplices continued on the tenth day of the trial, when Eryane Kahan took the stand, looking every bit as glamorous as the newspapers had reported. Tall, with strawberry blond hair, Kahan wore a wide-lapeled brown suit, a wool crew-neck sweater, long silk gloves, and a fashionable round hat trimmed with otter fur and tipped at a slight angle. She walked up to the front of the courtroom slowly, carrying a stylish handbag. Her dark-tinted glasses made her resemble an incognito Greta Garbo. She looked like she was in her late twenties or early thirties, rather than her actual age of fifty.

This mysterious woman was suspected of sending nine victims, all of them fellow Jews, to the escape network. The defense would try to show that she worked for the Gestapo and only sent Petiot traitors attempting to infiltrate his organization. The prosecution would take the position that Kahan could have worked out of any number of motives, ranging from a desire for commission profit, to the altruistic hope that she was helping desperate people escape the Nazi Occupation. For the prosecution, she was no collaborator, and more to the point of the trial, neither were the people she sent Petiot. Audience and jury alike would hang on every word of this important witness.

Kahan was visibly nervous as she started to testify. In a husky voice with a strong Slavic accent, she described how she first met Petiot through her friend and lover, Dr. Saint-Pierre, a physician well known in the underground for his criminal clients and connections. The meeting took place in a back room at Fourrier's hair salon, where Dr. Eugène, as she put it, questioned her about "the circumstances of my friends and me." She admitted referring the Wolff, Basch, and Schonker families to the escape organization. All of these people, she said, were delightful.

Given the portrayal of these families by the defense, Leser asked the witness if they were really opposed to the Nazis.

"Of course, Mr. Président," Kahan said. "They were not only anti-Nazi, but they also lived in terror of being arrested. There was no doubt of their sentiments." Each of the Jewish families was so happy about the opportunity to leave Occupied Paris that they viewed Petiot "as their God." They had praised the altruistic Frenchman who operated the escape agency, at great personal risk, to help Jews that he did not know. One journalist in the audience noted that the defendant stopped staring absentmindedly at the ceiling when he heard these words and looked like he felt a sudden sharp pain in his chest.

Kahan also testified to her desire to leave Paris, but Petiot had opposed it for the reason that she could be useful to the Resistance movement. "I understand now what a wonderful pawn I was."

The witness proceeded to describe how she had adored Dr. Eugène for his patriotic work on behalf of the Resistance. Even when the story broke in March 1944, she testified, she had not made a connection. She had never known him under the name Marcel Petiot, only Dr. Eugène, and all the talk of "injections, nightclubs, drugs, loose women" did not match the man she knew, who was "serious, levelheaded, composed, and very sensible." It was his photograph on the front page, she said, that caused her to discover the horrible truth.

As for why she did not simply go to the police with her story if she were as innocent as she claimed, Kahan reminded the prosecution that, as a Jew in the Occupation, she was "hunted as a harmful beast." At one point, she had considered going to the police, but she said that the attorney she consulted, René Floriot, advised her to "stay put."

Kahan's story and her motives were soon questioned by Floriot, and a spirited debate followed over her professed work for the Resistance. She became defensive. She struck the railing with her fist, and as she appeared flustered, her accent became more pronounced. Dupin came to her aid, noting that the police had found no evidence disputing her claims of having served the Resistance.

Floriot asked about a certain police report dated November 30, 1945, that identified Eryane Kahan as "an adventuress . . . who lies with skill." In the interviews following her arrest as an alleged Petiot accomplice in the autumn of 1944, Kahan could not name a single person she had worked with in the Resistance—and again, this was after the Liberation, when there was no lack of people claiming this distinction. Kahan had been found, Commissaire Poirier noted, with "many difficulties." Indeed, she was living in the 16th arrondissement, under the fake name of Odette Motte.

Another thing that Floriot knew was that the former leader of the French Gestapo, Henri Lafont, had picked her out from a list of photographs as a woman who had informed his gang about the activities and whereabouts of fellow Jews. Specifically, in a deposition signed December 21, 1944, Lafont stated that Kahan "came to us to give tips on the passages to Spain arranged by a doctor."

It was a lengthy cross-examination accompanied by a duel of glasses, as Floriot and Kahan removed and wiped their spectacles at regular intervals. Floriot focused first on establishing that Kahan had received a commission for every person she sent Dr. Petiot. He hounded the witness, citing the police report and the testimony of several witnesses. But Kahan refused to budge, and a heated exchange erupted between prosecution and defense attorneys. Insults and insinuations flew from both sides, prompting Leser to call a recess. When the court returned, Dupin withdrew his comments, which might have "offended the very legitimate sensitivities of my opponent."

Floriot nodded and then launched into a series of rapid-fire questions, suggesting that Kahan had enjoyed a close relationship with Occupation authorities. He asked about her friend, the German officer, and the fact that she had been seen riding in a German truck, which she could not deny. Her apartment building, Floriot continued, was often visited by three or four German officers. He mentioned the deposition of a former friend who believed that Kahan caused her husband's arrest by the Gestapo. Kahan countered that she had never heard that before.

When Floriot asked about Madame Cadoret's testimony, namely that she had been worried when Kahan was "saluted by a number of German soldiers," Kahan said that this was simply her friend Herbert Welsing and one or two of his Luftwaffe friends. Floriot noted that her memory had suddenly returned.

There was one last question, Floriot said. Kahan had been accused of "intelligence with the enemy" (Article 75 of the penal code), but what had happened to her dossier? Kahan denied having any knowledge of such a file. Jean-François Dominique, then covering the trial for Toulouse's *La Républic du Sud-Ouest*, thought that she was taken aback by the question.

"Since you do not appear to remember, the dossier is number 16582."

The prosecutor scribbled the number down with a great flourish, hoping to show the jurors that he intended to disprove this allegation. The judge ordered that this file, completed in April 1945, be retrieved and brought to the courtroom. It would not have any bombshells. But for the moment, it seemed that Kahan was a Gestapo agent.

Marcel Petiot had been unusually quiet. The president asked if he had any questions. Yes, he did, the defendant said. After inquiring about the baggage carried by the Wolff and Basch families and inviting the witness to clarify her financial situation, Petiot seemed most interested in the claim by Cadoret about his dirty hands. Had Kahan also noticed that? he asked.

"I have not looked at your hands," she said. "They did not interest me."

Perhaps they were dirty, Petiot responded. When he visited Kahan on rue Pasquier, he told the court, he had not felt safe and often changed the manual gearshift on his bicycle in case he needed to make a fast escape. Many people in the audience found it amusing to hear France's alleged most deadly serial killer claim that he did not feel safe on that particular street.

"If I did have dirty hands," Petiot then shouted, "at least I never dirtied them by raising them to swear an oath of loyalty to the traitor Pétain!"

"I forbid you to be insolent," Leser warned the defendant.

"Toward whom?" Petiot laughed. "Pétain?"

Leser reminded the court that magistrates had been required to swear oaths of allegiance to German authorities. The Act Constitutionel No. 9, drafted on April 4, 1941, made it law. Petiot said that he knew someone who had refused. Paul Didier was the most famous example of a judge who lost his position for his principled refusal.

Leser dismissed the witness. In the audience, Jean Galtier-Boissière found her intriguing and rather puzzling: "Was she tortured by remorse for having delivered three Jewish families who had confided in her to a killer?" Did she perhaps serve the Germans? After listening to her testimony the last two hours, Galtier-Boissière said that he still could not decide between "these equally plausible hypotheses."

The prosecution closed by calling a number of other witnesses to show that the Wolffs, the Basches, and the Schonkers could not have worked for the Gestapo. Three hotelkeepers from the quartier Saint-Sulpice testified that each of the Jewish families had fled the Nazis into France and were trying to flee again. Petiot had posed as their unfortunate answer.

33.

WALKOUT

THE FOREIGN PRESS DOES NOT APPEAR TO UNDERSTAND
FRENCH JUSTICE.

—Alex Ancel, *Parisien Libéré*, March 31, 1946

I N Floriot's hands, the interrogation of witnesses on days eleven and twelve sometimes became so fierce that it seemed that the question of a witness's or victim's honor overshadowed the issue of Petiot's guilt. The prosecution, outmaneuvered, labored to prove the obvious, namely, in Yvan Dreyfus's case, that he was a patriot who had been forced to sign two documents promising to aid the Third Reich. The defense used the evidence of his signature to argue that Dreyfus was a collaborator and a traitor who intended to infiltrate Petiot's Resistance organization.

After the radio engineer Jean-Claude Stern testified about Dreyfus's patriotism, an electrician imprisoned with him at Compiègne named Marcel Berthet also confirmed Dreyfus's Resistance credentials. "We respected Yvan Dreyfus as the most reliable Resistant, and I was keen to come here to declare it." One highlight of his testimony was telling the court how Dreyfus and several other prisoners nearly succeeded in digging a tunnel to escape the camp.

Maître Véron then read a telegram from Pierre Mendès-France, a future prime minister who at that time served as Charles de Gaulle's minister of national economy. After making a dramatic escape from a Vichy prison, Mendès-France joined the Free French forces in Britain. Mendès-France, then on a mission in New York, defended his fellow Resistant with passion. "I learn with amazement that PETIOT DARED DEFAME THE MEMORY OF YVAN DREYFUS." The allegations were "unthinkable to everyone who valued Dreyfus's character, courage, and patriotism." Petiot looked on, several eyewitnesses noted, with an expression that vacillated between boredom and disdain.

Paulette Dreyfus then took the stand, wearing a black dress suit with a black veil and a pearl necklace. Unlike most of the previous witnesses, Dreyfus did not look at Petiot when she testified, and the physician, for once, did not interrupt.

Dreyfus discussed, her voice trembling, how her husband wanted to leave Occupied France to join de Gaulle in London. She told of his capture, imprisonment at Compiègne, and fear of deportation to Drancy, followed by the sordid history of the negotiations over his release that ended with Yvan being forced to sign the Gestapo papers. "I was horrified," Dreyfus said. "His release was supposed to be unconditional."

Dreyfus told how then, after they had paid the ransom, the lawyer Jean Guélin came with yet another "last requirement" for her husband at Gestapo headquarters. Her husband left with him and she never saw him again.

"When your husband left, did he carry any suitcases?"

"No, Guélin took care of the luggage and loaned him some," Dreyfus said, thereby supporting the defense contention that the Gestapo attempted to infiltrate Petiot's organization. Floriot had already established that the first of the two letters her husband had been forced to sign bound him not to act in any way against the Third Reich. He now asked her about the second letter. Dreyfus's answer was exactly what the defense counsel wanted to hear: "To give information on the organization that managed the departures."

LIKE Madame Dreyfus, Fernand Lavie had been outraged by Dr. Petiot's assertion that he killed only "Germans, notorious collaborators, Gestapo, and *agents provocateurs*." His mother had been killed, he had earlier told the police, because she refused, "by her silence, or her declarations [to become] an accomplice of Dr. Petiot's trafficking in drugs." Lavie was the next witness called to the stand.

He retraced the background of the case from his half sister Raymonde Baudet's arrest for forged prescriptions to the strange postcards allegedly from his mother informing the family of her sudden departure for the unoccupied zone. "My mother never intended to leave," Lavie said, noting that she did not pack any personal belongings or take any money with her.

Floriot reminded the court that Khaït's husband David told the police that he believed Marthe had both written and delivered the letters, admitting also that she had previously expressed an interest in fleeing Occupied Paris. David Khaït was not available to testify because he had been arrested and deported by the Germans in June 1944. He had not returned.

"Do you know," Floriot then asked, "that three people, including a railroad employee, believed that they recognized your mother in June 1943?" This was fifteen months after her disappearance.

Lavie said he had not heard that.

"Didn't your mother come to drop off a letter with your attorney as your stepfather claimed?" The maid at the attorney's office had also recognized her, Floriot said. The attorney, of course, happened to be Véron, who was now serving as Lavie's representation in the civil suit. If this statement was correct, Floriot had found four witnesses who claimed to see Khaït after the time his client was accused of killing her.

"Let's call the maid to the stand," Véron said. The irony of the lawyer questioning the statement of his own maid was not lost.

Floriot asked about Lavie's half-sister, Raymonde Baudet, whose forged prescription began the original narcotics investigation. Lavie admitted that he had not heard from her and did not know her whereabouts. He only knew that she was living in the country.

"Yet she must know that we are discussing her at the Cour d'assises and that her presence here would be welcome," Dupin interjected, trying to cover the fact that the prosecution had neglected to call her to testify.

"How many witnesses does that make whom you haven't been able to produce?" Petiot asked. "Are we to conclude that they are dead? Did *you* murder them?"

Dupin then asked the witness if he had been shown a letter from Jean-Marc Van Bever, another alleged Petiot victim who disappeared within days of his mother in March 1942. Lavie said that he had. The police inspector had concealed the signature, but he thought the handwriting was the same as in the letters that arrived at their apartment supposedly from his mother.

The graphologist Edmond de Rougemont did not agree, Floriot noted.

"Maître, if you manage to explain this away," Véron said, "you will perhaps remove two reasons for condemning your client to death. There will still be twenty-five left."

MARGUERITE Braunberger took the stand on Saturday, March 30, the twelfth day of the trial and the last one for the prosecution witnesses. As the third widow to testify, Braunberger discussed her husband's disappearance on the morning of June 20, 1942, noting the mysterious phone call summoning him to a meeting at the L'Étoile métro station on the pretense of taking him to care for a patient at an unknown location on rue Duret.

An usher of the court opened one of the glass cages in the room and showed the witness a blue shirt with white pinstripes and a man's hat, size 50. Braunberger, embracing them, confirmed that they had been worn by her husband the day he disappeared.

"How do you explain this find?" asked Maître Perlès, the attorney for the Braunberger family.

"The moment has not come for me to answer," Petiot said.

"I would advise you to do so," Leser said.

Petiot refused, adding that he would respond after the other witnesses had testified.

"That gives you time to think of a reply," Perlès said.

"Petiot, I order you to answer."

The defendant held his ground, promising a rebuttal in half an hour.

"*Mon Dieu,* I'm not going to go anywhere." As the court would soon learn, Petiot actually had an unexpected answer to the accusations.

After Madame Braunberger left the stand, the prosecution called Raymond Vallée to testify about the relationship between Braunberger and Petiot. He was well placed to provide information. A friend of the Braunbergers and a cousin of Georgette Petiot, Vallée had hosted the luncheon where the victim and his alleged murderer met.

Vallée told the court about receiving a letter, purportedly from Braunberger, on June 24, 1942, asking him to bring his furniture to one of Petiot's properties near the Bois de Boulogne. Vallée admitted that he had been skeptical. He did not understand how Braunberger could have possibly known about the town house.

Petiot's expressions had been full of disdain, but at one point during the testimony, he lost his temper and jumped out of his chair, shouting at the witness. Leser ordered him to sit down and control himself. A guard, standing behind Petiot, indicated that he should comply, using the familiar *tu* form, not the formal *vous*.

"I forbid you to use *tu* with me!" Petiot yelled at the guard, who simply repeated the order.

"Fuck you!" Petiot screamed.

As the crowd jeered, Leser pounded the gavel and shouted for everyone to calm down. But then, as Petiot started to ask Vallée a question, Leser allowed the witness to leave the stand. Floriot smiled. The clerk of the court, alert to the possibility of a mistrial, whispered to Leser. An usher was sent to fetch Vallée. Moments later, he returned to answer Petiot's question. It was insignificant.

Other members of the Braunberger household took the stand, including the maid, the cook, and a nurse from Dr. Braunberger's medical practice. Each one identified the shirt and hat as belonging to the doctor.

Petiot now asked for the two pieces of evidence. "There was no reason for me to kill this old Jew." Not only did he barely know him, but Braunberger obviously didn't take any money or valuables with him the morning he left his apartment. There was nothing to gain, the defendant said. As for the shirt, Petiot disputed the prosecution's claims that it bore Braunberger's initials. "Do not speak to me anymore about this hat or shirt," he concluded, literally tossing the items at the clerk. Floriot would soon have more to say about these items.

During the break, Petiot was besieged by audience members wielding copies of his book *Le Hasard vaincu* and requesting autographs. Some asked for photographs with him. Petiot smiled, joked, and signed away, pausing at one point to sign a copy of his book that he would present as a gift to someone else. He inscribed on the title page: "Very sympathetically, to M. Leser."

WITNESSES were called next for the Kneller case, including their neighbor Christiane Roart, family friend Klara Noé, and young René's godfather, Michel Czobor, who told the court how they had also received postcards, allegedly from the Knellers, describing their arrival in South America and encouraging them to follow them abroad. Petiot did not refute anything of substance in the testimony, as it did not contradict his basic stance that he had helped the Knellers escape Occupied Paris.

During the testimony, the attorney for the family of Joseph Piereschi, Maître Dominique Stéfanaggi, again confronted the defendant about his relationship with the Germans: "Why were you released from prison by the Gestapo?"

Petiot clearly did not want to return to this subject. "To insinuate what you want to insinuate, you really have to be a bastard." He demanded that the attorney retract the question, before adding that he would hear from his cellmates at Fresnes.

Many attorneys jumped in, all speaking at once. Was Petiot threatening the attorney? It sounded that way to many people in the gallery, but actually Petiot was probably referring to a couple of witnesses who would soon testify for the defense. In the meantime, as Leser tried in vain to restore order, the sharp Marseille accent of Maître Charles

Henry, the representative of the Paulette Grippay family, drowned out the shouting. Henry suggested that the crux of the matter was not whether Petiot worked for the Resistance, but rather if he had served the Gestapo.

"Me? An agent of the Gestapo?" Petiot asked. "I was tortured and kept for eight months by the Germans." He boasted of not revealing anything about his fellow Resistance fighters, while "you lawyers of the alleged victims," on the other hand, launched desperate, last-minute attempts to slander him. "In other words, you are all bastards."

Maître Henry repeated that the case should be tried before the High Court of Justice, the new tribunal established by the Liberation government to hear cases of treason, which took precedence over a criminal trial. Leser interrupted, advising him not to suggest such a thing. Maître Stéfanaggi agreed with his civil attorney colleague. Petiot began to shout, and so did several other attorneys.

Enraged at the breakdown of protocol, Leser walked out of the courtroom. The magistrates, the clerk of the court, and other officials followed. Someone near Leser said he had actually adjourned the court, but few had heard it if he did. As this chaotic session wound down, Floriot looked pleased, no doubt contemplating cause for a mistrial on the grounds that the *président* of the tribunal left the room in the middle of the proceedings.

34.

NAUFRAGEUR

WHATEVER THE OUTCOME OF THIS TRIAL MIGHT BE, I WILL
ALWAYS BE GLAD TO HAVE SHARED A CELL WITH DR. PETIOT.

—Lieutenant Richard Héritier

AFTER a break Sunday, the trial would enter its third and final
week on Monday, April 1. By this time, all the prosecution witnesses had testified and the defense would begin calling its
witnesses. Tuesday and Wednesday would be devoted to the presenta-
tions of the civil suit attorneys, followed by the prosecution's closing
statement. On Thursday, Floriot would sum up the defense, and then the
jury would convene for its deliberations. This, at least, was the schedule
that Leser outlined for the court.

Rumors circulated that morning that the justices of the War Crimes
Trial at Nuremberg would take a break from their historic proceedings and attend the Petiot Trial. Many in the audience actually expected
Robert H. Jackson, chief justice of the U.S. Supreme Court, and his
fellow American, Soviet, British, and French justices of the Nuremberg
Commission to enter at any moment and assume the row of empty chairs
placed behind Leser. Others believed that this was just another unsub-
stantiated rumor that spread in the hothouse climate of this unorthodox
trial, perhaps even an April Fool's prank.

With April 1 also being day thirteen of the trial, several astrologers
and Tarot card readers were predicting a big day for Marcel Petiot. For
the first time since the opening, however, it was not difficult to find a
seat. Attendance was down considerably. Many Parisians had formed
their opinions and, no doubt, knew that the defense witnesses would not

offer as dramatic, or chilling, testimony. So for this brilliant spring day, even many regular trial attendees chose the boulevards, parks, and sidewalk cafés over the courtroom drama at the Palais de Justice.

Before the first witness took the stand, Maître Henry wanted to clarify what he had meant at the end of the previous day. He had not intended to propose that Petiot be charged for treason and the trial move to the High Court, no matter what the journalists and audience remembered. Instead, he claimed that he merely wanted to ensure that the defendant and his accomplices would be held responsible for their crimes. It was not a credible retraction. Leser stopped him to call the first witness.

François Comte, a decorated World War I veteran and shop owner in Villeneuve-sur-Yonne, spoke fondly of his experience as a patient at Petiot's clinic. He praised Petiot for his service to the poor, including his frequent treatment without charging a sou. Comte went on to explain how Petiot, an innocent man, ended up in such a predicament: the malicious slander of his enemies.

After this novel theory, which was championed with unusual vigor, Comte proceeded to elaborate on how many of Petiot's rivals, particularly conservative, right-wing townsmen, had opposed his expensive reforms. Other people, he said, resented that Petiot chose to marry Georgette Lablais, the daughter of a Seignelay pork butcher, rather than one of their own daughters.

Emile Pathier, a retired porter in his seventies who had previously served with Petiot on the municipal council, agreed, calling Villeneuve-sur-Yonne "a veritable fire-box of political intrigue." Still, Petiot had managed to improve the city in many ways. He had built a sewer system over the opposition of many critics and transformed the educational system from a "true nest of tuberculosis" into a quality institution. He was, simply, "incapable of doing the things that he had been accused of doing."

From the first witness, every Petiot defender spoke with conviction. Fellow townsmen and former patients alike praised the contributions of the popular, influential doctor. One witness told how Petiot cured a man who had suffered a serious injury from falling out of a poplar tree, visiting him every day for three years and nine months. Another witness testified that he had been overwhelmed by stress in his work and Petiot had even paid for his vacation. When the war came, he was said to hide British pilots and help patients avoid deportation to Germany by giving injections that made them temporarily ill. "Petiot was a Frenchman one hundred percent," Monsieur Mure said, before correcting himself. "Make that two hundred percent."

Not everyone in the courtroom was swayed by the testimony. Robert Danger of *France-Soir* concluded that Petiot had not been able to "kill everyone."

THE most effective witness for the defense was the decorated Resistance fighter Lieutenant Richard Héritier, a member of the SOE's RF unit that was dropped into Ruffey-sur-Seille in the Jura in February 1943. After his capture by the Germans, Héritier was imprisoned on June 10, 1943, at Fresnes, where for the next five months he had shared cell 440 with Marcel Petiot.

Héritier made several important claims about his cell mate. Given their many lengthy, detailed discussions in prison, often about the Fly-Tox organization and the clandestine escape network, Héritier had never doubted Petiot's Resistance credentials. Petiot had not only shown his inside knowledge of the movement, but he had also furnished Héritier with contact information of other Resistants in Paris, should he ever escape.

Among other things, Petiot had coached him on surviving the horrific interrogations of the Gestapo. He had surprised and even impressed hardened Resistance fighters with his audacity. Héritier testified that he had repeatedly been amazed by Petiot's almost complete lack of fear, to the point of taunting the Gestapo jailors. He was an inspiration to his prison mates, Héritier added, to a stunned courtroom, the audience and jury alike hanging on every word.

"You spent five months with him," Floriot said. "Do you think that a man can conceal his true feelings for five months?"

Héritier doubted that was possible. A prison cell was simply too intimate.

Floriot asked his opinion about the defendant.

"I think that first, Petiot did not act alone. Second, he was a member of a political party that was very active in the Resistance, but not the official Resistance that worked directly with the Allies. I believe that this party gave him orders which he carried out in his own way." The unidentified party was of course the Communists, which had furnished France and other countries in Occupied Europe with many Resistance fighters.

"After the beating he took in the press," Héritier continued, "the party that dared to claim Petiot would find itself sinking in the elections." Petiot had in other words "sacrificed himself for the cause," only to be unceremoniously discarded.

Petiot then asked the witness if a rational person could possibly think that he served the Gestapo.

"I don't believe so," Héritier said. "Whatever the outcome of this trial might be, I will always be glad to have shared a cell with Dr. Petiot."

After another Resistant and former cellmate, Roger Courtot, testified that Petiot was "without any question a real Resistant and a courageous one," the defense called to the stand Germaine Barré, a stylish blond dressmaker who had served in the British Secret Intelligence Service. She had been present in Jodkum's office when the Gestapo commissioner questioned Petiot.

Based on what she saw and heard, Barré was convinced that Petiot could not have worked for the Gestapo. She also told the court of Petiot's response when Jodkum asked if he would like to purchase his release for 100,000 francs: "I do not care whether you free me or not. I have stomach cancer and I do not have long to live anyway." Barré then testified that Jodkum called Petiot's brother to obtain the ransom.

Petiot asked the witness if she recalled his response when Jodkum wanted him to swear an oath never to engage in any activity against the German authorities. Yes, Barré answered. The defendant would not sign anything at all.

The court was hearing another side to Dr. Marcel Petiot. At the same time, one fundamental question remained. Although many witnesses had testified to Petiot's devotion as a doctor and his courage during his imprisonment by the Gestapo, had the defense been able to establish the crucial point—namely, that Petiot had served the French Resistance and killed only Germans and collaborators?

B Y the standards of the previous two weeks, attendance at the Petiot trial was once again low on the fourteenth and fifteenth days. "We're making a flop today" was how Petiot put it. The beautiful spring weather again offered many rival attractions, and the civil-suit attorneys, scheduled to present their cases, promised a great deal of repetition. On several occasions, Marcel Petiot would be seen and photographed sleeping in his box. One French newspaper summed it up as EVERYBODY SLEEPS AT THE PETIOT TRIAL.

Maître Archevêque outlined the Guschinow case, Véron the Dreyfus case; Maître Claude Perlès represented Madame Braunberger, Dominique Stéfanaggi the Joseph Piereschi estate, and Charles Henry the Grippay family. Very little new material emerged. Henry accused Petiot of working for a secret "anti-French terrorist organization" in close cooperation with the Germans—or, as he put it, a "Nazi faun that haunts the outskirts of the Gestapo."

Henry was often singled out for illustrating the problems of lengthy repetitive speeches that day. In the middle of his talk, in which he had promised to "cast light on the entire case," Petiot stood and said to much amusement: "I would like to remind the court that I am not paying for this lawyer's services." Henry spoke of everything in his closing statement, it seemed, except his client. At the end, Président Leser asked him "What about your client?"

"I am finished," Henry said. "I do not insist on anything further." Indeed, he had little to connect the disappearance of his client to the defendant, other than circumstantial evidence.

Andrée Dunant, the only female attorney in the trial, performed more effectively with her summary on behalf of the Rossmy family. Building on Petiot's admission on the third day of the trial that he had killed Gisèle Rossmy, Adrien the Basque's girlfriend, and reminding the jury of his reasoning, namely that "he did not know what else to do with her," Dunant argued that the court had no other course of action than to declare the defendant guilty. She stuck to the essentials, avoiding the extended, tedious, and frequent digressions that dogged her colleagues.

Spectators in the gallery might have complained about the lack of drama in the last session of the trial, but they did not know what had happened earlier outside the courtroom. At ten thirty that morning, a red-haired woman wearing a houndstooth jacket had entered the bicycle repair shop of one of the jurors, André Molvault. The customer wanted to know if her bike was repaired; Molvault apologized for the delay, telling her that he was serving at the Petiot trial. "Ah!" she said. "There are going to be reprisals, you know, believe me."

When Molvault asked if he should consider that a threat, the answer was yes, the woman said, storming out of the shop. In doing so, she had forgotten to take her bicycle and so Molvault was able to give a name to the police, who then traced it to a Dutch woman who lived in Lyon. Président Leser himself wrote an account of this incident and asked the police to pursue this case of juror intimidation.

On the fifteenth day, Wednesday, April 3, Maître Jacques Bernays summed up the civil case for the Wolff family. Maître Gachkel spoke for the Basches and Maître Léon-Lévy for the Knellers, both attorneys concentrating on showing that the victims simply could not have been collaborators or secret agents of the Gestapo. The defendant, Léon-Lévy said, united families—that is, by "uniting them in death." The most effective speech of the day, however, came from Maître Pierre Véron, who spoke this time for the Dreyfus family.

"I have the good fortune to defend an excellent case against a man who is only an imposter," Véron began, attacking Petiot's claims to have been a Resistant. Based on the latter's ignorance of basic facts and the many contradictions in his testimony, it was simply not possible that Petiot could have worked for the Resistance. A jury of eight-year-old children, Véron argued, could poke holes in his claims about his so-called secret weapon.

Véron provided one of the trial's memorable moments when he compared Petiot to a popular legend of *naufrageurs*, or ship wreckers:

> *Cruel men set lanterns on the cliffs to attract sailors in distress and make them believe that it was a port or harbor. The confident sailors, unable to conceive of such black deeds, crashed onto the reefs, losing their lives and property. Those who deceived them, by pretending to save them, then enriched themselves with the spoils. Petiot is just that: the false rescuer, the false refuge.*

The members of the French Resistance had not died in combat, torture chambers, or the execution grounds so that Dr. Petiot could "wrap himself in the folds of their flag."

Then, after reminding the jury of the fact that the Gestapo had released Petiot from prison, Véron pointed out that the Germans had certainly not been "very curious" about his activities. "I do not know if Petiot worked for the Gestapo or not," he said, "but one thing is certain: the smoke rising from the chimney of rue Le Sueur went to join . . . the smoke from the crematoria of Auschwitz or Belsen." Petiot was actually more hateful than the executioners at the Nazi death camps, Veron then argued, because he "dared to claim that he did this in the name of the Resistance."

For his unspeakable crimes, the jury must, Véron concluded, "condemn him to death." The court erupted in thunderous applause.

Amid the commotion, Petiot stood in his box shaking his fist and shouting insults at the attorney. Véron countered, as the applause died down, that he would attend his execution.

At this point, already well after five o'clock in the afternoon, Leser asked Dupin to begin the prosecution's closing arguments. Clearly he would not have time to finish the summary that day, and the obvious question was how much would splitting his concluding statement rob it of its power. Dupin began in an old-fashioned flowery rhetorical style, claiming "the records of the Cour d'assises de la Seine, preserved for more than a century, are unable to provide an example of another trial as monstrous." Petiot, looking down at his sketchpad, doodled and yawned.

"Yes, to find as many cadavers, to see as much blood, to witness as many killings one must go to the other side of the Rhine to the terrible charnel houses of Buchenwald or Auschwitz, where so many of our people have been systematically murdered by Nazi barbarians." On trial that day, however, was not a German war criminal but a Frenchman. Petiot, still sketching, acted as if he was barely able to stay awake.

Dupin described Petiot as "remarkably intelligent and a wonderful actor, devoid of all scruples, deeply perverted and sadistic." He covered his crimes by crafting his own personal "fictional romance of the Resistance." But in a few minutes, Dupin said, "I will show you without difficulty that all of this is only a tissue of lies." Petiot made a show of looking at the clock.

The prosecutor spoke for another two hours, blasting Petiot as "a murderer, a thief, a con man, and an impostor," that is, anything but a Resistant. To accomplish what he claimed, Petiot would have required personnel, matériel, and constant vigilance. "It's absurd," he concluded. Dr. Petiot was simply a criminal dominated by the twin desires of greed and cruelty. He was the "modern Bluebeard," that is, "a modern gangster" who "killed to rob." Dupin would not be able to finish his speech that evening. Leser adjourned the court at seven o'clock. The prosecutor's call for the death penalty would have to wait until the next day.

35.

THE VERDICT

PETIOT IS NOT A MURDERER.

—René Floriot

A s the sixteenth and final day of the trial opened at one o'clock on Thursday, April 4, socialites, actors, athletes, dignitaries, and many other spectators once again squeezed together in the crowded courtroom, as Pierre Scize of *Le Figaro* said, like "herrings in a cask." It was estimated to be the largest attendance at that time in the history of the Cour d'assises de la Seine.

Petiot, wearing the same gray suit and purple bow tie that he had on the first day of the trial, appeared confident as he scanned the gallery for Georgette, Gérard, and Maurice, all of them there as always. Dupin resumed his summary of the prosecution's case. Before he could launch into the bulk of his argument, however, there was a disruption in the audience. A woman or perhaps two women had fainted. People scrambled to help, and when the guards intervened, they also met resistance from spectators who refused to abandon hard-won seats. Président Leser seemed confused about what to do. The trial looked like it would end, as the correspondent for *Libé-Soir* put it, "in a scandalous buffoonery." Leser suspended proceedings at one forty-five.

Twenty-five minutes later, Dupin returned to his summary, reminding the court of the series of letters and postcards purportedly sent by victims after their disappearance. In each case, the content was similar, sometimes using almost identical language and word choices infrequently employed by the victim. Each time, too, the alleged writer signed his or her full name, even to a husband, a wife, or a lover.

Dupin classified Petiot's victims into three groups: Jews hoping to escape the Occupation; gangsters and their mistresses; and a final category of patients who in some way threatened to put his medical practice in jeopardy. The latter group was murdered to prevent them from testifying about his activities. The gangsters and their mistresses were killed for their wealth, and if any of them belonged to the Gestapo, Petiot did not know it at the time and only took advantage of the fact afterward. As for Petiot's calling the first group Gestapo agents and collaborators, this was a travesty. He had robbed and murdered Jews fleeing for their lives.

Petiot's claims that the human remains had been planted were preposterous. The bodies at rue Le Sueur had been worked on by a skilled surgeon. The patterns of dismemberment corresponded to the pieces that had washed up in the Seine between the spring of 1942 and January 1943. Petiot admitted sixty-three "executions," or liquidations as he called them, and Dupin reminded the court that there had probably been many more. He read a list of the twenty-seven people whom the state accused Petiot of murdering.

"No, Petiot, we will not allow anyone to desecrate the word 'Resistance' any longer," Dupin said. "No deception, Petiot. The hour of justice has sounded."

As soon as Dupin had uttered the words, Petiot stood and said, "Signed, the Procureur of the Vichy Régime." The defendant held up a drawing he had been sketching during the closing statement. It was a caricature of the prosecutor that elicited laughter from the audience.

"Petiot, the role of judge does not suit you," Dupin said.

"Nor you!"

The prosecutor, known for his reluctance to utter the words "death penalty," usually resorted to some circuitous way of calling for capital punishment. For several days now, journalists and commentators had enjoyed a parlor game of guessing the phrase Dupin would use. After a final reminder that psychiatric evaluations had confirmed the defendant's sanity and a claim that the death penalty had never seemed an "absolute necessity" more than now, Dupin was ready: "Let Justice be done and let us see Petiot soon join his victims." This was not a popular phrase among the families of the victims.

A T three o'clock that afternoon, Président Leser motioned for Floriot to begin the final plea of the defense. As customary before beginning his argument, Floriot had downed a single glass of champagne—later this day too, for the first time, he would drink a second one. Floriot approached the task ahead, as Pierre Scize put it, with "the pleasure of a hunting dog running a hare," a good comparison for the avid huntsman. Like many of the civil attorneys on the previous days, Floriot began by promising to be brief and deal strictly in known facts. His "short" summation would fill 339 typewritten pages and be one of the highlights of the trial.

Floriot confronted the prosecution head-on regarding the murder charges. The press had grossly distorted the facts, presenting the defendant as a "monster, an assassin, a thief, and perhaps even a sadist." The Occupation-controlled press systematically suppressed evidence of Petiot's work for France, embellishing instead his reputation as a terrorist and torturer. Never once was Petiot's arrest by the Gestapo mentioned. His client's image had been ruined.

The biases and mistakes in the media, moreover, were compounded by the inadequacies of the police investigation. Originally, Floriot said, the French police had wanted to accuse Petiot of one hundred murders, but with time, the number of victims had been steadily dropping as investigators discovered that he simply could not have killed them. In some cases, the real murderer was found; in other cases, the victim was discovered to be alive or to have been deported during the war. Sometimes, too, the victim had disappeared while Petiot was locked up at Fresnes. In the end, Floriot continued, the police were left with twenty-seven charges.

To secure conviction, detectives had searched for any piece of evidence that could be used against Floriot's client, while also ignoring the positive testimonies found along the way. Citing the statement of

Inspector Poirier, Floriot noted that the French police had interviewed two thousand of Petiot's clients and found that they had said overwhelmingly positive things about Petiot. The prosecution's statement had not reflected this reality.

Floriot retold Petiot's background from his perspective. A volunteer infantryman in World War I and a veteran wounded in battle and honorably discharged with 50 and eventually 100 percent disability, Petiot had proceeded to study medicine at the University of Paris. He had written a dissertation that earned high marks and then established his own medical practice in Villeneuve-sur-Yonne. Repeatedly his patients had testified about the quality of Petiot's work as a physician and his achievements as mayor. Then, after surviving the personal attacks from enemies who plotted his downfall, Petiot had moved to Paris and rebuilt his medical practice. All the while, he had remained a devoted husband and father. Like the police and prosecution statement Floriot just criticized, Floriot's was a blatantly one-sided portrait full of contradictions and omissions.

The same emphasis on service beyond the call of duty persuaded Petiot to throw his lot behind the Resistance—and what really, Floriot asked, was the Resistance? Was it necessary or sufficient to join an official organization? Shouldn't one also consider the importance of deeply held convictions?

Like it or not, Floriot argued, Petiot was a Resistant. Witnesses had confirmed his strong anti-German stance, and indeed there was not a single instance in the dossier that could show anything remotely pro-German. The advocate dwelled on how Petiot had provided false certificates for Frenchmen to avoid the German labor camps, or furnished prescriptions for drugs to make them sick on the day of the physical examination. Petiot had expanded his Resistance activities by working with Fly-Tox; Resistance fighters who knew him well, such as Lieutenant Richard Héritier, had no doubt about his Resistance past. Nor had the Gestapo, Floriot argued, reminding the jury of his client's almost eight months of torture and imprisonment.

Now, despite this service to his country, Petiot was on trial for twenty-seven murders. He admitted nineteen of them, claiming that each one was a Gestapo agent, an informer, or someone attempting to infiltrate the Fly-Tox organization and therefore subject to be "executed in the name of the Resistance and the name of France." This was not a crime, Floriot reminded the court, citing the wartime proclamation issued by General de Gaulle in Algiers: "There is no crime or misdemeanor when the crime or misdemeanor has been committed in the interest of France."

As for the other eight charges, Denise Hotin, Jean-Marc Van Bever, Marthe Khaït, Joachim Guschinow, Paul Braunberger, and Kurt, Greta, and René Kneller, Petiot denied them. Other than Guschinow and the Knellers, whom he had helped flee Occupied Paris, Petiot had no idea about the whereabouts of any of the other men and women. If the prosecution could provide sufficient evidence to pin a single one of these eight missing persons on his client, Floriot said, Petiot should be condemned. But the prosecution had not done so.

Floriot was meticulous, zooming in on each alleged victim and raising many doubts about the prosecution's evidence. In the case of René Kneller, for instance, it was true that a pair of child's pajamas had been found at 21 rue Le Sueur, the body of a young boy had washed up in the Seine, and, at the time of Petiot's arrest, a ration card formerly belonging to the seven-year-old René had been found in Petiot's possession with the surname changed to read Valeri.

Yet the prosecution had not managed to disprove Petiot's defense that he sent the family abroad. Perhaps the pajamas had simply been left behind as dirty laundry and the ration card handed over as a gift or in lieu of the fees the Knellers owed Petiot. As for the body of the boy in the Seine, that could have been one of many young children who tragically disappeared in those days. There was no evidence proving it was René, and nothing at all connecting the remains to Floriot's client. Petiot should not face the death penalty, the advocate argued, with so many questions remaining unanswered, and certainly not with such a glaring lack of evidence.

Turning to the disappearance of Dr. Paul Braunberger, Floriot proceeded to undermine the prosecution's main link to Petiot: the hat and shirt found on his property that Marguerite Braunberger claimed had belonged to her husband. Madame Braunberger, Floriot noted, was nearly blind. She had only identified the objects after reading a description of them in a catalogue and then looking specifically for them.

The evidence, moreover, had been treated sloppily. The suitcases in which the items were found had been packed by the police in the absence of Dr. Petiot. This was understandable given that Petiot was in flight at the time. But after his arrest, the suitcases were opened and closed a number of times without his or his attorney's presence. The fact that the seal was still intact was irrelevant. What was the guarantee of the integrity of the contents, Floriot asked, when the items had been "opened fifteen times in my absence and closed fifteen times in my absence?"

The hat and the shirt were not even found in the same location. The police claimed that they had been packed together, but that was incorrect. The shirt came from a suitcase in Neuhausen's attic, while the hat was found in a suitcase at rue Le Sueur that also included a pipe, a camera, an ink blotter, a medical flashlight for examining the throats of patients, and a small appointment book. If the hat and shirt belonged to Braunberger, then where were his jacket, waistcoat, trousers, and any other articles of clothing?

As for the shirt's supposed "P.B." initials, Floriot pointed out another problem. He asked the jury to look more closely at the shirt. Was it really P.B.? Could it perhaps be "B.P."? It also looked like "P.F." and "F.R." and some other combinations. Even Professor Sannié of the Identité Judiciaire, who had looked over the shirt closely with his microscope, could not say for certain that the initials had been "P.B." Floriot explained:

> When [Sannié can read the initials], he states it. Look at seal number thirty-five. On two other shirts, you see that someone has tried to remove the embroidered letters. A little further, he writes, "The initials which are found on the belt level of the left side have been removed. It is likely that they were A.E." As a result, when he is certain, he writes, "The letters are . . ." and

when he is less certain, he writes, "It is likely that . . ." But as
you cannot see any letters on the Braunberger shirt [seal num-
ber 44], he says nothing at all. You can see that some letters
have been removed; I do not dispute that, but you cannot assert
that they are P.B. They might be P.B., but they could also be a
number of other combinations.

As for the hat, Floriot called that "really something incredible."
Madame Braunberger had first told the police in an interview that her
husband owned a hat from the designer Gélot. But when the police
found a hat that matched her description, it carried the label of a different designer, "Berteil, rue du 4-Septembre." Braunberger still insisted
that the hat belonged to her husband because he had it repaired there in
1942 since, as she said, Gélot had then been closed.

Floriot challenged the statement. First of all, Gélot hats carry their
identification in the crown, and so the mark should have remained there,
even if the leather sweatband had been changed. Second, as Maison
Gélot only designed custom-made hats, Floriot had obtained the form
that the hatter used in designing the hat for "Doctor Braunberger, 207
Faubourg Saint-Denis, March 18, 1937."

With this information, Floriot invited the jury to compare the Gélot
form and the hat that the prosecution claimed had belonged to Braunberger. It was, Floriot said, "a disaster." The hat in question was "too
wide and much too short" for Braunberger's head. To be exact, it was
off by two and a half centimeters. "For a man who wore nothing but
custom-designed hats," Floriot noted, "a two-and-a-half-centimeter
gap is really quite a lot." It would either sit on "the top of your head" or
fall "to your ears."

Floriot then reminded the jury that Gélot had said Braunberger's hat
was patterned but the one exhibited in the courtroom was solid. When
he called Gélot himself to confirm this fact, he discovered something
remarkable. Gélot had actually given a sample of the fabric to the prosecution. "A sample?" Floriot asked. The prosecution had never informed
the defense that it had received such a thing.

"Gentlemen of the jury," Floriot said, taking out the replacement fabric provided by Gélot, "you may compare this sample with this hat." The exhibit was a solid, flat felt, but the sample was a patterned, rougher, felt *chiné*. "They resemble each other like night and day."

Not long after this demonstration, "hats off for the hat trick," as correspondent Géo London put it, Floriot approached the conclusion: Could Petiot, the doctor who treated a child suffering from leukemia for several days and nights, without being paid a sou, really be capable of killing little René Kneller? Could this Resistance fighter, who had been arrested, tortured by the Gestapo, with his teeth filed down three millimeters and his skull crushed until he bled from the nose, mouth, and ears, really be able to kill Jews fleeing from the Nazis? The patriot and hero Lieutenant Héritier told the court under oath that, regardless of its decision, he would always be proud of being a companion of Dr. Petiot.

"I commend Petiot to your hands," Floriot said, wrapping up a six-and-a-half-hour summary, the longest in his career. The jury, he was certain, would acquit his client.

Floriot received a standing ovation. The Associated Press Paris correspondent called it "the greatest defense summation in French criminal history." Indeed, at that moment, it seemed that all the bones in the basement, the bodies half-devoured in the pit of quicklime, and the countless remains pulled out of the Seine were forgotten in a stream of eloquence and applause.

As French law gave the last word to the defendant, Leser asked Petiot if he wanted to add anything. "I cannot . . . nothing," he said, emotional again from his lawyer's closing statement. "You are French. You know that I killed members of the Gestapo. You also know what you have to do."

THE jury was handed a list of 135 yes-or-no questions, five for each of the twenty-seven alleged victims: "Is the above mentioned, Marcel André Henri Petiot, guilty of having willfully put to death, in Paris or in any other part of France, [insert name]?" Follow-up questions asked if the defendant was guilty of the above "with malice afore-thought"? Was this also "accompanied by ambush and confinement"? or "by fraudulent appropriation of property"? Finally, did the defendant commit this voluntary homicide with the "aim of preparing, facilitating or affecting the fraudulent appropriation specified above?" A vote would be taken on each question for each victim. Two-thirds majority vote would suffice for the verdict.

As Leser, the two magistrates, and the members of the jury retired to the *chambre des délibérations* with the enormous dossier, they would enjoy a catered meal of sauerkraut and wine from a nearby bistro. Few spectators, meanwhile, dared to leave the courtroom, described by the writer Colette, covering the trial for *France-Soir*, as "suffocating and reeling." A large crowd waiting outside still hoped for a seat, in case someone made the mistake of visiting the cafeteria without having a friend reserve their place. Some members of the audience pulled sandwiches, dry sausages, and fruit from brown lunch bags; others smoked. In the back, binoculars were brandished.

A guard escorted Petiot into a side room. Three of the "Floriot's boys" took turns keeping him company. They would discuss everything from oriental carpets to the art of discovering bargains at auctions.

About 11:50 p.m., after two hours and fifteen minutes of deliberation, or roughly one minute per question, which was barely enough time to read the question aloud and vote, let alone debate the issue, the court clerk announced that the jury had reached its verdict. Petiot had already returned to the courtroom, where after signing copies of his book he had fallen asleep. He was awakened.

The jury and the magistrates soon entered the silent room. The clerk of the court read each of the questions. Petiot was found guilty of twenty-six of twenty-seven charges of murder. He was acquitted only in the case of Denise Hotin.

After asking the defendant to stand, Leser read the punishment: Marcel Petiot was sentenced to die on the guillotine.

Petiot looked calm and aloof. Bright flashes from the magnesium cameras popped, rendering his face paler and "hollowing out his sockets," as Henry Magnan wrote in *Le Monde*. One gasp was heard at the announcement, some believing it came from Georgette, others suggesting Maurice, Gérard, or perhaps someone unrelated to the defendant. Floriot promised to appeal the verdict.

As Leser announced the sentence, Petiot had looked right at his family. He rubbed his hands together as if washing them and then grinned with rage. Handcuffed again and escorted out of the courtroom by guards, Petiot turned and shouted, "I must be avenged!"

TIMBERS OF JUSTICE

DIVINE JUSTICE IS MY CONSOLATION.

—Georgette Petiot

I N a rare interview on the eve of the trial, Georgette Petiot had told reporters Maurice de Person and Christian Yve of *France-Soir* that she felt all alone and depressed. "Nothing more can now touch me," she said. "Public opinion is indifferent to me." As for her husband, he was innocent of the charges, simply another victim of Nazi propaganda and society's perpetual need for scandal. Although she and her son could not change the verdict, she was reconciled with its inevitability:

> *Life is made of many evil and dark hours. But it is also made of hours so beautiful that they can help clear up the dark hours. . . . And then there is hope. Hope that this life is not an end, but a means. Faith helps bear support at this present moment. Divine justice is my consolation.*

Eleven years after the trial, Georgette Petiot still maintained that her husband was innocent. One day, she said, she would prove it. She was reconstructing the dossier, piece by piece. At her small apartment near Montmartre cemetery, a photograph of Marcel Petiot adorned her dressing table.

Gérard would come to the attention of the French police one brief last time. In February of 1955, an anonymous letter reported that he was trying to sell valuables at a jewelry store on rue Provence. One of the shopkeepers, Léon Schpiglouz, told a detective that he had bought a microscope that had belonged to Dr. Petiot, but never any jewelry or other valuables. He also told police that his family, Jewish émigrés from Russia, had lived at 66 rue Caumartin during the war and Dr. Petiot had approached them several times to encourage them to leave Occupied Paris.

Gérard would eventually move to South America, settling in Rio de Janeiro, where he went into business with a cousin. Georgette, who worked a number of years as a baker, remarried in 1966. Both Georgette and Gérard shunned media and historians alike. They never spoke publicly about Marcel Petiot.

Although few people doubted that Petiot was guilty of taking many lives, it is difficult to argue that he received a fair trial. Trying to sort out the many unanswered questions of each case was a challenge in the best of circumstances, and squeezing all twenty-seven counts of murder into sixteen sessions in the volatile climate of Paris 1946 did not help the prospects for an impartial, informed examination of the evidence. The press, as René Floriot put it, had "cooked the case." A couple of jurors had given interviews to a reporter, which showed a strong bias against the defendant. Even Président Leser called Petiot a "terrifying monster." Twenty years after the verdict, one of the jurors confessed that he believed that he had made up his mind too hastily, and he was certain that Petiot did not have a fair trial.

It is also worth asking if the defense should have pleaded insanity. Article 64 of the French Penal Code then stipulated that there was "neither crime nor misdemeanor when the accused was in a state of dementia at the time of action, or if he were constrained by a force which he could not resist." The problem for Floriot was that Petiot, claiming to be a hero of the Resistance, refused to consider such a plea. Moreover, it is by no means certain that this argument would have persuaded the jury. In his last psychiatric evaluation, completed in December 1944, Petiot was found to suffer from no mental problem whatsoever.

Yet Petiot was no stranger to asylums. By the time he had turned forty, many psychiatrists had diagnosed him with a number of mental problems that rendered him "dangerous to himself and to others." Some of the early evaluations during World War I seem consistent with post-traumatic stress disorder. There were several reports of his delusions and hallucinations, and at least one diagnosis of dementia praecox, or schizophrenia. Just ten years before his trial, Petiot was diagnosed with cyclothymia, a mild case of manic-depressive psychosis, with feelings of paranoia and persecution. Indeed, right up to the jury deliberations, Petiot was apparently still receiving a pension for his mental disability.

Actually the prosecutor at the trial, Pierre Dupin, later expressed doubts about the defendant's sanity. Still, neither he, the defense attorney, the judge, nor Petiot wanted to deal with this part of his past. The jury was instructed to heed the latest mental evaluations: Petiot was not psychotic; he was amoral, completely lacking in conscience, empathy, and scruple and feeling no guilt or remorse.

After the verdict, the civil attorneys representing the families of the victims immediately sought financial compensation on behalf of their clients. The magistrates agreed on the following payments from the Petiot estate: Paulette Dreyfus would receive the largest amount (880,000 francs), influenced in part by the high ransom she had paid. Next was the widow of Dr. Braunberger, who received 700,000 francs, followed by Guschinow with 500,000 and 100,000 to the relatives of the Kneller family in Tel Aviv. Relatives of the Wolff family in Tennessee, Cuba, and Haifa were to share 300,000. The remaining five families all received 100,000 francs or less:

Grippay	100,000
Arnsberg	80,000
Rossmy	50,000
Khaït	50,000
Piereschi	10,000
Total:	2,770,000

The Petiot estate was also fined another 312,611.50 francs in court costs, making a total of 3,082,611.50 francs. Very little of this amount was ever paid.

=

A S Petiot awaited the outcome of his appeal, which Floriot had filed immediately, a routine search through his cell turned up a tiny vial sewn into the hem of his prison uniform. Authorities suspected it contained cyanide, but it was nothing more than a sedative. Otherwise, Petiot continued, as usual, smoking, drawing, writing poetry, and wondering, "When are they going to assassinate me?"

Jules-Henri Desfourneaux, meanwhile, was told to ready the guillotine. Sixty-nine years old, with a long white beard, Desfourneaux had been appointed grand high executioner, or *"Monsieur de Paris,"* in 1939 when his predecessor, Anatole Deibler, had suffered a heart attack on the way to his 401st public execution. Deibler had had no successor, and so the position would have gone first to his chief valet, André Obrecht, if he had been able to accept. The position of executioner was hereditary.

This instrument, introduced in April 1792 by its namesake, the French physician Joseph-Ignace Guillotin, was supposed to be a more humane form of capital punishment compared to the hooded ax man, who, after all, might miss, fail to use sufficient force, wield a dull blade, show up drunk, or all of the above. The guillotine would remove the head painlessly, Guillotin argued, and avoid the gruesome slaughter that sometimes accompanied executions.

After hiring a harpsichord maker to construct the first machine and then practicing it initially on straw, then sheep, and finally corpses, Guillotin had improved the device by adding weight and changing the shape of the blade from a crescent to a triangle. "The National Razor," "The People's Knife," "Guillotin's Daughter," and the "Timbers of Justice" were some of the popular nicknames for the instrument that would play such a prominent role in French history until its last exercise in 1977.

Desfourneaux's first execution had not been a success. On June 16, 1939, the neck of convicted murderer Eugen Weidmann did not sit properly in the lunette. One of the assistants had to yank his head forward, using what leverage he could, namely by grabbing the hair and tugging on the ears. Eyewitnesses spoke of fountains of blood, staring eyes, and the eerie whistling sound, or gasp from the windpipe, that comes, as witness Tennyson Jesse said, when the "last breath of air leaves the lungs." The audience came forward to dip handkerchiefs in the blood, as if the murderer had became a saint. Executions in the future, the government decided, would be held in private.

Now, seven years later, Desfourneaux would prepare to administer the Petiot death. He faced a number of problems. The guillotine had been severely damaged by Allied bombing raids and he needed money to repair it. When this was refused, Desfourneaux went on strike. Some critics not only wanted the government to decline his request for funds, but hoped that Desfourneaux himself would be sacked, as he had executed several French Resistance leaders on German orders. His valet, Obrecht, on the other hand, had worked for the Resistance, and would have even outranked Desfourneaux if the ancient family requirement weren't on the books.

Desfourneaux's supporters reminded his critics that Article 327 of the French Penal Code exonerated the executioner from any personal responsibility in administering state executions. Perhaps the whole dispute could be sidestepped, it was noted, by using a firing squad. Petiot, mocking the bumbling of the state's attempts to execute him, joked that he would die laughing.

EARLY on the morning of Saturday, May 25, Desfourneaux and three valets arrived at the inner courtyard of the Prison de la Santé with an old horse cart loaded with equipment. They assembled the machine quickly and quietly. The fifteen-foot uprights were hammered into place; the grooves inside the uprights had been greased. The heavy triangular steel blade had been sharpened and connected with the weight to ensure the knife fell only one time.

Petiot's appeal had been rejected by the Chambre Criminelle de la Cour de Cassation. Floriot had met with the president of France, Félix Gouin, but it was soon clear that there was not going to be a presidential pardon. And after a failed attempt on the twenty-fourth, when the guillotine was not working, the execution had been rescheduled for the following morning. At 4:10 a.m., everything was ready.

Four cars pulled up to the prison gates. The delegation consisted of Floriot, Dupin, Paul, Gollety, as well as Gollety's clerk Charles Schweich, Floriot's assistant Eugène Ayache, and several other police, court, and prison personnel. Président Leser, who did not come in person, sent a representative, one of the magistrates in the trial, Magistrate Meiis. Floriot's assistant Paul Cousin also demurred, claiming to be unable to watch the event.

Just before four forty-five a.m., the delegation entered cell 7 of Block 7. Petiot looked remarkably rested, as if his handcuffs, ankle irons, and the shadow of the guillotine had not disturbed his sleep. "Petiot, have courage," Dupin said. "The time has come." Petiot cursed him.

Dupin asked if he had any final requests. Petiot requested time to write a farewell letter to his wife and son. The irons were removed from his hands and feet, and after changing into the gray pin-striped suit he wore at the trial, Petiot sat down at the small desk beside his bed and started writing. "How long is he going to continue writing?" Meiis asked Dr. Paul, who said that he remembered some inmates composing letters for four hours. The delegation waited. Twenty minutes later, when he finished, Petiot glanced at Gollety, who looked pale enough to faint, and jokingly offered to give him an injection.

He looked at Dupin and Gollety: "Gentlemen, I am at your disposal."

As was customary in France, Petiot was offered a last cigarette and a glass of rum. He accepted the cigarette. The prison chaplain, Abbé Berger, offered confession and mass. Petiot declined, though he relented when he was told that it would please his wife. The delegation took Petiot down the long corridor, where fellow prisoners made noise in their cells to bid him farewell.

Leaving the Seventh Sector, they turned left onto an open area of the Fifth Sector and then descended the thirty-nine steps to the Sixth.

They arrived in the clerk's office, where Petiot signed the register, which released him from prison and into the hands of the executioner. The blinds in the office were down to prevent him from seeing the instrument for as long as possible. The handcuffs were removed and replaced by a cord. "I only see that condemnation to death distinguishes a man," Petiot said, citing the words of Mathilde de la Mole in Stendhal's *The Red and the Black*. "It is the only thing that you cannot buy."

Did Petiot have a last confession or any final words? "No," he said. "I am a traveler who is taking all his baggage with him."

After the nape of his neck was shaved, Desfourneaux tied Petiot's arms behind his back at the wrist and elbow. His shirt collar was ripped. "A pity," Petiot said. "So beautiful a shirt, which cost my wife so much. Think, it was a Christmas gift." According to Obrecht, present as the assistant executioner, Petiot then joked of a sudden crisis of uremia and asked to urinate.

"For the first time in my life," Dr. Paul noted, "I saw a man leaving death row, if not dancing, at least showing perfect calm. Most people about to be executed do their best to be courageous, but one senses that it is a stiff and forced courage. Petiot moved with ease, as though he were walking into his office for a routine appointment."

Outside, in the prison courtyard in the early-morning gray, Petiot smiled at the executioner and turned to the delegation that waited nearby. "Gentlemen, I have one last piece of advice. Look away. This will not be pretty to see."

His feet were tied together and he was strapped to the wooden tilting table and lowered into place with his neck in the lunette. A lever was released. At five minutes after five, the head rolled into the wicker basket with a thump.

37.

THE LOOT

THE SECRET OF ALL GREAT FORTUNES . . . IS ALWAYS SOME
FORGOTTEN CRIME—FORGOTTEN, MIND YOU, BECAUSE IT'S
BEEN PROPERLY HANDLED.

—Honoré de Balzac, *Père Goriot*

JO the Boxer's gold watch, Joachim Guschinow's fur coats, Lulu's emerald ring—the profits of the false escape agency can only be imagined. How much gold, silver, currency, how many diamonds, emeralds, signet rings, bonds, and other valuables were sewn into clothes, hidden in shoes, and packed into suitcases with dreams of a new life abroad? Add to this figure the fees Petiot collected for promising to supply forged papers and arrange the passage over rugged mountains, across a frontier, and then onto an ocean liner bound for Argentina.

Sometimes, too, the client had handed over property. Ilse Gang testified how Petiot carted away the Wolff furniture; Christiane Roart described the many attempts to gain possession of the Kneller property; and Raymond Vallée noted the strange messages, purportedly from Dr. Braunberger, asking him to transfer his furniture. Petiot also probably earned a percentage of the profits when he referred his clients to second-hand dealers, as both Joseph Scarella and René Marie experienced. As for the suits, shirts, shoes, dresses, coats, and wide variety of personal belongings in the suitcases found in Neuhausen's attic, how long was it before they ended up on the black market or sold to a German purchasing agency?

Without knowing the true number of victims or what each person carried to rue Le Sueur, there is no meaningful estimate of Petiot's profits. Indeed, no one has ever established the total number of victims, which could be anything from a handful to 26 (the court's opinion), 63 (Petiot's claim), 150 (Dr. Paul's off-the-record estimate), or perhaps even more (Director of the Police Judiciaire René Desvaux's guess). Clearly, however, the profits were substantial. The fifty-odd suitcases that had lined the back wall of the courtroom represented only a fraction of the lucrative enterprise.

But where was this fortune now?

Some of Petiot's wealth was clearly invested in property. Although rumors often exaggerated the number of buildings he owned, Petiot had snapped up several bargains as real estate prices plummeted during the Nazi Occupation. In addition to rue Le Sueur, he purchased buildings at 52 rue de Reuilly, as well as properties in nearby Auxerre, Villeneuve-sur-Yonne, and Seignelay. Some were purchased in his name, or that of his son, his brother, or his father-in-law. What about the rest of his treasure that he did not sink into real estate?

At one of the first interrogations, Petiot told Gollety that he kept the bulk of his fortune at rue Le Sueur. He never elaborated beyond that, and neither subsequent interrogations nor testimony at the trial had clarified the matter. In 1952, an architect bought the rue Le Sueur town house and proceeded to tear down the building "stone by stone." The demolition and rebuilding were closely watched, but no treasure was uncovered there or, as far as anyone knows, in any of his other properties.

As the defendant refused to discuss the fate of his alleged riches, rumor naturally filled in the gap. Some people believed that he had buried the treasure. At one point, René Nézondet claimed that Petiot had instructed him upon his release at Fresnes to relay a message to Georgette: "Go where you know to go and dig where you know to dig." This, however, was almost roundly dismissed. Some believed it was simply a joke on Petiot's part. Others interpreted it as another manifestation of Nézondet's tendency to exaggerate his own importance in the affair. At any rate, the likelihood of Petiot recruiting the talkative Nézondet for this special message was slim.

In 1968, the British writer Ronald Seth suggested that the fortune had been seized by the Communist Party. According to this theory, the Communists had protected Petiot during his flight from the police and therefore taken his wealth, securing his cooperation by threatening to harm his wife and son. Unfortunately, Seth did not cite any evidence. What he did not know, however, was that the man who had arrested Petiot, Captain Simonin, would later reveal that the suspect did in fact claim that the Communists had sheltered him. And from his own investigations, Simonin believed that this was probably correct. But that is a far cry from saying that the wealth ended up in Communist possession, and no evidence of that has ever emerged.

Indeed the climate in autumn of 1944—when Petiot presented himself to Communist leaders at the Reuilly armory—was dramatically different from the one that prevailed a few years before, when he was luring people to his town house on rue Le Sueur. Although the evidence is tenuous at best, there was probably a different protector at that time, and another possibility for where he hid his wealth.

I N early February 1944, two shiny black cars had pulled up in front of a small house in the town of Joigny, on the bank of the Yonne River. Among the arrivals was Marcel Petiot. He was accompanied by six men in flashy suits, flaunting gaudy rings on every finger. They had arrived for the funeral of the physician's distant cousin, Céline Petiot, a reclusive widow who had died poor and without children.

That night, Petiot volunteered to keep watch at the vigil while the members of the deceased's extended family got some much-needed rest. As the relatives went into the kitchen for a late snack, the physician entered the room where he would spend the night alone with the casket. He brought two large, bulging suitcases.

The next morning, when the pallbearers arrived, they discovered that the coffin, already nailed shut, was extraordinarily heavy. Immediately after the burial, Petiot and his entourage filed into their cars and sped away. The doctor's suitcases, this time, appeared to be very light.

One of the men in the car with Petiot was very curious about what

Petiot had buried in the grave of this relative. Several months later, in the autumn after the Liberation, he decided to take a look. Bringing along a friend, he returned to the grave site, removed the tombstone, and went to work with shovel and pickaxe. The two men opened the coffin. No treasure. Remarkably, however, there was no skeleton, either. There was nothing at all inside. Someone, they believed, had beaten them to the loot.

Whether Petiot actually hid his treasure, or more likely a part of it, in the grave of his relative is hard to say. But this small country funeral raises a number of questions. For one, only a couple of weeks earlier, Petiot had been released from Fresnes prison by the Gestapo. No one has ever adequately explained this release—arguments that the Gestapo would suddenly free him for only 100,000 francs or, as Jodkum said, by virtue of his insanity, strain credibility. The hypothesis that someone intervened on his behalf seems more plausible, but if so, then who was it, and more to the point, why did this protector allow Petiot to be arrested in the first place, let alone endure almost eight months of prison, including torture?

The timing of the funeral and the presence of the strange men at his side, on the other hand, suggest that the Gestapo men of office IV B-4 might well have released Petiot in order to follow him—not, as Petiot said at his interrogation, to arrest his so-called Resistance comrades, but rather to track down his treasure. Given that these Gestapo men sometimes tried to profit from their positions of authority, and unquestionably suspected that Petiot had accumulated a fortune, it is difficult to imagine that they would not have tried to lay their hands on it. A token payment would suffice to free their prisoner, and then Jodkum's men could follow him to the real source of his wealth, which Jodkum had hoped to seize from the moment they began seriously to investigate Dr. Eugène's organization.

Perhaps this attempt to conceal the treasure gives insight into another curiosity about the Petiot case that has never been adequately explained: the dangling panels, the ripped-up floorboards, cut-open divans, and holes in the walls found at rue Le Sueur when the French police arrived on March 11, 1944 (and later, too, at rue des Lombards in Auxerre). Was this evidence of a search of Petiot's property for concealed wealth?

But by whom? The Gestapo? As remarkable as it sounds given their interrogations and attempts to follow him after prison, there is no evidence that Jodkum and his men actually knew of his property at 21 rue Le Sueur before March 11. Someone else in Occupied Paris, however, did, and this brings us back to the men who accompanied Petiot to the funeral. Clearly they seem to have been providing protection, as one of them later admitted, and their identity would suggest that whatever Petiot carried in those suitcases was of significant value. This is because one of the men with the physician was Abel Danos, "The Mammoth" or "The Bloodthirsty."

A giant, cruel man with a long history of burglaries including a famous train robbery in 1936 and the first major holdup of the Occupation, a coup in February 1941 that resulted in some 8 million francs, Danos served the gangster Henri Lafont. In fact, Danos was one of Lafont's most valued toughs, belonging to the crime boss's inner circle or "war council" and selected to take on Lafont's most important tasks. The other men in Petiot's entourage—Gé les Yeux Bleus, François-le-Marseillais, André or Dédé-la-Mitraillette, Jo la Remonte—also worked for Lafont.

So if the coffin at Joigny might take us one step farther in seeing how Petiot dispersed his wealth, it does not ultimately reveal the fate of his treasure, which, alas, remains unknown. What it does offer, however, is support for an allegation first made by Adrien the Basque's brother, Emile Estébétéguy, of a Petiot-Lafont connection. Estébétéguy, also a member of Lafont's gang, claimed that Lafont had sent Adrien the Basque to Petiot. Lafont officially denied any knowledge of Petiot or rue Le Sueur, and the physician's name never appeared on the list of payments made by the French Gestapo. Nevertheless, it is not difficult to establish links between the two men.

One of Dr. Petiot's patients was Paul Jean Marie Joseph Clavié, a short, violent man who showed up at his office on rue Caumartin in the late 1930s, probably 1938, for treatment of gonorrhea. Clavié, then aged twenty-three, had selected Petiot, he said, because he was a respected "physician of the pissoir." Clavié was at this time a small-time hoodlum. A couple of years later, however, he was one of the most powerful men in the criminal underworld. Clavié was the nephew of Henri Lafont.

Lafont had, at this time, no immediate family, and he treated Clavié almost like a son. On January 10, 1941, while on an early mission with Lafont to establish an espionage center with radio transmitter-receptor at Cap Doumia, outside Algier, Clavié wrote a letter to Dr. Petiot, concluding with the postscript "my uncle greets you and will see you on his return." Lafont had just received permission from the Abwehr to expand his gang, along with hundreds of thousands of francs to finance his search for new recruits. By April 15, 1941, he was back in Paris doing just that, and by the end of May, he had moved into his office at rue Lauriston. That was the same week that Petiot purchased the property at rue Le Sueur. The physician paid the bulk of the price in cash, the source of which neither he nor anyone has ever been able to explain.

This, of course, does not mean that Lafont supplied or secured any of the funds for the town house. But assuming for the moment that Petiot could have raised the money from the profits of his medical practice, antiques dealing, and other assets, which is by no means certain, it is striking that he would choose to invest in that particular location. The Germans had already requisitioned numerous buildings in the neighborhood. What made Petiot so sure his newly purchased property would be immune from the ever-expanding ambitions of Occupation authorities to take over buildings in that area?

Oral testimony from a former member of the French Gestapo suggests that the relationship between Petiot and Lafont developed more significantly the following year. In early 1942, after breaking up a false escape organization in Tournus that pretended to take Jews across the line of demarcation (run by a police inspector who brought down the anger of the Germans when he stopped sharing his profits), the French Gestapo had been encouraged to continue this work, more actively seeking *passeurs* and escape organizations alike. By the early summer, an informer reported another such agency run by an unidentified physician who helped people escape Occupied Paris. Lafont's associate, Pierre Bonny, decided to investigate.

He sent three British men, who had served the gang since their desertion, to pose as downed Royal Air Force pilots hoping to flee to Spain. After a lengthy process, including help from Eryane Kahan to arrange the meeting, the physician, Dr. Eugène, received the pilots, heard their pleas, and then promptly doubled the asking price to 50,000 francs apiece. At the next meeting, in late June 1942, also arranged by Kahan, Bonny sent a team to follow the false pilots. Dr. Eugène inadvertently led the thugs straight to rue Le Sueur.

The men seized the physician, threw him to the ground, and snapped handcuffs on his wrists. At this point, Paul Clavié and an associate, Pierre Loutrel (later the notorious "Pierrot-le-Fou"), arrived, each wielding two pistols. Clavié was astonished. Dr. Eugène of the underworld was none other than his friend Marcel Petiot. The physician was released. With the tension diffused, Petiot offered everyone a drink. Before leaving rue Le Sueur, Bonny decided to take a look around the town house. It was his turn to be shocked. He saw jars with genitals in Formol, and two bodies in the process of being chopped up in the basement. Lafont, hearing of the butchery, apparently realized that he could make use of this doctor's scalpel and his willingness to wield it.

Lafont could not only take a cut from the profitable escape agency, but also use the opportunity to extend his reach farther. For instance, when a gang member committed a breach of confidence that could not be atoned for with the payment of a fine (he charged 1,000 to 10,000 francs for minor infractions), he soon realized that the only way to escape Lafont's wrath was to follow Jo the Boxer, Adrien the Basque, and their colleagues out of Occupied Paris. Alternatively, if Lafont did not want to make an example out of the offender, he could magnanimously allow that person to escape with his life, provided he left the country. Either way, Lafont would win, punishing irregularities that threatened to undermine his discipline and, at the same, turning a profit. And given the valuables that many gangsters were certain to carry, this could be substantial.

It was indeed this time—from the summer of 1942 to Petiot's arrest in May 1943—that represented the height of the Petiot reign of terror, when Dr. Paul started finding the first dismembered body parts, with the signature scalpel marks, pulled out of trunks from the Seine or parcels dropped around town. It was also after this summer confrontation that every known gangster sought Petiot's escape agency. Every one of them, too, had ties to Lafont. Indeed, given the extent of Lafont's power and knowledge of the criminal world, which was fueled by many informers, it is difficult to believe that an operation with the ambitions of Petiot's agency could have flourished without his awareness or approval.

The Liberation ended the golden age of crime for Lafont and his gang. The French Gestapo went on the run, its members fleeing to Spain, South America, Quebec, pre-Castro Cuba, or sometimes into the underground or hiding inside the Resistance. After handing out false papers to his own men, and insisting on the destruction of his gang files, Lafont fled to a small estate some forty-five miles from Paris, outside Bazoches. There, thanks to a tip from one of his own men, Joseph Joinovici, Lafont and Bonny and Paul Clavié were arrested on August 30, 1944.

One of Clavié's letters from his prison cell 120 on the quai de l'Horloge was intercepted by authorities. Writing to an unknown recipient, as he awaited his upcoming trial for treason, Clavié now urged that a certain "Dr. P" be immediately arrested. Clavié described how he had worked with him since 1938, and the physician was "very guilty." After confessing that he had found the doctor frightening, Clavié identified the reason why this man must be immediately arrested: the doctor "knows everything."

EPILOGUE

DESPITE winning a conviction for twenty-six murders, the prosecution never satisfactorily explained how the defendant was supposed to have killed his victims. In the opinion of the vast majority of biographers, Petiot used an injection, perhaps of strychnine or, as John V. Grombach proposed, an injection of an air bubble into the victim's veins. Other suggestions have included a distance-operated syringe, poison gas, or even a simple glass of wine laced with poison and drunk in a toast to the upcoming journey to freedom. Few, however, have offered any arguments or evidence for their theories.

Throughout the narrative, I have attempted to make clear what is fact and what is speculation. What follows is speculation, because no one knows for certain what Petiot did to his victims. He never made a full confession and authorities never cleared up the mystery.

There are good reasons for suspecting that Petiot used an injection. As a doctor, he could easily obtain poison and concoct a credible excuse to administer it. As both Renée Guschinow and Jean Gouedo testified, Joachim Guschinow was told by Petiot that he would require injections before his journey to South America. Ilse Gang also heard that the Wolff family would receive injections, and Michel Cadoret de l'Epinguen said that Petiot had personally told him that health regulations for entry into Argentina mandated them. The press latched on to the theory of injections, circulating it widely by the time of the trial, leaving a lasting impression on Petiot biographers for sixty-five years.

When I began researching this book, I also assumed that Petiot's modus operandi was an injection. I have since qualified my stance. Petiot did use one, but the aim was probably not to kill. Under the guise of vaccinations or inoculations for the journey, or visa health requirements, or some other excuse, Petiot probably used an injection to weaken the resistance of his victim. It was not poison—after all, no poison was ever found on the premises at rue Le Sueur, rue Caumartin, or any of his other properties. Morphine and peyote, on the other hand, were present in vast quantities.

These particular narcotics have powerful sedative effects. They would allow the victim to cooperate with Petiot's demands, whatever these might have been. At the same time, either of these drugs would allow the victim to remain coherent enough to copy a text or take dictation. The victims then wrote out the short letters to relatives, which Petiot said he would send once he had confirmed their safe arrival. This use of drugs would also account for the curious claims in many of the letters (Braunberger's, Guschinow's, and Kneller's, for example) that the writer or a family member had fallen sick on their journey, thereby explaining in advance any irregularities in the handwriting. Then, after writing the cards, the victim would be moved into the triangular room. The use of morphine or peyote would also explain another fact that puzzled observers, namely, how Petiot could handle strong gangsters like Adrien the Basque—and then also why investigators never found any physical evidence of anyone having attempted to break out of the small room.

As for the triangular room, was it really necessary for Petiot to make extensive renovations if he simply planned to kill by injection? Was it by chance that he had hired a firm that had just that year finished the construction of a major municipal slaughterhouse in Limoges? The particular changes he made are indeed curious: Petiot was creating a small room, located separately from the main building, with no windows, very thick, reinforced walls with a viewing lens on the outside, and all of this also being soundproof and almost airtight—and it could be made so, Professor Griffon testified at the trial, by the mere insertion of a rug under the door. Even if the prosecution could not produce a rug, Petiot, a dealer in antiques, would not have had any difficulty. As for the gas masks inspectors found, all of these did not necessarily have to have belonged to the victims, and the gas mask found in Petiot's office may not have been only for covering the stench of the cadavers. And when Petiot explained his renovations to the builders, he told them he was constructing a radiation chamber—a good alibi, I suspect, for his real purpose: a gas chamber.

My doubts about death by injection grew over the years, but increased most of all when I had the good fortune of unearthing a rare source about Marcel Petiot, published in Belgium in March 1944, only a couple of weeks after the discovery of the remains at rue Le Sueur. The small book, Albert Massui's *Le cas du Dr Petiot,* was indeed valuable, but it had one piece of extraordinary testimony: a firsthand account of a young man who applied to Petiot's escape organization and claimed to have lived through the entire selection process. Could this possibly be genuine? After much consideration, I believe so.

The man was identified only as Raphaël K. His last name was withheld because at the time of publication, the Nazis still occupied Paris and he hoped to find a way to flee Europe. His family urged him to remain quiet. People would be skeptical, he was told, and indeed, this was an all-too-frequent occurrence at that time (1942), when the first Jews who escaped from Nazi camps tried to warn other people about the shocking, incomprehensible atrocities that they had experienced. Note, too, that this young man's account appeared in print before Petiot's methods were widely known.

In June 1942, Raphaël K applied to Petiot's escape organization. After paying his fees, which were lower than any other known charge (5,000 francs), Raphaël received instructions very similar to other clients'. He was told to arrive at the corner of rue Championnet and rue Damrémont, in the 18th arrondissement, where he was taken in a disorienting way across the city until he arrived at the hair salon. There, in a back room, Raphael reconfirmed his intention to leave Paris. "I do not have to know why," the doctor told him. "I am sure it is for excellent reasons."

After learning that the young man wished to leave as soon as possible, the doctor told him of his "extraordinary luck" in that a group was leaving the following morning. He would travel through Casablanca, as Guschinow had been told five months earlier. "Given the circumstances," Petiot said, "I would advise you to take with you as much money as possible."

Raphaël was instructed to write letters to relatives. As he was single, he wrote to his parents, telling them not to worry and that he would return home when the situation improved. In Raphaël's case, he was asked to write the letters before he arrived at the meeting with the physician. This was not likely standard procedure. For one thing, in the case of other letter writers, like Van Bever, Khaït, and Braunberger, each one had disappeared without warning, and as they did not carry any luggage, it is not likely that they carried any letters informing of their departure, either. It is also possible that the procedure was later changed. Raphaël would have been one of the early travelers in the false network.

The evening of the departure, Petiot escorted Raphaël to rue Le Sueur. "Still decided? Are you really afraid?" Petiot asked his new client, who answered that he was not. "Good, so much the better." He took the young man into his office, which was where Massu placed it, in the outside building, with the polished desk, armchairs, and magazines on the table. The applicant was told to enter a room down the corridor where he should await departure. This was the triangular room. He was told he would leave from this room, exiting onto a side street, today's rue Bois de Boulogne. A chauffeur would soon arrive to take him on his journey to freedom. Raphaël did not know this, but the so-called exit was the false door inspectors found glued onto the wall.

"You see, it is important that you completely master your nerves," Petiot advised his client, explaining the difficulties that lay ahead. Raphaël remembered the physician telling him that he would probably have to go three days at least without sleep. To help him cope with the physical and mental challenges of the escape from Occupied Paris, Petiot offered an injection.

The injection was not by a distance-operated syringe, as Nézondet claimed, attributing the story to Maurice Petiot. It was probably an ordinary hypodermic needle; it did not elicit any special description or commentary. After the injection was administered, Dr. Petiot escorted Raphaël into the small room and returned to his "office." Raphaël was now alone in the triangular room. There was no forced entry or incarceration. He was free to walk around the room. He stared at the bare walls. No windows, a door with a button, and an odd array of hooks. He waited. He sat down on one of his suitcases. It was completely silent.

As he described the sensation, he began to feel weak. His head became heavy, his heartbeat seemed to slow, and he felt a sudden sense of fatigue. There was still no sign of the chauffeur or the doctor, who he thought must have been detained by a patient. Then, as Raphaël described it, he felt an "unbearable torpor seize [him]."

After what seemed like several hours, though of course he could not say for sure, Raphaël woke up in a great deal of pain. He compared it to being "spread out on a pile of wood or on iron bars." His wrists, he discovered, were now locked in iron bolts, and so were his ankles. A rope, tied from the ceiling, passed around his body. He was now hanging on the wall, suspended from the iron hooks. He could not move. He felt exhausted and nauseous, with an excruciating pain in his back. His ears buzzed, his muscles cramped, and he saw visions. His head was more congested than at any time of his life. His body was one big overwhelming pain. Everything felt hopeless, he said, but he knew that his only chance of survival was to maintain hope.

Suddenly it became difficult to breathe. As he described it, the room was overtaken by a "stinking atmosphere." He believed it was carbon monoxide, but as he was not a chemist and that particular gas has no odor or taste, this could not be correct. A gas of some sort, however, had entered the room. What was it?

In the 1980s, an unidentified former member of the French Gestapo living in South America gave a startling admission to a French historian using the pen name "Henry Sergg" while writing the book *Paris Gestapo*. In a wide-ranging conversation, accompanied by a glass or two of tequila, the former French Gestapo member mentioned that some people in his gang knew how Dr. Petiot killed his victims. The standard theory of death by injection was, as he put it, "a load of crap." What Petiot did was gas them. Of course, a single anonymous source cited by a historian using a pseudonym is hardly ideal evidence (at the time, historians researching the French Gestapo still received death threats). That comment passed without much notice and no other biographer besides Sergg has mentioned it.

But in light of Raphaël's testimony, this claim deserves more consideration. In fact, the former French Gestapo member identified the gas as hydrogen cyanide. HCN, or "prussic acid" for its blue color, is a highly poisonous gas that enters the body not only through the lungs, but also the eyes, the skin, the gastrointestinal tract, and the mucous membranes. It attacks the oxygen in the blood and the central nervous system, causing the organism's cells and living tissue literally to suffocate. Hydrogen cyanide is also the gas that the Nazis used at Auschwitz and other death camps.

When Petiot began his renovations at 21 rue Le Sueur, the first known Nazi experiments with this particular gas had taken place in Block 11 of the Auschwitz Main Camp on September 3, 1941. It was a doctor, SS Colonel Dr. Viktor Brack, who had first suggested hydrogen cyanide to the Nazi elite, who were then looking for a more efficient and faster way than carbon monoxide to implement the "Final Solution." Six months after this first experiment, which killed some six hundred Soviet POWs and three hundred Poles and Polish Jews, the Nazis had begun using hydrogen cyanide at the new gas chamber at Auschwitz-Birkenau. By this time, Petiot's triangular room had been completed for nine months.

Petiot did not need Zyklon B, the commercial form of hydrogen cyanide that the Nazis used. He could create the deadly gas by dropping pellets of cyanide of potassium into a bucket of sulfuric acid and distilled water—which is indeed what the French Gestapo member said that he did. As for the electric heater that Massu found outside the triangular room and stood on to look through the Lumvisor lens, it probably had a different purpose. Hydrogen cyanide gas only becomes volatile at seventy-five degrees Fahrenheit. On cold days of winter and spring, Petiot's electric heater would raise the temperature enough to begin vaporization.

When the lethal gas attacks the cells, preventing them from processing oxygen, the victim gasps for air, sometimes gurgling or foaming at the mouth, the head moving up and down to the chest and side to side. The victim may then writhe in pain, with violent body spasms and convulsions. The heart might start and stop again for minutes in a prolonged, agonizing confusion of life and death. It is a horrific demise. Petiot installed a Lumvisor to watch every detail.

Or did he? Since the first use of the gas chamber, actually by the Nevada State Penitentiary at Carson City on February 8, 1924, the chambers have been equipped with a viewing lens as a safety precaution. As this particular gas forms clouds that would fill the room, the question arises: did Petiot really intend to enjoy the spectacle, or was it simply a means of indicating when it was safe to reenter the room and begin airing it out? At any rate, the triangular room was indeed a torture chamber, an even more disturbing one than imagined.

So, almost sixty years later, while a number of probable solutions have emerged, there are still many unanswered questions. How many people did he kill, and how exactly did he do it? How close were his ties to the French Gestapo or, for that matter, the French Resistance? What happened to his loot? We may never know for certain the answers to these and other questions. Petiot did indeed take many of his secrets with him.

What we do know is that this story is an important one that should never be forgotten. It is not simply about a prolific and profitable serial killer, one of the most profitable in history. Behind the ominous cloud of smoke that poured from the chimney in the heart of Paris's chic

16th arrondissement was a terrifying tragedy. A predator had brutally exploited opportunities for gain, slaughtering society's most vulnerable and desperate people, the majority of them being Jews fleeing persecution. Dr. Petiot had become the self-appointed executioner for Hitler, gassing, butchering, and burning his victims in his own private death camp.

Acknowledgments

A MONG the many people who helped me over the years I spent researching and writing this book, I would like to thank, first of all, Suzanne Gluck at William Morris Endeavor. Suzanne is the best agent on the planet, and it is an immense privilege and pleasure to work with her. I am also most fortunate to have John Glusman as my editor. John has supported this project in every possible way, and I am grateful for his many outstanding suggestions.

It is also my pleasure to thank someone else whose help has been extraordinarily beneficial: Françoise Gicquel, *Commissaire Divisionnaire* of the Service de la Mémoire et des Affaires Culturelles, who granted me access to the entire Petiot dossier, which has been classified and locked away since the discovery of the crimes. Thanks to her support, I was able to read the Brigade Criminelle's original reports, interrogations, and searches, not to mention Petiot's own personal notebooks and some of his poetry. I am forever grateful for this opportunity. I would also like to thank Oliver Accarie-Pierson, Magali Androuin, Emmanuelle Broux-Foucaud, Orlanda Scheiber, and Jean-Daniel Girard for their expertise, professionalism, and hospitality. All of you did so much to welcome me at the Archives de la Préfecture de Police, and you made my stays in Paris so valuable.

I would like to thank Jacques Delarue, who, in addition to his pioneering works of scholarship that have long helped historians understand the Occupation, kindly gave me access to some sensitive archives at the Bibliothèque de documentation internationale contemporaine. Thank you, Aldo Battaglia and the team at BDIC for making this possible. I would also like to thank the Centre de documentation juive contemporaine for allowing me to read captured Gestapo records, and for their kindness and expertise. Sincere thanks, too, to everyone at the Archives de Paris for the opportunity to read the material on the Petiot trial that they had available and the Archives Nationales for an invaluable stenographic account that supposedly never existed. Thanks to Jason Clingerman at the National Archives in College Park and Mark Stout at the International Spy Museum for helpful advice. I would also like to thank Pete Kandianis, a detective whom I am proud to call a friend; his reading suggestions and book loans certainly helped me gain a better understanding of challenges Commissaire Massu and the Brigade Criminelle faced in their hunt for Dr. Petiot. A special thank-you also goes to Professor David Olster for sharing his scholarship and friendship over the years, and to the late Professor Raymond F. Betts for his profound influence, not least his infectious love of France. I would also like to thank many dear friends, both in Lexington and around the globe, who have shown such keen interest in this project, many of them since I first became fascinated by this story years ago when I was preparing one of my World War II lectures at the University of Kentucky.

I would like to thank everyone in the interlibrary loan department at the University of Kentucky for providing me with many rare books from dozens of libraries around the world. These included a wide variety of memoirs and diaries written by doctors; diplomats; detectives; historians; actresses; Americans; sons of gangsters; Resistance fighters; rescuers; Gestapo, Abwehr, and Wehrmacht officers; a millionaire son of a founder of a major bank; a brothel madam; and many others. For books that were rarer and apparently not owned by any of the ten thousand libraries in the system, I would like to thank my antiquarian book dealers. It was exciting to open each new package, which included no less than Commissaire Massu's "other" memoir, the memoir of Dr. Petiot's oldest friend, a forgotten book on Petiot (the first major book on the subject and actually published in Berlin), and a fascinating small book published just three weeks after the discovery of the crimes at rue Le Sueur—this last one proving far more valuable than I'd expected. Of course, any remaining errors in this book are my responsibility alone.

I would also like to thank my parents, Van and Cheryl King, for all their love and encouragement over the years, and I am deeply grateful for everything. As always, it is a joy to thank my wife, Sara, for all her love and excitement. She is an exceptional critic, and her many suggestions were hugely valuable. Thanks, and I love you! Finally, a special thank-you to Julia and Max for enlivening and enriching my world, and it is to you that I dedicate this book with all my love.

Selected Bibliography

ARCHIVES

AN   Archives Nationales
AP   Archives de Paris
APP   Archives de la Préfecture de Police
BDIC   Bibliothèque de documentation internationale contemporaine
CDJC   Centre de documentation juive contemporaine

BOOKS

Abetz, Otto. *Histoire d'une politique franco-allemand 1930–1950: mémoires d'un ambassadeur.* Paris: Librairie Stock, 1953.

Amouroux, Henri. *Les beaux jours des collabos, juin 1941–juin 1942.* Paris: Robert Laffont, 1978.

———. *Joies et douleurs du peuple libéré, 6 juin 1944–1 er Septembre 1944.* Paris: Robert Laffont, 1988.

———. *Un printemps de mort et d'espoir, novembre 1943–6 juin 1944.* Paris: Robert Laffont, 1985.

———. *La vie des français sous l'occupation.* Paris: Fayard, 1961.

Angeli, C., and P. Gillet. *La police dans la politique (1944–1954).* Paris: Éditions Bernard Grasset, 1967.

Aronson, Ronald. *Camus & Sartre: The Story of a Friendship and the Quarrel That Ended It.* Chicago: The University of Chicago Press, 2004.

Assouline, Pierre. *Simenon: A Biography.* Translated by Jon Rothschild. New York: Alfred A. Knopf, 1997.

Aubrac, Lucie. *Outwitting the Gestapo.* Translated by Konrad Bieber with the assistance of Betsy Wing. Lincoln: University of Nebraska, 1993.

Auda, Grégory. *Les belles années du "milieu" 1940–1944: Le grand banditisme dans la machine répressive allemande en France.* Paris: Éditions Michalon, 2002.

Avni, Haim. *Argentina and the Jews.* Translated by Gila Brand. Tuscaloosa: The University of Alabama Press, 1991.

———. *"The Zionist Underground in Holland and France and the Escape to Spain," Rescue Attempts During the Holocaust: Proceedings of the Second Yad Vashem International Historical Conference, Jerusalem, April 8–11, 1974.* Jerusalem: Yad Vashem, 1977

Azéma, Jean-Pierre. *De Munich à la Libération 1938–1944.* Paris: Éditions du Seuil, 1979.

Azéma, Jean-Pierre with François Bédarida, eds. *La France des années noires*. I–II. Paris: Seuil, 1993.

Aziz, Philippe. *Tu Trahiras sans vergogne. Histoire de deux "collabos" Bonny et Lafont*. Paris: Fayard, 1970.

Bacelon, Jacques. *Dans les dossiers de la Gestapo*. Paris: Jacques Grancher 1988.

Baronnet, Jean. *Les Parisiens sous l'occupation: Photographies en couleurs d'André Zucca*. Paris: Gallimard, 2008.

Barret, Claude. *L'affaire Petiot*. Paris: Gallimard, 1958.

Beavan, Colin. *Fingerprints: The Origins of Crime Detection and the Murder Case That Launched Forensic Science*. New York: Hyperion, 2001.

Beevor, Anthony, and Artemis Cooper. *Paris After the Liberation 1944–1949*. New York: Penguin Books, 2004.

Berlière, Jean-Marc, with Laurent Chabrun. *Policiers français sous l'occupation: d'après les archives de l'épuration*. Paris: Perrin, 2009.

Bertin, Claude. *Les assassins hors-série: Gilles de Rais, Petiot*. Vol. 10 of *Les grands procès de l'histoire de France*. Paris: Éditions de Saint-Clair, 1967.

Bonny, Jacques. *Mon père l'inspecteur Bonny*. Paris: Robert Laffont, 1975.

Brée, Germaine. *Camus and Sartre: Crisis and Commitment*. New York: Delacorte Press, 1972.

Brenner, Jacques. *La race des seigneurs. Petit supplément à l'essai de Thomas de Quincey de l'assassinat considéré comme un des beaux-arts*. Paris: Éditions Albin Michel, 1966.

Bresler, Fenton. *The Mystery of Georges Simenon*. New York: Beaufort Books, Inc., 1983.

Brissaud, André. *The Nazi Secret Service*. Translated by Milton Waldman. New York: W.W. Norton & Company, 1974.

Bruce, David K. E. *OSS Against the Reich: The World War II Diaries of Colonel David K. E. Bruce*. Edited by Nelson D. Lankford. Kent, Ohio: Kent State University Press, 1991.

Brunelle, Gayle K., and Annette Finley-Croswhite. *Murder in the Métro: Laetitia Toureaux and the Cagoule in 1930s France*. Baton Rouge: Louisiana State University Press, 2010.

Buisson, Patrick. *1940–1945 Années érotiques: Vichy ou les infortunes de la vertu*. Paris: Albin Michel, 2008.

Burrin, Philippe. *France Under the Germans: Collaboration and Compromise*. Translated by Janet Lloyd. New York: The New Press, 1996.

Cabanne, Pierre. *Pablo Picasso: His Life and Times*. New York: William Morrow and Company, Inc., 1977.

Calet, Henri. *Les Murs de Fresnes*. Paris: Éditions des Quatre Vents, 1945.

Camus, Albert. *Camus at Combat: Writing 1944–1947*. Edited and annotated by Jacqueline Lévi-Valensi. Translated by Arthur Goldhammer. Princeton, New Jersey: Princeton University Press, 2006.

———. *Notebooks 1942–1951*. Translated by Justin O'Brien. New York: Paragon House, 1991.

Cancés, Claude, with Dominique Cellura, Alissia Grifat, and Franck Hériot. *Histoire du 36, Quai des Orfèvres*. Paris: Jacob-Duvernet, 2010.

Cathelin, Jean, and Gabrielle Gray. *Crimes et trafics de la Gestapo française*. Vols. I–II. Paris: Historama, 1972.

Cesaire, Frédérique. *L'Affaire Petiot. Grands procès de l'histoire*. Paris: Éditions De Vecchi S.A., 1999.

Charbonneaux, Hubert. "Hommage à Jean Charbonneaux (1918–1943)." Chantran. vengeance.free.fr/Doc/Charbonneaux05.pdf

Chenevier, Charles. *La Grande maison*. Préface de Jean Marcilly. Paris: Presses de la Cité, 1976.

Christofferson, Thomas R., and Michael S. *France During World War II: From Defeat to Liberation*. New York: Fordham University Press, 2006.

Cobb, Richard. *French and Germans, Germans and French: A Personal Interpretation of France Under Two Occupations 1914–1918/1940–1944*. Hanover: Brandeis University Press by University Press of New England, 1983.

Cohen-Solal, Annie. *Sartre: A Life*. Translated by Anna Cancogni. New York: Pantheon Books, 1987.

Collins, Larry, with Dominique Lapierre. *Is Paris Burning?* New York: Pocket Books, Inc., 1966.

Crankshaw, Edward. *Gestapo: Instrument of Tyranny*. New York: Da Capo Press, 1994.

D'Albert-Lake, Virginia. *An American Heroine in the French Resistance: The Diary and Memoir of Virginia d'Albert-Lake*. Edited by Judy Barret Litoff. New York: Fordham University Press, 2006.

Dallas, Gregor. *1945: The War That Never Ended*. New Haven: Yale University Press, 2005.

Dank, Milton. *The French Against the French: Collaboration and Resistance*. Philadelphia: J.B. Lippincott Company, 1974.

Decaux, Alain. *C'était le xxe siècle: la guerre absolue 1940–1945*. Paris: Perrin, 1998.

de Gaulle, Charles. *The Complete War Memoirs of Charles de Gaulle*. Translated by Jonathan Griffin and Richard Howard. New York: Carroll & Graf Publishers Inc., 1998.

Delarue, Jacques, with Anne Manson. *"L'affaire Landru de la Libération: Docteur Petiot 21, Rue Lesueur."* In Gilbert Guilleminault et al., eds., *Les lendemains qui ne chantaient pas*. Paris: Denoël, 1962.

———. *The Gestapo: A History of Horror*. Translated by Mervyn Savill. New York: Paragon House, 1987.

———. *Trafics et crimes sous l'occupation*. Paris: Fayard, 1968.

Demory, Jean-Claude. *Pompiers dans Paris en guerre (1939–1945)*. Paris: Éditions Altipresse, 2004.

Desprairies, Cécile. *Paris dans la Collaboration*. Préface de Serge Klarsfeld. Paris: Seuil, 2009.

Destaing, Philippe. *Missions en France*. Paris: Les Éditions de Minuit, 1946.

Devoyod, R. P. *Les délinquants*. Reims: Matot-Braine, 1955.

Dominique, Jean-François. *L'affaire Petiot: médecin, marron, gestapiste, guillotiné pour au moins vingt-sept assassinats*. Paris: Éditions Ramsay, 1980.

Dreyfus, Jean-Marc. " 'Almost-Camps' in Paris: The Difficult Description of Three Annexes of Drancy—Austerlitz, Lévitan, and Bassano, July 1943 to August 1944." Jonathan Petropoulos and John K. Roth, eds. *Gray Zones: Ambiguity and Compromise in the Holocaust and Its Aftermath*. New York: Berghahn Books, 2005.

Dubois, Edmond. *Paris sans lumière*. Lausanne: Payot, 1946.

Dupont, Victor. *Témoignages*. Chantran.vegeance.free.fr/Doc/VicDupontv10.pdf

Eder, Cyril. *Les Comttesses de la Gestapo*. Paris: Bernard Grasset, 2006.

Fabre-Luce, Alfred. *Vingt-cinq années de liberté*. Vol. II, *L'Épreuve (1939–1946)*. Paris: René Julliard, 1963.

Faralicq, René. *The French Police from Within*. London: Cassell and Company, 1933.

Fittko, Lisa. *Escape Through the Pyrenees*. Translated by David Koblick. Evanston, Illinois: Northwestern University Press, 1991.

Fogelman, Eva. *Conscience and Courage: Rescuers of Jews During the Holocaust*. New York: Doubleday Dell Publishing Group Inc., 1994.

Floriot, René. *Les Erreurs judiciares*. Paris: Editions J'ai lu, 1968.

———. Préface in Montarron, Marcel. *Les grands procès d'assises*. Paris: Éditions Planète, 1967.

Foot, M. R. D. *Resistance: European Resistance to Nazism 1940–45*. New York: McGraw-Hill Book Company, 1977.

———. *SOE in France: An Account of the Work of the British Special Operations Executive in France 1940–1944*. Frederick, Maryland: University Publications of America, Inc., 1984.

Foot, M. R. D., and J. M. Langley. *MI9: Escape and Evasion 1939–1945*. Boston: Little, Brown, and Company, 1980.

Frenay, Henri. *Combat*. Paris: Société des Éditions Denoël, 1945.

———. *The Night Will End: Memoirs of a Revolutionary*. Translated by Dan Hofstadter. New York: McGraw-Hill Book Company, 1976.

Fuligni, Bruno, ed. *Dans les secrets de la police: quatre siècles d'histoire, de crimes et de faits divers dans les archives de la Préfecture de police*. Paris: L'Iconoclaste, 2008.

Galtier-Boissière, Jean. *Mon journal dans la drôle de paix*. Paris: La Jeune Parque, 1947.

———. *Mon journal pendant l'Occupation*. Garas: La Jeune Parque, 1944.

Gerassi, John. *Talking with Sartre: Conversations and Debates*. New Haven: Yale University Press, 2009.

———. *Jean-Paul Sartre: Hated Conscience of His Century*. Chicago: University of Chicago Press, 1989.

Gilbert, Martin. *The Holocaust: A History of the Jews of Europe During the Second World War*. New York: Henry Holt and Company, 1985.

Gildea, Robert. *Marianne in Chains: Daily Life in the Heart of France During the German Occupation*. New York: Picador, 2002.

Gisevius, Hans Bernd. *To the Bitter End*. Translated by Richard and Clara Winston. New York: Da Capo Press, 1998.

Glass, Charles. *Americans in Paris: Life and Death Under Nazi Occupation*. New York: The Penguin Press, 2010.

Goñi, Uki. *The Real Odessa: Smuggling the Nazis to Perón's Argentina*. London: Granta Books, 2003.

Gordeaux, Paul. *Le Docteur Petiot, "Le crime ne paie pas."* Paris: Editions Minerva, 1971.

Gordon, Bertram M. *Collaborationism in France during the Second World War*. Ithaca, New York: Cornell University Press, 1980.

Grombach, John V. *The Great Liquidator*. New York: Zebra Books, 1980.

Grou-Radenez, Frédérique. *Les Perles noires*. Preface by Henri Amouroux. Paris: Grasset, 1971.

Guéhenno, Jean. *Journal des Années Noires (1940–1944)*. Paris: Gallimard, 1947.

Guillaume, Commissaire. *Trente-sept ans avec la pègre*. Paris: Editions de France, 1938.

Guilleminault, Gilbert, et al., eds., *Les lendemains qui ne chantaient pas*. Paris: Denoël, 1962.

Guillon, Éric. *Abel Danos, dit "le mammouth": entre Résistance et Gestapo*. Paris: Fayard, 2006.

Halimi, André. *La délation sous l'Occupation*. Paris: Editions A. Moreau, 1983.

Hastings, Max. *Overlord: D-Day and the Battle for Normandy*. New York: Simon & Schuster, 1985.

Heller, Gerhard. *Un allemand à Paris 1940–1944*. Paris: Éditions du seuil, 1981.

Heppenstall, Rayner. *Bluebeard and After: Three Decades of Murder in France*. London: Peter Owen, 1972.

Hilberg, Raul. *The Destruction of the European Jews*. New Haven: Yale University Press, 2003.

Hitchcock, William I. *The Bitter Road to Freedom: A New History of the Liberation of Europe*. New York: Free Press, 2008.

Hoffman, Stanley. Introduction to Marcel Ophuls's *The Sorrow and the Pity* (1972). Filmscript translated by Mireille Johnston. New York: Berkley Publishing Corporation, 1975.

Hoobler, Dorothy and Thomas. *The Crimes of Paris: A True Story of Murder, Theft, and Detection*. New York: Little, Brown and Company, 2009.

Horne, Alistair. *Seven Ages of Paris*. New York: Alfred A. Knopf, 2002.

Huffington, Arianna. *Picasso: Creator and Destroyer*. New York: Avon Books, 1988.

Humbert, Agnès. *Résistance: A Woman's Journal of Struggle and Defiance in Occupied France*. Translated by Barbara Mellor. New York: Bloomsbury, 2008.

Jäckel, Eberhard. *Frankreich in Hitlers Europa. Die deutsche Frankreichpolitik im Zweiten Weltkrieg*. Stuttgart: Deutsche Verlags-Anstalt, 1966.

Jackson, Julian. *France: The Dark Years 1940–1944*. Oxford: Oxford University Press, 2001.

Jacquemard, Serge. *La Bande Bonny-Lafont*. Paris: Fleuve Noir, 1992.

————. *Petiot, Docteur Satan*. Paris: FleuveNoir, 1993.

Jamet, Fabienne. *One Two Two*. Translated into English as *Palace of Sweet Sin*. London: W. H. Allen, 1977.

Josephs, Jeremy. *Swastika Over Paris: The Fate of the Jews in France*. New York: Arcade Publishing, 1989.

Jouve, Pierre. *Brigade Criminelle: L'enquête inédite*. Paris: Denoël, 2004.

Jucker, Ninetta. *Curfew in Paris: A Record of the German Occupation*. London: The Hogarth Press Ltd., 1960.

Jullian, Marcel. *Le mystère Petiot*. Paris: Edition No. 1, 1980.

Jünger, Ernst. *Premier journal parisien, II: 1941–1943*. Paris: Christian Bourgeois, 1980.

————. *Second journal parisien, III: 1943–1945*. Paris: Christian Bourgeois, 1980.

Kaspi, André. *Les juifs pendant l'occupation*. Paris: Seuil, 1997.

Kedward, H. R. *Occupied France: Collaboration and Resistance 1940–1944*. Oxford: Basil Blackwell, 1985.

Kernan, Thomas. *France on Berlin Time*. Philadelphia: J.B. Lippincott Company, 1941.

Kershaw, Alister. *Murder in France*. London: Constable & Company, 1955.

Kitson, Simon. *The Hunt for Nazi Spies: Fighting Espionage in Vichy France*. Translated by Catherine Tihanyi. Chicago: The University of Chicago Press, 2008.

Kladstrup, Don and Petie. *Wine and War: The French, the Nazis, and the Battle for France's Greatest Treasure*. New York: Broadway Books, 2001.

Klarsfeld, Serge. *Le calendrier de la persécution des juifs de France*. I–III. Paris: Fayard, 1993–2001.

————. *Vichy-Auschwitz: le rôle de Vichy dans la solution finale de la question juive en France—1942*. Paris: Fayard, 1983.

————. *Le mémorial de la déportation des juifs de France*. Paris: Klarsfeld, 1978.

Koreman, Megan. *The Expectation of Justice: France, 1944–1946*. Durham, North Carolina: Duke University Press, 1999.

Larue, André. *Les Flics*. Paris: Fayard, 1969.

Le Boterf, Hervé. *La vie parisienne sous l'occupation = Paris bei Nacht*. Paris: Éditions France-Empire, 1974.

Le Clère, Marcel. *Histoire de la police*. Paris: Presses Universitaires de France, 1947.

Lefébure, Antoine. *Les conversations secrètes des francais sous l'Occupation*. Paris: Plon, 1993.

Les Dossiers du Clan. *Paris 40–44: La vie artistique, cinématographique, journalistique et mondaine pendant l'occupation*. Revue trimestrielle. Numero 2. Mai 1967.

Lifton, Robert Jay. *The Nazi Doctors: Medical Killing and the Psychology of Genocide*. New York: Basic Books, 2000.

Lloyd, Christopher. *Collaboration and Resistance in Occupied France: Representing Treason and Sacrifice*. New York: Palgrave Macmillan, 2003.

Locard, Edmond. *Manuel de technique policière*. Paris: Payot, 1923.

Lottman, Herbert R. Albert *Camus: A Biography*. Garden City, New Jersey: Doubleday & Company, Inc., 1979.

Lucas, A. *Forensic Chemistry and Scientific Criminal Investigation*. London: Edward Arnold & Co., 1946.

Maeder, Thomas. *The Unspeakable Crimes of Dr. Petiot*. Boston: Little, Brown and Company, 1980.

Marnham, Patrick. *Crime and the Académie Française*. London: Penguin Books, 1994.

————. *The Man Who Wasn't Maigret: A Portrait of Georges Simenon*. New York: Farrar, Straus, Giroux, 1993.

Marrus, Michael R., and Robert O. Paxton. *Vichy France and the Jews*. New York: Basic Books, Inc., 1981.

Martelli, George. *The Man Who Saved London: The Story of Michel Hollard*. Garden City: Doubleday & Company, Inc., 1961.

Massu, Georges. *Aveux Quai des Orfèvres. Souvenirs du Commissaire Massu*. Paris: La Tour Pointue, undated/1951.

————. *L'enquête Petiot: La plus grande affaire criminelle du siècle*. Paris: Librairie Arthème Fayard, 1959.

Massui, Albert. *Le cas du Dr Petiot*. Brussels: E.D.C., 1944.

May, Ernest R. *Strange Victory: Hitler's Conquest of France*. New York: Hill and Wang, 2000.

Mesplède, Claude. "*Petiot, le docteur Satan: un industriel du crime*." In Bruno Fuligni, ed. *Dans les secrets de la police: quatre siècles d'histoire, de crimes et de faits divers dans les archives de la Préfecture de police*. Paris: L'Iconoclaste, 2008.

Michaud, Stephen G., and Roy Hazelwood. *The Evil That Men Do: FBI Profiler Roy Hazelwood's Journey into the Minds of Sexual Predators*. New York: St. Martin's Press, 1998.

Mitchell, Allan. *Nazi Paris: The History of an Occupation, 1940–1944*. New York: Berghahn Books, 2008.

Montagnon, Pierre. *42, rue de la Santé: une prison politique, 1867–1968*. Paris: Pygmalion/Gérard Watelet, 1996.

Montarron, Marcel. *Les grands procès d'assises*. Paris: Éditions Planète, 1967.

Mortimer, Edward. *The Rise of the French Communist Party 1920–1947*. London: Faber and Faber, 1984.

Neave, Airey. *Saturday at M.I.9: A History of Underground Escape Lines in North-West Europe in 1940–5 by a Leading Organiser at M.I.9*. London: Leo Cooper, 2004.

Nézondet, René. *Petiot "le Possédé."* Paris: L'Imprimerie Express, 1950.

Noguères, Henri with Marcel Degliame-Fouché and Jean Louis Vigier. *Histoire de la Résistance en France de 1940 à 1945*. Paris: Robert Laffont, 1967–1981.

Novick, Peter. *The Resistance Versus Vichy: The Purge of Collaborators in Liberated France*. New York: Columbia University Press, 1968.

Obrecht, André, with Jean Ker. *Le Carnet noir du bourreau. Mémoires d'André Obrecht, l'homme qui exécuta 322 Condamnes.* Paris: Editions Gerard de Villiers, 1989.

Odic, Charles. *Stepchildren of France: A Doctor's Account of Paris in the Dark Years.* New York: Roy Publishers, 1945.

Ophuls, Marcel. *The Sorrow and the Pity.* Filmscript translated by Mireille Johnston. New York: Berkeley Publishing Corporation, 1975.

Ory, Pascal. *Les Collaborateurs, 1940–1945.* Paris: Seuil, 1976.

Ottis, Sherri Greene. *Silent Heroes: Downed Airmen and the French Underground.* Lexington, Kentucky: The University Press of Kentucky, 2001.

Ousby, Ian. *Occupation: The Ordeal of France 1940–1944.* New York: St. Martin's Press, 1997.

Ouzoulias, Albert. *Les bataillons de la jeunesse: Le colonel Fabien et d'autres jeunes dans la résistance, dans les maquis et l'insurrection parisienne.* Paris: Éditions Sociales, 1967.

Paillole, Colonel Paul. *Fighting the Nazis: French Military Intelligence and Counterintelligence 1935–1945.* New York: Enigma Books, 2003.

Paxton, Robert O. *Vichy France: Old Guard and New Order 1940–1944.* New York: Columbia University Press, 2001.

Perrault, Gilles, and Pierre Azéma. *Paris Under the Occupation.* New York: The Vendome Press, 1989.

———. *The Red Orchestra.* Translated by Peter Wiles. New York: Schocken Books, 1989.

Perry, Jacques, and Jane Chabert. *L'affaire Petiot.* Paris: Gallimard, 1957.

Petiot, Marcel. *Le Hasard vaincu.* Paris: Roger Amiard, 1946.

Petropoulos, Jonathan, and John K. Roth, eds. *Gray Zones: Ambiguity and Compromise in the Holocaust and Its Aftermath.* New York: Berghahn Books, 2005.

Piédelièvre, René. *Souvenirs d'un médecin légiste.* Paris: Flammarion, 1966.

Piketty, Guillaume. *Pierre Brossolette un héros de la résistance.* Paris: Jacob 1998.

Planel, Alomée. *Docteur Satan ou l'affaire Petiot.* Paris: Éditions Robert Laffont, 1978.

Pontaut, Jean-Marie, and Éric Pelletier, Solenne Durox, and Julien Arnaud. *Chronique d'une France Occupée: Les rapports confidentiels de la gendarmerie 1940–1945.* Paris: Éditions Michel Lafon, 2008.

Porch, Douglas. *The French Secret Services: A History of French Intelligence from the Dreyfus Affair to the Gulf War.* New York: Farrar, Straus, and Giroux, 1995.

Pryce-Jones, David. *Paris in the Third Reich: A History of the German Occupation, 1940–1944.* New York: Holt, Rinehart and Winston, 1981.

Rees, Laurence. *Auschwitz: A New History.* New York: PublicAffairs, 2005.

Reile, Oscar. *L'Abwehr: Le contre-espionnage allemand en France.* Preface by Colonel Rémy. Paris: Éditions France-Empire, 1970.

Rémy, Colonel. *La Ligne de démarcation.* Paris: Perrin, 1964–1971.

———. *Passeurs clandestins.* Paris: Fayard, 1954.

Riding, Alan. *And the Show Went On: Cultural Life in Nazi-Occupied Paris.* New York: Alfred A. Knopf, 2010.

Rougeyron, André. *Agents for Escape: Inside the French Resistance 1939–1945.* Translated by Marie-Antoinette McConnell. Baton Rouge: Louisiana State University Press, 1996.

Roussel, Christine. *Lucien Romier (1885–1944): Historien, économiste, journaliste, homme politique.* Preface by Michel François, of l'Institut. Paris: Éditions France-Empire, 1979.

Rousso, Henry. *Le syndrome de Vichy: de 1944 à nos jours.* Paris: Editions du Seuil, 1990.

Rowley, Hazel. *Tête-à-Tête: Simone de Beauvoir and Jean-Paul Sartre.* New York: HarperCollinsPublishers, 2005.

Safrian, Hans. *Eichmann's Men.* Translated by Ute Stargardt. Published in assocation with the United States Holocaust Memorial Museum. Cambridge: Cambridge University Press, 2010.

Saint-Exupéry, Antoine de. *Wartime Writings 1939–1944.* Translated by Norah Purcell. New York: Harcourt Brace Jovanovich, 1986.

Sanders, Paul. *Histoire du marché noir 1940–1946.* Paris: Perrin, 2001.

Sannié, Charles. *The Scientific Detection of Crime.* Annual Report of the Board of Regents of the Smithsonian Institution. Publication 4190 (1954). Washington: 1955.

Sannié, Charles, and D. Guérin. *Élements de police scientifique.* Vols. I–IV. Paris: Hermann & Cie Éditeurs, 1938–1940.

Sartre, Jean-Paul. *The Aftermath of War (Situations III).* Translated by Chris Turner. New York: Seagull Books, 2008.

Schall, Roger. *Paris au quotidien 1939–1945.* Paris: Le Cherche Midi, 2005.

Schiff, Stacy. *Saint-Exupéry: A Biography.* New York: Henry Holt and Company, 2006.

Schoenbrun, David. *Soldiers of the Night: The Story of the French Resistance.* New York: E.P. Dutton, 1980.

Schroeder, Liliane. *Journal d'occupation: Paris, 1940–1944: Chronique au jour le jour d'une époque oubliée.* Paris: François-Xavier de Guibert, 2000.

Seaton, Albert. *The German Army 1933–1945.* New York: New American Library, 1982.

Sergg, Henry. *Paris Gestapo.* Paris: Grancher, 1989.

Seth, Ronald. *Petiot: Victim of Chance.* London: Hutchinson of London, 1963.

———. *A Spy Has No Friends.* Foreword by Sir Ambrose Sherwill. London: Andre Deutsch, 1952.

Shiber, Etta, in collaboration with Anne and Paul Dupre. *Paris-Underground.* New York: Charles Scribner's Sons, 1943.

Sigot, Jacques. *1946: Le procès de Marcel Petiot.* Paris: Editions C.M.D., 1995.

Sorel, Cécile. *An Autobiography.* Translated by Philip John Stead. New York: Staples Press, 1953.

Spotts, Frederic. *The Shameful Peace: How French Artists and Intellectuals Survived the Nazi Occupation.* New Haven: Yale University Press, 2008.

Stead, Philip John. *The Police of Paris.* London: Staples Press Limited, 1957.

————. *Second Bureau*. London: Evans Bros., 1959.

Steinberg, Lucien. "Jewish Rescue Activities in Belgium and France." In *Rescue Attempts During the Holocaust: Proceedings of the Second Yad Vashem International Historical Conference, Jerusalem, April 8–11, 1974*. Jerusalem: Yad Vashem, 1977. Pages 603–615.

Stemmle, R. A. *Reise ohne Wiederkehr: Der Fall Petiot*. Berlin: Non Stop-Bücherei, 1951.

Stephan, Yann. *A Broken Sword: Policing France During the German Occupation*. Chicago: University of Illinois, Office of International Criminal Justice, 1991.

Stout, Mark. "The Pond: Running Agents for State, War, and the CIA: The Hazards of Private Spy Operations," in *Studies in Intelligence*, 48, No. 3, available at CIA.Gov/library/center-for-the-study-of-intelligence/csi-publications/csi-studies/studies/vol48no3/article07.htn

Sullivan, Rosemary. *Villa Air-Bel: World War II, Escape, and a House in Marseille*. New York: HarperCollins, 2006.

Sweets, John F. *Choices in Vichy France: The French Under Nazi Occupation*. Oxford: Oxford University Press, 1994.

Tartière, Drue, and M. R. Werner. *The House Near Paris: An American Woman's Story of Traffic in Patriots*. New York: Simon & Schuster, 1946.

Tavernier, René. *Alors rôdait dans l'ombre le docteur Petiot*. Paris: Presses de la Cité, 1974.

Teissier du Cros, Janet. *Divided Loyalties*. Preface by D.W. Brogan. London: Hamish Hamilton, 1962.

Thorwald, Jürgen. *The Century of the Detective*. Translated by Richard and Clara Winston. New York: Harcourt, Brace, & World, Inc., 1965.

Todd, Olivier. *Albert Camus: A Life*. Translated by Benjamin Ivry. New York: Alfred A. Knopf, 1997.

Toesca, Maurice. *Cinq ans de patience 1939–1944*. Paris: É. Paul, 1975.

Tomlins, Marilyn Z. *Die in Paris: A True Story of Compulsion and Murder*. New York: Raider Publishing International, 2010.

Tooze, Adam. *The Wages of Destruction: The Making and Breaking of the Nazi Economy*. New York: Viking, 2007.

Varaut, Jean-Marc. *L'abominable Dr. Petiot*. Paris: Balland, 1974.

Vaughan, Hal. *Doctor to the Resistance: The Heroic True Story of an American Surgeon and His Family in Occupied Paris*. Washington, D.C.: Brassey's Inc., 2004.

Veale, F. J. P. *War Crimes Discreetly Veiled*. New York: The Devin-Adair Company, 1959.

Villiers, Gérard de. *La brigade mondaine: Dossiers secrets révélés par Maurice Vincent, officier de police principal honoraire*. Paris: Presses de la Cité, 1972.

Vinen, Richard. *The Unfree French: Life Under the Occupation*. New Haven: Yale University Press, 2006.

Wagman, Fernande. *The Demarcation Line: A Memoir*. Xlibris, 2004.

Walter, Gérard. *Paris under the Occupation*. Translated by Tony White. New York: The Orion Press, 1960.

Weisbrot, Robert. *The Jews of Argentina: From the Inquisition to Péron*. Philadelphia: The Jewish Publication Society of America, 1979.

Werth, Léon. *Déposition: Journal 1940–1944*. Paris: Viviane Hamy, 2000.

Wetterwald, François. *Vengeance: Histoire d'un corps franc*. Paris: Mouvement Vengeance, 1946.

Yonnet, Jacques. *Paris Noir: The Secret History of a City*. Translated by Christine Donougher. London: Dedalus, 2006.

Zasloff, Tela. *A Rescuer's Story: Pastor Pierre-Charles Toureille in Vichy France*. Madison: The University of Wisconsin Press, 2003.

Zimmer, Lucien. *Un Septennat policier: Dessous et secrets de la police républicaine*. Paris: Fayard, 1967.

Zuccotti, Susan. *The Holocaust, the French, and the Jews*. New York: BasicBooks, 1993.

NEWSPAPERS

Associated Press
L'Aube
L'Aurore
Chicago Daily Tribune
Combat
Le Cri du Peuple
Le Figaro
France-Soir
Franc-Tireur
Front National
L'Humanité
Libération-Soir
Le Matin
Le Monde
Life
Newsweek
New York Herald Tribune (International Edition)
New York Times
L'Oeuvre
Le Parisien Libéré
Paris-Matin
Paris-Soir
Le Petit Parisien
Résistance
Time
United Press
Washington Post

Notes

PREFACE

1 *A thick black smoke* Brigade Criminelle Report, March 14, 1944, APP, Série J, affaire Petiot, carton n° II; *Le Matin*, March 13, 1944.

1 *unusually warm weather* Robert Delannoy to Alain Decaux, *C'était le xxe siècle: la guerre absolue 1940–1945* (Paris: Perrin, 1998), 257.

1 *burnt caramel, burnt rubber* *Le Pays*, March 5, 1946, and Albert Massui, *Le Cas du Dr Petiot* (Brussels: E.D.C., 1944), 10.

1 *"Do something"* Andrée Marçais, *Audition*, undated, APP, Série J, affaire Petiot, carton n° II.

1 *two-and-a-half-story* Many books refer to the building as four or four and a half stories. This was not the case in 1944. The town house had an extensive renovation in 1952.

2 *"Away for a month"* Charles Deforeit, Report, March 11, 1944, APP, Série J, affaire Petiot, carton n° III.

2 *The concierge . . . informed them* Marie Pageot, *Nouvelle Audition*, APP, Série J, affaire Petiot, carton n° III.

2 *"Have you entered"* Joseph Teyssier, *Audition*, undated, APP, Série J, affaire Petiot, carton n° V; *Report*, March 15, 1944, APP, Série J, affaire Petiot, carton n° V.

2 *second-floor balcony* *Rapport des pompiers*, March 11, 1944, APP, Série J, affaire Petiot, carton n° I. All references to floors, unless otherwise noted, are by the American convention.

3 *human hand* Avilla Boudringhin, *Audition*, March 16, 1944, APP, Série J, affaire Petiot, carton n° III, and Charles Deforeit, Report, March 11, 1944, APP, Série J, affaire Petiot, carton n° III.

3 *one of the younger men leaned* Jacques Delarue and Anne Manson, *"L'affaire Landru de la Libération: Docteur Petiot 21, Rue Lesueur,"* in Gilbert Guilleminault et al. (eds.), *Les lendemains qui ne chantaient pas* (Paris: Denoël, 1962), 15.

3 *"Gentlemen, come and take a look"* Avrilla Boudringhin, *Audition*, March 16, 1944, and Joseph Teyssier, *Audition*, same day, APP, Série J, affaire Petiot, carton n° III.

3 *walked up to the fire chief* Robert Boquin, *Audition*, March 17, 1944, APP, Série J, affaire Petiot, carton n° III.

3 *"Are you good"* Joseph Teyssier, *Audition*, undated from 1945, and Joseph Teyssier, *Audition*, undated, APP, Série J, affaire Petiot, carton n° V.

3 *"What kind of question" . . . "I must destroy"* Ibid.

4 *Sympathetic to the work* Teyssier, or "Olive," was a member of the police resistance group Honneur de la police.

4 *Later, when Teyssier* *Paris-Soir,* April 13, 1944.

4 *"I still remember"* Georges Massu, *L'enquête Petiot: La plus grande affaire criminelle du siècle* (Paris: Librairie Arthème Fayard, 1959), 7.

4 *"stabbing in the vicinity of Montmartre"* Massu, *L'enquête Petiot,* 9.

5 *"somber and deserted" . . . "uneasy curiosity"* Massu, *L'enquête Petiot,* 12.

5 *The French actress* Cécile Sorel interview, *Le Matin,* March 14, 1944. She did not discuss this fact in her book, *Cécile Sorel: An Autobiography* (New York: Staples Press, 1953).

6 *"The name Marcel" . . . Dante's Inferno* Massu, *L'enquête Petiot,* 13, 15, 18–19.

6 *a decomposed body* Charles Deforeit, March 11, 1944, APP, Série J, affaire Petiot, carton n° III.

7 *a polished desk* Report, March 13, 1944, APP, Série J, affaire Petiot, carton n° III.

8 *His assistants, however* Massu, *L'enquête Petiot,* 23.

8 *Commissaire Massu had made* Jean-Marc Berlière, with Laurent Chabrun, *Policiers français sous l'occupation: d'après les archives de l'épuration* (Paris: Perrin, 2009), 140.

8 *but he had never seen* Massu, *L'enquête Petiot,* 15.

8 *"nightmare house"* Massu *L'enquête Petiot,* 22.

8 *"the crime of the century"* The epithet would become the subtitle of Massu's memoir. See *L'enquête Petiot,* 229 and 244.

Chapter 1. German Night

9 *The duke of Windsor* David Pryce-Jones, *Paris in the Third Reich: A History of the German Occupation, 1940–1944* (New York: Holt, Rinehart and Winston, 1981), 8.

9 *"the laboratory of the"* Frederic Spotts, *The Shameful Peace: How French Artists and Intellectuals Survived the Nazi Occupation* (New Haven: Yale University Press, 2008), 11, 7–8.

9 *no farther than Portbou* Lisa Fittko, *Escape through the Pyrenees,* trans. David Koblick (Northwestern University Press, Evanston, 1991), 113–115.

9 *On the afternoon of* Edmond Dubois, *Paris sans lumière* (Lausanne: Payot, 1946), 57. The air raid is used with effect by Irène Némirovsky in the opening of her novel *Suite Française,* trans. Sandra Smith (New York: Vintage, 2006), 3–5.

10 *"like a badly-cut"* Alexander Werth, *The Last Days of Paris: A Journalist's Diary* (London: H. Hamilton, 1940), 124.

10 *from the north, the east, and* Charles de Gaulle, *The Complete War Memoirs of Charles de Gaulle,* trans. Jonathan Griffin and Richard Howard (New York: Carroll & Graf Publishers Inc., 1998), 59.

10 *More often, residents* Roger Langeron, préfect de police, watched from his window, June 11–13, 1940, *Paris juin 40* (Paris: Flammarion, 1946), 16, 28–29.

10 *Rumors thrived* See, for example, the telephone conversations intercepted by commission de contrôle de Dijon, Antoine Lefébure, *Les Conversations Secrètes des francais sous l'Occupation* (Paris: Plon, 1993), 58–62.

10 *estimated six to ten million* Julian Jackson, *France: The Dark Years 1940–1944* (Oxford: Oxford University Press, 2001), 120.

10 *Paris saw its population* Jean-Pierre Azéma, *De Munich à la Libération 1938– 1944* (Paris: Éditions du Seuil, 1979), 62.

10 *"a boot had scattered"* Antoine de Saint-Exupéry, *Flight to Arras* (New York: 1942; edition 1968), 68.

11 *"There never has been"* Robert Murphy, *Diplomat Among Warriors* (Garden City: Doubleday & Company, Inc., 1964), 42.

11 *At least sixteen* This figure only includes known cases in Paris, and not those outside, including Albert Einstein's nephew Carl in the Pyrénées. Ian Ousby, *Occupation: The Ordeal of France 1940–1944* (New York: St. Martin's Press, 1997), 170–171.

11 *stuck his arm* Nossiter, *Algeria Hotel: France, Memory, and the Second World War* (Houghton Mifflin, 2001), 3. There is some question on his method and the reasons for his suicide. See, for instance, Thomas Kernan, *France on Berlin Time* (Philadelphia: J.B. Lippincott Company, 1941) and Herbert R. Lottman, *The Fall of Paris: June 1940* (New York: HarperCollins, 1992), 354–355.

12 *"the rights of the occupying power"* Article III of the Armistice Convention. For more on the exploitation, Jacques Delarue, *Trafics et crimes sous l'occupation* (Paris: Fayard, 1968).

12 *"working together"* Robert O. Paxton, *Vichy France: Old Guard and New Order 1940–1944* (New York: Columbia University Press, 2001), 19.

12 *There were lavish* Otto Abetz, of course, downplays this part of his work in his postwar memoir, *Histoire d'une politique franco-allemand 1930–1950: mémoires d'un ambassadeur* (Paris: Librairie Stock, 1953).

13 *"dancing with false"* *Time*, March 27, 1944.

13 *As of October 3, 1940* Serge Klarsfeld, *Le calendrier de la persécution des juifs de France 1940–1944* (Paris: Fayard, 2001), I, 29–33.

13 *"Aryanized"* For more on Aryanization, see Jean-Marc Dreyfus, *Pillages sur ordonnances. Aryanisation et restitution des banques en France, 1940–1953* (Fayard: Paris, 2003).

13 *"eliminate all"* Law of July 22, 1941, translation by Paxton, *Vichy France*, 179.

13 *"special train 767"* Serge Klarsfeld, *Vichy-Auschwitz: le rôle de Vichy dans la solution finale de la question juive en France—1942* (Paris: Fayard, 1983), 42–43.

13 *75,721* Michael R. Marrus and Robert O. Paxton, *Vichy France and the Jews* (New York: Basic Books, Inc., Publishers 1981), note to p. 343. This figure includes 815 Jews arrested in Nord and Pas-de-Calais, noted by Serge

Klarsfeld in *Le mémorial de la déportation des juifs de France* (Paris: Klarsfeld, 1978).

13 *four darkest years* Alistair Horne, *Seven Ages of Paris* (New York: Alfred A. Knopf, 2002), 353.

14 *A French law* Jean-François Dominique, *L'affaire Petiot: médecin, marron, gestapiste, guillotiné pour au moins vingt-sept assassinats* (Paris: Éditions Ramsay, 1980), 99.

14 *Massu could have* He had, of course, worked around the legal hour before. See, for instance, Georges Massu, *Aveux Quai des Orfèvres. Souvenirs du Commissaire Massu* (Paris: La tour pointue, undated/1951), 230.

14 *a total of forty thousand agents* This figure is taken from the size of the Gestapo in 1944, recorded in, for instance, Edward Crankshaw, *Gestapo: Instrument of Tyranny* (New York: Da Capo, 1994), 95.

15 *The garage at No. 22* Organization Todt requisitioned the garage on September 8, 1940.

15 *"calm and order"* . . . *"attacks of the communists"* C. Angeli and P. Gillet, *La police dans la politique (1944–1954)* (Paris: Éditions Bernard Grasset, 1967), 17.

15 *The subordination was to be* This was the view of Philip John Stead in *The Police of Paris* (London: Staples Press Limited, 1957), 162, and others at the time, such as Maurice Toesca, who emphasized the risks of militia taking over in *Cinq ans de patience 1939–1944* (Paris: É. Paul, 1975), 168.

16 *Commissaire Massu arrived* Georges Massu, *L'enquête Petiot: La plus grande affaire criminelle du siècle* (Paris: Librairie Arthème Fayard, 1959), 30.

16 *At ten o'clock* Jacques Delarue and Anne Manson, *"L'affaire Landru de la Libération: Docteur Petiot 21, Rue Lesueur,"* in Gilbert Guilleminault et al. (eds.), *Les lendemains qui ne chantaient pas* (Paris: Denoël, 1962), 22.

16 *"Petiot has"* Alomée Planel, *Docteur Satan ou L'affaire Petiot* (Paris: Éditions Robert Laffont, 1978), 38.

16 *"Radio Paris lies"* Fernande Wagman, *The Demarcation Line: A Memoir* (Xlibris, 2004), 112.

17 *Patrolmen Fillion and Teyssier still* Teyssier *Audition*, March 16, 1944, and Fillion *Audition* of same date, APP, Série J, Affaire Petiot, carton n° III.

17 *"it smells like death"* . . . *"If I told you"* Albert Massui, *Le cas du Dr Petiot* (Brussels: E.D.C., 1944), 10–12.

CHAPTER 2. THE PEOPLE'S DOCTOR

19 *"At the death of my sister"* Henriette Bourdon, *Audition*, March 21, 1944, APP, Série J, affaire Petiot, carton n° III.

19 *the layers of rumor* See, for instance, *Le Matin*, March 18–19, 1944; APP, Série J, affaire Petiot, carton n° I.

19 *Even his favorite* René Nézondet, *Petiot "le Possédé"* (Paris: Express, 1950), 12–14.

20 *One former classmate* Jean Delanove to Alain Decaux, December 2, 1975, Alain Decaux, *C'était le xxe siècle: la guerre absolue 1940–1945* (Paris: Perrin, 1998), 263.

20 *"intelligent, but not enjoying"* *Dossier de réforme*, July 7, 1920, APP, Série J, affaire Petiot, carton n° V.

20 *"incapable of [making]"* Ibid.

21 *Young Petiot seemed* Jean-François Dominique, *L'affaire Petiot: médecin, marron, gestapiste, guillotiné pour au moins vingt-sept assassinats* (Paris: Éditions Ramsay, 1980), 17–27.

21 *On January 11, 1916* Ministry of Pensions Report, APP, Série J, affaire Petiot, carton n° I.

22 *A hand grenade* Etat Général des Services et Campagnes, 91 ème régiment d'infanterie, Report on Petiot (1097), APP, Série J, affaire Petiot, carton n° V.

22 *"mental disequilibrium, neurasthenia"* Extrait du registre du contrôle de psychiatrie de la Vo Région (February 26, 1918–March 29, 1918), Report, October 15, 1936, APP, Série J, affaire Petiot, carton n° V.

22 *"Here, what is"*. . . *"it is the law"* Communication of "Lucien B," January 13, 1976, Decaux *C'était le xxi siècle*, 263–265.

23 *"mental imbalance, along with sleepwalking"* 8 ème Corps d'Armée, 15 ème Division, 30 ° Brigade, Place de Dijon, Committee Report on Petiot, APP, Série J, affaire Petiot, carton n° V.

23 *Petiot was discharged* Dossier No 363831 in police report, March 15, 1944, APP, Série J, affaire Petiot, carton n° I.

23 *"continuous surveillance"* Ministry of Pensions Report, April 1944, APP, Série J, affaire Petiot, carton n° I.

23 *"delicate and nervous"*. . . *"very intelligent and understands"* *Dossier de réforme* (July 7, 1920), APP, Série J, affaire Petiot, carton n° V.

24 *The first two years . . . He completed his third* Faculty of Medicine, January 9, 1945, APP, Série J, affaire Petiot, carton n° V.

24 *His thesis* This was entitled *Contribution à l'étude de la paralysie ascendante aiguë.*

24 *a legitimate degree-holder* Faculty of Medicine, January 9, 1945, APP, Série J, affaire Petiot, carton n° V.

24 *"very banal"* Dominique, *L'affaire Petiot*, 34.

25 *"Dr. Petiot is young"* Prospectus for Petiot's medical practice, APP, Série EA, carton n° 181.

25 *One recurring rumor* Marcel Jullian, *Le mystère Petiot* (Paris: Edition No. 1, 1980), 61.

25 *Madame Husson* Dominique *L'affaire Petiot*, 42.

26 *"Horse cures!"* Nézondet, *Petiot "le Possédé,"* 27.

27 *"that could kill an adult"* AN 334 AP65, 3310.

27 *"It was a veritable"*. . . *"I think I will"* Nézondet, *Petiot "le Possédé,"* 32, 7, 18, 34–35; Tomlins, *Die in Paris*, 156.

28 *the approximate equivalent* Thomas Maeder, *The Unspeakable Crimes of Dr. Petiot* (Boston: Little, Brown and Company, 1980), 134.

28 *"That's nothing"* Dominique *L'affaire Petiot*, 57.

CHAPTER 3. PRELIMINARY FINDINGS

29 *"the charred remains"* *Paris-Midi*, March 12, 1944.

29 *a sickening sweet . . . "it smelled just like"* Jean-François Dominique, *L'affaire Petiot: médecin, marron, gestapiste, guillotiné pour au moins vingt-sept assassinats* (Paris: Éditions Ramsay, 1980), 10.

29 *"a pile of skulls"* René Piédelièvre, *Souvenirs d'un médecin légiste* (Paris: Flammarion, 1966), 73.

30 *"respectable people"* Massui, *Le cas du Dr Petiot* (Brussels: E.D.C.1944), 11.

30 *"it was impossible to tell"* Marie Lombre, Report, June 3, 1944, APP, Série J, affaire Petiot, carton n° III.

30 *"cries for help"* Victor Avenelle in report, March 17, APP, Série J, affaire Petiot, carton n° II, and elaborated in his *Audition*, May 30, 1944, in carton n° III. See also *Paris-Soir*, March 28, 1944.

30 *Others claimed to hear* APP, Série J, affaire Petiot, carton n° II; Several biographers also cite the testimony of another Petiot family living on rue Le Sueur. There was none in 1944. But eighty-two-year-old Amais Petiot had lived on the fourth floor of No. 18 until 1942, and her husband Eugène until his death in 1935. The second oldest of their four children was also named Marcel Petiot.

30 *smaller pile of lime . . . brown suitcase* Objets saisis rue Le Sueur, 13/3 PV No. 4, March 14, 1944, APP, Série J, affaire Petiot, carton n° I.

30 *a cart* Report, March 13, 1944, APP, Série J, affaire Petiot, carton n° III. The cart, lime, gas mask, needle, bust, the jars, and other items here were sealed as evidence by March 15, as outlined in Charles Deforeit's report, APP, Série J, affaire Petiot, carton n° III.

31 *a black satin dress* Report, *Objets saisis*, March 14, 1944, APP, Série J, affaire Petiot, carton n° I.

31 *old-fashioned woman's hat* As police learned, the former owner of 21 rue Le Sueur, Princess Colloredo-Mansfeld, had purchased it for a friend, Georgette Mazeaublanc, who lived in the house between 1932 and 1939. This woman left the hat there when she moved out. Report, March 28, 1944, APP, Série J, affaire Petiot, carton n° II.

31 *twenty-two toothbrushes* Georges Massu, *L'enquête Petiot: La plus grande affaire criminelle du siècle* (Paris: Librairie Arthème Fayard, 1959), 198–199.

32 *specimens of human genitals* Report, March 15, 1944, APP, Série J, affaire Petiot, carton n° III.

32 *"Order from German"* Massu, *L'enquête Petiot*, 234; Maeder, *The Unspeakable Crimes of Dr. Petiot* (Boston: Little, Brown, 1980), 10.

32 *then a twenty-four-year-old* Inspector Hernis, in his investigations, later discovered her age. Note, March 22, 1944, APP, Série J, affaire Petiot, carton n° II.

33 *René Nézondet remembered* René Nézondet, *Petiot "le possédé"* (Paris: Express, 1950), 34–35.

33 *"If she returns"* Frédérique Cesaire, *L'Affaire Petiot: Grands procès de l'histoire* (Paris: Éditions De Vecchi S.A., 1999), 14.

33 *Petiot was seen loading* Nézondet, *Petiot "le Possédé,"* 38.

34 *"A murder is"* Massu, *L'enquête Petiot*, 13.

34 *Massu was a native* Massu "Biographie," APP, KA 108, n° 93298.

34 *In January 1908* Massu personnel record, APP, KA 108, n° 93298.

34 *"Motor Car Bandits"* Dorothy and Thomas Hoobler, *The Crimes of Paris: A True Story of Murder, Theft, and Detection* (New York: Little, Brown and Company, 2009), 208–248. See also Richard Parry, *The Bonnot Gang* (London: Rebel Press, 1987).

35 *"good training"* Georges Massu, *Aveux Quai des Orfèvres. Souvenirs du Commissaire Massu* (Paris: La Tour Pointue, undated/1951), 11. The methods used at the time are described by a former chief of police judiciaire, Commissaire Guillaume, in *Trente-sept ans avec la pègre* (Paris: Editions de France, 1938), 44–48, 202–205.

35 *"without raising the voice"* Massu, *Aveux Quai des Orfèvres*, 13–14, 244.

36 *The massive, unruly* Janet Flanner, *Paris Was Yesterday 1925–1939* (New York: Harcourt Brace Jovanovich, 1972), 216–217; *Life*, July 10, 1939. George Sand's granddaughter testified at the trial, for the defense.

36 *"about forty years old"* . . . *"considered dangerous"* Arrest notice, March 13, 1944, APP, Série J, affaire Petiot, carton n° III.

36 *"The steps of an investigation"* . . . *"an idiot"* Massu, *Aveux Quai des Orfèvres*, 8.

37 *about nine thirty* Alice Denis, *Audition*, March 12, 1944, APP, Série J, affaire Petiot, carton n° II.

37 *"Yesterday evening"* Raymonde Denis, *Audition*, March 12, 1944, APP, Série J, affaire Petiot, carton n° II.

38 *a veritable prewar café* Massu, *L'enquête Petiot*, 226.

38 *504 vials Réquisitoire définitif,* December 31, 1945, APP, Série J, affaire Petiot, carton n° VII, and for the conclusion of a large amount far surpassing the average, AN 334 AP 65, 3361.

38 *"diabolical and grimacing"* Report, March 16, 1944, APP, Série J, affaire Petiot, carton n° III.

Chapter 4. Two Witnesses

39 *no fewer than ninety-five* AN 334, AP 65, 3313 and 3422. This part of Petiot's practice was already being reported by *Le Matin*, March 14, 1944.

39 *Massu now learned* Georges Massu, *L'enquête Petiot: La plus grande affaire criminelle du siècle* (Paris: Librairie Arthème Fayard, 1959), 45–46.

39 *In early 1942* André Larue discusses some of the drug seizures at this time in *Les Flics* (Paris: Fayard, 1969), 213, and another view is in Gérard de Villiers,

La brigade mondaine: Dossiers secrets révélés par Maurice Vincent, Officier de police principal honoraire (Paris: Presses de la Cité, 1972).

39 *Jean-Marc Van Bever* APP, Série J, affaire Petiot, carton n° I, particularly folder 13.

40 *the most exposed* See, for instance, Lucien Zimmer, *Un Septennat policier: Dessous et secrets de la police républicaine* (Paris: Fayard, 1967), 143–154.

40 *Petiot had written* AN 334 AP 65, 4168.

41 *"go out and steal."* . . . *"only known cure"* John V. Grombach, *The Great Liquidator* (New York: Zebra Books, 1980), 141.

41 *He had, however, become* AN 334 AP 65, 4171.

42 *"Perhaps Jeannette had"* Thomas Maeder, *The Unspeakable Crimes of Dr. Petiot* (Boston: Little, Brown and Company, 1980), 23.

42 *In November 1941* AN 334 AP 65, 4182–4183.

43 *"It is no longer necessary"* . . . *a fine* Grombach, *The Great Liquidator,* 144.

44 *"14 vials of heroin"* AN 334, AP 65, 4193–4194.

44 *It was hardly his fault* AN 334, AP 65, 4192–4193. Both Baudet and Desrouet would later blame each other.

44 *According to the police report* Fernand Lavie, *Audition,* March 14, 1944, APP, Série J, affaire Petiot, carton n° III.

45 *Petiot offered to make* Ibid.

46 *"Do not trouble yourself"* Claude Bertin, *Les assassins hors-série: Gilles de Rais, Petiot,* vol. 10 of *Les grands procès de l'histoire de France* (Paris: Éditions de Saint-Clair, 1967), 165.

46 *Khaït also recalled* AN 334, AP 65, 4201.

47 *The maid, who received the letters* AN 334, AP 65, 4206.

47 *"You wretch!"* *Le Matin,* March 14, 1944, and Petiot's reply, Massu, *L'enquête Petiot,* 51.

48 *"Rest assured"* Marcel Jullian, *Le Mystère Petiot* (Paris: Edition No. 1, 1980), 142; Georges Massu reports the incident with slightly different words in *L'enquête Petiot,* 52.

Chapter 5. "100,000 Autopsies"

49 *"The New Landru"* *Le Petit Parisien,* March 13, 1944.

49 *"burned alive"* *L'Oeuvre,* March 13, 1944.

49 *"demonic, erotic"* *Le Matin,* March 14, 1944.

50 *double life* The question of a double life was also posed in French papers, for instance *Le Petit Parisien,* March 16, 1944.

50 *"shady ladies"* . . . *"twisted corpse"* Associated Press, May 28, 1944.

50 *spotlights* The United Press, in turn, broadcast the report in various newspapers, for instance, *Milwaukee Journal,* March 15, 1944. The claim had already been reported by *Le Matin,* March 14, 1944.

50 *"You have often heard"* Georges Massu, *Aveux Quai des Orfèvres. Souvenirs du Commissaire Massu* (Paris: La Tour Pointue, undated/1951), 242–243.

51 *"catastrophic"* Ibid.

51 *many bodies, but no signs* Jacques Perry and Jane Chabert, *L'affaire Petiot* (Paris: Gallimard, 1957), 20.

51 *"I should have been"* Albert Massui, *Le cas du Dr Petiot* (Brussels: E.D.C., 1944), 35.

51 *"A shiver ran down"* . . . *"His black eyes"* Associated Press, May 4, 1944.

52 *"horrible and icy"* Georges Massu, *L'enquête Petiot: La plus grande affaire criminelle du siècle* (Paris: Librairie Arthème Fayard, 1959), 184.

53 *having trouble sleeping* Massu, *L'enquête Petiot*, 83.

53 *"Boss"* . . . *"It's almost certain"* Massu, *L'enquête Petiot*, 86. Rumors of Petiot's drug habit were soon circulated further, *Le Petit Parisien*, March 15, 1944.

53 *"did not want to provide"* Report, March 14, 1944, APP, Série J, affaire Petiot, carton n° I.

53 *"very bad reputation"* Ibid.

53 *On March 11, 1930* Report, March 14, 1944, APP, Série J, affaire Petiot, carton n° I.

55 *"Furiously, he pressed"* Seguin's testimony appears in Jean-François Dominique, *L'affaire Petiot: médecin, marron, gestapiste, guillotiné pour au moins vingt-sept assassinats* (Paris: Éditions Ramsay, 1980), 51. Petiot's fingerprints are found in folder 42 of APP, Série J, carton n° I.

55 *Speculations rose* Paris-Soir, March 20, 1943, and more fully in *Paris-Soir*, March 21, 1943.

56 *"by accident"* Jean-Marc Varaut, *L'abominable Dr. Petiot* (Paris: Balland 1974), 51.

56 *"anthropometric" techniques* Marcel Le Clère, *Histoire de la police* (Paris: Presses universitaires de France, 1947), 105–107; Colin Beavan, *Fingerprints: The Origins of Crime Detection and the Murder Case That Launched Forensic Science* (New York: Hyperion 2001), 76–93.

57 *five million measurements* Claude Cancès with Dominique Cellura, Alissia Grifat, and Franck Hériot, *Histoire du 36, quai des Orfèvres* (Paris: 2010), 53.

57 *"enthusiastic admiration"* Sir Arthur Conan Doyle, "The Adventure of the Naval Treaty," in Dorothy and Thomas Hoobler, *The Crimes of Paris: A True Story of Murder, Theft, and Detection* (New York: Little, Brown and Company, 2009), 153.

57 *"A right foot"* Dr. Paul's testimony in F.A. Mackenzie, *Landru* (London: Geoffrey Bles, 1928), 201. This book was reissued in 1995 in *The Notable Trials Library* of Gryphon Editions with an introduction by Alan M. Dershowitz.

58 *"the doctor of"* . . . *"thigh bones, craniums, shinbones"* Massu, *L'enquête Petiot*, 78–79.

58 *Massu and Paul* Massu, *Aveux Quai des Orfèvres*, 212; Massu, *L'enquête Petiot*, 80.

58 *In most cases* Premier Rapport préliminaire et succinct, APP, carton n° VII.

59 *"three garbage cans"* Le Petit Parisien, March 15, 1944.

59 *"It's not an autopsy"* Massu, *L'enquête Petiot*, 79.

Chapter 6. The Woman with the Yellow Suitcase

61 *"I realized"* Simone de Beauvoir, *The Prime of Life*, translated by Peter Green (London: Penguin Books, 1988), 13.

61 *Sartre's friend Jean Paulhan joked* Annie Cohen-Solal, *Sartre: A Life*, translated by Anna Cancogni (New York, Pantheon Books, 1987), 187.

62 *"the strongest heterosexual"* Ronald Aronson, *Camus & Sartre: The Story of a Friendship and the Quarrel That Ended It* (Chicago: The University of Chicago Press, 2004), 20.

62 *"We were like"* Ibid.

62 *"Imagine what she"* Olivier Todd, *Camus: A Life*, translated by Benjamin Ivry (New York, Alfred A. Knopf, 1997), 231.

63 *"He has no right"* French police report printed in Pascal Bonafoux, *"Picasso, Français?": Questions sur la naturalisation de l'artiste*, in Bruno Fuligni, ed., *Dans les secrets de la police: quatre siècles d'histoire, de crimes et de faits divers dans les archives de la Préfecture de police* (Paris: L'Iconoclaste, 2008), 230–231. See also *Pablo Picasso: dossiers de la préfecture de police, 1901–1940* by Pierre Daix and Armand Israël (Moudon, Switzerland: Editions Acatos, 2003).

63 *"Very illegally"* Maurice Toesca, *Cinq ans de patience 1939–1944* (Paris: É. Paul, 1975), 179.

63 *stacks of manuscripts* Gerhard Heller, *Un allemand à Paris 1940–1944* (Paris: Éditions du Seuil, 1981), 26–28.

63 *heart beating with excitement* Ibid., 117–118, his first visit to Picasso, June 1942.

63 *the drab palette* Pierre Cabanne, *Pablo Picasso: His Life and Times* (New York: William Morrow and Company, Inc., 1977), 343.

64 *a roadside restaurant* Georges Massu, *L'enquête Petiot: La plus grande affaire criminelle du siècle* (Paris: Librairie Arthème Fayard, 1959), 87; time and placement of the stop in police report, March 14, 1944, APP, Série J, affaire Petiot, carton n° I.

64 *"roasted barley"* Massu, *L'enquête Petiot*, 88.

65 *Maurice Petiot was not there* He is invariably placed in the shop, but the Brigade Criminelle report indicates he was not, March 14, 1944, APP, Série J, affaire Petiot, carton n° I. Other reports, along with interviews with Maurice cited below, confirm the fact.

65 *thirty-one-year-old* Monique would turn thirty-one in nine days.

65 *"the most extraordinary"* Le Matin, March 23, 1944.

65 *Albert Neuhausen* Report April 6, 1944, APP, Série J, affaire Petiot, carton n° I.

66 *"We spoke of things"* Report, March 13, 1944; APP, Série J, affaire Petiot, carton n° I.

66 *a black skirt* Paris-Matin, March 15, 1944.

66 *a few locks* Le Petit Parisien, March 16, 1944.

66 *before collapsing* Massu, *L'enquête Petiot*, 90–91.

66 *One young man* Ibid. *Le Matin*, March 15, 1944.

66 *Maurice, who had been apprehended* Report, March 24, 1944, APP, Série J, affaire Petiot, carton n° I.

66 *"short sobs"* Massu, *L'enquête Petiot*, 91, and Report, March 16, 1944, APP, Série J, affaire Petiot, carton n° II.

CHAPTER 7. "BESIDE A MONSTER"

67 *"the intrusion of"* Georges Massu, *Aveux Quai des Orfèvres. Souvenirs du Commissaire Massu* (Paris: La Tour Pointue, undated/1951), 28–29.

68 *Massu stalled* Georges Massu, *L'enquête Petiot: La plus grande affaire criminelle du siècle* (Paris: Librairie Arthème Fayard, 1959), 94.

68 *two million bicycles* Gilles Perrault and Pierre Azéma, *Paris Under the Occupation* (New York: The Vendome Press, 1989), 41.

68 *"Well, Madame Petiot"* Massu, *L'enquête Petiot*, 94.

68 *"I must say"* Georgette Petiot, *Audition*, March 14, 1944, APP, Série J, affaire Petiot, carton n° III.

68 *in a low, barely audible* Massu, *L'enquête Petiot*, 94–95.

69 *"old books and antiquities"* . . . *one hour and a half later* Georgette Petiot, *Audition*, March 14, 1944, APP, Série J, affaire Petiot, carton n° III.

69 *Raymonde Hanss* Report, June 18, 1936, APP, Série J, affaire Petiot, carton n° V.

69 *"Pull yourself"* . . . *"Perhaps rue des Lombards?"* Massu, *L'enquête Petiot*, 96–102; *Le Petit Parisien*, March 16, 1944; Report, March 18, 1944, APP, Série J, affaire Petiot, carton n° II.

72 *Wives of criminals* . . . *In which category* Massu, *L'enquête Petiot*, 91.

72 *"a little chill"* . . . *"I have never known"* Maurice Petiot, *Audition*, March 14, 1944, APP, Série J, affaire Petiot, carton n° III.

CHAPTER 8. A DELIVERY

74 *"Paris had been"* Jean-Paul Sartre, "Paris Under the Occupation," originally published in *La France libre* (1945), and reprinted in *The Aftermath of War* (Situations III), translated by Chris Turner (New York: Seagull Books, 2008), 22. Turner has a slightly different translation.

74 *Potatoes were peeled* Lucie Aubrac, *Outwitting the Gestapo*, translated by Konrad Bieber, with the assistance of Betsy Wing (Lincoln: University of Nebraska Press, 1993), 19.

75 *Wartime diets in France* Julian Jackson, *France: The Dark Years 1940–1944* (Oxford: Oxford University Press, 2001), 233. A possible exception, of course, was Italy. Robert O. Paxton, *Vichy France: Old Guard and New Order* (New York: Columbia University Press, 2001), 360. Paxton also thinks that France was worse off than "Eastern Europe, Rumania, Bulgaria, Hungary, and the Protectorate of Bohemia-Moravia."

75 *the "ballet of buds"* Georges Massu, *L'enquête Petiot: La plus grande affaire criminelle du siècle* (Paris: Librairie Arthème Fayard, 1959), 130.

75 *"Did she confess?"* Massu, *L'enquête Petiot,* 103.

75 *"Gentlemen"* . . . *"Simple mania"* Massu, *L'enquête Petiot,* 131, 103–106.

76 *"Assassins!"* Le Petit Parisien, March 16, 1944.

77 *Georgette Petiot was driven* Report March 20, 1944, APP, Série J, affaire Petiot, carton nº II.

77 *Georgette's father* Report, February 6, 1945, APP, Série J, affaire Petiot, carton nº V.

78 *"humming, whistling, and"* Jean-François Dominique, *L'affaire Petiot: médecin, marron, gestapiste, guillotiné pour au moins vingt-sept assassinats* (Paris: Éditions Ramsay, 1980), 45.

79 *"love the people"* Dominique, *L'affaire Petiot,* 58.

79 *"Drain Petiot"* John V. Grombach, *The Great Liquidator* (New York: Zebra Books, 1980), 78.

80 *"It's a vile political"* Claude Barret, *L'affaire Petiot* (Paris: Gallimard, 1958), 44.

80 *twenty-one residents* Report, March 18, 1944; APP, Série J, affaire Petiot, carton nº II.

81 *According to Alicot* Report, March 18, 1944, APP, Série J, affaire Petiot, carton nº II. The stays, from September 11, 1940, to February 22, 1944, are listed, with room numbers, in a Brigade Criminelle report two days later, also in carton nº II. See also René Kracmer's interview with Madame Alicot in *Le Matin,* March 28, 1944.

CHAPTER 9. EVASION

82 *"Dr. Petiot was"* René Piédelièvre, *Souvenirs d'un médecin légiste* (Paris: Flammarion, 1966), 78.

82 *young and beautiful* Sylvie Givaudan, Marseille Police Report, March 28, 1944, APP, Série J, Affaire Petiot, carton nº I. See also *Paris-Soir,* March 20, 1944, and *Le Parisien* of the same day.

82 *Joséphine Aimée Grippay* Grippay is "Josephine G" in Georges Massu, *L'enquête Petiot: La plus grande affaire criminelle du siècle* (Paris: Librairie Arthème Fayard, 1959), 137–143.

82 *"It was good"* Massu, *L'enquête Petiot,* 138.

82 *"La Chinoise"* Marseille Police, March 28, 1944, APP, Série J, affaire Petiot, carton nº I.

82 *By the time* Piereschi police record, forwarded from Marseille, APP, Série J, affaire Petiot, carton nº I. He is "P" in Massu's memoir.

83 *"sunny farmhouse"* Fabienne Jamet, *One Two Two: [122 rue de Provence]* (Paris: O. Orban, 1975), translated by Derek Coltman as *Palace of Sweet Sin* (London: W.H. Allen, 1977), 10–11.

83 *Petiot had drawn* APP, Série J, affaire Petiot, carton nº I.

83 *"the same reasons"* Report, May 20, 1944, APP, Série J, affaire Petiot, carton nº I.

84 *"nearly all the drug addicts"* Report, June 29, 1944, APP, Série J, affaire Petiot, carton n° I.

84 *"It is through"*... *"pinch nipples"* Jean-François Dominique, *L'affaire Petiot: médecin, marron, gestapiste, guillotiné pour au moins vingt-sept assassinats* (Paris: Éditions Ramsay, 1980), 31.

84 *"All human preoccupations"*... *"a foul muddle"* Piédelièvre *Souvenirs*, 11, 73–79.

86 *clearly after the skin* Premier Rapport préliminaire et succinct, APP, Série J, affaire Petiot, carton n° VII.

86 *"The smallest testimony"* Massu, *L'enquête Petiot*, 145.

86 *"Would you please"*... *"It is for you to prove"* Maurice Petiot, *Audition*, March 15, 1944, APP, Série J, affaire Petiot, carton n° III.

87 *"He told me it"* Enquête Auxerre, March 16, 1944, APP, Série J, affaire Petiot, carton n° III.

87 *"Have you seen any lime"* Maurice Petiot, *Audition*, March 15, 1944, APP, Série J, affaire Petiot, carton n° III.

88 *Maurice hesitated* Massu, *L'enquête Petiot*, 111.

88 *"the electrical material"*... *"I should tell you"* Maurice Petiot, *Nouvelle Audition*, March 15, 1944, APP, Série J, affaire Petiot, carton n° III.

89 *"As long as"* Massu *L'enquête Petiot*, 114.

89 *Maurice Petiot, protesting* Le Petit Parisien, March 17, 1944.

89 *That night, he and Bernard discussed* Massu, *L'enquête Petiot*, 114–116.

Chapter 10. "Goodbye Arrogance"

90 *a success popularized* Stephen G. Michaud with Roy Hazelwood, *The Evil That Men Do: FBI Profiler Roy Hazelwood's Journey into the Minds of Sexual Predators* (New York: St. Martin's Press, 1998), 6.

90 *"homicidal triad"* John Douglas and Mark Olshaker, *Mindhunter: Inside the FBI's Elite Serial Crime Unit* (New York: Pocket Books, 1995), 105.

90 *the third was* The fire and suspicions of Dr. Petiot, Inspector Hernis report, March 22, 1944, APP, Série J, affaire Petiot, carton n° II.

91 *Detectives searched banks* Report, March 18, 1944, APP, Série J, affaire Petiot, carton n° III.

91 *staking out the auction houses* Surveillance report, March 18, 1944, APP, Série J, affaire Petiot, carton n° II.

91 *"I have never noticed anything"* Marie Le Roux, *Audition*, March 13, 1944, APP, Série J, affaire Petiot, carton n° III.

92 *"nothing suspicious"* Transport et Perquisition, March 15, 1944, APP, Série J, affaire Petiot, carton n° III.

92 *to "kill the bugs"* Maurice Petiot, *Nouvelle Audition*, March 16, 1944, APP, Série J, affaire Petiot, carton n° III.

92 *"Goodbye arrogance"* Georges Massu, *L'enquête Petiot: La plus grande affaire criminelle du siècle* (Paris: Librairie Arthème Fayard, 1959), 118.

93 *"My brother did not"* . . . *"I wanted to know"* Maurice Petiot, *Nouvelle Audition*, March 16, 1944, APP, Série J, affaire Petiot, carton n° III.

93 *as Massu soon learned* Report, March 24, 1944, APP, Série J, affaire Petiot, carton n° IV.

93 *"I am convinced"* Albert Massui, *Le cas du Dr Petiot* (Brussels: E.D.C., 1944), 56.

CHAPTER 11. SIGHTINGS

94 *Monster of rue Le Sueur* Variants were also used, particularly the *"Vampire de l'Etoile"* (*Le Petit Parisien*, March 23, 1944) and *"Vampire de la rue le Sueur"* (*Le Petit Parisien*, March 29, 1944).

94 *the Werewolf of Paris* *Chicago Daily Tribune*, April 10, 1946.

94 *In the métro* *Paris-Soir*, March 25, 1944.

95 *scalping* *Le Cri du Peuple*, March 26, 1944.

95 *The police* *Le Cri du Peuple*, April 8–10, 1944.

95 *"Satan in person"* A reporter for *Le Matin* heard similar comments, March 18–19, 1944.

95 *A psychic claimed* Letter, March 22, 1944, APP, Série J, affaire Petiot, carton n° V.

95 *on a country road in Yonne* Or, in a variant form, in the river, though this was proved false, the *New York Times* reported, March 25, 1944.

95 *"If Petiot is still alive"* Georges Massu, *L'enquête Petiot: La plus grande affaire criminelle du siècle* (Paris: Librairie Arthème Fayard, 1959), 238.

95 *Fifty thousand concierges* Maurice Toesca, *Cinq ans de patience 1939–1944* (Paris: É. Paul, 1975), entry dated March 12, 1944, 218.

96 *A man in Orléans* *Le Petit Parisien*, March 20, 1944. There is also a police report from Orléans of a sighting about this time in Report, March 17, 1944, APP, Série J, affaire Petiot, carton n° III.

96 *"Pity"* Albert Massui, *Le cas du Dr Petiot* (Brussels: E.D.C.,1944), 59.

96 *"freemason brothers"* *Paris-Soir*, April 1, 1944.

96 *"It is a myth"* March 29, 1944, Léon Werth, *Déposition: Journal 1940–1944* (Paris: Viviane Hamy, 2000), 594.

97 *"Petiot, he runs"* Massu, *L'enquête Petiot*, 238.

97 *"fatal injections"* . . . *"crowded war news"* *Time*, March 27, 1944. The author of the piece also noted the belief that Petiot was a fabrication.

97 *"Madame, your bones"* Jean-Marc Varaut, *L'abominable Dr. Petiot* (Paris: Balland, 1974), 160.

97 *"real-life equivalent"* *St. Petersburg Times*, May 28, 1944.

97 *"Will Dr Petiot"* *Paris-Soir*, March 18, 1944.

97 *"Who would have believed"* Massu, *L'enquête Petiot*, 75–76.

98 *about nine fifteen or nine twenty* Verification, March 18, 1944, APP, Série J, affaire Petiot, carton n° III; Maria Vic, *Audition*, March 24, 1944, also in n° III.

98 *"Burn the papers!"* Report, March 18, 1944, APP, Série J, affaire Petiot, carton n° III.

98 *purchased about three hundred kilos* Report, March 19, 1944, APP, Série J, affaire Petiot, carton n° III.

99 *Redouté would later* Georges Redouté, *Audition,* November 4, 1944, APP, Série J, affaire Petiot, carton n° V.

99 *The concierge* Report, November 4, 1944, APP, Série J, affaire Petiot, carton n° V.

99 *"only went out"* Ibid.

100 *If only, he mused . . . "impatient as a young dog"* Massu, *L'enquête Petiot,* 56, 58, 60–61, and 74.

100 *"debris of bones"* *Le Matin,* March 22, 1944.

101 *Massu said that he knew* Massu, *L'enquête Petiot,* 152.

101 *"field of vision"* Massu, *L'enquête Petiot,* 132.

101 *"reduced to hypotheses"* Massu, *L'enquête Petiot,* 153.

102 *"at the level of the neck"* Report, August 31, 1942, APP, Série J, affaire Petiot, carton n° VII.

102 *"trace of violence"* Ibid.

102 *two human hands* Police report of Courbevoie, August 22, 1942, APP, Série J, affaire Petiot, carton n° VII.

103 *"a man of the lecture hall"* *Le Petit Parisien,* March 22, 1944.

103 *"We forensic scientists"* Ibid.

103 *four thighs alone* Report, November 19, 1942, APP, Série J, affaire Petiot, carton n° VII.

103 *"a storm cloud of mosquitoes"* Massu, *L'enquête Petiot,* 154.

104 *"Is it tomorrow"* Massu, *L'enquête Petiot,* 156.

Chapter 12. The Gestapo File

105 *According to one* Gestapo report, May 8, 1943, APP, Série J, affaire Petiot, carton n° I.

106 *Jodkum* Jodkum or Jodkun is usually called director of IV B-4. He was not. The leader of IV B-4, at this time, was SS First Lieutenant Heinz Röthke, who assumed duties in July 1942 from Theodor Dannecker. Background on Jodkum comes from captured Gestapo records and interviews at CDJC, XCVI Service allemand anti-juif en France, and Service IVB-4, particularly the testimony of Kurt Schendel and Henri Jalby on B.d.s. IV 4 b.

106 *Although also nominally* See particularly Henri Joseph Jalby testimony at CDJC, "Service Jodkun" XCVI, 58–62, 76 as well as Grégory Auda, *Les belles années du "milieu" 1940–1944* and *Le grand banditisme dans la machine répressive allemande en France* (Paris: Éditions Michalon, 2002), note 1, 109.

106 *"contraband of persons"* Report, Sipo (SD) KD Paris, IV E 2a15016, May 22, 1943, APP, Série J, affaire Petiot, carton n° I.

106 *Dreyfus was a thirty-five-year* Der Kommendeur der Sicherheitspolizei und des SD in Paris, Tgb. Nr. V B1—4065/44, June 23, 1944, APP, Série J, affaire Petiot, carton n° II.

107 *"I am a Frenchman"* AN 334, AP 65, 4434.

107 *at Montpellier* Report, October 7, 1944, APP, Série J, affaire Petiot, carton n° I.

108 *"hotel or a doctor's office"* Gestapo report, May 8, 1943, APP, Série J, affaire Petiot, carton n° I.

108 *The organization under scrutiny* Gestapo report, May 21, 1943, and forwarded to the French police, APP, Série J, affaire Petiot, carton n° I.

109 *"The management"* Ibid.

109 *"remarkably efficient"* Gestapo report, May 21, 1943, APP, Série J, affaire Petiot, carton n° I.

109 *"unexpected costs"* AN 334, AP 65, 4439–4440.

109 *signing two important documents* AN 334, AP 65, 4398–9.

110 *By this time* Guélin had prepared the way for three months of work, according to hairdresser Raoul Fourrier. AN 334, AP 65, 4403.

110 *"We climbed a dirty, dark"* Gestapo report, May 14, 1943, printed in Jacques Perry and Jane Chabert, *L'affaire Petiot* (Paris: Gallimard, 1957), 100.

110 *counted as numerous* Report, Sipo (SD) KD Paris, IV E 2a15016, May 22, 1943, APP, Série J, affaire Petiot, carton n° I.

110 *Once this was accomplished* Gestapo report, May 21, 1943, APP, Série J, affaire Petiot, carton n° I.

112 *"the doctor showed it"* Gestapo report, May 16, 1943, APP, Série J, affaire Petiot, carton n° I.

112 *"thirty-five to thirty-eight"* VM-X report to Gestapo, May 18, 1943, APP, Série J, affaire Petiot, carton n° I.

112 *serial numbers* Ibid.

112 *He ordered his* Report, Sipo (SD) KD Paris, IV E 2a15016, May 22, 1943, APP, Série J, affaire Petiot, carton n° I.

113 *They also arrested* Der Kommandeur der Sicherheitspolizei und des SD, Tgb. Nr. V B1—4065/44, June 23, 1944, APP, Série J, affaire Petiot, carton n° II.

113 *"a den of murderers"* Hans Bernd Gisevius, *To the Bitter End: An Insider's Account of the Plot to Kill Hitler, 1933–1944*, foreword by Allen W. Dulles, translated by Richard and Clara Winston (New York: Da Capo Press, 1998), 50.

114 *"with his hand"* Ibid.

114 *"three days and two nights"* Alomée Planel, *Docteur Satan ou l'affaire Petiot* (Paris: Éditions Robert Laffont, 1978), 191.

114 *"the bath"* Jacques Delarue, *Trafics et crimes sous l'occupation* (Paris: Fayard, 1968), 42.

114 *Sometimes prisoners* Edward Crankshaw, *The Gestapo: Instrument of Tyranny* (New York: Da Capo Press, Inc., 1994),128–129, based on the evidence amassed by the French prosecuting counsel at Nuremberg.

114 *"running a prisoner"* Cooks on the second floor complained of the screams from the interrogation rooms on the fifth. Jacques Delarue, *The Gestapo: A History of Horror*, translated by Mervyn Savill (New York: Paragon House, 1987), 234–236.

115 *"June 1943"* . . . *"Vive le fin"* Henri Calet, *Les Murs de Fresnes* (Paris: Editions des Quatre Vents, 1945), 29, 57, 25, 53.

115 *"a pitiful sight"* René Nézondet, *Petiot "le Possédé"* (Paris: Express, 1950), 59.

115 *According to his confession* Nr IV-B Report, Le Chef de la Sû
reté et du SD en France, June 11, 1943, APP, Série J, affaire Petiot, carton n° I.

116 *"All I knew"* Ibid.

116 *"I never saw"* Ibid.

116 *The file in front of Massu* The Gestapo rarely released prisoners, that is, except to a German tribunal, a concentration camp, or at least a French prison. For more, see Jacques Delarue, *The Gestapo*, 241–242.

116 *to "turn" prisoner* A tactic described, for instance, from an Abwehr perspective, in Oscar Reile, *L'Abwehr: Le contre-espionnage allemand en France,* preface by Colonel Rémy (Paris: Éditions France-Empire, 1970), 281–282.

117 *in return for 100,000 francs* This was confirmed by a man attached to Jodkum in the Gestapo office, Henri Jalby, in an undated report, APP, Série J, affaire Petiot, carton n° II.

CHAPTER 13. POSTCARDS FROM THE OTHER SIDE

118 *On September 27, 1940* Serge Klarsfeld, *Le Calendrier de la persécution des juifs de France 1940–1944* (Paris: Fayard, 2001), I, 26–28. *"Enterprise juive"* comes from paragraph 4 of this law.

118 *The following month* For more, see Susan Zuccotti, *The Holocaust, the French, and the Jews* (New York: Basic Books, 1993), 56–64, and Michael R. Marrus and Robert O. Paxton, *Vichy France and the Jews* (New York: Basic Books, Publishers, 1981), 75–114.

118 *In early May 1941* Serge Klarsfeld, *Vichy-Auschwitz* (Paris: Fayard, 1983), 15–18. Klarsfeld also shows the breakdown into Polish, Czech, and former Austrian Jews, and by arrondissement.

119 *Three months later* Klarsfeld, *Vichy-Auschwitz*, 25–27.

119 *As Gouedo explained* Jean Gouedo declaration, March 15, 1944, APP, Série J, affaire Petiot, carton n° I. See also his interrogation, March 23, 1944 in carton n° III.

120 *On January 2* Renée Guschinow, *Audition*, March 21, 1944, APP, Série J, affaire Petiot, carton n° III.

121 *"I have arrived"* . . . *"sell all [her] belongings"* Renée Guschinow, *Audition*, March 21, 1944, APP, Série J, affaire Petiot, carton n° III. AN 334, AP 65, 3372–3373.

121 *Marcel Petiot had purchased* Robert Sens-Olive, *Audition*, March 18, 1944, APP, Série J, affaire Petiot, carton n° II, and report March 24, 1944, in carton n° I.

122 *Jean Minaud . . . said* Jean Minaud, *Audition*, March 21, 1944, APP, Série J, affaire Petiot, carton n° III.

122 *"electric transformer"* Gaston Dethève, *Audition*, March 23, 1944, APP, Série J, affaire Petiot, carton n° III.

123 *"Aryanized"* For more on Aryanization, see note to page 13.

124 *Porchon, tempted* Roland Porchon, *Audition*, March 17, 1944, APP, Série J, affaire Petiot, carton n° III.

124 *"the King of the Gangsters"* Roland Porchon, *Audition*, March 17, 1944, APP, Série J, affaire Petiot, carton n° III.

124 *"sixteen corpses stretched out"* . . . *"I suppose he asked them"* Ibid.

125 *"He didn't seem"* . . . *"forgotten about it"* René Bouygues, *Audition*, March 19, 1944, APP, Série J, affaire Petiot, carton n° III; Lucien Doulet, *Audition*, April 24, 1944; also in Jean-François Dominique, *L'affaire Petiot: médecin, marron, gestapiste, guillotiné pour au moins vingt-sept assassinats* (Paris: Éditions Ramsay, 1980), 105–107.

125 *even after fireman* Avilla Boudringhin, *Audition*, March 16, 1944, APP, Série J, affaire Petiot, carton n° III.

126 *"At no point"* Joseph Teyssier, *Audition*, March 16, 1944, APP, Série J, affaire Petiot, carton n° III.

126 *Fillion supported* Emile Fillion, *Audition*, March 17, 1944, APP, Série J, affaire Petiot, carton n° III.

126 *evidence was mounting* For instance, Roger Berody, *Audition*, March 16, 1944, APP, Série J, affaire Petiot, carton n° III, and on the following day, additional confirmation from eyewitnesses Robert Bouquin and Maurice Choquat, also in carton n° III.

126 *"the brother of the owner"* Emile Fillion, *Audition*, March 18, 1944, APP, Série J, affaire Petiot, carton n° III.

126 *Teyssier also now acknowledged* Joseph Tessyier, *Audition*, March 18, 1944, APP, Série J, affaire Petiot, carton n° III. Newspapers later covered the story—for instance, *Le Cri du Peuple*, April 7 and 14, 1944, and *Paris-Soir*, April 13, 1944.

126 *"At that moment"* Emile Fillion, *Audition*, March 18, 1944, APP, Série J, affaire Petiot, carton n° III.

126 *jumping out of a window* Luc Rudolph (coordination), *Au coeur de la Préfecture de police: de la résistance à la liberation. 2e Partie. La Préfecture de police: une résistance oubliée 1940–1944* (Paris: 2010), 56.

Chapter 14. Destination Argentina

128 *"verbal trance [that] gave free rein"* Brassaï, *Conversations with Picasso*, translated by Jane Marie Todd (Chicago: University of Chicago Press, 1999), 200.

128 *"humor and inexhaustible spirit of invention"* Ibid.

128 *As the play ended* Maurice Toesca, *Cinq ans de patience 1939–1944* (Paris: É. Paul, 1975) 220–221.

128 *"A year before"* Simone de Beauvoir, *The Prime of Life*, translated by Peter Green (London: Penguin Books, 1988), 569.

128 *"We constituted"* Simone de Beauvoir, *The Prime of Life*, 575.

129 *"filled with the joy"* Ibid.

129 *Fourrier appeared nervous* Georges Massu, *L'enquête Petiot: La plus grande affaire criminelle du siècle* (Paris: Librairie Arthème Fayard, 1959), 160–161.

129 *Fourrier told* Raoul Fourrier, *Audition*, March 19, 1944, APP, Série J, affaire Petiot, carton n° III.

129 *"the doctor is a charming"* . . . *"nice commission"* Massu, *L'enquête Petiot*, 163.

130 *"Jo la Ric"* Raoul Fourrier, *Nouvelle Audition*, March 19, 1944, APP, Série J, affaire Petiot, carton n° III. "Iron Arm Jo" or "Iron Arm Géo" were often reported, for instance, in *Le Matin*, March 27, 1944.

130 *"no choirboy"* Massu, *L'enquête Petiot*, 169.

130 *Hesse* Chamberlin, *Audition*, September 8, 1944, BDIC, Fonds Delarue, F° Delta RES 787 4.

131 *"discretion, efficiency"* Philippe Aziz, *Tu Trahiras sans vergogne. Histoire de deux 'collabos' Bonny et Lafont* (Paris: Fayard, 1970), 76.

131 *"François the Corsican"* A police report from Lyon described him as a "dangerous individual," April 21, 1944, APP, Série J, affaire Petiot, carton n° I.

131 *"dark-haired and elegant"* Ibid.

131 *"La Poute"* Report, April 17, 1944; APP, Série J, affaire Petiot, carton n° I.

131 *"difficult, even impossible"* Massu, *L'enquête Petiot*, 168.

132 *"gave him the chills"* Paul Georges Jobert, *Audition*, March 21, 1944, APP, Série J, affaire Petiot, carton n° III.

132 *François the Corsican went first* Many writers, including Massu later in his memoirs (page 168), mistakingly make Jo depart first.

132 *at the end of October 1942* APP, Série J, affaire Petiot, carton n° I.

132 *an estimated 1.4 million* Paul Georges Jobert, *Audition*, March 21, 1944, APP, Série J, affaire Petiot, carton n° III.

133 *"Really, did you not"* . . . *Massu, after the interview, felt* Massu, *L'enquête Petiot*, 168–169.

133 *network Vengeance* Some of its exploits are in François Wetterwald, *Vengeance: Histoire d'un corps franc* (1946), Victor Dupont's memoir *Témoignages,* and the archive on the organization Wetterwald donated to the BDIC. See also the website Turma Vengeance, at chantran.vengeance.free.fr.

133 *"set Europe ablaze"* M. R. D. Foot, *SOE in France: An Account of the Work of the British Special Operations Executive in France 1940–1944* (Frederick, Maryland: University Publications of America, Inc., 1984), 11.

133 *Section DF was smuggling* M.R.D. Foot, *SOE in France*, 94.

133 *British Military Intelligence Section 9 (MI 9)* M. R. D. Foot and J. M. Langley, *MI9: Escape and Evasion 1939–1945* (Boston: Little, Brown, and Company, 1980).

134 *not least in* Raising morale was another important consequence, a "marvellous effect" in the words of Airey Neave in *Saturday at M.I.9* (London: Hodder, 1969), 20.

134 *at least 313 Jews* Susan Zuccotti, *The Holocaust, the French, and the Jews* (New York: Basic Books, 1993), 257.

134 *Smugglers had long* See Lisa Fittko, *Escape Through the Pyrenees*, translated by David Koblick (Evanston, Illinois: Northwestern University Press, 1991) as

well as the works by Émilienne Eychenne, such as *Montagnes de la peur et de l'espérance: Le franchissement de la frontière espagnole pendant la seconde guerre mondiale dans le département des Hautes Pyrénées* (Paris: Édouard Private, 1980) and *Les Pyrénées de la liberté* (Paris: France–Empire, 1983).

135 *"the people of the port"* Daniel Judah Elazar and Peter Medding, *Jewish Communities in Frontier Societies: Argentina, Australia, and South Africa* (New York: Holmes & Meier, 1983), 67. See also Robert Weisbrot, *The Jews of Argentina: From the Inquisition to Péron* (Philadelphia: The Jewish Publication Society of America, 1979).

135 *"The federal government"* Haim Avni, *Argentina and the Jews*, trans. Gila Brand (Tuscaloosa: The University of Alabama Press, 1991), 9.

135 *"deny visas"* . . . *"uncorrupted"* Uki Goñi, *The Real Odessa: Smuggling the Nazis to Perón's Argentina* (London: Granta Books, 2003), 28–37.

137 *"Monsieur le commissaire"* . . . *"I am unable"* Massu, *L'enquête Petiot*, 170–174.

137 *Pintard would eventually say* Edmond Pintard, *Audition*, March 20, 1944, APP, Série J, affaire Petiot, carton n° III, and another one on March 22, 1944, also in carton n° III.

CHAPTER 15. WAR IN THE SHADOWS

139 *"The cause of France"* Charles de Gaulle, *The Complete War Memoirs of Charles de Gaulle*, translated by Jonathan Griffin and Richard Howard (New York: Carroll & Graf Publishers Inc., 1998), 83–84.

139 *"Whatever happens"* Ibid.

139 *Most of de Gaulle's* The figure for the entire movement is in Robert O. Paxton, *Vichy France: Old Guard and New Order 1940–1944* (New York: Columbia University Press, 2001), 44; the role of Bretons in Thomas R. Christofferson with Michael S. Christofferson, *France During World War II: From Defeat to Liberation* (New York: Fordham University Press, 2006), 136–137.

139 *seven thousand patriots* Robert O. Paxton, *Vichy France*, 44.

140 *"capable of using"* Although exaggerated, Tillion makes a point. See Christopher Lloyd's analysis, *Collaboration and Resistance in Occupied France: Representing Treason and Sacrifice* (New York: Palgrave Macmillan, 2003), 34.

140 *Liliane Schroeder reported* Liliane Schroeder, *Journal d'occupation, Paris 1940–1944: Chronique au jour le jour d'une époque oubliée* (Paris: François-Xavier de Guibert, 2000), February 13, 1941, 68.

141 *On the morning of August 21* Albert Ouzoulias (Colonel André), *Les Batillons de la jeunesse: le colonel Fabien et d'autres jeunes dans la résistance, dans les maquis et l'insurrection parisienne* (Paris: éditions sociales, 1967), 130–131.

141 *"corresponding to the gravity of the case"* Oscar Reile, *L'Abwehr: Le contre-espionnage allemand en France*, preface by Colonel Rémy (Paris: Éditions France-Empire, 1970), 163.

142 *"All close male relatives"* Ibid., 174–175.

142 *"a good occupation"* Point number 33 in Jean Texcier's "Advice to the Occupied" for Bastille Day 1940, Milton Dank, *The French Against the*

French: Collaboration and Resistance (Philadelphia: J.B. Lippincott Company, 1974), 66.

143 *"Total war has been"* Combat, Underground No. 55, March 1944, printed in *Camus at Combat: Writing 1944–1947,* edited and annotated by Jacqueline Lévi-Valensi, translated by Arthur Goldhammer (Princeton: Princeton University Press, 2006), 3.

143 *He missed his favorite* Olivier Todd, *Albert Camus: A Life,* translated by Benjamin Ivry (New York: Alfred A. Knopf, 1997), 36.

143 *For a time* Ibid., 161–162; previous experience, Herbert R. Lottmann, *Albert Camus: A Biography* (Garden City: Doubleday & Company, 1979), 235.

144 *The German-controlled press* John Gerassi, *Talking with Sartre: Conversations and Debates* (New Haven: Yale University Press, 2009), 108–109.

144 *"total dependence"* John Gerassi, *Jean-Paul Sartre: Hated Conscience of His Century Vol I: Protestant or Protester?* (Chicago: University of Chicago Press, 1989), 184.

144 *"spiritual leader"* Annie Cohen-Solal, *Sartre: A Life,* translated by Anna Cancogni (New York, Pantheon Books, 1987), 268.

144 *"golden age"* Ibid., 214.

145 *handsome young SS men* Fabienne Jamet, with René Havard and Albert Kantof *One Two Two: [122 rue de Provence]* (Paris: O. Orban, 1975), translated by Derek Coltman as *Palace of Sweet Sin* (London: W.H. Allen, 1977), 92.

145 *"horrible creatures"* . . . *"threw their money"* Ibid., 117–119.

Chapter 16. The Attic

146 *"the most passionate"* Georges Massu, *L'enquête Petiot: La plus grande affaire criminelle du siècle* (Paris: Librairie Arthème Fayard, 1959), 232–234.

146 *"Adrien the Basque"* Philippe Aziz, *Tu Trahiras sans vergogne: Histoire de deux 'collabos' Bonny et Lafont* (Paris: Fayard, 1970), 44; APP, Série J, affaire Petiot, carton n° I; AN, 334, AP 65, 4317–4318.

146 *A forty-five-year-old* Grégory Auda, *Les belles années de "milieu," 1940–1944* (Paris: Editions Michalon, 2002), 63, and AN, 334 AP 65, 4317–4318.

147 *Devisenschützkommando* Jacques Delarue, *Trafics et crimes sous l'occupation* (Paris: Fayard, 1968), 40.

147 *some thirty-eight thousand apartments* Jean-Marc Dreyfus, "Almost-Camps" in Paris: The Difficult Description of Three Annexes of Drancy—Austerlitz, Lévitan, and Bassano, July 1943 to August 1944," in Jonathan Petropoulos and John K. Roth, eds., *Gray Zones: Ambiguity and Compromise in the Holocaust and Its Aftermath* (New York: Berghahn Books, 2005), 225.

147 *Approximately one thousand cases* Detailed description from a victim of one such case in October 1943 is in BDIC, Fonds Delarue F Delta RES 787 6.

148 *with a scar two inches long* Report, March 27, 1944, APP, Série J, affaire Petiot, carton n° I.

148 *"Gine Volna"* Report, April 15, 1944; APP, Série J, affaire Petiot, carton n° I.

148 *"La Chinoise"* Marseille Police, March 28, 1944, APP, Série J, affaire Petiot, carton n° I.

148 *100-franc note* Fourrier acknowledged that this was a sign. *Nouvelle Audition,* March 19, 1944, APP, Série J, affaire Petiot, carton n° III, and discovery at rue Caumartin, *Perquisition,* March 15, 1944, also in n° III. See also Report, May 6, 1944, in same carton and later media attention, such as *Le Petit Parisien,* March 23, 1944.

149 *An inspector observing . . . "to simmer"* Massu, *L'enquête Petiot,* 179 180.

150 *"1000 to 2000 bottles of cognac"* René Nézondet, *Audition,* March 17, 1944, APP, Série J, affaire Petiot, carton n° III.

150 *"white as a sheet" . . . distance-operated syringe* René Nézondet, *Audition,* March 22, 1944, APP, Série J, affaire Petiot, carton n° III; this also appears in René Nézondet, *Petiot "le Possédé"* (Paris: Express, 1950), 70–75.

151 *"Why did you not inform" . . . "horrible truth"* Ibid.

151 *Commissaire Massu asked* Massu, *L'enquête Petiot,* 185.

151 *"fainted, or almost fainted"* Nézondet, *Petiot "le Possédé,"* 80. Aimée Lesage did not believe the faints were genuine interrogation, March 25, 1944, APP, Série J, affaire Petiot, carton n° III.

152 *an old truck* Augusta Debarre, *Audition,* March 18, 1944, APP, Série J, affaire Petiot, carton n° III.

152 *the vehicle was gray* Andrée Marçais, *Audition,* March 18, 1944, APP, Série J, affaire Petiot, carton n° III.

152 *"With my daughter"* Yvonne Staeffen, *Audition,* March 18, 1944, APP, Série J, affaire Petiot, carton n° III.

153 TRANSPORTS AVENUE DAUMESNIL Angèle Lalanne, *Audition,* March 18, 1944, APP, Série J, affaire Petiot, carton n° III.

153 *One of them* Report, undated, APP, Série J, affaire Petiot, carton n° III.

153 *Lion verified* Maurice Lion, *Audition,* March 31, 1944, APP, Série J, affaire Petiot, carton n° III.

153 *A quick visit* Brigade Criminelle Report, September 10, 1944, APP, Série J, affaire Petiot, carton n° VI.

153 *His wife, Simone-Andrée* Report, April 1, 1944, APP, Série J, affaire Petiot, carton n° II.

154 *Half of the village* Massu, *L'enquête Petiot,* 214–215.

154 *"the most tragic cargo"* Massu, *L'enquête Petiot,* 219.

154 *Rain splashed* Massu, *L'enquête Petiot,* 219–220.

154 *a luggage room* Ibid.

154 *The contents* Report, April 6, 1944, APP, Série J, affaire Petiot, carton n° I.

154 *311 handkerchiefs* Another tally found 366.

155 *Massu hoped* Massu, *L'enquête Petiot,* 221–222.

CHAPTER 17. FRUSTRATION

156 *"I do not read the newspapers"* Albert Neuhausen, *Audition,* March 31, 1944, APP, Série J, affaire Petiot, carton n° III.

156 *In the bedroom* Their son Christian Neuhausen admitted to the gifts. April 1, 1944, APP, Série J, affaire Petiot, carton n° III.

156 *He had also used* Two suitcases, however, were found at Hôtel Alicot. April 1, 1944, APP, Série J, affaire Petiot, carton n° III.

157 *"Now that Dr. Petiot"* Albert Neuhausen, *Nouvelle Audition*, March 31, 1944, APP, Série J, affaire Petiot, carton n° III.

157 *Neuhausen had other information* Ibid.

157 *a white shell necklace . . . Detectives also found* Search of rue Le Sueur, April 4, 1944, APP, Série J, affaire Petiot, carton n° III.

158 *"During my time with Dr. Petiot"* Geneviève Cuny, Procès-Verbal, March 23, 1944; APP, Série J, affaire Petiot, carton n° II.

158 *"Yes," she said, "Dr. Petiot often"* Ibid.

158 *One friend predicted* Le Matin, March 16, 1944.

158 *suicide* Le Petit Parisien, March 16, 1944

158 *After living his first five years* Gerhardt Petiot, *Audition*, March 30, 1944, APP, Série J, affaire Petiot, carton n° III.

159 *"I went there three different times"* Ibid.

160 *thirty-three thousand Jews alone* Serge Klarsfeld, *Vichy-Auschwitz: le rôle de Vichy dans la solution finale de la question juive en France—1942* (Paris: Fayard, 1983), 8.

160 *"You would phone"* Jean-Paul Sartre, "Paris Under the Occupation," originally published in *La France libre* (1945) and reprinted in *The Aftermath of War (Situations III)* translated by Chris Turner (London: Seagull Books, 2008), 15.

160 *The case of* APP, Série J, affaire Petiot, carton n° I, folders 46 and 50.

161 *The former husband* Charles Bartholomeus, *Audition*, March 21, 1944, APP, Série J, affaire Petiot, carton n° III.

161 *Mayor Hotin would deny* Henry Hotin, *Audition*, April 18, 1944, APP, Série J, affaire Petiot, carton n° I.

161 *"on her own initiative"* Pauline Hotin, *Audition*, April 18, 1944, APP, Série J, affaire Petiot, carton n° I.

161 *Wearing a yellow orange dress* Jean Hotin, *Audition*, April 18, 1944, APP, Série J, affaire Petiot, carton n° I.

161 *an enigmatic letter* Report, April 20, 1944, APP, Série J, affaire Petiot, carton n° I.

161 *"miscarriage" . . . "I am very sad"* Thomas Maeder, *The Unspeakable Crimes of Dr. Petiot* (Boston: Little, Brown and Company, 1980), 95–96.

162 *Jean said that he had first* Gendarmerie Nationale Report, May 25, 1944, APP, Série J, affaire Petiot, carton n° I.

162 *Denise's family* Report, March 24, 1944, APP, Série J, affaire Petiot, carton n° I.

162 *"It was half past"* Jean-Marc Varaut, *L'abominable Dr. Petiot* (Paris: Balland 1974), 242.

CHAPTER 18. NINE MORE

164 *Confirmation came from* Henri Chamberlin, *Audition,* November 22, 1944, APP, Série J, affaire Petiot, carton n° VII.

165 *Max Stocklin* Henri Chamberlin, *Audition,* September 8, 1944, BDIC, Fonds Delarue F° Delta RES 787, 4.

165 *"Otto agency"* Jacques Delarue, *Trafics et crimes sous l'occupation* (Paris: Fayard, 1968), 29–31; Grégory Auda, *Les belles années du "milieu" 1940–1944: Le grand banditisme dans la machine répressive allemande en France* (Paris: Éditions Michalon, 2002), 42–48.

165 *rue Tiquetonne* He answered to the "bureau Otto," which had expanded from three buildings, 18, 23, and 24 square du Bois de Boulogne. Henri Amouroux, *Les beaux jours des collabos: Juin 1941–Juin 1942* (Paris: Éditions Robert Laffont, 1978), 514.

166 *"you will talk"* Philippe Aziz, *Tu Trahiras sans vergogne: Histoire de deux "collabos" Bonny et Lafont* (Paris: Fayard, 1970), 45.

166 *The leader of the Abwehr* Oscar Reile, *L'Abwehr: Le contre-espionnage allemand en France,* preface by colonel Rémy (Paris: Éditions France-Empire, 1970), 76.

166 *The Abwehr had found* Grégory Auda, *Les belles années du "milieu" 1940–1944* (Paris: Éditions Michalon, 2002), 18–23, 48, 53–64.

166 *Adrien the Basque* Adrien Estébéteguy was one of the first selected. Report by Section Spéciale, August 30, 1944, BDIC, Fonds Delarue F° Delta RES 787, I.

167 *naturalized German citizen* Henri Chamberlin, *Audition,* September 8, 1944, BDIC, Fonds Delarue F° Delta RES 787, 4, and Paul Clavié, *Audition,* September 19, 1944, BDIC, Fonds Delarue F° Delta RES 787, VI.

167 *anonymous letter* APP, Série J, affaire Petiot, carton n° I, folder 7.

168 *There was nothing* Georges Massu, *L'enquête Petiot: La plus grande affaire criminelle du siècle* (Paris: Librairie Arthème Fayard, 1959), 196.

168 *the commissaire released* Le Petit Parisien, March 25, 1944.

168 *"Madame W"* APP, Série J, affaire Petiot, carton n° I, folder 7.

169 *Seventy-eight percent* 110,000 of 140,000 in the Netherlands, compared with 25 percent in France. Christopher Lloyd, *Collaboration and Resistance in Occupied France: Representing Treason and Sacrifice* (New York: Palgrave Macmillan, 2003), 25.

169 *When the Wolff family* APP, Série J, affaire Petiot, carton n° I, folder 7.

169 *Hôtel du Danube* Research on hotels in folder 18, APP, Série J, affaire Petiot, carton n° I.

169 *"a spy on the Orient Express"* Marcel Jullian, *Le Mystère Petiot* (Paris: Edition No. 1, 1980), 134.

170 *"We always need"* Eryane Kahan, *Audition,* September 8, 1944, APP, Série J, affaire Petiot, carton n° VI.

170 *"a man of vast culture"* Thomas Maeder, *The Unspeakable Crimes of Dr. Petiot* (Boston: Little, Brown and Company, 1980), 89.

170 *Maurice Wolff concealed* AN, 334, AP 65, 3394.

170 *"twelve bullets in my carcass"* John V. Grombach, *The Great Liquidator* (New York: Zebra Books, 1980), 188.

171 *Gilbert Basch* Charles Nodier, *Audition,* April 25, 1944, APP, Série J, affaire Petiot, carton n° I.

171 *Chaïm Schonker* Hoofdbureau van politie te Amsterdam, June 1944, APP, Série J, affaire Petiot, carton n° I.

171 *She had declined* Ilse Gang, *Audition,* APP, Série J, affaire Petiot, carton n° III.

CHAPTER 19. THE LIST

172 *"doctoress Iriane"* Anonymous letter, March 26, 1944, APP, Série J, affaire Petiot, carton n° I.

172 *masseuse* AN, 334 AP 65, 4354–4355.

172 *close friend* Louise Nicholas, Report, April 26, 1944, APP, Série J, affaire Petiot, carton n° I.

172 *Welsing had little to say* Herbert Welsing, *Audition,* April 26, 1944, APP, Série J, affaire Petiot, carton n° I.

173 *It was about March 20* Fernande Goux, *Audition,* in Report, April 26, 1944, APP, Série J, affaire Petiot, carton n° I.

173 *On April 12* List, April 12, 1944, APP, Série J, affaire Petiot, carton n° III.

173 *His wife, Marie, feared* Marie Lombard, *Audition,* March 27, 1944, APP, Série J, affaire Petiot, carton n° III.

174 *But police soon learned* Report, May 1, 1944, APP, Série J, affaire Petiot, carton n° I.

174 *A number of invoices* Report, May 6, 1944, APP, Série J, affaire Petiot, carton n° II.

174 *The list of probable victims* Report, May 10, 1944, APP, Série J, affaire Petiot, carton n° III.

174 *"the most difficult and complicated"* Stephen E. Ambrose, *Eisenhower: Soldier and President* (New York: Simon & Schuster, 1990), 142; Winston S. Churchill, *The Second World War* (New York: Bantam Books, 1962), Volume V, 499–512, 528–544.

175 *He introduced himself* Charles Rolland, *Audition,* June 24, 1944, APP, Série J, affaire Petiot, carton n° III.

175 *It was in Marseille* Ibid.

176 *"He seemed in a"* Ibid.

177 *later criticized* Massu discusses it briefly in *L'enquête Petiot: La plus grande affaire criminelle du siècle* (Paris: Librairie Arthème Fayard, 1959), 241–242.

177 *"The Greatest Bluebeard"* *New York Times,* July 26, 1944.

177 *Three weeks later* *Washington Post,* August 17, 1944.

CHAPTER 20. APOCALYPTIC WEEKS

178 *"told me that"* Georges Suard, *Audition,* October 9, 1944, APP, Série J, affaire Petiot, carton n° VI.

178 *de Brinon would ever* Count Fernand de Brinon, *Audition,* October 20, 1945, APP, Série J, affaire Petiot, carton n° VI, and again in the report of December 1945, in APP, Série J, affaire Petiot, carton n° VI. See also *Le Pays,* March 13, 1946, for another speculation about his intervention. Brinon passes over the spring of 1944 quickly in his *Mémoires* (Paris: La Page Internationale, 1949).

179 *"vain flight"* United Press, April 21, 1944; *Le Petit Parisien,* April 21, 1944; *Le Cri du Peuple,* April 24, 1944.

179 *But Massu was not* Jean-François Dominique makes this point well in *L'affaire Petiot: médecin, marron, gestapiste, guillotinée pour au moins vingt-sept assassinats* (Paris: Éditions Ramsay, 1980), 110. See also AN, 334 AP 65, 3368.

180 *four thousand tons* Omar N. Bradley, *A Soldier's Story* (New York: Henry Holt and Company, 1951), 386–387.

180 *"the key to France"* Anthony Beevor and Artemis Cooper, *Paris After the Liberation 1944–1949* (New York: Penguin Books, 2004), 36.

180 *De Gaulle wanted* Charles de Gaulle, *The Complete War Memoirs of Charles de Gaulle* (New York: Carroll & Graf Publishers Inc., 1998), 631–632.

181 *"Paris must not"* Larry Collins with Dominique Lapierre, *Is Paris Burning?* (New York: Pocket Books, Inc., 1966), unpaginated introduction; Samuel W. Mitcham Jr., *Retreat to the Reich: The German Defeat in France, 1944* (Westport, CT: Praeger, 2000), 189.

181 *The French police rebelled* C. Angeli and P. Gillet, *La police dans la politique (1944–1954)*(Paris: Éditions Bernard Grasset, 1967), 57–74.

181 *Under the leadership* Marcel Le Clère describes the role of the guardians of peace in particular in *Histoire de la police* (Paris: Presses Universitaires de France, 1947), 124–125.

182 *The pilot believed* Gregor Dallas, *1945: The War That Never Ended* (New Haven: Yale University Press, 2005), 179; Charles de Gaulle's version, *The Complete War Memoirs,* 634–635.

182 *"To this city"* Collins, *Is Paris Burning?,* 30.

183 *"sparkling torpedoes"* Beevor and Cooper, *Paris After the Liberation 1944–1949,* 34.

183 *"purple-faced generals"* Ibid.

183 *"crossroads of death"* Willis Thornton, *The Liberation of Paris* (New York: Harcourt, Brace & World, 1962), 167.

183 *With forces estimated* Beavor and Cooper, *Paris After the Liberation 1944–1949,* 33.

184 *Grand Palais* Edmond Dubois, *Paris sans lumière* (Lausanne: Payot, 1946), 208.

184 *"roped to the turret"* Collins with Lapierre, *Is Paris Burning?,* 175.

184 "Tous Aux Barricades" Comité parisien de Libération, Albert Ouzoulias (Colonel André), *Les Batillons de la jeunesse: le colonel Fabien et d'autres jeunes dans la résistance, dans les maquis et l'insurrection parisienne* (Paris: Éditions Sociales, 1967), 439–440.

184 *"What the hell, Brad"* . . . *"Is Paris burning?"* Collins with Lapierre, *Is Paris Burning?*, 203, 220, 221, 302.

186 *"olive drab jeeps"* Flint Whitlock, *The Rock of Anzio: From Sicily to Dachau: A History of the U.S. 45th Infantry Division* (Boulder: Westview Press, 1998), 398.

187 *"The greatness of man"* . . . *"The night of truth,"* *Combat*, August 25, 1944, printed with a slightly different translation in *Camus at Combat: Writing 1944–1947*. Jacqueline Lévi-Valensi Trans. Arthur Goldhammer (Princeton: Princeton University Press, 2006), 18.

187 *"Paris," he shouted* Gregor Dallas, *1945*, 21; De Gaulle later described it as an "improvised reply," *The Complete War Memoirs of Charles de Gaulle*, 649–650.

187 *"I was drunk"* Gilles Perrault and Pierre Azéma, *Paris Under the Occupation* (New York: The Vendome Press, 1989), 56.

187 *"the loveliest, brightest"* Collins and Lapierre, *Is Paris Burning?*, 322.

Chapter 21. "P.S. Destroy All My Letters"

188 *"provisionally released"* *Réquisitoire définitif*, December 31, 1945, APP, Série J, affaire Petiot, carton n° VII.

188 *Massu, a firm believer* Georges Massu, *Aveux Quai des Orfèvres. Souvenirs du Commissaire Massu* (Paris: La Tour Pointue, undated/1951), 151.

189 *"I was almost arrested"* . . . *"P.S. Destroy"* Marguerite Braunberger to juge d'instruction, September 6, 1944, printed in Jacques Perry and Jane Chabert, *L'affaire Petiot* (Paris: Gallimard, 1957), 62–63; AN 334, AP 65, 3378.

190 *"ma chère amie"* Ibid.

190 *"Ma chère Maggi"* Ibid; Marguerite Braunberger, *Audition*, December 4, 1944, APP, Série J, affaire Petiot, carton n° V.

191 *"a baptism or first communion"* Ibid.

191 *"either a genius or a madman"* Raymond Vallée, *Audition*, December 5, 1944, APP, Série J, affaire Petiot, carton n° V.

191 *"I'm going to give"* . . . *anything else, other than* Marguerite Braunberger, letter to juge d'instruction, September 6, 1944, and Report, December 11, 1944, APP, Série J, affaire Petiot, carton n° V. Marcel Braunberger confirmed receiving a letter as well. Marcel Braunberger, *Audition*, December 8, 1944, also in carton n° V.

192 *she reported her husband's disappearance* Report, March 26, 1946, APP, Série J, affaire Petiot, carton n° III.

192 *The case was closed* Braunberger dossier, No. 95, 543 closed on January 9, 1943, APP, Série J, affaire Petiot, carton n° III.

Chapter 22. At Saint-Mandé-Tourelle Station

193 *"The Mad Butcher"* . . . *"a swarthy, sinister-looking"* United Press, August 31, 1944.

193 *"He is only too real"* Ibid.

193 *"We have identified 54 victims"* Ibid; *Washington Post*, November 3, 1944. The

first part of this quote was also published by the *New York Times,* August 31, 1944.

193 *a twenty-nine-year-old Italian woman* Laetitia Toureaux is the subject of a fascinating new book by Gayle K. Brunelle and Annette Finley-Croswhite, *Murder in the Métro: Laetitia Toureaux and the Cagoule in 1930s France* (Baton Rouge: Louisiana State University Press, 2010).

194 *"hooded ones"* Maurice Pujo coined the term after the Ku Klux Klan. Bertram M. Gordon, *Collaborationism in France During the Second World War* (Ithaca: Cornell University Press, 1980), 58.

194 *Perhaps he had New York Times,* August 31, 1944.

194 *forwarded by attorney* Jacques Yonnet, *Audition,* November 7, 1944, APP, Série J, affaire Petiot, carton n° V.

194 *"Dear Mr. Editor"* . . . *"Having lost"* *Résistance,* October 18, 1944. Special thanks to Magali Androuin at the archives of the Préfecture de Police for showing me the original letter, which, given its state (ripped to pieces), is held outside the dossier.

196 *Colonel Rol* *Liberation-Soir,* November 4, 1944. For more on Colonel Rol's life in general, see Roger Bourderon, *Rol-Tanguy* (Paris: Tallandier, 2004).

196 *The first priority in the reckoning* Megan Koreman, *The Expectation of Justice: France, 1944–1946* (Durham: Duke University Press, 1999), 92.

197 *An estimated ten to twenty thousand women* Fabrice Virgili estimates twenty thousand in *Shorn Women: Gender and Punishment in Liberation France* (Oxford: Berg Publishers, 2002), 1.

197 *A recent study* Jean-Paul Picaper and Ludwig Norz, *Enfants Maudits*: ils sont 200,000, on les appelait les "enfants de Boches" (Paris: Syrtes, 2004).

197 *In all, about 310,000 cases* Philippe Burrin, *France Under the Germans: Collaboration and Compromise,* translated by Janet Lloyd (New York: The New Press, 1996), 459.

197 *More recent studies* Henry Rousso, "L'épuration en France: une histoire inachevée" *Vingtième Siècle* no. 33 (January–March, 1992); H. R. Kedward put the number between 10,000 and 12,000 in *Occupied France: Collaboration and Resistance 1940–1944* (Oxford: Basil Blackwell, 1985), 77, and a few studies, returning full circle, place the figure higher. For more on the debate, see Christopher Lloyd's first-rate *Collaboration and Resistance in Occupied France: Representing Treason and Sacrifice* (New York: Palgrave Macmillan, 2003), 39–40.

198 *"stock market in a moment"* Douglas Porch, *The French Secret Services: A History of French Intelligence from the Dreyfus Affair to the Gulf War* (New York: Farrar, Straus, and Giroux, 1995), 266.

198 *France, he said, was using* René Nézondet, *Petiot "le Possédé"* (Paris: Express, 1950), 117.

198 *At 10:45* Captain Simonin, *Arrest of Dr. Petiot,* APP, Série J, affaire Petiot, carton n° V.

198 *as he punched his ticket* letter to Decaux, Alain Decaux, *C'était le xxe siècle: la*

guerre absolue 1940–1945 (Paris: Perrin, 1998), 293, and asking for the time comes from an interview with one of the officers, in *France-Soir*, December 3, 1975.

198 *"no longer sully the honor"* Jean-Marc Varaut, *L'abominable Dr. Petiot* (Paris: Ballard, 1974), 185.

198 *The murder suspect carried* Captain Simonin, Report, APP, Série J, affaire Petiot, carton n° V; Commission Rogatoire, November 2, 1944, also in carton n° V.

199 *"We believe we have fulfilled"* Thomas Maeder, *The Unspeakable Crimes of Dr. Petiot* (Boston: Little, Brown and Company, 1980), 155. See also the *Front-National*, November 3, 1944, and *L'Humanité*, November 3, 1944.

199 *the DGER* The BCRA had become DGSS and then DGER in what Lucien Zimmer called a "ballet of initials" in *Un Septennat policier: Dessous et secrets de la police républicaine* (Paris: Fayard, 1967), 216.

199 *He was later identified* *Résistance*, March 13, 1946. The article was written by Jacques Yonnet, the same journalist who penned the previous "Petiot, *Soldat du Reich*." APP, Série J, affaire Petiot, carton n° III.

200 *"It's unbelievable"* . . . *"To think that I have been alone"* Dylma interview in *L'Oeuvre*, November 3, 1944.

200 *He was accused of four specific charges* Massu's *Epuration* dossier, APP, KB 74.

200 *"dining on several occasions"* Jean-Marc Berlière with Laurent Chabrun, *Policiers français sous l'occupation: d'après les archives de l'épuration* (Paris: Perrin, 2009), 141–142.

201 *"the end of a rope"* Commission Rogatoire, November 2, 1944, the first of thirty-three identified items in his possession, APP, Série J, affaire Petiot, carton n° V.

201 *suicide attempt* . . . *"anti-national act"* Berlière, *Policiers français*, 141, 145; Massu's *Epuration* dossier, APP, KB 74.

201 *"A good colleague"* Massu, *L'enquête Petiot*, 239.

201 *"haunted the Palais de Justice"* *Télé Programme Magazine*, February 2–8, 1958, 4th year—N° 119, 7–9, translation by Stephen Trussel, December 2003. For more on Simenon and Maigret, see his excellent website, trussel.com.

201 *"I took all my models"* Ibid.

Chapter 23. Interrogations

202 *"a hero of the Resistance"* . . . *later Simonin would say* Simonin to Decaux, Alain Decaux, *C'était le xxe siècle*, 293, 284–288.

203 *Petiot denied* . . . *He returned to rue Le Sueur* Marcel Petiot, *Procès-verbal d'interrogatoire*, October 31, 1944, APP, Série J, affaire Petiot, carton n° V.

206 *Years later* Simonin told this to Marcel Jullian, *Le Mystère Petiot* (Paris: Edition No. 1, 1980), 203.

206 *"My conscience does not"* Alomée Planel, *Docteur Satan ou L'affaire Petiot* (Paris: Éditions Robert Laffont, 1978), 250; *Front National*, November 3, 1944.

206 *"A demon for detail"* *Time*, July 28, 1967. See also *Françoise Giroud vous présente le tout-Paris. Préface de Marcel Achard* (Paris: Gallimard, 1952), 88–93.

206 *Mussolini, who at the height* Information on Magda Fontages's relationship with Mussolini comes from his chaffeur, Ercole Boratto, whose memoir was discovered by Mario J. Cereghino in 2004, in his work with Giorgio Cavalleri and Franco Giannantoni, *La Fine: Gli ultimi giorni di Benito Mussolini nei documenti dei servizi segreti americani (1945–1946)* (Milan: Garzanti, 2009).

207 *Petiot's sector was reserved* Pierre Montagnon, *42, rue de la Santé: une prison politique, 1867–1968* (Paris: Pygmalion/Gérard Watclet, 1996), 259.

207 *"I have been"* . . . *"A five-ton truck"* Marcel Petiot, November 2, 1944, published in Planel, *Docteur Satan*, 254–258.

207 *When a handful* Megan Koreman, *The Expectation of Justice: France, 1944–1946* (Durham: Duke University Press, 1999), 50.

207 *"too uncultivated"* Jean-François Dominique, *L'affaire Petiot: médecin, marron, gestapiste, guillotiné pour au moins vingt-sept assassinats* (Paris: Éditions Ramsay, 1980), 179.

208 *"in a great disorder"* . . . *"I was absolutely bewildered"* Jacques Perry and Jane Chabert, *L'affaire Petiot* (Paris: Gallimard, 1957), 111–112.

210 *April 4, 1936* Report, April 6, 1936, APP, Série J, affaire Petiot, carton n° V.

210 *"bash his face in"* Ibid.

210 *According to this document* Reports of April 6 and June 18, 1936, APP, Série J, affaire Petiot, carton n° V.

211 *"If I hadn't given it"* Ibid.

211 *"wept convulsively"* Dr. Ceillier, *Rapport Medico-Legal*, July 22, 1936, APP, Série J, affaire Petiot, carton n° V.

211 *"mental debility"* . . . *"dangerous to himself and others"* Ibid.

212 *The physician arrived* APP, Série J, affaire Petiot, carton n° I, folder 43.

212 *"cyclothymic"* Dr. Achille Delmas, August 15, 1936, APP, Série J, affaire Petiot, carton n° V.

212 *"to justify his past acts"* Ibid.

212 *"attempting a variety of simultaneous tasks"* Ibid.

212 *"calm, lucid, and non-delirious"* Dr. Rogues de Fursac, Medical Report, August 18, 1936, APP, Série J, affaire Petiot, carton n° V.

212 *"a state of mental equilibrium"* Dr. Achille Delmas, August 25, 1936, *Extrait du registre du contrôle de psychiatrie de la Vo Région*, APP, Série J, affaire Petiot, carton n° V.

212 *"I am absolutely sane in mind"* Marcel Petiot to the procureur de la république, August 18, 1936, APP, Série J, affaire Petiot, carton n° V.

212 *"amoral and unbalanced"* . . . *"should not weigh excessively"* *Rapport Medico-Legal*, December 19, 1936, APP, Série J, affaire Petiot, carton n° V.

Chapter 24. Beating Chance?

214 *"Cigarette Butt"* Petiot signed a poem with this nickname. APP, Série J, affaire Petiot, carton n° VII.

214 *"It would be marvelous"* Ibid.

215 *"If Petiot is condemned"* René Nézondet, *Petiot "le Possédé"* (Paris: Express, 1950), 123–124.

215 *"very cultivated, very intelligent"* France-Soir, March 16, 1946.

215 *"I never saw"* Nézondet, *Petiot "le Possédé,"* 128.

215 *"meatballs"* . . . *"virgin forest"* Marcel Petiot, *Le Hasard vaincu* (Paris: Roger Amiard, 1946), 14, 341, 1, 5–6.

217 *"Petiot Exposition"* Jacques Delarue and Anne Manson, *"L'affaire Landru de la Libération: Docteur Petiot 21, Rue Lesueur,"* in Gilbert Guilleminault et al., eds., *Les lendemains qui ne chantaient pas* (Paris: Denoël, 1962), 54.

217 *"very esteemed"* Jean Duchesne, *Audition*, November 27, 1944, APP, Série J, affaire Petiot, carton n° V.

217 *"he had belonged to a group"* Ibid.

218 *"participated in the murder"* Jean Duchesne, *Audition*, November 28, 1944, APP, Série J, affaire Petiot, carton n° V.

218 *the owner of the five-room apartment* Yvonne Salvage, *Audition*, December 10, 1944, APP, Série J, affaire Petiot, carton n° V.

218 *About nine o'clock one evening* . . . *"make the cadavers disappear"* Georges Redouté, *Audition*, November 4, 1944, APP, Série J, affaire Petiot, carton n° V.

219 *a "Corsican"* Ibid. Marguerite Durez, *Audition*, November 5, 1944, APP, Série J, affaire Petiot, carton n° V.

219 *"During the time"* . . . *"always alone"* Georges Redouté, *Audition*, November 4, 1944, APP, Série J, affaire Petiot, carton n° V.

219 *"a drum with German colors"* Perquisition, November 4, 1944, APP, Série J, affaire Petiot, carton n° V.

219 *Petiot had called this* Georges Redouté, *Audition*, November 4, 1944, APP, Série J, affaire Petiot, carton n° V.

220 *a "game of poker"* Ibid.

220 *"I was convinced at that moment"* . . . *"the war, the Germans"* Emilie Bézayrie, *Audition*, November 6, 1944, APP, Série J, affaire Petiot, carton n° V.

220 *"true patriot"* . . . *"I did not go to the police"* Jacques Perry and Jane Chabert, *L'affaire Petiot* (Paris: Gallimard, 1957), 113.

222 *Petiot, laughing, offered* Delarue and Manson, *"L'affaire Landru,"* 51.

222 *Lieutenant Jacques Yonnet* Many biographers confuse the surname and the alias. The correct surname is Yonnet.

222 *wounded by a German grenade* Jacques Yonnet was still feeling the effects June 16, 1944, describing how fragments "roam about in my side, my hip, my neck. They tickle, prick, scratch, throb, and sometimes leave me prostrate with attacks of absolutely unbearable convulsive pain." Jacques Yonnet, *Paris Noir: The Secret History of a City*, translated by Christine Donougher (London: Dedalus, 2006), 165.

223 *the twenty-five-year-old Charbonneaux* Hubert Charbonneaux, "Hommage à Jean Charbonneaux (1918–1943)," last updated December 22, 2007, which can

be read at the recommended Turma Vengeance website, at chantran.vengeance.
free.fr/Doc/Charbonneaux05.pdf

223 *inventor of the bath torture* Jacques Delarue, *Trafics et crimes sous l'occupation*
(Paris: Fayard, 1968), 45–52.

224 *identifying one hundred V-1* George Martelli, *The Man Who Saved London: The
Story of Michel Hollard* (Garden City: Doubleday & Company, Inc, 1961), 8,
154–155, 167.

224 *No one in Agir* Many other Resistants who would have moved in his circles
denied any knowledge as well, including Claire Davinroy, *Audition*,
October 31, 1944; Dr. Vic Dupont, *Audition*, November 13, 1944; and widows
of fallen leaders, such as Gilberte Brossolette, Report, March 21, 1945, APP,
Série J, affaire Petiot, carton n° V.

224 *"A guy who did nothing"* DGER Report, *Conclusions*, May 3, 1945, APP,
Série J, affaire Petiot, carton n° V and IV.

CHAPTER 25. THE KNELLERS

225 *"Shit! I'll run over there"* Hazel Rowley, *Tête-à-Tête: Simone de Beauvoir and
Jean-Paul Sartre* (New York: HarperCollins Publishers, 2005), 147.

226 *"land of freedom and equality"* Ibid, 150.

226 *"that doctrine which makes"* . . . *"Existentialism defines"* Annie Cohen-Solal,
Sartre: A Life, translated by Anna Cancogni (New York: Pantheon Books,
1987), 249–251.

226 *"Too Many Attend Sartre"* Ronald Aronson, *Camus & Sartre: The Story of a
Friendship and the Quarrel That Ended It* (Chicago: The University of Chicago
Press, 2004), 47.

227 *"the hairy adolescents"* . . . *P.T. Barnum* Annie Cohen-Solal, *Sartre*, 261.

227 *what the historian Ronald Aronson* Ronald Aronson, *Camus & Sartre*, 48.

227 *A journalist asked* Jean-François Dominique, *L'affaire Petiot: médecin, marron,
gestapiste, guillotiné pour au moins vingt-sept assassinats* (Paris: Éditions
Ramsay, 1980), 171.

227 *"constitutional delinquent"* . . . *"completely amoral"* John V. Grombach, *The
Great Liquidator* (New York: Zebra Books, 1980), 266–269.

229 *"[Petiot's] hesitations, his contradictions"* DGER Report, *Conclusions*, May 3,
1945, APP, Série J, affaire Petiot, carton n° V and IV.

229 *On September 11, 1944* Marthe Wetterwald, *Audition*, November 20, 1944,
APP, Série J, affaire Petiot, carton n° V.

229 *He wanted to help* Petiot had obtained Wetterwald's name after trying the same
method two days before offering to help in the release of another physican,
who, in the middle of his pitch, walked into the room. Marguerite Gérard,
Audition, November 20, 1944, APP, Série J, affaire Petiot, carton n° V.

230 *He was a leader* François Wetterwald, *Audition*, November 13, 1944, APP,
Série J, affaire Petiot, carton n° V. See also Wetterwald's memoir, *Vengeance:
Histoire d'un corps franc* (Paris: Mouvement Vengeance, 1946).

231 *12,884 Jewish men, women, and children* There were 3,031 men, 5,802 women, and 4,051 children between the ages of two and sixteen. Serge Klarsfeld, *Vichy-Auschwitz* (Paris: Fayard 1983), 121–122.

232 *"I know, this appears suspect"* Ernest Jorin, *Audition,* November 6, 1944, APP, Série J, affaire Petiot, carton n° IV.

232 *Roart was struck* Report, October 10, 1944, APP, Série J, affaire Petiot, carton n° IV.

233 *a woman's black coat* Ibid.

233 *though she could not say for certain* Ibid.

234 *the mutilated remains of a young boy* Asnières report, August 19, 1942, APP, Série J, affaire Petiot, carton n° VII.

234 *Petiot suddenly refused* L'*Aurore,* November 6, 1945, and *Franc-Tireur,* November 9, 1945.

234 *"On what date did you buy"* . . . *"Write 'ditto' "* The interrogation is in Jacques Perry and Jane Chabert, *L'affaire Petiot* (Paris: Gallimard, 1957), 162.

234 *all charges would be dropped* Combat, January 4, 1946.

235 *"Yet it is certain that"* Réquisitoire définitif, December 31, 1945, APP, Série J, affaire Petiot, carton n° VII.

CHAPTER 26. THE PETIOT CIRCUS

For the trial of Marcel Petiot, most diligent biographers draw upon the text in Jacques Perry and Jane Chabert, *L'affaire Petiot* (Paris: Gallimard, 1957), hereafter PC. I have also supplemented my account with the *Extrait des minutes de la cour d'assises de la Seine,* preserved in the Archives de Paris 30.W.4 and the stenographic record in the Archives Nationales at AN 334 AP 65. For the reactions of attorneys, jurors, and members of the audience, I have drawn upon a number of testimonies in newspapers, memoirs, diaries, and other eyewitness accounts. Citations are used for direct quotations or for more contentious points. Unless otherwise stated, all translations are my own.

236 *"the most sensational"* Washington Post, March 18, 1946.

237 *All jurors* The drawing of the jurors is covered in *Extrait des Minutes du Greffier de la Cour d'Appel de Paris,* APP, Série J, affaire Petiot, carton n° III.

237 *His assistant . . . to the prosecution* Thomas Maeder, *The Unspeakable Crimes of Dr. Petiot* (Boston: Little, Brown and Company, 1980), 192, 185.

238 *"devil's poet"* Claude Bertin, *Les assassins hors-série: Gilles de Rais, Petiot,* vol. 10 of *Les grands procès de l'histoire de France* (Paris: Éditions de Saint-Clair, 1967), 142.

238 *Petiot took off* Alain Decaux, present that day, described it in *C'était le xxe siècle: la guerre absolue 1940–1945* (Paris: Perrin, 1998), 298.

238 *"Gentlemen, please"* Bertin, *Les assassins hors-série,* 143.

238 *"willful homicide"* PC, 175; Maeder, *The Unspeakable Crimes,* 194.

239 *stooped over* Spokane Daily Chronicle, March 19, 1946.

239 *"like the edge"* PC, 174.

239 *he looked younger* New York Times, March 19, 1946.

239 *The dark circles under his eyes* Jean Galtier-Boissière, *Mon journal dans la drôle de paix* (Paris: La jeune Parque, 1947), 206.

239 *"famous hypnotic stare" Sydney Morning Herald*, March 19, 1946. The *Chicago Daily Tribune* noted the staring sometimes at victims' families, and Francine Bonitzer said it was a murderous glare in *L'Aurore*, March 19, 1946.

239 *"What about Colonel"* . . . *"She told everyone"* Bertin, *Les assassins hors-série*, 143–148. Report, February 6, 1946, APP, Série J, Affaire Petiot, carton n° III.

240 *"Don't mention it"* Reported by Jean-François Dominique, who covered the trial as a reporter for *La Républic du Sud-Ouest*, in his *L'affaire Petiot: médecin, marron, gestapiste, guillotiné pour au moins vingt-sept assassinats* (Paris: Éditions Ramsay, 1980), 199.

241 *"My first murder"* PC, 176.

241 *Petiot had good* Le Figaro, March 22, 1946.

241 *St. Antony* Galtier-Boissière, *Mon journal*, 206.

241 *"That was a story"* . . . *"Yes, I was convicted"* PC, 176–177.

241 *"Next you are going to tell"* Maeder, *The Unspeakable Crimes*, 195.

242 *"the prospectus of a quack!"* . . . *"No one ever knows"* PC, 177–178.

243 *"Nothing is simpler"* . . . *"there was no Resistance"* PC, 179–180.

244 *public that looked back* The low opinion of the legal profession, particularly judges, is described by Megan Koreman in *The Expectation of Justice: France, 1944–1946* (Durham: Duke University Press, 1999), 98.

244 *After a heckler suggested* René Nézondet, *Petiot "le Possédé"* (Paris: Express, 1950), 145.

244 *One film producer* John V. Grombach, *The Great Liquidator* (New York: Zebra Books, 1980), 294.

245 *"What are plastic explosives?"* Bertin, *Les assassins hors-série*, 156.

245 *"Is this"* . . . *"Why?"* PC, 181–182. Reactions and Petiot's words at the end are in *L'Aube*, March 19, 1946, and *Le Pays*, March 19, 1946.

CHAPTER 27. "NOT IN DANGER OF DEATH"

246 *"hundreds of marriage proposals"* A.A.P. correspondent, *Sydney Morning Herald*, March 20, 1946.

247 *"It is very simple"* AN 334, AP 65, 4458.

247 *"I have detected them"* Ibid.

247 *"How did you get rid"* . . . *"My client"* PC, 183–184.

247 *"He was served"* John V. Grombach, *The Great Liquidator* (New York: Zebra Books, 1980), 305–306. Jean-Marc Varaut finishes the words of his friend Floriot in *L'abominable Dr. Petiot* (Paris: Balland 1974), 222.

248 *"Simonin, or under his real name"* Leser wanted an investigation into Yonnet's allegations. *Vérification*, March 28, 1946, APP, Série J, affaire Petiot, carton n° III.

248 *"Shut up"* . . . *"minister of Pétain"* PC, 184–186. For a different wording of Véron, see Jean-François Dominique, *L'affaire Petiot: médecin, marron, gestapiste, guillotiné pour au moins vingt-sept assassinats* (Paris: Éditions Ramsay, 1980), 208.

249 *"What are the names of the people"* Thomas Maeder, *The Unspeakable Crimes of Dr. Petiot* (Boston: Little, Brown and Company, 1980), 202.

249 *"Oh, you know"* Ibid.

249 *"At [Chalon-sur-Saône]"* PC, 186.

249 *"cloak and dagger novel"* Claude Bertin, *Les assassins hors-série: Gilles de Rais, Petiot,* vol. 10 of *Les grands procès de l'histoire de France* (Paris: Éditions de Saint-Clair, 1967), 160–161.

249 *"It was the famous Jodkum"* Ibid., 162.

250 *"What about the bodies"* . . . *"Oh, no!"* Maeder, *The Unspeakable Crimes,* 202–203.

250 *One journalist noticed* Chicago Daily Tribune, March 20, 1946.

250 *"You know well"* . . . *"I should hope so"* PC, 187.

250 I AM NOT IN DANGER *L'Aurore,* March 20, 1946.

252 *"What about me?"* . . . *"What, are you bored?"* PC, 191; Bertin *Les assassins hors-série,* 166.

252 *"a demon"* New York Herald Tribune (international edition), March 20, 1946.

252 *"the guillotine is too swift"* Ibid.

CHAPTER 28. TWO TO ONE

253 *"calm and dignity"* René Nézondet, *Petiot "le Possédé"* (Paris: Express, 1950), 152. Gollety investigates the author of the *New York Herald Tribune* article, May 9, 1946, APP, Série J, affaire Petiot, carton n° IV.

254 *"the expert in clandestine passages"* PC, 192–193.

254 *"an affliction I don't care to name"* . . . *"any more than you have seen"* Thomas Maeder, *The Unspeakable Crimes of Dr. Petiot* (Boston: Little, Brown and Company, 1980), 207.

254 *"You are forgetting that Argentina"* . . . *"Do you respect"* PC, 193–197.

256 *"What gave you the right"* Maeder, *The Unspeakable Crimes,* 210.

256 *"If there had been"* Ibid.

257 *the towering stack of evidence started* Paris-Matin, March 21, 1946.

257 *he joked* Ibid.

257 *"The Wolffs were Jews"* . . . *"If Kahan had sent"* PC, 198.

258 *"What about the Schonkers?"* . . . *"Why didn't you"* Maeder, *The Unspeakable Crimes,* 211.

259 *"never been more amused"* Jean-François Dominique, *L'affaire Petiot: médecin, marron, gestapiste, guillotiné pour au moins vingt-sept assassinats* (Paris: Éditions Ramsay, 1980), 197.

CHAPTER 29. INSIDE MURDER HOUSE

260 *"four hundred prostitutes"* John V. Grombach, *The Great Liquidator* (New York: Zebra Books, 1980), 314.

260 *"If he's a Jew"* Jean-Marc Varaut, *L'abominable Dr. Petiot* (Paris: Balland 1974), 247.

261 *Nézondet's allegation* René Nézondet, *Petiot "le Possédé"* (Paris: Express, 1950), 73–74.

261 *"an informer of the"* . . . *"Dreyfus was"* PC, 202.

261 *"Petiot ranted, roared, stamped"* *Sydney Morning Herald,* March 23, 1944.

262 *"Yes . . . he was"* *Combat,* March 22, 1946.

262 *" 'Was' is the operative word"* Thomas Maeder, *The Unspeakable Crimes of Dr. Petiot* (Boston: Little, Brown and Company, 1980), 214.

262 *"Those must be"* . . . *"You could have"* PC, 202–204; Claude Bertin, *Les assassins hors-série: Gilles de Rais, Petiot,* vol. 10 of *Les grands procès de l'histoire de France* (Paris: Éditions de Saint-Clair, 1967), 181–182.

262 *Dupin stood* *Le Pays,* March 22, 1946.

262 *"I do not know if it is"* Associated Press, March 22, 1946.

263 *"face of a kindly boxer"* *France Soir,* March 22, 1946.

264 *a rainy Friday* *Le Pays,* March 23, 1946.

264 *wooden barricades* Associated Press, March 22, 1946.

264 *Other people looked out* *L'Aube,* March 23, 1946.

265 *from Place Dauphine* Report, March 25, 1946, APP, Série J, affaire Petiot, carton n° III.

265 *"enlightened justice"* Maeder, *The Unspeakable Crimes,* 217.

265 *"a strange conglomeration"* *Time,* April 1, 1946.

265 *"the leprous walls"* *Le Figaro,* March 23, 1946.

266 *"Where is the viewer?"* . . . *"Stories like this"* PC, 207–209.

267 *"It is here at the bottom"* . . . *"half a corpse"* Grombach, *The Great Liquidator,* 319.

267 *"This sack is"* PC, 210.

267 *"This is truly incredible"* Ibid. Maeder, *The Unspeakable Crimes,* 219.

268 *rugby scrum* *L'Aurore,* March 23, 1946.

268 *"Do you want to see the boiler?"* Dominique Jean-François, *L'affaire Petiot: Médecin, marron, gestapiste, guillotiné pour au moins vingt-sept assassinats* (Paris: Éditions Ramsay, 1980), 211, and house invaded, *L'Aube,* March 23, 1946.

268 *"human shin bones"* *Le Pays,* March 23, 1946.

268 *"Death to the assassin!"* *L'Aurore,* March 23, 1946.

Chapter 30. Black Fingernails

269 *"It is absurd"* Claude Bertin, *Les assassins hors-série: Gilles de Rais, Petiot,* vol. 10. *Les grands procès de l'histoire de France.* Paris: Éditions de Saint-Clair, 1967, 191.

269 *"Did you find any"* PC, 210.

269 *"No, we did not"* Ibid.

270 *"Why do these civil servants"* *Le Figaro,* March 23, 1946.

270 *Although he had not* Georges Massu, *L'enquête Petiot: La plus grande affaire criminelle du siècle* (Paris: Librairie Arthème Fayard, 1959), 245, 247–250, 253–254.

271 *"I can assert"* . . . *"Who is the criminal"* PC, 213–215.

271 *"Yet you have"* Bertin, *Les assassins hors-série*, 197.

272 *"how many"* *Paris-Matin*, March 25, 1946; *L'Aurore*, March 25, 1946.

272 *"completely unknown"* Bertin, *Les assassins hors-série*, 199.

272 *"an adventurer without scruple"* Jean-Marc Varaut, *L'abominable Dr. Petiot* (Paris: Ballard, 1974), 213.

272 *"Before he accused Petiot"* Thomas Maeder, *The Unspeakable Crimes of Dr. Petiot* (Boston: Little, Brown and Company, 1980), 226–227.

272 *"the Parisian newspapers continue"* PC, 216–217. One example of such a photograph is *Paris-Matin*, March 23, 1946.

273 *"thin as an umbrella"* Maeder, *The Unspeakable Crimes*, 227.

273 With quivering voice *St. Petersburg Times*, March 26, 1944.

273 *"You are very intelligent"* . . . *"render us invisible"* PC, 219–223. Cadoret de l'Epinguen elaborated his points in a series of interviews and police reports from December 1944, in APP, Série J, affaire Petiot, carton n° VI.

276 *Robert Malfet Liberation-Soir,* January 27, 1945, and a report of January 12, 1945, APP, Série J, affaire Petiot, carton n° VI.

276 *"The mad doctor"* Maeder, *The Unspeakable Crimes,* 232. Petiot scoffing is in *Paris-Matin*, March 26, 1946.

276 *"his secretary"* Report, December 13, 1945, APP, Série J, affaire Petiot, carton n° VI.

276 *"He had black stains"* AN, 334, AP 65, 3365–3366.

276 *"It's very important"* PC, 224.

277 *"Will we have the pleasure"* Ibid.

CHAPTER 31. "A TASTE FOR EVIL"

278 *"grit its teeth"* Le Pays, March 27, 1946.

278 *"one hundred bony pieces"* . . . *"globular"* L'Ordre, March 27, 1945, APP, Série EA, carton n° 181.

278 The latter included . . . *"very mummified"* Dérobert, Paul, *et* Piédelièvre, Report, January 10, 1945, APP, Série J, affaire Petiot, carton n° VII.

279 *"We were able to conclude"* PC, 226.

279 *"No, not a scrap"* Paul was referring to his section, *"Examen des cheveux et des poils,"* in Report, January 10, 1945, APP, Série J, affaire Petiot, carton n° VII.

279 *"Five were men, five women"* AN 334, AP 65, 3323.

279 *"We can say that these"* AN, Ibid.

280 *"Not a single"* . . . *"Pardon me"* PC, 226–227.

281 *"putrefied and damaged"* . . . *"diptera and coleoptera"* Thomas Maeder, *The Unspeakable Crimes of Dr. Petiot* (Boston: Little, Brown and Company, 1980), 235. Elaboration about the seven tubes of insects as well as the musca, muscina, ophyra, calliphoridae, drosophilidae, phoridae, piophilidae, and others is in "Rapport entomologique" inside Dérobert, Paul, *et* Piédelièvre, Report, January 10, 1945, APP, Série J, affaire Petiot, carton n° VII.

281 *"Yes, you know"* L'Aurore, March 27, 1946.

281 *Petiot agreed and invited himself* Paris-Matin, March 27, 1946.

281 *"that does not mean"* . . . *"It would have been easy"* Claude Bertin, *Les assassins hors-série: Gilles de Rais, Petiot,* vol. 10 of *Les grands procès de l'histoire de France* (Paris: Éditions de Saint-Clair, 1967), 212–213.

281 *"That's only a hypothesis"* . . . *"I see"* Maeder, *The Unspeakable Crimes,* 235–236, PC, 228–229.

282 *"I have examined"* Bertin, *Les assassins hors-série,* 213.

282 *"fully responsible"* . . . *"His thesis received"* PC, 229.

282 *"'mediocre' in dissection"* The laughter following this statement was noted by the Reuters correspondent, March 28, 1944.

283 *"She is in good health"* Bertin, *Les assassins hors-série,* 214.

283 *"Sorry, but Petiot"* Ibid.

283 *Rougemont detected* AN, 334, AP 65, 3380–3384.

283 *"Monsieur de Rougemont is"* Bertin, *Les assassins hors-série,* 215.

283 *"If we had asked"* Maeder, *The Unspeakable Crimes,* 238.

284 *Petiot's Resistance credentials* In 2010, when the CIA declassified thousands of documents from the secretive American semi-private espionage group known as the Pond, the media widely reported that Petiot had in fact been one of its informers. This was a suggestion first made by the organization's leader, John V. Grombach, and it is not impossible. The problem is that, even with the new documents thus far released, there is still no verifiable evidence of his work as an informer. The new files contain "no reference to Petiot," except for a short, two- or three-sentence "summary of a report about conviction." E-mail to author from Mark Stout, author of a forthcoming book on the Pond.

285 *"Organized Resistance has never"* Dewavrin to Marcel Jullian, *Le Mystère Petiot* (Paris: Edition No. 1, 1980), 153. See also Dupin's theory that Fly-Tox was the name the British used for an individual and Petiot merely adopted it, AN, 334 AP, 65, 3352.

285 *"I refuse to tell you"* . . . *"Obviously"* Bertin, *Les assassins hors-série,* 217.

285 *doubtful* Reuters, for example, March 27, 1946.

285 *"Monsieur Ibarne"* Maeder, *The Unspeakable Crimes,* 240; PC, 232; *L'Aurore* describes Petiot as showing extreme anger at this witness, March 27, 1946.

285 *"On the contrary"* PC, 232.

CHAPTER 32. THE HAIRDRESSER, THE MAKEUP ARTIST, AND THE ADVENTURESS

288 *"neither of business nor politics"* PC, 235.

288 *"The journeys begin and end at rue Le Sueur"* Nézondet told his view also in his interrogation, March 22, 1944, APP, Série J, affaire Petiot, carton n° III, and in his memoir, René Nézondet, *Petiot "le Possédé"* (Paris: Express, 1950), 71.

289 *"No, I concluded"* . . . *"None"* PC 236–237.

290 *"The longer this trial goes"* Ibid.

290 *hat trimmed with otter fur* Le Pays, March 29, 1946.

291 *a strong Slavic accent* Jean Galtier-Boissière, *Mon journal dans la drôle de paix* (Paris: La Jeune Parque, 1947), 207–208.
291 *"the circumstances of my friends"* AN 334, AP 65, 4566.
291 *delightful* AN, 4570–4571.
291 *"Of course, Mr. President"* AN 334, AP 65, 4571.
291 *"They were not only anti-Nazi"* Ibid.
291 *"as their God"* Ibid.
291 *"I understand now"* AN 334, AP 65, 4575.
292 *"injections, nightclubs, drugs"* AN 334, AP 65, 4576.
292 *"hunted as a harmful beast"* AN 334, AP 65, 4577.
292 *"stay put"* Ibid.
292 *"an adventuress . . . who lies"* AN 334, AP 65, 4592.
292 *"many difficulties"* AN 334, AP 65, 4608.
292 *"came to us to give tips"* AN 334, AP 65, 4355–4356.
293 *Insults and insinuations* AN 334, AP 65, 4609–4610.
293 *"offended the very legitimate sensitivities"* AN 334, AP 65, 4611.
293 *"saluted by a number of German"* AN 334, AP 65, 4614.
293 *"Since you do not appear to remember"* AN 334, AP 65, 4615.
293 *The judge ordered* Request for Dossier No. 16582, March 28, 1944, APP, Série J, affaire Petiot, carton n° III.
294 *"I have not looked at your hands" . . . "Pétain?"* AN 334, AP 65, 4623–4624.
294 *"Was she tortured"* Galtier-Boissière, *Mon journal*, 211.
294 *"these equally plausible"* Ibid.

CHAPTER 33. WALKOUT

295 *"We respected Yvan" . . . "To give information"* PC, 247–249.
296 *"Germans, notorious collaborators"* Fernand Lavie in a letter of November 30, 1944, APP, Série J, affaire Petiot, carton n° IV.
297 *"My mother never intended to leave" . . . "Yet she must know"* PC, 249–251.
297 *"How many witnesses"* Thomas Maeder, *The Unspeakable Crimes of Dr. Petiot* (Boston: Little, Brown and Company, 1980), 251. Emphasis added. Many other important witnesses were not found, not least of which was Georges Redouté, who had left town. Report, March 12, 1946, APP, Série J, affaire Petiot, carton n° III.
298 *"Maître, if you manage"* PC, 251.
298 *"How do you explain this find?"* Claude Bertin, *Les assassins hors-série: Gilles de Rais, Petiot*, vol. 10 of *Les grands procès de l'histoire de France* (Paris: Éditions de Saint-Clair, 1967), 245.
298 *"The moment has not come" . . . "Do not speak"* PC, 252–254.
300 *"Very sympathetically"* John V. Grombach, *The Great Liquidator* (New York: Zebra Books, 1980), 268–269.
300 *"Why were you released" . . . "To insinuate"* PC, 255.
301 *"Me? An agent"* Bertin, *Les assassins hors-série*, 248.
301 *"you lawyers of the alleged victims"* Grombach, *The Great Liquidator*, 356–357.

301 *this chaotic session* The *New York Times* correspondent calls it a "screaming contest." *New York Times,* March 31, 1946.

Chapter 34. *Naufrageur*

303 *"a veritable fire-box of political intrigue"* Claude Bertin, *Les assassins hors-série: Gilles de Rais, Petiot,* vol. 10 of *Les grands procès de l'histoire de France* (Paris: Éditions de Saint-Clair, 1967), 255.

303 *"true nest of tuberculosis"* Ibid, 256.

304 *"Petiot was a Frenchman"* PC, 256.

304 *"kill everyone"* France-Soir, April 2, 1946.

305 *"You spent five months with him"* . . . *"Whatever the outcome"* PC, 257–258; Bertin, *Les assassins hors-série,* 258–259.

305 *"without any question a real Resistant"* John V. Grombach, *The Great Liquidator* (New York: Zebra Books, 1980), 364.

305 *stylish Paris-Matin,* April 2, 1946.

305 *"I do not care"* PC, 258.

306 *"We're making a flop"* Petiot repeated this several times when the size of the audience fell. Claude Barret, *L'affaire Petiot* (Paris: Gallimard, 1958), 145.

306 EVERYBODY SLEEPS AT THE PETIOT TRIAL *L'Aurore,* April 3, 1946.

306 *"Nazi faun that haunts"* . . . *"I do not insist"* PC, 260–261.

307 *"he did not know"* This was Petiot's statement on March 20, 1946, as noted on page 256.

307 *"Ah!" she said* Leser, April 2, 1946, APP, Série J, affaire Petiot, carton n° III.

307 *"uniting them in death"* Grombach, *The Great Liquidator,* 367.

307 *"I have the good fortune"* AN 334, AP 65, 4432.

308 *"Cruel men set lanterns"* AN 334, AP 65, 4474.

308 *The members of the French Resistance* . . . *"wrap himself"* AN 334, AP 65, 4471.

308 *"very curious"* . . . *"I do not know if Petiot"* AN 334, AP 65, 4470–4474.

308 *"condemn him to death"* AN 334, AP 65, 4475.

309 *"the records of the Cour d'assises de la Seine"* AN 334, AP 65, 4006, and Dupin's handwritten version, AN 334, AP 65, 4086.

309 *"Yes, to find as many cadavers"* AN 334, AP 65, 4007.

309 *"remarkably intelligent"* AN 334, AP 65, 3306.

309 *"I will show you"* AN 334, AP 65, 3341.

309 *Petiot made a show Paris-Matin,* April 4, 1946.

309 *"modern Bluebeard"* AN 334, AP 65, 3311.

309 *"a modern gangster"* Ibid.

Chapter 35. The Verdict

310 *"herrings in a cask"* Le Figaro, April 5, 1946.

310 *"in a scandalous buffoonery"* Libé-Soir, April 5, 1946.

311 *Dupin classified Petiot's victims* AN 334, AP 65, 3385.

311 *"No, Petiot, we will not allow"* AN 334, AP 65, 3444.

311 *"Signed, the Procureur"* . . . *"Nor you!"* PC, 267, and Dupin's continuation, AN 334 AP 65, 3445.

311 *"Let Justice be done"* AN 334, AP 65, 3449.

312 *"the pleasure of a hunting dog"* Le Figaro, April 5, 1946.

312 *"monster, an assassin, a thief"* AN 334, AP 65, 4092.

313 *what really, Floriot asked* AN 334 AP 65, 4119–4120.

314 *"executed in the name of the Resistance"* AN 334, AP 65, 4120.

314 *"There is no crime or misdemeanor"* AN 334, AP 65, 4340–4341.

315 *Madame Braunberger, Floriot noted* AN 334, AP 65, 4274.

315 *"opened fifteen times"* AN 334, AP 65, 4277.

315 *Could it perhaps be "B.P."* AN 334, AP 65, 4280.

315 *he states it* AN 334, AP 65, 4282; PC, 280.

316 *"really something incredible"* . . . *"to your ears"* AN 334, AP 65, 4289–4292.

316 *"A sample?"* . . . *"They resemble each"* AN 334, AP 65, 4300–4301.

317 *"hats off for the hat trick"* Jean-Marc Varaut, *L'abominable Dr. Petiot* (Paris: Balland, 1974), 261.

317 *The patriot and hero* Many accounts make Floriot end by saying that he, too, would always be proud of having defended Petiot, but those words are not in the stenographic account.

317 *"I commend Petiot to your hands"* AN 334, AP 65, 4430.

317 *"the greatest defense summation"* Associated Press, April 5, 1946.

317 *"I cannot . . . nothing"* AN 334 AP 65, 4430.

317 *"Is the above mentioned"* Claude Bertin, *Les assassins hors-série: Gilles de Rais, Petiot*, vol. 10 of *Les grands procès de l'histoire de France* (Paris: Éditions de Saint-Clair, 1967), 283; Thomas Maeder, *The Unspeakable Crimes of Dr. Petiot* (Boston: Little, Brown and Company, 1980), 277.

318 *"suffocating and reeling"* France-Soir, April 5, 1946.

318 *Marcel Petiot was* AP 30.W.4, 17.

318 *"hollowing out his sockets"* Le Monde, April 5, 1946.

319 *"I must be avenged!"* PC, 292.

CHAPTER 36. TIMBERS OF JUSTICE

320 *"Nothing more can"* . . . *"Life is made of"* Frédérique Cesaire, *L'Affaire Petiot. Grands procès de l'histoire* (Paris: Editions De Vecchi S. A., 1999), 48.

320 *In February of 1955* Report, February 8, 1955, APP, Série J, affaire Petiot, carton n° III.

321 *"cooked the case"* Canberra Times (Australia), April 6, 1946.

321 *"terrifying monster"* New York Herald Tribune (international edition), March 20, 1946.

321 *"dangerous to himself and to others"* Ceiller, Rapport Medico-Legal, July 22, 1936, citing the Law of 1838, APP, Série J, affaire Petiot, carton n° V.

322 *later expressed doubts* According to John V. Grombach, Dupin "definitely stated that he believed Petiot to be positively insane." John V. Grombach, *The Great Liquidator* (New York: Zebra Books, 1980), note to page 297.

322 *Paulette Dreyfus would receive* AP, 30.W.4.18–27.

322 *Guschinow with 500,000* Not 100,000 as invariably reported. AP 30. W.4.21.

322 *Relatives of the Wolff family* Despite the portrait in Petiot biographies, the relatives of the Wolff and Kneller families did receive compensation, AP 30.W.4.23 and AP 30.W.4.25.

323 *Authorities suspected Paris-Matin,* May 23, 1946.

323 *"When are they going"* Thomas Maeder, *The Unspeakable Crimes of Dr. Petiot* (Boston: Little, Brown and Company, 1980), 285.

323 *Anatole Deibler, had suffered* Janet Flanner, *Paris Was Yesterday 1925–1939* (New York: Harcourt Brace Jovanovich, Publishers, 1972), 217.

323 *a harpsichord maker* This was Tobias Schmidt. See Stanley Karnow's portrait in *Paris in the Fifties* (New York: Times Books, 1999), 166–167.

324 *"last breath of air"* Rayner Heppenstall, *Bluebeard and After: Three Decades of Murder in France* (London: Peter Owen, 1972), 158.

324 *Petiot, mocking* Jean-Marc Varaut, *L'abominable Dr. Petiot* (Paris: Balland, 1974), 9. Varaut heard the story from René Floriot, in *L'Aurore,* April 30, 1974.

325 *"Petiot, have courage"* Varaut, *L'abominable Dr. Petiot,* 7.

325 *"How long is he"* Varaut, *L'abominable Dr. Petiot,* 8.

325 *"Gentlemen, I am"* PC, 294.

326 *"I only see"* Serge Jacquemard, *Petiot, Docteur Satan* (Paris: FleuveNoir, 1993), 214.

326 *"No," he said* Marcel Jullian, *Le mystère Petiot* (Paris: Edition No. 1, 1980), 167.

326 *"A pity"* Jacquemard, *Petiot, Docteur Satan,* 214.

326 *According to Obrecht* André Obrecht, *Le Carnet noir du bourreau: Mémoires d'André Obrecht, l'homme qui exécuta 322 condamnés* (Paris: Editions Gerard de Villiers, 1989), 197.

326 *"For the first time"* Maeder, *The Unspeakable Crimes,* 287; Varaut, *L'abominable Dr. Petiot,* 12.

326 *"Gentlemen, I have"* Claude Barret, *L'affaire Petiot* (Paris: Gallimard, 1958), 9.

CHAPTER 37. THE LOOT

328 *"stone by stone"* *Parisien-Libéré,* July 5, 1952; *Franc-Tireur,* April 23, 1953; APP, Séric EA, carton n° 181.

328 *"Go where you know"* Georges Massu, *L'enquête Petiot: La plus grande affaire criminelle du siècle* (Paris: Librairie Arthème Fayard, 1959), 213.

329 *According to this theory* Ronald Seth, *Petiot: Victim of Chance* (London: Hutchinson, 1963), 206.

329 *In early February* Serge Jacquemard, *La Bande Bonny-Lafont* (Paris: Fleuve Noir, 1992), 181–183.

331 *As remarkable as it sounds* There were German searches of rue Caumartin, as well as rue de Reuilly, but never rue le Sueur. AN 334 AP 65, 4394. Reports of German visitors to the property were not confirmed by the police, and one admitted visit (they left the lights on by mistake) was from June 1944. Kriminalpolizei, *Bericht,* June 12, 1944, APP, Série J, affaire Petiot, carton n° II.

331 *Danos served the gangster* Éric Guillon, *Abel Danos, dit "le mammouth": entre Résistance et Gestapo* (Paris: Fayard, 2006).

331 *Adrien the Basque's brother* By the autumn of 1944, Jacques Yonnet was also making this comment to investigators. Jacques Yonnet, *Audition*, November 7, 1944, APP, Série J, affaire Petiot, carton n° V.

331 *Lafont officially denied* Henri Chamberlin, *Audition*, November 22, 1944, APP, Série J, affaire Petiot, carton n° VII.

332 *"physician of the pissoir"* . . . *"my uncle"* Jean-François Dominique, *L'affaire Petiot: médecin, marron, gestapiste, guillotiné pour au moins vingt-sept assassinats* (Paris: Éditions Ramsay, 1980), 81–84.

332 *Cap Doumia, outside Algier* Grégory Auda, *Les belles année du "milieu" 1940–1944: Le grand banditisme dans la machine répressive allemande en France* (Paris: Éditions Michalon, 2002), 65–66. Lafont purchased the farm in Clavie's name, BDIC, Fonds Delarue Report September 10, 1944, and September 19, 1944, F Delta RES 787 6.

332 *Lafont had just received* Philippe Aziz, *Tu Trahiras sans vergogne: Histoire de deux 'collabos' Bonny et Lafont* (Paris: Fayard, 1970), 49–53.

332 *Oral testimony* Henry Sergg, *Paris Gestapo* (Paris: Grancher, 1989), 80–82. Petiot also admitted that some members of the French Gestapo had in fact been inadvertently led back to rue Le Sueur in his *Audition*, November 5, 1944, APP, Série J, affaire Petiot, carton n° VII.

334 *It was indeed this time* APP, Série J, affaire Petiot, carton n° VII contains many reports of the findings.

334 *"Dr. P"* . . . *"knows everything"* Dominique, *L'affaire Petiot*, 118. Petiot hints that he knew many unknown things about Lafont's gang on rue Lauriston in *Audition par Section Spéciale*, November 10, 1944, APP, Série J, affaire Petiot, carton n° V.

Epilogue

335 *distance-operated syringe* René Nézondet, *Petiot "le Possédé"* (Paris: Express, 1950), 76–78.

337 *"I do not have to know"* . . . *"stinking atmosphere"* Albert Massui, *Le cas du Dr Petiot* (Brussels: E.D.C., 1944), 66–76.

340 *"a load of crap"* Henry Sergg, *Paris Gestapo* (Paris: Grancher, 1989), 88.

340 *Raphaël's testimony* Raphaël K escaped Petiot, he said, thanks to some extraordinary good fortune. The door to the triangular room had somehow not latched shut. He managed to wiggle out, exit through the narrow corridor, and after coming out of a window into the courtyard, reach the street. Petiot, due to some "incomprehensible distraction," was nowhere in sight. Raphaël was sick for some time afterward.

340 *He could create* This is very similar to the method adopted by Nevada in June 1930, when they changed their execution procedure. Scott Christianson, *The Last Gasp: The Rise and Fall of the American Gas Chamber* (Berkeley: University of California Press, 2010), 98–99.

Illustration Credits

1. © Albert Harlingue / Roger-Viollet / The Image Works
2. © LAPI / Roger-Viollet / The Image Works
3. © LAPI / Roger-Viollet / The Image Works
4. Rue des Archives / The Granger Collection, New York
5. Albert Harlingue / Roger-Viollet / The Image Works
6. Courtesy of *Le Matin*, photographer unknown
7. Photo by author, used with permission of the Service des Archives et du Musée de la Préfecture de police
8. © LAPI / Roger-Viollet / The Image Works
9. © LAPI / Roger-Viollet / The Image Works
10. © LAPI / Roger-Viollet / The Image Works
11. Courtesy of *Le Matin*, photographer unknown
12. © LAPI / Roger-Viollet / The Image Works
13. Rue des Archives / The Granger Collection, New York
14. Rue des Archives / The Granger Collection, New York
15. French Photographer (20th century) Private Collection / Archives Charmet / The Bridgeman Art Library
16. © LAPI / Roger-Viollet / The Image Works
17. Photo by author, used with permission of the Service des Archives et du Musée de la Préfecture de police
18. Photo by author, used with permission of the Service des Archives et du Musée de la Préfecture de police
19. © Roger-Viollet / The Image Works
20. Marcel Petiot, *Le hasard vaincu* (1946)
21. Marcel Petiot, *Le hasard vaincu* (1946)

Index